PSYCHOPATHOLOGY: Contributions from the Biological, Behavioral, and Social Sciences
edited by Muriel Hammer, Kurt Salzinger, and Samuel Sutton

ABNORMAL CHILDREN AND YOUTH: Therapy and Research
by Anthony Davids

PRINCIPLES OF PSYCHOTHERAPY WITH CHILDREN
by John M. Reisman

AVERSIVE MATERNAL CONTROL: A Theory of Schizophrenic Development
by Alfred B. Heilbrun, Jr.

INDIVIDUAL DIFFERENCES IN CHILDREN
edited by Jack C. Westman

EGO FUNCTIONS IN SCHIZOPHRENICS, NEUROTICS, AND NORMALS: A Systematic Study of Conceptual, Diagnostic, and Therapeutic Aspects
by Leopold Bellak, Marvin Hurvich, and Helen K. Gediman

INNOVATIVE TREATMENT METHODS IN PSYCHOPATHOLOGY
edited by Karen S. Calhoun, Henry E. Adams, and Kevin M. Mitchell

THE CHANGING SCHOOL SCENE: CHALLENGE TO PSYCHOLOGY
by Leah Gold Fein

INNOVATIVE TREATMENT METHODS
IN PSYCHOPATHOLOGY

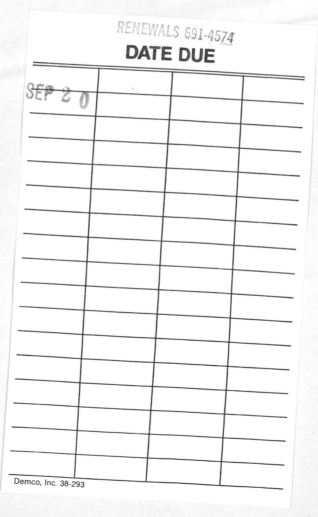

INNOVATIVE TREATMENT METHODS IN PSYCHOPATHOLOGY

Edited by

KAREN S. CALHOUN
HENRY E. ADAMS
KEVIN M. MITCHELL
University of Georgia, Athens

A WILEY-INTERSCIENCE PUBLICATION

JOHN WILEY & SONS, New York ● London ● Sydney ● Toronto

Copyright © 1974 by John Wiley & Sons, Inc.

All rights reserved. Published simultaneously in Canada.

Library of Congress Cataloging in Publication Data:
Calhoun, Karen S

  Innovative treatment methods in psychopathology.
  (Wiley series on personality processes)
  "A Wiley-Interscience publication."
  Includes bibliographies.
  1. Behavior therapy. 2. Psychology, Pathological.
3. Biofeedback training. I. Adams, Henry E.,
1931-   joint author. II. Mitchell, Kevin M.,
joint author. III. Title. [DMLM: 1. Psychopathology. 2. Psychotherapy. WM100 I55 1974]

RC489.B4C34   616.8'914   73-21968

ISBN 0-471-12995-X

Printed in the United States of America

10 9 8 7 6 5 4 3 2 1

Contributors

HENRY E. ADAMS, Ph.D., Professor of Psychology and Coordinator of Clinical Training, University of Georgia

DAVID H. BARLOW, Ph.D., Director of Clinical Psychology Internship Program, Department of Psychiatry, University of Mississippi Medical Center

EDWARD B. BLANCHARD, Ph.D., Associate Professor of Psychiatry (Psychology), University of Mississippi Medical Center.

JASPER BRENER, Ph.D., Professor of Psychology, University of Tennessee

KAREN S. CALHOUN, Ph.D., Assistant Professor of Psychology, University of Georgia

ROBERT S. DAVIDSON, Ph.D., Coordinator of Psychological Research, Clinical Research Psychologist, VA Hospital, Miami, Florida

JOHN DAVIS, B.A., Research Technician, Clinical Research Unit, Camarillo State Hospital, Camarillo, California

PETER M. LEWINSOHN, Ph.D., Professor of Psychology, University of Oregon

ROBERT P. LIBERMAN, M.D., Director, Laboratory for Behavior Modification and the Clinical Research Unit, Camarillo State Hospital, Camarillo, California

W. ROBERT NAY, Ph.D., Assistant Professor of Psychology, Virginia Commonwealth University

ROBERT W. SCOTT, Ph.D., Assistant Professor of Psychiatry (Psychology), University of Mississippi Medical Center

JAMES TEIGEN, M.S.W., Psychiatric Social Worker, Clinical Research Unit, Camarillo State Hospital, Camarillo, California

CHARLES WALLACE, Ph.D., Program Coordinator, Clinical Research Unit, Camarillo State Hospital, Camarillo, California

RONALD L. WEBSTER, Ph.D., Chairman and Associate Professor of Psychology, Hollins College, Hollins College, Virginia

Series Preface

This series of books is addressed to behavioral scientists interested in the nature of human personality. Its scope should prove pertinent to personality theorists and researchers as well as to clinicians concerned with applying an understanding of personality processes to the amelioration of emotional difficulties in living. To this end, the series provides a scholarly integration of theoretical formulations, empirical data, and practical recommendations.

Six major aspects of studying and learning about human personality can be designated: personality theory, personality structure and dynamics, personality development, personality assessment, personality change, and personality adjustment. In exploring these aspects of personality, the books in the series discuss a number of distinct but related subject areas: the nature and implications of various theories of personality; personality characteristics that account for consistencies and variations in human behavior; the emergence of personality processes in children and adolescents; the use of interviewing and testing procedures to evaluate individual differences in personality; efforts to modify personality styles through psychotherapy, counseling, behavior therapy, and other methods of influence; and patterns of abnormal personality functioning that impair individual competence.

IRVING B. WEINER

Case Western Reserve University
Cleveland, Ohio

Preface

The modification of abnormal behavior is a field that is undergoing radical and rapid change. Although many clinicians may be threatened by changes from traditional methods and theories, the benefits of these changes in thinking and technology to the public are rapidly becoming evident. Not only are these new treatment methods less time consuming, less expensive, and more effective with the usual disorders of interest to behavioral scientists and clinicians, but they are also being used in areas where the former treatment of choice was custodial care because other methods were ineffective and/or too expensive. Some examples are mental retardates, institutionalized individuals with long-term psychotic disorders, and criminals. Another aspect of this change is the emerging development of techniques to control psychophysiologic and other physiological disorders, long considered the territory of the profession of medicine. This indicates a developing and needed rapport between physicians and behavioral clinicians, which will perhaps eliminate the schism caused, in part, by the controversy over the disease model of abnormal behavior. It is an exciting era of change, controversy, and advancement in the behavioral sciences.

This book was designed to sample innovative techniques in psychopathology at various stages of their development. In general, each author gives a brief survey of his topic, his theoretical approach to the disorder, a general description of the treatment technique, and research. When appropriate, research on efficiency and effectiveness of the technique is given with follow-up data. In some cases, this search for effective modification techniques yields valuable clues to the causes of the disorder.

We would like to thank Charles L. Darby, Head, Department of Psychology; H. Boyd McWhorter, former Dean, College of Arts and Sciences; Victor S. Mamatey, Dean, College of Art and Science; and other administrators, faculty, and graduate students whose cooperation and support made this project possible. We especially appreciate the help of Perrie Lou Bryant, our secretary, who did much editing as well as typing. The patience and assistance of Gardner M. Spungin of John Wiley and Sons was particularly helpful. We would like to acknowledge the courtesy of publishers and authors who gave permission to include copyright material in this volume. This project was also supported in part by the National Institute of Mental Health, Training Grant No. 5T01MH08924.

KAREN S. CALHOUN

HENRY E. ADAMS

KEVIN M. MITCHELL

Athens, Georgia
September 1973

Contents

INNOVATIVE TREATMENT METHODS
IN PSYCHOPATHOLOGY

CHAPTER 1

Innovations in the Treatment of Abnormal Behavior

HENRY E. ADAMS and KAREN S. CALHOUN

No area of scientific endeavor has been as open to critical scrutiny, subjective bias, and emotional reactions as the changing of human behavior. The fact that the science of human behavior overlaps with and is often seen as conflicting with philosophical and religious views of the nature of man has contributed to this controversy. Consequently, techniques for modifying man's adjustment have been a function of the *Zeitgeist* more than of the nature of human behavior, and changes or modifications of these treatment techniques from trephining to moral therapy have been primarily a function of changing religious and political climates rather than dissatisfaction with the effectiveness of the treatment methods. For example, Bochoven (1963) claimed that moral treatment, popular during the nineteenth century, was more successful than present-day treatment techniques. This method is based on the belief that behavioral disorders are a result of severe psychological and social stresses and can be treated by friendly association, discussion of the problem, and the daily pursuit of purposeful activity. As the climate of the times changed, however, deviant individuals became regarded as "ill" people, and moral treatment has now been discarded.

Many professionals and others engaged in the modification of behavior, from the minister counseling the individual to adhere to a more strict observation of the Ten Commandments to the humanistic therapist attempting to help the individual to a more meaningful life, have viewed with disdain and skepticism attempts to apply the scientific method to the investigation of human behavior and techniques for changing it. This skepticism has ranged from dogmatic statements that human behavior cannot be understood in scientific terms to the proposition that the scientific method was developed in animal laboratories and should be altered to make it more appropriate for the study of human behavior. To further compound the problem, most theories of normal and abnormal behavior could scarcely be called scientific in nature. Treatment techniques es-

1

poused by these theories were often a complex mixture of ingredients which even their proponents had difficulty defining in meaningful terms. As a result, empirical evaluation of these treatment methods was impossible.

Freud and Rogers

One of the most significant innovations in treatment methods in modern history was the introduction of psychoanalysis by Sigmund Freud. With Freud's emphasis on irrational man, psychic determinism, and unconscious forces, insight and verbal psychotherapy methods of changing behavior soon dominated the field. Although later Freudians and neo-Freudians contributed minor variations of this basic theme in terms of guesses about etiology, briefer treatments, and the therapist-patient relationship, the basic assumption of psychodynamic psychology that insight causes attitude and consequently behavioral changes was not seriously challenged. Innovations during this period of the dominance of psychodynamic theory were minor and largely ignored. Strangely enough, this also seemed to be the case with biological as well as psychological techniques. Various physiologic techniques such as electroshock treatment that were introduced during the 1930s were regarded as symptomatic treatments and not widely used until the early 1950s.

For the last twenty years, however, increasing attention has been focused on innovative techniques of behavior change. In psychological treatment, client-centered therapy as proposed by Carl Rogers (1951) became a popular treatment method. Although insight is still a major element in Rogerian therapy, the techniques of psychotherapy, the manner by which insight is fostered, had changed drastically to provide a therapeutic environment in which the individual could grow and insight would occur. However, the most significant contribution of Rogers and his students is their insistence on the evaluation of the effectiveness of psychotherapy and the active ingredients in the treatment procedure (i.e., the process versus outcome paradigm). Whereas the methods, response measures, and procedures were primitive and plagued by problems of unreliability and lack of validity, these researchers fostered a change from an attitude of passive acceptance and belief to one of healthy skepticism and scientific weighing of the evidence regarding psychotherapeutic procedures.

CAUSES OF RECENT INNOVATIONS

The 1950s and 1960s were marked by a disenchantment with traditional treatment techniques and the introduction of a large number of new approaches and techniques for modifying abnormal behavior. These innovations ranged from effective methods in some cases to ridiculous schemes in others. Psychoanalysis and traditional psychodynamic psychotherapy were clearly on the decline and were even held in contempt by many therapists, where formerly their prestige was not challenged. The reasons for this critical reappraisal of theories and techniques seemed to come from the following sources: (a) the research evidence on the ineffectiveness of traditional psychotherapy; (b) the critical appraisal and decline of the mental illness model; (c) the development of basic scientific psychology and a new interest in applying it to behavioral disorders; and (d) a change in the political and social climate.

The Effectiveness of Traditional Psychotherapy

Perhaps the most devastating attack on traditional psychotherapy was Eysenck's (1952) classic review of the effects of psychotherapy. He presented evidence that the published studies did not indicate that psychotherapy produced a greater remission rate in treated neurotics than spontaneous recovery in untreated neurotic patients and suggested that more methodologically sophisticated studies should be conducted with newer techniques, whatever the cost. The reactions to Eysenck's article were varied and sometimes puzzling. They ranged from complete misunderstanding of Eysenck's position to personal attacks on his veracity, virility, ancestry, and professional qualifications. At times the rejoinders to Eysenck's statements became absurd. For example, Raush (1954) stated, "It is not the point to discuss the efficacy or lack of efficacy of psychotherapy. Psychotherapy is a method for studying the human psyche. Whether it is a good or bad method is not an issue." This attitude was not uncommon and some traditional psychotherapists maintained either implicitly or explicitly that their theories and treatment methods were valid. Since the evidence did not support the theories and techniques, some even suggested that the scientific method should be discarded as an invalid approach to the study of human behavior. Astin (1961) discussed the remarkable resistance to change among traditional psychotherapists and suggested that psychotherapy of the traditional type has become functionally autonomous and not susceptible to influence by data.

One of the puzzling effects of this controversy has been the position assumed by some psychodynamic theorists and humanistic therapists. This position, as exemplified by Raush (1954), quoted above, simply states that psychoanalysis or other humanistic or traditional theories are methods (as alternatives to the scientific method) for studying human behavior and that outcome study of the efficiency of the clinical methods with behavioral disorders is irrelevant. A similar position has been taken by many humanistic psychotherapists who disdain outcome studies of their treatment methods and make no claim of therapeutic benefits in the usual sense. Instead, they indicate that they are interested in growth of the individual, happiness, understanding, and the like. In fact, many traditional and humanistic psychotherapists have accepted the proposition that their treatment techniques are not effective methods for modifying deviant behavior. Yet, as Astin indicated, they persist in using the techniques in the absence of demonstrated effectiveness.

More recent evidence regarding the efficacy of traditional psychotherapy has not altered Eysenck's initial conclusions about its effectiveness (Levitt, 1963). In fact, these data have led some researchers to conclude that further studies of therapeutic success in traditional psychotherapy as well as the evaluation of outcome resulting from traditional therapeutic practice are a waste of time and money (Bergin and Strupp, 1970).

Mental Illness and the Medical Model

At approximately the same time, serious questions regarding the validity of the medical model of abnormal behavior were being raised (Szasz, 1960). In essence, the medical model is based on analogy with disease entities, proposing that abnormal behavior is symptomatic of underlying processes just as fever is a symptom of an underlying disease process. Consequently, as in physiologic disorders, treatment procedures should be directed at eliminating the underlying cause or causes of the symptoms. If the symptom were treated directly, it would leave the underlying cause or causes intact and another, perhaps more severe symptom would develop. In actuality, Bandura (1969) and Yates (1970) report that the phenomenon of symptom substitution has not been substantiated. Many behavioral scientists accepting this model have claimed that mental illness is basically no different from other disease processes and the difference between mental and bodily disease is that in the former the brain is affected, causing the symptoms to manifest themselves by mental disorders.

The most appropriate criticism of this position was stated by Adams (1964), who indicated that the concept of functional mental illness is a verbal analogy. He suggested that it is appropriate to regard neurological disorders as true organic diseases, since they are similar to organic illnesses involving the circulatory or digestive system, but it is questionable to apply the term "illness" to arbitrarily defined patterns of behavior, particularly where there is no evidence of physiological malfunction. Szasz (1960) indicated that mental illness is simply a term to describe "problems in living" and not diseases of the brain. Illness implies a deviation from a clearly defined physiological norm, whereas behavioral disorders are deviations from social and psychological norms. Consequently, organic malfunction or disease and so-called "mental illness" are defined by different criteria and are modified or "cured" by fundamentally different principles. This challenge to the medical model, combined with other factors, facilitated the disenchantment with treatment approaches such as traditional psychotherapy which were intimately associated with the mental illness model and stimulated the search for other techniques to modify behavior.

Application of Basic Psychological Principles

For change to occur, newer and more effective techniques must become increasingly available. It could be argued that the field of psychology has, by this time, progressed to a point where it is feasible to attempt application of basic psychological knowledge to behavioral disorders. This seems to be particularly true in the field of learning, where the basic principles of operant conditioning, as formulated by Skinner, and classical conditioning, as initiated by Pavlov and further developed by Tolman, Hull, Spence, and others, were fairly well established. This is not to claim that there is a well-developed theory of learning that can be applied to deviant behavior.

Contrary to the assumption of Breger and McGaugh (1965), the development of treatment techniques in behavior modification does not necessarily require a well-established theory or theories of learning. In fact, basic principles of conditioning and empirical data are sufficient to facilitate the development of behavior change technology. As London (1972) indicates, theories are not only unnecessary, but developing technology can often correct bad theory or contribute new theory.

In addition, research on experimental neurosis by Pavlov, Watson, Gantt, Masserman, Wolpe, and Liddell indicate the relevance of animal and human analogs of behavioral disorders to formulations of abnormal behavior. These trends reflected the imminent wedding of animal analogs, scientific methodology, and clinical application, which has resulted in the rapidly developing field of behavior modification. As we will see in later chapters of this book, the effective application of basic psychological principles to clinical problems has become an established fact.

The *Zeitgeist*

Perhaps the single most important factor in the multitude of innovative treatment techniques that have been developed in the last two decades is the change in the *Zeitgeist*. The political and social atmosphere, particularly in the United States and Europe, was in a period of rapid change. This period was marked by rebellion against established authority, greater interest in human problems, and a marked affinity for change. The public became interested in poverty, discrimination against minority groups, political changes, and individual freedom. In the behavioral sciences similar changes were occurring. It was no longer intellectually fashionable to be interested in a phenomenon simply for the sake of scientific knowledge, and various investigators began to feel that scientific knowledge should be applied to social problems.

Along with this changing attitude within the behavioral sciences was the concurrent and correlated trend of critically questioning established theories and practices. Consequently, some scientists and clinicians began to admit that psychotherapy, particularly psychoanalysis, was not effective in handling human problems; that it took too long; that the cost of the psychotherapeutic method made it available only to the financially elite; and that training and expertise in these methods was so complex, long term, and expensive that it would be impossible to train enough therapists to treat realistically all those who need it.

The conflict became even more severe when data indicated that undergraduate students and housewives with no special training could be as effective as professionals (Poser, 1966; Rioch, Elkes, Flint, Usdansky, Newman, and Silber, 1963). These facts supported Schofield's (1964) claim that psychotherapists are essentially offering their clients a supportive, substitute friendship which does not require professional training and that clients could probably receive the same benefits by talking to trustworthy colleagues or friends. Schofield further suggested that the psychotherapist could better invest his time in community psychology, becoming a consultant to technicians administering treatment, a better utilization of his professional skills. The logic of this position is incompatible with a set of skills that can be implemented only by professionals. In addition, training parents, teachers, or paraprofessionals in skills that have not been shown to be effective would simply increase the number of people who are unable to modify deviant behavior.

A similar suggestion by some professionals interested in community psychology is that the role of the behavioral consultant should be to modify the community rather than the individual—an interesting proposition, since psychological scientists seem to be even more ignorant of community problems and how to modify them than they are of individual problems. Nevertheless, the *Zeitgeist* with its emphasis on application of basic principles and empirical facts of psychology to behavioral disorders, emphasis on community psychology and social problems, and an interest in the individual and his search for freedom and meaning within the culture has stimulated the search for and development of innovative methods.

THE DEVELOPMENT OF INNOVATIVE TECHNIQUES

The disenchantment with traditional techniques has led to a plethora of novel techniques for modifying behavior. Although it is probably true with traditional methods, as Lazarus and Davison (1971) claim, that the majority of clinical techniques for modifying behavioral disorders have come from clinical experimentation and innovation rather than controlled research or field studies, this is not always the case with innovative techniques, nor should it necessarily be. One approach that seems feasible is the combination of clinical and basic research in development of modification techniques where new methods are devised by the creative clinician who is well versed in the basic principles, empirical data, and current research in the behavioral sciences. In general, the following sequence, which is illustrated in many of the later chapters, seems to have the most utility.

Assessment and Definition of the Target Behavior

The first step would be a careful assessment of the deviant behavior. Thorough case histories, interviews, observations of responses in the environment, stimuli eliciting the behavior, reinforcement histories of target behaviors, and other characteristics of the behavioral disorder are a necessary first step. Careful assessment leads to a definition and a description of the essential characteristics of the disorder, which allows the clinician to classify individuals as to whether or not they exhibit the behavior. A thorough assessment and understanding of the target behavior is a prerequisite to a search of the relevant animal, human, and clinical research literature that may be helpful in establishing the parameters of the behavior and an initial formulation of the disorder.

A good example of this is the approach used by Meyer and Levy (1973) in defining and classifying compulsive rituals. A search of the research literature on ritualistic behavior in animals and humans indicated that variations of response prevention could be effective in decreasing rituals, and they have successfully utilized this technique in a series of cases.

The Use of Human and Animal Analogs

At this stage, the clinical researcher may decide that a human or animal analog study would be useful in further investigating the parameters of the target behavior or the effectiveness of certain techniques for modifying it. An example of such an approach is seen in Wolpe's (1958) work using animals to study analogs of phobias. Although these research analogs are plagued with numerous problems, it cannot be denied that in some cases they furnish useful information about the nature of the behavioral disorder or the treatment technique. Many examples of the use of analogs are reported in the following chapters.

Initial Formulation and Clinical Trial

After an assessment and definition of the behavioral disorder, a search of the previous research, and, on occasion, research with animal and human analogs, the clinical researcher is in a position to devise methods that may increase or decrease the occurrence of the target behavior. At this stage, an initial formulation or hypothesis of the effects of the innovative method on the behavior is possible. The next step is the clinical trial.

If Roger's greatest contribution to psychotherapy is the emphasis on research, then the greatest contribution of the behavioral movement is research methodology. As Eysenck (1970) stated, "The greatest contribution of behavior therapy has been from the beginning not only the substantial improvement in clinical practice, vital though that has been, but even more the insistence on theoretical rigor, experimental proof, and clinical checks" (p. 14). This contribution has been most evident in the development and modification of the case history into the single case experimental design. The single case design, which emanated from psychoanalysis on one hand and the laboratory of operant psychology on the other, has resulted in a very powerful method, easily applied to clinical problems. The theoretical and logical aspects of this methodology have been discussed in detail by Barlow and Hersen (1973), Duke (1965), Chassan (1960), Baer, Wolf, and Risley (1968), Davidson and Costello (1969), and Sidman (1960) and deserve careful study and investigation by the student of research methodology and behavioral change.

The method as applied to clinical problems has been discussed by Shapiro (1961) and has a number of advantages. By first taking a careful assessment of the target behavior or symptom, the clinician can determine the frequency, intensity, and other characteristics of the response under various stimulus conditions. Treatment can then be introduced and the behavior again observed to note changes. This gives a continuous evaluation of treatment and, by removing the treatment, it can be demonstrated that the treatment has effectively changed the behavior if it returns to the baseline frequency of occurrence. There are several variations of the single case design which can be utilized in various situations to estimate whether the treatment procedure is actually controlling or affecting the target behavior.

It has been assumed frequently that the single case design is simply a poor substitute for the multiple subject design. Often the two designs are seen as antagonistic approaches, and some psychological journals will not publish single case studies, whereas others will not publish studies with multiple subject designs. In actuality, each design has advantages and disadvantages (see Barlow and Hersen, 1973; Chassan, 1960; Baer, Wolf, and Risley, 1968; Davison and Costello, 1969; Paul, 1969; Sidman, 1960). The difficulties with the single case design have been elaborately described by Paul (1969); the limitations of the multiple subject design and the advantages of single case design have been described by Sidman (1960) and Chassan (1960). Whether a clinical researcher decides to use one approach or the other depends on the nature of the behavior under investigation, the nature of the variables to be controlled, the purpose of the investigation, and practical limitations such as the time and the number of subjects available. An extensive discussion of these issues is not the aim of this chapter, but it can be stated that the single case design is generally most appropriate during the development and the clinical trial of an innovative method. If it can be shown that the treatment technique does affect the target behavior, the research clinician is in a position to tease out the "active ingredient" in the procedure, which can then be combined with other active ingredients or methods to improve the technique. The use of the single case design as one method for determining therapeutic active ingredients in a complex treatment program will be seen in several of the following chapters. The multiple subject design is more appropriately used to evaluate the general effectiveness of the complex or multivariate treatment method about which less is known or with behaviors not yet subjected to laboratory controls, and perhaps too variable to allow observation of steady states. The group design may also be particularly appropriate to outcome or other clinical studies where important stimulus control factors (e.g., natural environments) cannot be controlled. Of course, both approaches can be used exclusively or conjointly.

In general, the strategy of careful assessment of the target behavior, a search for relevant research principles, animal or human analog studies, formulation of a treatment method, clinical trials, reformulation and search for the active ingredients of the procedure while evaluating other variables such as demand characteristics and placebo effects, and, finally, multiple subject evaluation of the effectiveness of the treatment seems to be the most desirable method of developing and evaluating innovative treatment procedures. The following chapters present numerous examples of this sequence with different contributors at different stages of the sequence. It should be noted that this sequence of development is not limited to behavioral research but is adaptable to research in chemotherapy as well as other forms of treatment.

EVALUATION OF INNOVATIVE TREATMENT METHODS

With the explosion of new techniques and treatment methods, evaluation of these innovations becomes crucial. The following factors are essential in this evaluation.

The Basic Requirement

The initial step in the evaluation process is to determine if the target behavior and the innovative treatment are clearly defined and described so that evaluation is possible. This means that scientific terminology, operational definitions, classification, and the specification of the data language are prerequisites for objective evaluation of therapeutic techniques. Unfortunately, many of the recent innovations such as those used in Gestalt therapy, encounter groups, and similar techniques developed primarily from humanistic psychology do not meet these criteria. Consequently, realistic evaluation of these techniques is impossible. To further add to this dilemma, many of the proponents of these approaches do not feel that scientific methodology and procedures are appropriate for their therapeutic methods. If the initial prerequisites for measurement are not met, evaluation of a technique is not possible, and whether such approaches and techniques are effective becomes a philosophical rather than a scientific issue.

Effectiveness

The second major criterion is the effectiveness of the particular procedure. This involves the question of whether the particular technique is more effective than no treatment, placebo, or competing treatment methods. In general, this evaluation involves administering the treatment in question, the competing treatment method, and necessary control methods to a random sample of groups from the population for which the method was designed.

In this case the research clinician is dealing with an outcome paradigm and a group design, since the question is whether the technique is adaptable to the majority of individuals in the defined sample, irrespective of individual differences. If there are large individual differences in the effectiveness of the therapeutic method between subjects in the population, and if the characteristics of the individual which are responsible for these differences can be identified, then it is permissible to restrict the use of the technique to that part of the population for which it is most effective. For example, it has been suggested that systematic desensitization, a technique designed principally for phobias, is very effective with monosymptomatic phobias but is less effective with agoraphobia, social phobias, and other types of phobias where high arousal levels are elicited by vague, constant stimuli. In other words, a careful definition of the population of clients and specific behaviors for which the therapeutic technique is designed are necessary for determining its effectiveness.

Efficiency and Complexity

A third criterion is the efficiency of the technique. Although a given treatment method may be 90 percent effective with a given disorder, the cost and the requirements for administering the treatment might render it useless. A good example of this lack of efficiency is classic psychoanalysis. The client is seen four or five times a week for a period of two or three years or more. This means that approximately 500 hours of treatment are required. Furthermore, since it is a "talking" therapy where insight of an intellectual nature is required, one of the prerequisites for treatment is above-average intellectual functioning and education. Training of the psychoanalyst is expensive and the cost of treatment is extremely high (approximately $10,000 where a minimum cost of $20 per hour is estimated). Other prerequisites for treatment include absence of psychosis, brain damage, mental retardation, or advanced age. Consequently, the feasibility of this treatment technique is extremely limited regardless of effectiveness because of the high cost and the restricted population.

If a therapeutic procedure is very complex (such as the broad-spectrum therapies), its usefulness is reduced. One of the reasons that behavior modification techniques have become so popular is the fact that some of the behavioral techniques are fairly simple and can be taught to teachers, parents, technicians, and other individuals who do not have extensive backgrounds in psychology or medicine. Consequently, the role of the professional becomes one of assessing the problem, developing the treatment program, and teaching or consulting with various types of behavioral engineers. This means that the ratio of individuals who can implement the treatment to the number of individuals who need the treatment becomes small, which, combined with the fact that the usual behavioral treatment approaches require moderate lengths of time, make these techniques extremely feasible. In other words, the simpler the method, both in terms of teaching it to technicians and amount of time required to implement it, the more desirable the treatment technique. Although it is true that there may always be certain behavioral disorders requiring extremely complex techniques administered by highly trained professional staff, the goal always is to develop simple techniques that can be easily taught to and implemented by paraprofessionals.

Side Effects

A problem that has often been ignored in behavioral treatment is the potential side effects of the method. This variable is emphasized in chemotherapy, but it has been largely neglected in behavioral research because it is seldom observed in most behavioral treatment techniques. Nevertheless, it can seriously detract from the effectiveness of a therapeutic technique. For example, an individual who was treated for a fetish by aversion therapy became impotent with his wife because he had been maintaining heterosexual behavior through use of deviant fantasies. Although this particular individual was treated successfully for impotence, it is possible that an alternate procedure might have been preferred to aversion because of the undesirable side effects which aggravated his life situation.

There are often beneficial side effects of a treatment method which, in some cases, are examples of response generalization. For example, successful treatment of a social phobia by systematic desensitization may enhance the client's sex life and vocational happiness and decrease his rate of drinking. Such dividends greatly increase the value of a treatment technique.

Heuristic Value

The heuristic value of the therapeutic technique refers to the amount of research it generates, perhaps because of the number of questions it leaves unanswered or issues it raises. A particular technique which is tied directly into a theoretical position or a set of psychological principles is more likely to meet this criterion than a technique which is vague and/or exclusively empirical. The former is more likely to generate research where the active elements and the principles responsible for the effectiveness of the technique are more closely specified. Research generates refinement and improvement in the procedure.

There are a number of good examples of this in the behavior modification literature. One example is the research on systematic desensitization where it has been demonstrated that the original method is most effective when combined with *in vivo* or contact desensitization (Bandura, 1969). Another is the utilization of aversion therapy (Rachman and Teasdale, 1969; Cautela, 1969). Aversion therapy has been modified greatly since the earlier clinical work on nausea-producing drugs with alcoholics and Feldman and MacCulloch's (1965) early work with homosexuals. The search for the active ingredients and better procedures when combined with the theoretical controversies in the arena of aversion therapy have certainly led to improvement in aversion techniques including the development of new methods such as covert sensitization. Controversy usually leads to improvement in a treatment technique when it is associated with an increase in research activity.

In summary, the usefulness of an innovative technique is not determined solely by the percentage of the target behavior it eliminates as compared to competing techniques and other nonspecific factors. Other parameters are equally important and an innovative treatment must be weighed against all of the criteria.

PRESENT AND FUTURE TRENDS

In the following chapters various innovative treatment methods are described. Some of these contributions are in advanced stages of development and look extremely promising in terms of the foregoing criteria for evaluation of innovative techniques. Other methods, such as the biofeedback techniques described by Brener as well as Blanchard and Scott, are in their infancy. These chapters are important because they illustrate how we are beginning to apply basic research to psychophysiological disorders. The next major breakthrough in treatment methods may be in the area of physiological psychology, just as in the last 10 to 15 years therapeutic advances have been made in the field of learning.

The following chapters also illustrate how the formulation of a particular disorder can lead to the development of a treatment method or how the search for a treatment method can give clues to promising hypotheses in the theoretical formulation of a behavioral disorder. These chapters also illustrate that traditional clinical theories of behavior such as psychoanalysis, which result in very complex, broad-spectrum treatment methods such as psychotherapy are declining in influence. More specific formulation of a particular behavioral disorder with specific treatment methods is becoming common. With this development, a premium is now being placed on the skill of the clinician to select a specific treatment method for a particular disorder, which is a novel development in the field of abnormal behavior. Another trend is the emphasis on the community setting and the generalization of adaptive responses acquired in the clinical setting to the natural environment.

The present contributions are behavioral (a term which has lost much of its meaning since it is becoming a synonym for the scientific approach). There are two reasons for this. First, a majority of innovations in behavior change techniques are coming from clinicians and researchers with a behavioral orientation, Second, other orientations, such as humanistic psychology, simply have not gone through the sequence of development described in this chapter nor do they meet the evaluation criteria. This is not meant to imply that other theoretical orientations or fields of psychology cannot or will not contribute to innovative behavioral change procedures. As long as the basic rules of science are followed, any area or field of behavioral sciences can contribute to modification of abnormal behavior.

The myth among clinicians that general and theoretical psychology has little to contribute to the field of abnormal psychology and its modification is rapidly being replaced by demonstrations to the contrary. The following chapters should aid in the elimination of this myth and contribute to the position that the application of the knowledge, methods, and principles of psychology and the behavioral sciences to abnormal behavior will aid in the effective control and prevention of behavior disorders. In the final analysis, it is absurd to maintain the dualism of one theory of behavior for abnormal psychology and another for general psychology. This book represents an attempt to contribute to eliminating that absurdity.

REFERENCES

Adams, H.B. Mental illness or interpersonal behavior? *American Psychologist*, 1964, **19**, 191–197.

Astin, A.W. The functional autonomy of psychotherapy. *American Psychologist*, 1961, **16**, 75–78.

Baer, D.M., Wolf, M.M., and Risley, T.R. Some current dimensions of applied behavior analysis. *Journal of Applied Behavior Analysis*, 1968, **1**, 91–97.

Bandura, A. *Principles of Behavior Modification.* New York: Holt, Rinehart and Winston, 1969.

Barlow, D.H., and Hersen, M. Single case experimental designs: Use in applied clinical research. *Archives of General Psychiatry,* 1973, **29**, 319–327.

Bergin, A.E., and Strupp, H.H. New directions in psychotherapy research. *Journal of Abnormal Psychology,* 1970, **76**, 13–26.

Bockoven, J. S. *Moral Treatment in American Psychiatry.* New York: Springer, 1963.

Breger, L., and McGaugh, J.L. Critique and reformulation of "learning theory" approaches to psychotherapy and neuroses. *Psychological Bulletin,* 1965, **63**, 338–358.

Cautela, J.R. Behavior therapy and self-control: Techniques and implications. In C.M. Franks (Ed.), *Behavior Therapy: Appraisal and Status.* New York: McGraw-Hill, 1969.

Chassan, J.P. Statistical inference and the single case in clinical design. *Psychiatry,* 1960, **23**, 173–184.

Davidson, P.O., and Costello, C.G. (Eds.) *N = 1: Experimental Studies of Single Cases.* New York: Van Nostrand-Reinhold, 1969.

Duke, W.F. N. = 1. *Psychological Bulletin,* 1965, **64**, 74–79.

Eysenck, H.J. The effects of psychotherapy: An evaluation. *Journal of Consulting Psychology,* 1952, **16**, 319–324.

Eysenck, H.J. Behavior therapy and its critics. *Journal of Behavior Therapy and Experimental Psychiatry,* 1970, **1**, 5–15.

Feldman, M.P., and MacCulloch, M.J. The application of anticipatory avoidance learning to the treatment of homosexuality. 1. Theory, technique and preliminary results. *Behaviour Research and Therapy,* 1965, **2**, 165–183.

Lazarus, A.A., and Davidson, G.C. Clinical innovation in research and practice. In A.E. Bergin and S.L. Garfield (Eds.), *Handbook of Psychotherapy and Behavior Change: An Empirical Analysis.* New York: Wiley, 1971.

Levitt, E.E. Psychotherapy with children: A further evaluation. *Behaviour Research and Therapy,* 1963, **1**, 45–51.

London, P. The end of ideology in behavior modification. *American Psychologist,* 1972, **27**, 913–920.

Meyer, V., and Levy, R. Modification of behavior in obsessive-compulsive disorders. In H.E. Adams and I.P. Unikel (Eds.), *Issues and Trends in Behavior Therapy.* Springfield, Ill.: Thomas, 1973.

Paul, G.T. Behavior modification research: Design and tactics. In C.M. Franks (Ed.), *Behavior Therapy: Appraisal and Status.* New York: McGraw-Hill, 1969.

Poser, E.G. The effects of therapists' training on group therapeutic outcome. *Journal of Consulting Psychology,* 1966, **30**, 283–289.

Rachman, S., and Teasdale, J.D. Aversion therapy: An appraisal. In C.M. Franks (Ed.), *Behavior Therapy: Appraisal and Status.* New York: McGraw-Hill, 1969.

Raush, H.L. Comment on Eysenck's "Further comments on 'Relations with psychiatry.'" *American Psychologist,* 1954, **2**, 588–589.

Rioch, M.J., Elkes, E., Flint, A.A., Usdansky, B.C., Newman, R.G., and Silber, E. National Institute of Mental Health pilot study in training mental health counselors. *American Journal of Orthopsychiatry*, 1963, **33**, 678–689.

Rogers, C.R. *Client Centered Therapy*. Boston: Houghton, 1951.

Schofield, W. *Psychotherapy: The Purchase of Friendship*. Englewood Cliffs, N.J.: Prentice-Hall, 1964.

Shapiro, M.B. A method of measuring psychological changes specific to the individual psychiatric patient. *British Journal of Medical Psychology*, 1961, **34**, 151–155.

Sidman, M. *Tactics of Scientific Research*. New York: Basic Books, 1960.

Szasz, T. The myth of mental illness. *American Psychologist*, 1960, **15**, 113–118.

Wolpe, J. *Psychotherapy by Reciprocal Inhibition*. Stanford, Calif.: Stanford University Press, 1958.

Yates, A.J. *Behavior Therapy*. New York: Wiley, 1970.

CHAPTER 2

A Behavioral Analysis of Stuttering: Treatment and Theory

RONALD L. WEBSTER

The purpose of this chapter is to suggest that stuttered speech constitutes a problem that can be most effectively understood and corrected when it is dealt with in strictly physical terms. It appears as if the phenomenon has been generally misunderstood because both researchers and clinicians have focused for too long on apparent relationships between emotionality and stuttering; covariation has been mistaken for causation. The problem has been obscured by an overabundance of inadequate theories, deficiencies in the use of quantification in research and therapy settings, and by an apparently studied indifference of workers in the area to reliable, observed relationships between specifiable stimulus and response events in stuttering.

Perhaps one of the most striking characteristics of the literature on stuttering is the lack of success that has been achieved in providing verbal, working definitions of the phenomenon. As Beech and Fransella (1968) pointed out, the specification of what stutterers do when they are stuttering provides a basis for much conjecture. At the same time, it seems somewhat surprising to note that investigators of stuttering have a minimum amount of difficulty in distinguishing between their experimental and control groups. Apparently, most investigators can recognize stuttering (except in borderline cases), but no one seems to have described it very well. In fact, there seems to be a general reluctance on the part of workers in the area to accept even any limited definition that may serve to generate information on lawful relationships between types of stimulus variables and observed aspects of stuttered speech. Attempts have been made to provide limited, operational definitions of stuttering; however, the established authorities on stuttering have consistently rejected such attempts at defining the problem. For example, Van Riper (1971, p. 14) said of Wingate's (1964) definition (which shall be presented later in this chapter), "such catalog descriptions are incomplete and all stutterers do not show all the behaviors listed." It would be the remarkable behavior problem, indeed, which had all cases manifesting all aspects of the problem. Other objections come from those who feel that stuttering is defined essentially in terms of the stutterer's perceptions and feelings. To them, the measurable characteristics of stuttering are not representative of the true problem. Attention to the measurement of stuttering neglects the "whole person."

Much of the confusion in the analysis of stuttering probably has derived from a reliance on conceptions of stuttered speech that focus on assumptions about the phenomenon rather than on observable aspects of the problem. Both the clinician and the researcher have been quick to move beyond the physicalistic description of stuttering to assess the veiled meaning of speech forms manifested by stutterers. For example, Brutten and Shoemaker (1967, pp. 29–30) discussed stuttering in the following terms: "Stuttering is not seen as an instrumental response that depends on reinforcement for acquisition and maintenance, but as a fluency failure caused by cognitive and motoric disorganization associated with negative emotion." Negative emotion is the term used by these authors in reference to anxiety, fear, or reactions to stressful situations. An earlier view of stuttering was presented by Van Riper (1957, p. 879): "Stuttering, as a disorder of communication rather than of speech, always involves a disturbance in interpersonal relationships. No matter what its origin might have been, in its advanced stages, it is accompanied by fear and by compulsive, stereotyped reactions which its possessor cannot control." Fenichel (1945) described stuttering as a neurotic phenomenon that could be attributed to defective personal control. A more recent approach to stuttering has emphasized the role properties of the stutterer. Sheehan (1968, p. 72) viewed stuttering as "a false role disorder. It is not a speech problem per se, but an interpersonal communicative disorder. It is a fault in the social presentation of the self, a self-role conflict."

Although there are some problems with objectively based definitions of stuttering, it does appear as if these definitions provide the best starting point for trying to understand the phenomenon. Indeed, there seem to be few alternatives open if stuttering is to be studied with the methods of science. One of the more adequate attempts at defining stuttering has been provided by Wingate (1964, p. 488) and is quoted below in its entirety:

1. (a) Disruption in the fluency of verbal expression which is (b) characterized by involuntary, audible or silent, repetitions or prolongations in the utterance of short speech elements, namely; sounds, syllables, and words of one syllable. These disruptions (c) usually occur frequently or are marked in character and (d) are not readily controllable.

2. Sometimes the disruptions are (e) accompanied by accessory activities involving the speech apparatus, related or unrelated body structures, or stereotyped speech utterances. These activities give the appearance of being speech-related struggles.

3. Also, there are not infrequently (f) indications or report of the presence of an emotional state, ranging from a general condition of "excitement" or "tension" to more specific emotions of a negative nature such as fear, embarrassment, irritation, or the like.

Table 1. Some Characteristics that Differentiate Stuttered Speech from Normal Types of Speech Disfluencies

Type of Behavior	Form of Disfluency in Normal Speakers	Form of Disfluency in Stutterers
Syllable repetitions		
Frequency per word	Less than 2	More than 2
Frequency per 100 words	Less than 2	More than 2
Tempo	Normal tempo	Faster than normal
Airflow	Rarely interrupted	Often interrupted
Prolongations		
Duration	Less than 1 second	Longer than 1 second
Frequency	Less than 1 per 100 words	More than 1 per 100 words
Silent pauses		
Within the word	Absent	May be present
Prior to the speech attempt	Not marked	Unusually long
Phonation		
Phonatory arrest	Absent	May be present

(Modified from Van Riper, C. *The Nature of Stuttering*. Englewood Cliffs, N.J.: Prentice-Hall, 1971. Copyright (1971) by Prentice-Hall. Reproduced by permission)

(g) The immediate source of stuttering is some incoordination expressed in the peripheral speech mechanism; the ultimate cause is presently unknown and may be complex or compound.

Beech and Fransella (1968) pointed out that the frequent qualifiers which occur in many of Wingate's statements produce some difficulty in understanding the definition. Although one must agree with the criticism, it should be noted that this type of criticism can be met by improving the adequacy of the quantification procedures used in measuring stuttering. Additional research employing proper methods of quantification will provide some solution to these definitional matters.

Still another set of guidelines for using objectively specifiable measures to differentiate stuttering from normal speech disfluencies has been provided by Van Riper (1971). A series of 26 specific points is presented, along with observations which seem to be useful in differentiating the characteristics of stuttered speech from the disfluencies normally seen in the speech of fluent speakers. A few of the differences in stuttered versus normal speech noted by Van Riper are presented in Table 1.

The value of these objective definitions lies in (1) their parsimony; (2) the increased reliability of measurement made possible both within and across investigators; and (3) the increased ease of discovering relationships between measurable response events in stuttering and various types of stimulus conditions. Improvements in the definition of stuttering must come from the continuous refining and delineating of empirically specifiable dimensions.

It should be made clear that the present account of stuttering employs definitions that are generally congruent with Wingate's statement and with Van Riper's catalog.

AN OVERVIEW OF CONCEPTIONS OF STUTTERING

A brief chronology of the general approaches that have been applied to stuttering in this century is useful in establishing a preliminary perspective on current therapeutic and research efforts. No attempt is made here to present a detailed, inclusive review of the literature on stuttering. Brief summary statements are presented on major developments in theory and treatment.

The first period of work on stuttering in this century has been referred to as the antistuttering period (Williams, 1968) and extended from about 1900 to 1925. The treatments employed in this interval involved direct, manipulative attempts to alter the characteristics of stuttered speech. The basic idea was to employ techniques that would keep an individual from stuttering. Among the procedures used were speech sound drills, exercises in breathing, suggestion, attempts at generating speech rate control, and the use of various abnormal speech patterns (Van Riper, 1970). This was also the period of time in which various "schools" of stuttering therapy were established. The treatment programs in these schools, for example, the Bogue and the Lewis schools, were based on the application of certain types of antistuttering techniques. One of the common procedures was to employ some form of rhythmic stimulation, such as arm-swinging, to cue the rhythmic release of syllables. The general lack of success of these early, direct manipulative attempts at improving the speech fluency of stutterers led to a disillusionment with such approaches that still persists in our time. The limited empirical orientation of the early 1900s (and the years immediately preceding) was subsequently replaced by the development of more systematic and elaborate theoretical accounts of stuttering (Van Riper, 1970).

The second period, extending from about 1925 to the present, has been characterized generally by the emergence of a variety of theoretical views on stuttering. One common element runs through most of these theoretical accounts: in some way or another the emotional status of the stutterer is implicated as a factor in the production of disfluent speech. Williams (1968) has referred to this as the antianxiety period of stuttering theorizing. It is possible to place the theories of stuttering which emerged during this period into a number of categories. For example, there are the disintegration theories, conditioned anticipation theories, psychoanalytic theories, learning theories, and servomechanism theories. Some general characteristics of these theories will be considered here. A more complete discussion of theoretical orientations in stuttering may be found in Beech and Fransella (1968), Bloodstein (1969), and Van Riper (1970, 1971).

The disintegration theories were among the early prominent systematic conceptual developments in stuttering. Travis (1931) presented a theory of stuttering based on the concept that the necessary integration of hemispheric functions was different in stutterers than in normally fluent speakers. It was assumed that increases in emotionality led to increases in the magnitude of interference in cortical cooperation required for guiding speech. A somewhat similar concept, that of dysphemia, was advanced by West (1936). Dysphemia was considered to take the form of rather encompassing constitutional abnormalities. The basic idea was that stutterers had an inherited predisposition toward a breakdown of the central mechanism which controls speech functions. This concept was also employed to account for frequency differences shown in stuttering by the two sexes, hereditary factors in stuttering, and other similar biologically determined variables. West (1958) later discussed stuttering as a possible type of epilepsy which was specific to the motor system in speech. A somewhat related view regarding possible organic factors involved in stuttering was put forth by Eisenson (1958), who considered stuttering to be a form of motor and sensory perseveration based on constitutional factors.

A number of theories were developed which dealt with the role of anticipation as an important contributor to stuttering. Central to these theories is the idea that the stutterer has come to believe that he will experience difficulty in speaking, and because of this belief, interference occurs in speech production. Conditioned anxiety is generally held to be the fundamental cause of the speech disorder. A good example of this type of approach is seen in the work of Wendell Johnson (1955), who presented what has commonly been designated as a "diagnosogenic" theory of stuttering. According to Johnson, stutterers as young children were not differentiated from nonstutterers. Both groups of children, or more properly all children, were thought to experience a range of disfluencies in their speech as a natural concomitant of language acquisition. A critical point in the development of stuttering was thought to be attained when adults in the child's world labeled him as a stutterer. The act of calling attention to the child's speech was thought to serve as a source of anxiety to the child. The resulting increases in attentiveness to the act of speaking served to yield increases in the frequency and possibly the severity of speech disfluencies.

Bloodstein (1958) and Bloodstein, Alper, and Zisk (1965) presented a similar view of the probable basis for stuttering. This view suggested that the continuing occurrence of speech disfluencies in the presence of pressure to maintain communication increases the severity and duration of the normal types of disfluencies, which, in turn, leads to the expectancy of difficulty in future similar communication situations.

Van Riper (1954) also presented a more refined version of the conditioned anxiety hypothesis. A comprehensive attempt was made to describe the condition of the stutterer just before an attempt to say a feared or difficult-to-say word. It was assumed that a characteristic "set" was established by the stutterer prior to speaking a feared or difficult word. Increases in muscle tension and incorrect placement of articulatory mechanisms were judged to make it difficult for the stutterer to produce the intended word.

Psychoanalytically derived theories constitute another general form of conceptualization that has been applied to stuttering. This type of approach, often termed the "medical" model, applies generally not only to stuttering but to other maladaptive behaviors. The deviant responses are considered to be symptoms of an internalized emotional conflict. Thus, when considered from this point of view, the observable characteristics of stuttering are thought to be symptomatic of an unconscious conflict or a neurotic need. In contemporary literature on speech pathology there are discussions of approaches to the treatment of stuttering based on "symptomatic therapies" versus what some workers apparently believe to be the valid forms of therapy. The considerable attention received by the medical model conception of deviant behavior within psychiatry and psychology has carried over into many current considerations of stuttering. The pervasive impact of these views has been reflected in the variety of forms in which psychotherapy has become an important component in many attempts to treat stuttering.

With the development of learning theory in psychology, a variety of systematic attempts were made to conceptualize the problem of stuttering within a framework of learning principles. Wischner (1950) illustrated the potential utility of a learning theory approach by pointing out how reinforcement for stuttering might be derived from reductions in anxiety which occurred with the termination of a speech block. In addition, Wischner showed that the adaptation effect, observed reductions in the number of disfluencies that result from repeated oral reading of a passage, could be interpreted in terms of learning principles. Another learning theory interpretation was offered by Sheehan (1958), who held that stuttering could be based on a double-approach avoidance conflict model similar to that described by Miller. In Sheehan's paradigm stuttering represented an oscillatory speech pattern that was based on changes in the relative strength of the desire to speak versus the relative strength of the motivation to avoid speaking. Different sources of speech avoidance motivation were postulated, ranging from past conditioning of anxiety to specific words to needs to avoid threats associated with potential success or failure in communication.

An additional learning paradigm was suggested by Shames and Sherrick (1963). These authors did not appeal to elaborate hypothetical constructs and intervening variables in their approach. Stuttering was discussed in terms of operant behavior. Shames and Sherrick considered the possible roles of positive reinforcement, negative reinforcement, and schedules of reinforcement in the development of stuttering, and suggested that in children normal disfluent speech responses could be strengthened by a variety of conditioning principles.

Subsequent to a demonstration that stuttering frequency could be reduced by punishment (Flanagan, Goldiamond, and Azrin, 1958) it was shown by Goldiamond (1965) that the disfluent speech of stutterers could be reshaped into fluent speech through the use of operant conditioning procedures. The Goldiamond study was significant because it showed that operant response shaping techniques could reliably lead to improvements in speech fluency, at least within the confines of the laboratory. In a number of cases, success was reported in the transference of improved speech fluency into the stutterer's everday life.

Brutten and Shoemaker (1967) presented another interpretation of stuttering as learned behavior. These authors stressed the role of classical conditioning in establishing connections between cues in situations that evoked negative emotion (autonomic activity) and the response of stuttering. Disfluent speech was considered to be caused by cognitive and motoric disorganization which stems directly from the autonomic bodily activities labeled as negative emotion. Various situational cues then become conditioned stimuli for the elicitation of the learned autonomic activity which, in turn, produces stuttering. Brutten and Shoemaker's form of desensitization therapy is based on this specific paradigm.

There remains one general class of theories pertaining to stuttering. Servosystem paradigms are based on analogies between self-regulating systems (often mechanical or electrical systems are used for purposes of comparison) and the mechanisms of speech. Experiments by Lee (1950a, 1950b, 1951) showed that the speech of normally fluent subjects was disrupted by delayed auditory feedback, thus suggesting that a closed feedback loop was involved in speech control. Closed-loop servosystems function by producing an output of some type which is sensed and compared with a reference value. Differences between the reference value and the output are detected and when the difference exceeds a predetermined value, an adjustment is automatically made to the input source, which, in turn, restores the output characteristics to the desired value.

Fairbanks (1954) presented a theoretical account of the speech mechanism as a servosystem. In this model, acoustic and somesthetic signals associated with speech were fed back and compared with the characteristics of the intended output. A variety of hypothetical entities was postulated to account for the regulation of speech output. Mysak (1959, 1960) also presented a servosystem theory. In his theory Mysak suggested that disturbance in feedback loops could conceivably result in disruptions of the flow of speech. More recently, Webster and Lubker (1968) presented a somewhat more parsimonious and more empirically oriented servosystem model of stuttering. These investigators held that muscles in the middle ear, which contract in a speech-associated mode, could be responsible for producing disruption in properties of auditory feedback signals which are normally used in speech guidance.

None of the existing accounts of stuttering provides a satisfactory theoretical framework for integrating information in this area. Theories of stuttering are somewhat reminiscent of the theorizing seen in psychology from the late 1930s through the 1950s. The theories are broad in scope, use an excess of loosely identified intervening variables, and pay too little attention to the objectively measurable aspects of stuttering. Assumptions have taken precedence over careful observation and experimentation. A redress of this situation is required if theories dealing with stuttering are to assume scientific maturity.

OVERVIEW OF TREATMENT METHODS

Various treatments have been employed in attempts to alleviate the problem of stuttering. Once more, to provide some perspective on general treatment forms, an overview is presented of selected developments which have occurred in this century. Before describing the types of treatment used, it should be pointed out to those readers who have little previous knowledge of stuttering that the problem has not yielded readily or reliably to treatment by any procedure or combination of procedures.

With the advent of theoretical treatments of stuttering, systematic, logically derived forms of therapy were developed. Perhaps the most pervasive treatment devised for stuttering was psychotherapy. Stuttering was seen by the psychoanalytically oriented workers as a neurotic symptom. The focus of treatment involved the identification of unconscious conflict and the subsequent restructuring of personality. There have been few concrete data presented to suggest that psychotherapy is an effective procedure for the treatment of stuttering. Even so, the impact of psychoanalytically oriented procedures may be seen in the majority of the forms of therapy that have been devised for stuttering. One particularly deleterious aspect of the strong psychoanalytic orientation has been to deter therapists from attempts to manipulate stuttered speech. Removal of a stutterer's defenses by reducing disfluencies was judged to be a dangerous undertaking. It was feared that the successful removal of stuttering could result in the appearance of some other neurotic symptom that could be more harmful than stuttering.

Other developments in therapy during the decade of the 1930s were derived from the cerebral dominance theory of Travis (1931) and the dysphemia notion of West (1936). Among the procedures used were a shifting of hand use and the use of coincident speech and writing in an effort to shift the dominance of cerebral functioning. As part of the treatment, attempts were made to cause the stutterer to attend to his speech more carefully. The idea was to move speech to a less automatic and more directly controlled level.

Formal developments in speech therapy were closely linked to the emergence of a discipline concerned with speech and hearing disorder. At the University of Iowa, under the supervision of Lee Edward Travis, a group of researchers and clinicians brought this interest to bear on problems of speech and hearing. Among prominent developments that emerged from the University of Iowa during the 1930s were the different therapies set forth by Bryngelson, Johnson, and Van Riper. The ideas of these men have had a profound and continuing effect on the training of most contemporary workers in the area of stuttering. Their contributions to theory and therapy extend over a period of 30 years or more.

Bryngelson's (1943) approach involved stressing the stutterer's acquisition of an objective attitude about his problem. The client was taught to accept the problem, to speak freely about it, and to go ahead and stutter freely without attempting to hide or introduce word substitutions or other devices to mask the problem. Bryngelson encouraged the use of voluntary stuttering in addition to work on attitude change. In essence, the stutterer was encouraged to stutter voluntarily so that he might be better able to control the involuntary instances of stuttering when they occurred. Attempting to teach the stutterer to accept his condition was a reasonable goal since the basic problem was judged to be organic in nature. Parenthetically, it is interesting to note that this attitude has been carried over into much of the contemporary training in stuttering therapy. Many therapists still seek to teach the stutterer to accept his condition.

A somewhat different approach was taken by Johnson (1955), who maintained that stuttering was based on reactions to environmental pressures and not on organic factors. The basic concept underlying Johnson's theory was that there were no genuine differences between stutterers and fluent speakers. Any observed differences were thought to have resulted from pressures placed on the child by his caretakers as he passed through a period of "normal" disfluencies. The emotional responses generated by calling attention to the child's speech were judged to be responsible for increasing the frequency and duration of his disfluencies. The goals in Johnson's therapy were to teach the stutterer to manage speech situations without embarrassment or fear. At first, the technique of voluntary stuttering was used by Johnson. The concept was that voluntary stuttering could be used to weaken the tendency to stutter and to transform instances of stuttering into the type of disfluencies that were similar to those of so-called normal speakers. Of particular importance to Johnson were the perceptions the stutterer had of himself. Subsequent developments in Johnson's approach involved trying to implement changes in the stutterer's self-appraisal by focusing on the meaning of the language he used in describing himself. The personal meanings of words applied to the self, such as "stutterer," were examined in order to establish how the stutterer perceived himself as being different from other speakers. In addition, the stutterer was led to an awareness that the speech-associated activities which were actually interfering with his communication efforts were, in fact, self-produced. Through an increased awareness of his own activities and increased clarity of self-perception, it was expected that the stutterer would progressively improve in his ability to talk without emitting the interfering stuttering behaviors.

Still another approach was taken by Van Riper (1937, 1958), who chose to deal primarily with treatment of the stutterer's fears. Van Riper did not dwell extensively on the fundamental reasons for stuttering. Instead, he focused on the role of anticipatory reactions in stuttering. The therapeutic goal was to teach the stutterer how to stutter "fluently." Specific steps in therapy were designed to change the stutterer's preparatory set through (1) initiating speech with the articulators in a resting state (2) making the first speech sound as a smooth-flowing movement into the next sound and (3) initiating the flow of air through the larynx in an immediate effort to say the intended word. Additional steps included teaching the stutterer techniques of "pullout," a smooth prolongation of a word begun with blockage, and "cancellation," a renewed and improved effort to say a word on which a speech block had just occurred. The effects of these manipulations were interpreted by Van Riper in terms of internalized changes in the stutterer's ability to cope with his fears or, in other words, as a nonverbal form of psychotherapy.

Brutten and Shoemaker (1967) presented a program of therapy based on counterconditioning procedures. It was assumed in their approach that the speech disruptions of stuttering were produced by internalized fear responses which had been classically conditioned to speech situations. The therapeutic effort consisted of two parts. First, new and incompatible responses were conditioned to specific conditioned fear stimuli. A primary response to be acquired was that of deep-muscle relaxation (Jacobson, 1938). Next, the stutterer progressively worked through a hierarchy of feared speech situations, gradually acquiring and extending the ability to maintain a relaxed state in the presence of conditioned fear stimuli. The second portion of therapy aimed at the reduction of the instrumental responses associated with stuttering. These responses include escape and avoidance behaviors, eye blinks, sudden inhalations, and similar behaviors often regarded as "symptoms" of stuttering. Instrumental responses were to be inhibited by the use of extended periods of response repetition. The idea was that reactive inhibition and conditioned inhibition would eventually serve to reduce the frequency with which these undesirable behaviors occurred. This type of orientation toward stuttering therapy has become quite popular, possibly because of the prominent belief that stuttering is emotional in its origin.

The observation that stuttering decreases when speech accompanies a rhythmic stimulus has served as a basis for a form of therapy developed by Brady (1969, 1971). In this program, the stutterer wears a small metronome on the ear, much like a hard-of-hearing person wears a hearing aid. Stutterers are trained to initiate words in accompaniment with the clicks from the metronome. Whenever possible, the stutterer's reliance on the metronome is gradually reduced to the point where he can maintain fluent speech without it. This form of therapy has not been well regarded by those with a "traditional" background in the speech area. It has been maintained that the metronome is nothing more than a "distraction" and that it is essentially impossible for the stutterer to remain fluent because the effects of the distraction will eventually wear off. Speech workers seem to have ignored the significance of the point that rhythmic cueing stimuli, as well as other clearly specifiable stimuli, demonstrably attenuate stuttering. Rather than search for mechanisms that could realistically explain the observations, the trend has been to dismiss the phenomenon and to retain the vague concept of distraction.

In 1965 Goldiamond presented a detailed report outlining operant shaping procedures he employed to establish fluent speech in stutterers. This report by Goldiamond was significant for a number of reasons. It brought the following to bear on stuttering: (1) the systematic, direct manipulation of the observable properties of stuttered speech; (2) the application of operant conditioning principles that were well understood and based on extensive laboratory research; (3) a strong bias toward observing the characteristics of stuttering rather than theorizing about the problem; and (4) reliable improvements in speech fluency were produced, which seemed to have significant potential for further analysis. Goldiamond's basic procedure was to employ delayed auditory feedback in conjunction with prolonged speech to establish an initial, manipulable fluent speech pattern on an oral reading task. Delayed auditory feedback gradually was faded out and slow, prolonged speech remained. The program then proceeded gradually to accelerate the rate of speech of the subjects. Fluent oral reading was established in all stutterers. In a number of cases, a schedule of home exercises was initiated. The stutterers would read for a short period of time at home with the very slow and then the normal fluent rates that had been established in the laboratory. After completing the reading, the subjects would engage in conversation with others for a short period of time. The amount of time spent in conversation was increased by small increments until the stutterers were able to maintain fluent conversational speech for long periods of time. A number of Goldiamond's subjects were successful in generalizing the new fluent speech pattern to their everyday life settings.

As Williams (1968) indicated, many of the stuttering therapies in use today reflect a mixture of procedures. Often these procedures have incompatible goals. For example, the therapies employed by those who adhere to the disintegration theories have two essential goals: the first is to teach the stutterer to accept the condition of stuttering, and the second is to try to teach the person how to reduce the degree of effort involved in stuttering. Williams has pointed out that many of the current therapeutic efforts still involve helping the individual to accept the fact that he is a stutterer when, very often, other aspects of the same therapy are treating stuttering as a form of learned behavior. This apparent contradiction in orientations is very much a characteristic of current efforts to treat the problem of stuttering.

It is interesting to compare the general and rather vague treatments used for stuttering with the nature of treatments rendered for more specific problems, for example, articulatory defects. Relatively few speech therapists have any hesitation in attempting to correct the production of deficient speech sounds. There may be some lack of agreement regarding the specific type of instructional technique used in instruction, but vigorous attempts at restructuring articulatory patterns are made, usually with substantial success. However, in marked contrast to their approach in dealing with articulation defects, speech therapists usually have not attempted to apply systematic, direct, manipulative techniques to stuttering. The old taboos associated with the "distraction" forms of therapy and the apparent fear of symptom substitution, or the hesitancy in calling attention to stuttering in young children for fear of causing them to perceive themselves as stutterers, have impeded most of the directive attempts to deal with the problem.

At the present time, there seems to be no specific type of stuttering therapy which has a history of reliably and efficiently eliminating or markedly reducing the problem. A number of the important theories of stuttering have been originated by men who are themselves stutterers. It appears as if many of the theorists have selected a point of view and have tried to elaborate on that point of view without following the precepts of rigorous scientific investigation. In fact, it may be fairly said that many of the theories of stuttering and their associated therapies are based on more or less extended common sense interpretations and/or impressionistic data, rather than on carefully conducted studies which meet acceptable standards of scientific rigor and objectivity.

An examination of most reports on stuttering therapies gives few, if any, quantitative data on the performance of those being treated. In general, most therapies have focused on global aspects of personality rather than on measurable speech properties. Attempts seem to have been largely devoted to defining how the stutterer reacts in various speaking situations, to understanding the stutterer's attitudes, feelings, and emotions, and to restructuring his attitudes toward himself and his listeners. Relatively little objective information has accompanied the reports on stuttering therapy. For example, even Van Riper's (1958) well-respected report on experiments in stuttering therapy is rich in qualitative description and deficient in quantitative information on speech behavior. Although the methods of evaluation available include overall severity ratings by clinicians (Cullinan, Prather, and Williams, 1963), estimates of tension and struggle (Rousey, 1958), self-ratings, and measures of disfluency durations and frequencies, in actual clinical practice there seems to be little reliance on measurement.

Speech evaluations of stutterers received by the Hollins Stuttering Research Project support the previous statement. Approximately one out of ten evaluations we receive gives any form of quantification based on observable, measurable speech characteristics. About half the reports use general descriptive terms like mild, moderate, or severe without specifying what these terms mean. Close to half the reports mention apparent levels of tension manifest in speech attempts. Any evaluations of progress in therapy have almost exclusively been limited to statements regarding improvements in attitudes toward one's self or speaking situations.

Meaningful statements about the comparative efficacy of traditional therapies simply cannot be made in the absence of quantitative data. Existing therapies have not been documented to produce reliable improvements in the speech fluency of treated clients.

St. Onge and Calvert (1964, p. 159) offer a particularly cogent comment: "The scholar who attempts to teach in the area of stuttering spends most of his time clarifying what the majority of experts disbelieve about stuttering, simply because the area of disbelief so greatly exceeds the consensus." This statement would become less applicable if more attention were given to studying the observable aspects of stuttered speech.

DEVELOPMENT OF THE FLUENCY SHAPING PROGRAM AT HOLLINS COLLEGE

Our present fluency shaping program has evolved through five different identifiable versions. Each of the revisions has generated advancements in (1) the transfer of improved fluency from the laboratory to the stutterer's everyday life, (2) the retention of improved fluency following completion of the program, (3) the specificity of the skills learned in the program, and (4) the reliability and the ease with which the fluency shaping program itself could be administered. Our goal in establishing the program has been to provide, whenever possible, a standardized, reliable form of therapy which does not rely on expensive apparatus or highly specialized, long-term training.

It is important to make the point that it was essentially our rejection of cumbersome, poorly defined theoretical notions about stuttering which led to the current program. We have focused on an empirical analysis of the variables that control fluency establishment and retention in stutterers. We have carefully avoided traditional attempts to treat the "whole person" in the derivation of the program. We have attempted to manipulate only those components of stuttering that are directly observable. Our rationale has been that by first studying and manipulating the clearly observable behavioral aspects of stuttering, we shall eventually be in a better position to deal with less tangible characteristics of the problem.

Dependent Variable Measure

The dependent variable measure used in our program has been the number (or percentage) of disfluent words produced by the subject. A disfluent word is scored if a subject displays one or more of the following behaviors: struggle concurrent with speech initiation, silent stops, forced breathing, facial grimaces, or repetitions of sounds, syllables, or words. We used this measure for the following reasons: (1) it is a sensitive response measure; (2) it is a reliable response measure [the reliability of disfluent word counts by two different and independent observers has consistently ranged from 90 to 100 percent in our laboratory (Webster and Dorman, 1970)]; (3) the measure is convenient to use in a clinical or research setting where large quantities of data are handled; and (4) the measure seems to covary well with subjective estimates regarding the overall severity of stuttering. We have not counted the total number of disfluencies that occur on a given word, because observer reliability in scoring is decreased.

Our considerations of stuttering do not involve a dichotomy of stutterer versus nonstutterer. Instead, we think of a continuum of fluency-disfluency, which ranges from highly fluent speech at one extreme to severe stuttering at the other. The fluency shaping program moves the stutterer toward the fluent end of the continuum. In the context of our program we do not think in terms of "curing" the stutterer. The term "cure" is not especially useful because of the variety of its meanings. We can state, however, with accuracy and reliability that a given stutterer has been moved from one region to another on the fluency-disfluency continuum.

Program I. The first program was conducted with two severe stutterers and was essentially a replication of Goldiamond's (1965) procedures. We found that excellent laboratory fluency was generated in both subjects. These subjects reported difficulty in maintaining a slow rate of speech outside the laboratory. Extensive sessions in the laboratory did not markedly improve their ability to employ a fluent speech pattern away from the laboratory. Nor was there a reduction in speech disfluencies in daily life when home practice included exercises involving the use of a tape recorder.

Program II. This program was a revision based on several items of information generated in our laboratory. First, we had been aware of the fact that continuous presentation of delayed auditory feedback was sufficient to increase speech fluency in stutterers (Webster, Schumacher, and Lubker, 1970). Hence we eliminated the contingent relationships specified by Goldiamond. Next, we chose to avoid using elaborate apparatus to control the subject's reading rates. Finally, we added a step involving rate discrimination training. The general steps used in the second program are described next. (Each subject was advanced through the program on the basis of his progress within each step. Unless otherwise noted, subjects read from prepared texts.)

During each of the first three days, 40-minute baseline recordings of oral reading were made and disfluent words were counted. As the first step in the program, the subjects, using a hand counter, recorded each instance of a disfluent word. When the counts for the subject and experimenter were approximately equal, the next stage was begun.

Several variables were introduced next. The first was the continuous presentation of delayed auditory feedback. The subject wore headphones and spoke into a microphone connected to a delayed auditory feedback tape recorder set for a 0.2-second delay interval. At the same time, the subject was instructed to prolong his speech by markedly increasing the duration of vowel sounds. The nature of the correct responses was illustrated to the subject by the experimenter and then the subject tried prolongation until he was able to make correct responses. The subject thus began reading with very slow, prolonged speech on delayed auditory feedback. The effect of this treatment was to produce fluent speech in all subjects. Delayed auditory feedback was gradually faded out by turning down the volume control knob on the recorder. From approximately the fifth or sixth session, the subjects continued to produce self-maintained fluent speech without delayed auditory feedback. The rate of speaking was approximately 30 words per minute at this point in the program.

Our next step involved what we designated as "smoothing out" the slow speech. Smoothing was done by instructing the subject in how to decrease the speed and initial amplitude with which he made consonant sounds while maintaining prolongation of vowel sounds. The instruction sequence at this point included having the subjects learn to make gradual transitions from one speech sound to another within words. When gradual sound transitions were achieved, the speech rate of the subject was gradually increased to approximately 100 to 120 words per minute. In the event that stuttering occurred at any point in the speed-up process, the first instruction to the subject was to smooth out his sound transitions. If this instruction did not immediately improve fluency, then the speech rate was slowed. Following the recovery of fluency at the slower rate, the speech rate was increased and the program continued until speech reached a slow, normal rate (approximately 120 words per minute).

The succeeding step was labeled "rate discrimination training." Here the subject was taught to identify and to speak at one of two different rates of speech. The subject was instructed to speak at approximately 110 words a minute for two minutes and then was switched to a rate of about 75 words a minute for a two-minute period. At two-minute intervals, a cue was given to switch from one rate to the other. After achieving reliable rate discrimination, the steps of conversation were initiated. The subject was given a magazine and told to describe in one short sentence a picture or an advertisement. The speech rate was approximately 120 words per minute. When the subject was able to describe the pictures with short sentences, he was instructed to produce more elaborate descriptions using longer sentences or chains of sentences. When performance at this stage of the program was stable (i.e., no stuttering after approximately one hour of sessions), actual conversations began between the subject and the experimenter. Next, the subject was asked to use his fluent speech in conversation within the laboratory building. After a few days of conversation in the laboratory environment, the subject was asked to use his new speech pattern for short periods of time at home. He was told that if he was successful in utilizing the new fluent pattern, he was to continue using it. In the event he had any difficulty in maintaining fluent speech, he was to do one of two things, either (1) to concentrate more completely on the new speech pattern and to use it correctly or, failing that, (2) to completely give up any attempts to use the new fluent speech pattern while away from the laboratory. In general, we found that once the subjects began to use fluent speech in the home, they could extend this to other areas of conversation. During the portion of the program that was concerned with transfer, training in conversation within the laboratory continued. Subjects terminated the program when they reported that they were experiencing less than approximately five instances of speech blockage during the day.

All subjects ($N = 16$) eventually succeeded in transferring fluent speech (defined here as less than a 2 percent disfluent word rate) to settings away from the laboratory. For some, the transition was relatively easy. For others, however, the process was very slow and unstable. After approximately 10 months following completion of the program, all subjects reported that their speech was markedly improved. Most of the subjects reported that they could maintain good speech fluency; however, they reported that great concentration was required on their part and that even then they were not able to maintain good fluency at all times. Several subjects reported a recurrence of stuttering at approximately their previous levels. One of these was brought back to the laboratory and run through the rate discrimination and conversation steps. He subsequently reported that his speech was improved but careful concentration was required to maintain fluency. The others were not able to receive additional training.

Program III. This version of the program was developed after a variety of attempts were made to improve upon Program II. The second program had been uniformly successful in establishing absolutely excellent speech fluency in stutterers within the laboratory. The fact that all stutterers showed substantial improvement in speech fluency outside the laboratory was also somewhat gratifying. However, the relative difficulty in attaining the use of fluent speech in settings away from the laboratory exceeded what we regarded as acceptable limits. At first we felt that the process of transferring fluent speech into everyday speaking situations merely required constructing finer gradations of tasks in the approximation to normal speech environments. After trying changes of this type in the program, we noted little improvement in terminal performance. Other variations of the program were tried: the experimenter accompanied stutterers into speech situations outside the laboratory and delivered reinforcements for fluent speech episodes; training in relaxation was tried; further training employing techniques of desensitization were also tested; a variety of pep talks were used; and some stutterers were even subjected to various types of punishment for instances of disfluent speech in situations outside the laboratory. Much to our dismay, none of these modifications had the desired effect of stabilizing fluent speech outside the laboratory. Finally, we considered the possibility that perhaps we had been asking the subjects to learn too many different kinds of behavior at one time.

Speech consists of chains of phonemes, syllables, words, phrases, and sentences. It occurred to us that specific desired articulatory gestures might be more readily discriminable to the subject at the level of the word or syllable than they would be when embedded in longer chains. In addition, the adequacy of vowel prolongation and gentle consonant initiation in single sounds could be detected more readily by the experimenter and this information could be relayed with increased precision to the subject as a means of aiding his learning.

To increase the specificity of the training, we chose to initiate Program III with single words. Individual words were presented to the subject. Instructions were given in how to prolong vowel sounds. The subject was given an opportunity to practice on successive trials, with the experimenter feeding back statements to him regarding the adequacy of his performance. Next, the gentle initiation of speech sounds was taught. After that, the subject moved progressively through a series of several hundred single words, gradually reducing the degree of prolongation to the point where the word durations were approximately the length that would occur at speech rates of approximately 100 to 130 words per minute. After achieving a stable level of performance with prolongation and gentle sound onsets, the subject began to make up two- and three-word sentences from the single words. The subject moved on to construct progressively longer self-generated sentences. Conversation was phased-in in the laboratory setting, and then transferred to other locations within the building in which the laboratory was located. The fluent speech pattern was then transferred into everyday life. We asked the subject to use fluent speech during designated periods throughout the day and gradually extended the duration of these periods until he was reporting good speech fluency throughout the entire day. The training in the production of single words and self-generated sentences in conversation continued in the laboratory as the transfer phases were taking place.

It soon became evident that we were at last beginning to isolate some of the critical variables involved in the transfer and retention of fluent speech. A significant observation was made with the first subjects who went through this version of the program. In all cases, these subjects offered much less resistance to initiating the activities involved in transferring speech to settings outside the laboratory. The subjects did not offer excuses that would prevent them from going outside the laboratory to practice their new speech in real situations, and they did not require the extensive "prodding" that had been required by some of the subjects in earlier versions of the program. A second benefit appeared to be the increase in certainty of the subjects' knowledge of what they were doing in order to remain fluent. It appeared to us as if the subjects were more aware of the specific articulatory gestures involved in the production of fluent speech. By increasing the specificity of what the stutterers learned in the laboratory, we were better able to insure that they could practice these new responses upon moving to new and different environments.

Program IV. The fourth edition of the fluency shaping program further increased the specification of the tasks to be learned by the stutterers. Instead of starting with a nonsystematic presentation of words of different lengths, we initiated the program with one-syllable words, moved next to two-syllable words, three-syllable words, short, self-generated sentences, longer sentences, conversation, then the transfer of fluent speech to settings outside the laboratory.

In earlier versions of the program we found that the experimenter often became a discriminative stimulus for the subject's speech fluency. Transfer of fluent speech to everyday life settings became more difficult to achieve when the experimenter served as a cue for fluent speech. A number of subjects verbalized that they could speak fluently with some degree of confidence as long as the experimenter was there to serve as a reminder of what they were supposed to do. An analysis of our procedures for feeding performance evaluations back to the subjects led us to conclude that we had inadvertently structured the learning environment in a way that interfered with the establishment of the desired terminal fluent speech behavior. Before beginning each section of the program, the subjects had been instructed in the form of the responses to be made. Illustrations of the responses were given to them by the experimenter and the subject was then asked to try to produce the correct behaviors. On each trial, the experimenter verbally fed back information to the subject, telling him whether or not the word had been spoken correctly, and if it had not been spoken correctly, how it was to be spoken on the next trial. The apparent flaw in this procedure is that extensive feedback of information provided a crutch on which some subjects came to rely. Thus, at this point, we decided that it would be important to reduce the participation of the experimenter in the therapeutic interaction.

Our next step was to alter the procedures for feeding back information about the adequacy of subjects' responses. We decided to reduce the continuous verbal, instructional participation of the experimenter. Initial instructions specifying the correct responses were given and a few trials were then made by the subject, who was corrected by the experimenter. After that, feedback to the subjects in Program IV was provided through a light and counter which were controlled by the experimenter and the subject. After the subject emitted the speech response, he pressed his button. If, in the experimenter's judgment, the response just emitted had met the criteria that were sought, a green light went on in front of the subject and a point was added to the counter. If the response was incorrect, nothing happened when the subject pressed his button and that trial was repeated. The introduction of the self-correction procedure and the further increase in the structure within the program once more increased the ease with which the subjects went about transferring fluency into their everyday life and resulted in further improvements in the retention of fluency.

The findings from Programs III and IV were particularly gratifying. Each time we improved the specificity of the subject's tasks, we found that the activities involving transfer and retention of fluency were handled with greater ease. It no longer became necessary to give subjects pep talks or to deliver external reinforcements or punishments to have them sustain a fluent speech pattern outside the laboratory. It was becoming increasingly evident that once the subjects knew precisely what behaviors had to be produced to yield fluent speech, the intrinsic reinforcers for fluency would apparently sustain the activity.

Program V. The main thrust of our observations through four versions of the program had been to indicate that *precision of instruction regarding small response units was probably the critical variable* in determining the success or failure of the program in establishing fluency in any given stutterer. To learn more about what specific skills should be taught, we examined the speech sound characteristics of approximately 60 stutterers who ranged in severity from slight stuttering to very severe stuttering. In every case, when in tests the stutterer sufficiently reduced the initial intensity of speech onset below that of his stuttered speech and simultaneously increased the duration of speech sounds, disfluencies did not occur. It was clear that certain specific physical movements and certain forces were characteristic of disfluent speech while other movements and forces were characteristic of fluent speech in the same individuals. This information led to a rather simple, basic premise which underlies Program V: *stutterers make the sounds of speech incorrectly.* (At this point, we will make no attempt to infer why stutterers make speech sounds incorrectly, nor will we try to specify what proportions of speech sounds are made incorrectly; we are only reporting a generalization based on our observations.)

The fluency shaping program was now seen as a systematic means of purposefully modifying the characteristic movements and forces in the speech of stutterers. At the most parsimonious level of specification, it seemed that we were teaching three basic skills: (1) the gentle initiation of phonation (or, more precisely, how to produce speech which had "correct" amplitude versus time contours rather than the "incorrect" amplitude versus time contours of disfluent speech); (2) how to produce unvoiced consonants in such a way that the "correct" phonetory activity could occur following those sounds; and (3) how to slightly increase the duration of most speech sounds.

The fifth edition of the program was constructed during the summer and fall of 1969. A sequence of speech tasks was assembled which began with the acquisition of simple phonetory and articulatory skills at the level of sounds and syllables. The sounds of American English were placed into the following four functionally defined classes: class I, vowels; class II, vowel-like consonants (sounds represented by the letters L, R, M, N, V, J, W, Y, and Z); class III, sounds that were easy to modify in terms of duration and were characterized by the passage of air through a constricted vocal opening prior to the onset of phonation (fricative sounds represented by the letters F, S, H, SH, CH, and the voiceless TH; and class IV, the stop-consonants (plosive sounds represented by the letters P, B, G, K, D, and T). Our experience indicated that each class of sounds in the progression was slightly more complex and difficult to modify than the preceding class.

A series of reference sounds, or speech sound targets, was established for each step within the program. The subject had examples of correct speech sound targets presented to him before beginning each portion of the program. After each trial, the subject pressed a button. If, in the experimenter's judgment, the subject's response was correct, a green light flashed in front of the subject and he then went on to the next trial. If the subject's response was incorrect, the experimenter pressed a button which prevented the signal light from coming on. The subject then repeated the trial until he got it correct several times in succession.

After completing the section containing sounds and syllables, the subject started a segment of the program consisting of one-syllable words. This portion of the program contained a sequence of words that began with class I sounds. Words beginning with class II sounds were next, followed by words beginning with class III sounds and, finally, words beginning with class IV sounds. The next section of the program consisted of two-syllable words. The progression from class I through class IV sounds in the initial position was again used here. The next section of the program contained words with three or more syllables and again the progression went from words starting with class I through class IV sounds. Throughout the sections on sounds, syllables, and individual words, a variety of important sound blends was also practiced.

The duration of the one-syllable words was greatly exaggerated at the outset. With increased proficiency in attaining the gentle onset and duration speech targets, the amount of prolongation was reduced until, by the time the subjects were working with three-syllable words, they were producing words of a duration that would be associated with the speech rate of 100 to 130 words per minute. At the next stage of the program the subjects constructed short sentences. After that, longer sentences were constructed by defining the meaning of single words. Speech rates were maintained at approximately 100 to 130 words per minute in conversation.

The transfer activities in this version of the program were initiated in parallel, successive stages beginning very early in the program. Subjects began to transfer practice on single words into their home environment early in the program, to practice some limited conversation at home using an exaggerated slow speech pattern, and then as the progression through the program continued, they transferred longer and more comprehensive fluent speech behavior into their everyday lives. As the final transfer portions of the program were taking place, laboratory training on the basic skills continued.

The fluency shaping program now consists of three major items: (1) a 650-page programmed text which the stutterer works through under the guidance of a therapist; (2) a therapist's guide which sets forth the administration procedures for the entire program; and (3) a series of tape recordings used to illustrate the speech targets at different stages through the program. These materials are now being readied for public distribution.

Normal administration of Program V has ranged from 40 to 60 laboratory hours per individual. The program has been used in a slightly simplified form with children at 6 to 8 years of age. It is intended for use with individuals over approximately the ages of 10 to 12. The oldest person to go through the program was 57 years of age. A total of 55 stutterers have gone through this version of the program.

We have found that the program requires a minimum of six hours per week to produce its effects in an efficient manner. Typical therapy sessions, one hour in duration, several times a week, are spaced too far apart for significant learning to occur. In most of our cases, subjects go through an intensive three-week program, working 4 to 7 hours a day for 15 to 21 days. This type of schedule permits a dramatic, rapid improvement in speech fluency. The rapid rate of fluency acquisition is probably an important form of reinforcement that contributes to the success of the program.

RESULTS OBTAINED WITH PROGRAM V

A randomly selected sample of 17 male and 3 female stutterers was examined approximately two years after their completion of Program V. It should be noted that this specific version of Program V did not involve the parallel transfer aspects used in the current version. The transfer activities were still confined to the end of the program. Subjects ranged in age from 8 to 52 years. The median age at treatment was 25 years. The median time since program completion in this follow-up study was 25 months.

Table 2 shows disfluent word frequencies and self-reports on speech quality obtained in the follow-up study. The disfluent word frequencies observed in the baseline sessions, prior to the initiation of the fluency shaping program, are also shown. The distributions of disfluent word frequencies before and again approximately two years after the program are shown in Figure 1.

Figure 1 shows that the posttreatment measures shifted toward the low end of the disfluency continuum. In the posttreatment oral reading task, 13 out of 20 subjects had disfluent word frequencies at or below 1 percent. In the posttreatment conversation measure, 9 out of 20 subjects scored at or below 1 percent disfluencies. In all cases, decreases in disfluent word frequencies occurred from pretreatment to posttreatment measures. The pretreatment and posttreatment differences for both conversation and reading are significantly different at

Table 2. Pretreatment and Posttreatment Data

Subject	Age	Sex	Treatment-Follow-Up Interval (months)	Disfluent Words Prior to Treatment (Reading only) (%)	Disfluent Words after Treatment (%)		FOLLOW-UP DATA					
					Reading	Conversation	Subject's Report of Posttreatment Speech Quality vs. Pretreatment Speech Quality			Subject Satisfied with Current Level of Speech Fluency?		
							Better	Same	Worse	Yes	Somewhat	No
P.P.	20	M	30	19	<1	3	X			X		
P.J.	40	M	27	6	1	3	X			X		
G.K.	52	F	33	15	2	1	X				X	
F.T.	8	M	24	4	3	1	X			X		
P.J.	36	M	29	8	1	1	X					X
P.J.	33	M	33	3	<1	<1	X			X		
M.G.	16	M	30	33	9	4	X			X		
C.B.	23	M	28	6	<1	0	X					X
W.C.	21	F	26	1	<1	<1	X			X		
R.C.	27	M	27	16	<1	<1	X			X		
C.J.	45	M	6	6	1	0	X			X		
B.J.	28	M	8	20	1	1	X			X		
C.R.	14	M	12	12	7	8		X				X
Z.G.	27	M	26	11	3	4	X					X
P.G.	33	M	4	20	3	5	X			X		
S.R.	22	M	4	11	3	2	X			X		
O.R.	34	M	15	47	<1	1	X			X		
S.L.	17	F	21	27	0	10	X					X
T.M.	12	M	11	17	5	5	X					X
G.W.	22	M	10	19	4	3	X				X	

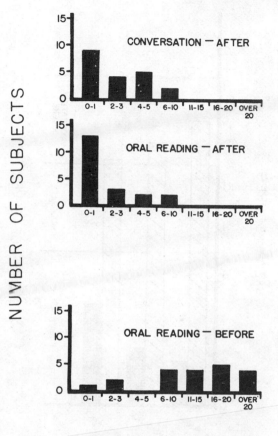

Figure 1. Percentage of disfluent words in the speech of stutterers prior to and then a median time of 25 months following participation in the fluency shaping program.

or beyond the .005 level when tested with the Wilcoxon signed-ranks test.

Limited self-reports were obtained from the entire sample. Of 20 subjects, 19 indicated that their posttreatment speech quality was improved when compared with pretreatment levels. One subject reported his speech was the same as it had been before coming into the program, and none said his speech was worse. The self-reports are consistent with the observed changes in the disfluent word rates. Twelve of the subjects reported that they were satisfied with their current levels of speech fluency. Two said they were somewhat satisfied but felt they could do better, and six said they were not satisfied with their current levels of speech fluency because they were clearly aware of the fact that they had done and could do better. One case, P. J., indicated that he was not satisfied with his current level of speech fluency, even though he scored at an essentially

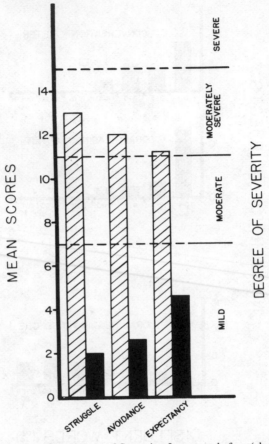

Figure 2. Scores on the Perceptions of Stuttering Inventory before (slashed bars) and then approximately four months following completion of the fluency shaping program (solid bars).

normal level of fluency. Upon further discussion with this subject, he said that he should have completely fluent speech.

Perceptions of Stuttering Inventory

Self-report data have been collected on another sample of 19 stutterers who completed Program V. Only one stutterer occurs in both samples reported in this chapter. The self-report form used was an instrument designated as the *Perceptions of Stuttering Inventory* (Woolf, 1967). The instrument consists of 60 items. The person taking the inventory checks whether or not each item is characteristic of him at that time. There are three scales, each of which is based on 20 items.

The first scale deals with struggle (repeating a sound or word with effort, prolonging a sound or word while trying to push it out, etc.). The second scale is concerned with avoidance (avoiding talking with others of his own age group, avoiding talking to one or both of his parents, etc.). The third scale deals with expectancy (wondering whether you will stutter or how you will speak if you do stutter, postponing speaking for a short time until certain you can be fluent, saying words slowly or rapidly preceding the word on which stuttering is expected).

Although the instrument is essentially a research instrument and much remains to be learned about its reliability and validity, a previous form of the instrument (Rothenberg, 1963) showed reliability coefficients in the middle to high .80s. Figure 2 shows the mean before-after scores on the *Perceptions of Stuttering Inventory*. The mean time between testing was approximately four months. The mean before-treatment scores were all in the moderately severe area of the scale. In the follow-up data, the mean scores are at the mild end of the scale. It is not unusual to find that the expectancy score is somewhat higher than the struggle and avoidance scores. Since several items on the inventory pertain to various aspects of attention to speaking before producing sounds (saying words slowly or rapidly preceding the word on which stuttering is expected; concentrating on how you are going to speak, e.g., thinking about where to put your tongue or how to breathe), we do not take this score to mean that there is expectancy of the actual act of stuttering. The slightly higher expectancy scores are generally indicative of the fact that the subjects are attending to the task of speaking fluently. It is worth noting that most of the subjects on whom the inventory scores were collected went through the program using the early initiation of transfer. We have observed that there is greater stability of fluency when the early transfer procedure is systematically employed.

General Observations

We observed other changes in our subjects. First, there is usually a decided increase in the amount of verbal output as the subjects progress through the program. Apparently, as it becomes easier to speak fluently, the amount of verbal behavior increases. Second, we also observed that many of the stutterers seem to become more socially aggressive. That is, they display an increased willingness to go into situations that were previously uncomfortable. Third, we observed some dramatic behavioral changes in our subjects in their everyday life situations. For example, one subject, a major in the military service who was a moderate stutterer (approximate 10 percent disfluent word rate), felt that he would not be promoted because of his stuttered speech. After completing the fluency shaping program, he was placed on the promotion list, attended Staff and General Command School, and during oral presentations in classes there was never given less than the top rating. He reported that it was unlikely that anyone at Staff and General Command School knew he was a stutterer. This subject now holds a command position at a large military base in Europe. He spends extensive portions of each day in pressured communication situations and spends much time on the telephone. Personal observation of his fluency made by our staff in his current situation have shown that he speaks with excellent speech fluency (now about 30 months after completing the program). His estimated disfluent word rate in conversations, including telephone conversations, was less than 1 percent. Other subjects have initiated college programs that they had not previously attempted because of their speech deficiencies, and some have undertaken new jobs that could not have been handled previously, for example, becoming newspaper reporters, teachers, and businessmen. Also, three physicians have completed the program and in each case they reported that their professional responsibilities became much easier to handle. Another of the characteristics we observed is that unmarried stutterers who improve the quality of their speech usually show dramatic increases in the frequency and intensity of their contacts with members of the opposite sex.

The results indicate that stutterers generally can and do retain high levels of fluency after a single three-week period of intensive training. It is significant that in many instances the stuttering behavior had existed for 20 or more years prior to the training. It may be concluded that the fluency shaping program is sharpening the focus on how we should approach the problem of stuttering. In those cases where there has been some difficulty in retaining fluent speech, the main problem has been that the stutterers failed to acquire (or maintain) the correct basic skills in sound production. It appears that as long as the stutterer obeys certain "rules of speech mechanics" he will produce speech sounds that are fluent. However, when the movement and forces of speech gestures exceed certain values, at that point the stutterer manifests disfluent speech. Our experience to date indicates that it is quite probable that there are few reasons why an individual who stutters must continue to experience the existing level of his speech handicap. We have worked with mental retardates, cases with cerebral palsy, and instances of stuttering that were so severe that it was virtually impossible to obtain the disfluent word rates on the baseline measures. An exciting and highly significant finding is that *in every instance* it has been possible to establish fluent speech in the laboratory and at worst, to demonstrate some lasting improvements in fluency in the everyday speech of most subjects.

THE PROBABLE BASIS FOR STUTTERING

The preceding discussion of the fluency shaping program was based on observations resulting from the direct manipulation of stuttered speech. The procedures were empirically derived and did not follow from an elaborate set of theoretical assumptions. However, we have developed a conceptual scheme that can account for many of the important phenomena seen in stuttering.

Because we can establish fluent speech in stutterers with a systematic training program, it is tempting to conceptualize stuttering as learned behavior. However, this would probably be an oversimplification. Stuttering is unique because it enters into some interesting lawful relationships with a number of stimulus conditions. For example, the dramatic improvement in speech fluency seen under conditions of auditory masking or delayed auditory feedback seem to preclude any simple view of stuttering as learned behavior.

It appears as if a multiple-feedback-loop servosystem model can satisfactorily account for many of the observed phenomena seen in investigations of stuttering. Such a model is described following a review of several classes of data on specific stimulus-response relationships in speech which are especially relevant for the development of the model. The data reviewed implicate sensory feedback variables in stuttering.

The Effects of Delayed Auditory Feedback in Normal Speech Guidance

Experiments which have manipulated auditory feedback in normally fluent speakers indicate that this particular variable exerts substantial control over the characteristics of speech. The first reports by Lee (1950a, 1950b, 1951) and later reports by Fairbanks (1954, 1955), Fairbanks and Guttman (1958), Black (1954, 1955), Chase, Sutton, First, and Zubin (1961), and Goldiamond, Atkinson, and Bilger (1962) demonstrate very clearly that the speech of normally fluent speakers was markedly disrupted by the delayed air-conducted auditory signal produced in speech. General types of changes in speech associated with delayed auditory feedback involve voice quality, intensity, fundamental frequency, number of articulation errors, and general overall slowing of speech rate. Other interesting reports by Peters (1954) and Davidson (1959) indicate that speech rates increase when auditory feedback is accelerated beyond normal limits. Taken together, these data suggest that the variable of auditory feedback is important in controlling certain characteristics of speech production.

The Effects of Delayed Auditory Feedback on Stutterers

Experiments have shown that delayed auditory feedback can serve as a stimulus which decreases the disfluencies in the speech of stutterers (Chase, Sutton, & Rapin, 1961; Goldiamond, 1965; Webster and Lubker, 1968; Webster, Schumacher, and Lubker, 1970). An interpretation was offered that could account for the decreased disfluencies seen during delayed auditory feedback with stutterers. Feedback of the auditory signal produced during the first portion of speech initiation is judged to be responsible for precipitating the blockage in stuttered speech. Fluency improvement witnessed during delayed auditory feedback could occur because the delay interval retards the return of the interfering air-conducted auditory feedback signal until the specific response which originated that signal was well under way or terminated. This specific interpretation also accounts for the rapid generation of fluency seen when stutterers are placed on continuous delayed auditory feedback and for the rapid increase in disfluencies seen when delayed auditory feedback is discontinued.

The Effects of Attenuating Auditory Feedback in Stutterers

When the auditory feedback to a stutterer is attenuated or eliminated by external causes, decreases usually occur in the frequency of disfluencies. The intensity of auditory speech feedback cues can be reduced by the variables of masking noise, deafness, or use of whispered speech.

Experiments on auditory masking have shown that loud stimulation with white noise yields marked decreases in stuttering (Cherry and Sayers, 1956; Maraist and Hutton, 1957; Sutton and Chase, 1961; Webster and Dorman, 1970). The Sutton and Chase and the Webster and Dorman studies employed four conditions: (1) noise onset made contingent on phonation; (2) noise cessation made contingent on phonation; (3) a continuous noise condition; and (4) a no-noise control condition. In these experiments, all noise conditions yielded significantly less stuttering than the no-noise control conditions. Webster and Dorman indicated that the most plausible way of interpreting the effects of the contingent noise conditions is to consider the probable role of the middle ear muscles during the various experimental conditions.

It has also been suggested that there is a very low incidence of stuttering among deaf children (Backus, 1938; Harms and Malone, 1939; Albright and Malone, 1942). Webster and Lubker (1968) suggested that severe attenuation of auditory feedback in the speech of the deaf eliminated the possibility for middle ear mechanisms to interfere with air-conducted auditory feedback signals.

It has also been observed that fluency improves when stutterers whisper (Johnson and Rosen, 1937; Cherry and Sayers, 1956). Whispering could reduce stuttering for one of two reasons: first, it produces reduced auditory feedback; or, probably more importantly, it involves a marked change in the use of the phonetory apparatus.

The Effects of Rhythmic Cueing Stimulation on Stuttered Speech

An important but not well understood variable that yields fluency in stutterers is the use of a rhythmic cueing stimulus. Stutterers speaking in time with a metronome, finger taps, arm swings, or similar rhythmic events have been observed to speak with increased fluency (Barber, 1939, 1940; Bloodstein, 1950; Bluemel, 1960; Van Dantzig, 1940; Brady, 1969). Webster and Lubker (1968) hypothesized that rhythmic stimuli provided an external stimulus which a stutterer could use as a cue to govern the initial release of the syllables to be produced. Thus certain aspects of speech feedback control would be transferred from auditory feedback to the external stimulus.

The Adaptation Phenomenon in Stuttering

Studies have shown that the frequency of disfluencies rapidly decreases as the stutterer continues to reread materials (Tate, Cullinan and Ahlstrand, 1961; Trotter, 1955; Newman, 1954; Wingate, 1966). Various concepts have been used in an attempt to account for the adaptation effect in stuttering: reduction in fear or anxiety; increased familiarity with the reading material; changes involving decreased propositionality of the reading material; and the extinction of learned anxiety responses (Wingate, 1966). None of these interpretations has been adequate for providing understanding of adaptation phenomena (Beech and Fransella, 1968).

Studies by Webster and Dorman (1971), James (1971), and James (1972) have suggested that the adaptation phenomenon may result from temporary reductions in the reliance on auditory feedback cues used in speech guidance. Webster and Dorman gave normally fluent subjects practice on a standard oral reading task and then tested their subjects under delayed auditory feedback. During tests under delayed auditory feedback, subjects who had experienced six previous oral reading trials on a standard passage under normal auditory feedback made significantly fewer articulation errors and had significantly shorter reading times than subjects who did not have prior reading practice. Tests of practiced subjects versus nonpracticed subjects under normal auditory feedback showed no significant differences in articulation errors or reading times. Whispered practice (James, 1971) produced reduction in the degree of disruption by delayed auditory feedback. Reading by mouthing of the passage without voicing also produced decreases in the degree of disruption produced by delayed auditory feedback (James, 1972), but silent reading of the passage did not result in decreases in disruption when compared with control subjects. Thus it seems likely that for normally fluent subjects, temporary changes in reliance on auditory feedback cues can take place. It appears as if there are shifts from auditory feedback usage to the cues generated from muscle and other sensory feedback channels.

Webster and Dorman (1971) suggested that it would be useful to consider the possibility that the phenomenon of stuttering adaptation could involve temporary changes in the subjects' relative reliance on auditory feedback cues. This hypothesis merits consideration because it provides a parsimonious means of accounting for the basic shape of the typical adaptation curve, for the "spontaneous recovery" of stuttering following adaptation, and for a number of the other effects that have been observed in studies of this phenomenon.

Observations on Self-Recovery from Stuttering

Although these data do not result directly from experimentation, they do suggest that some characteristic changes in articulation activity occur in stutterers who become fluent. The studies by Shearer and Williams (1965) and Sheehan and Martyn (1966) have some significance. Shearer and Williams found that 69 percent of the stutterers who eventually attained fluent speech indicated that speaking more slowly was a critical factor. Sheehan and Martyn also presented data showing that slowing down and relaxing were contributing factors in the spontaneous recovery from stuttering.

A MULTIPLE-FEEDBACK-LOOP SERVOSYSTEM MODEL OF STUTTERING

A servosystem model of speech control does not rely on elaborate systems of hypothetical constructs or intervening variables. The term "model" is used here in the manner indicated by Marx (1963): it is tentative and only serves the purpose of showing that the speech mechanism *acts as if* it is a known type of system. The critical point to be remembered in evaluating the model is that when the properties of auditory feedback are experimentally manipulated, the changes in speech fluency observed are like those changes that occur when similar variables are manipulated in certain existing servosystems. The parallels between known servosystems and stuttering emphasize the potential importance of physically specifiable variables which may be determinants of stuttered speech.

At the present time it seems superfluous to present an elaborate theoretical schema like those of Fairbanks (1954) and Mysak (1966). No significant purpose would be served by elaborating the potential central brain processes or brain locations that may be involved in the actual control of speech. However, it may be assumed that these central processes do take place and that various types of feedback control are involved. For example, the brain is judged to be responsible for encoding messages to be communicated in a speech form, preparing a sequence of motor commands that can result in the appropriate movements of the speech musculature, and in releasing the patterns of motor commands to produce the speech output. It is likely that a variety of feedback channels exist at the central level which are used to compare the output of various brain subsystems with the instruction sets used to run the system.

Although we can only speculate about the central processes, it is possible to manipulate directly various aspects of speech feedback and thereby derive some information about the probable role of different types of sensory feedback channels in speech guidance. Among the obvious prominent feedback channels to be considered are the somesthetic and auditory. The model presented here assumes that properties of auditory and somesthetic feedback cues are used to assist in the guidance of speech output. Stuttering is hypothesized to result *from an aberration of auditory feedback signals* that are normally employed in speech guidance. Of the many behaviors that may be associated with developed stuttering, one is assumed to be primary in importance and first in order of appearance in the development of stuttering: stuttering is considered to be fundamentally a blockage of the phonetory activity associated with the production of an intended speech sound. Usually this is a sound at the beginning of an utterance. The blockage is hypothesized to result directly as a function of the faulty characteristics of the muscle mechanisms located in the middle ear canal of the stutterer and not from conditioned or unconditioned anxiety responses nor from a neurological deficit.

The apparent speech guidance functions of somesthetic and auditory feedback require the assumption that a multiple-feedback-loop model is involved. Multiple-loop control systems are not unusual and appear to be common in living organisms. For example, Fender and Nye (1961) proposed that a linear multiple-feedback-loop system controls eye movements when a continuously moving visual target is being tracked. Their experiments indicate that three different feedback loops are involved: (1) a loop dealing with signals emanating from the image on the retina of the eye; (2) a loop processing signals coming from nerves attached to the extraocular muscles; and (3) a loop processing signals coming from proprioceptors giving the difference between the desired visual goal and the degree of achievement in attaining the goal for any movement. Fender (1964) also discussed closed-loop control systems involved in accommodation, convergence, and pupil dilation. Priban and Fincham (1965) and Priban (1969) suggested a multiple-feedback-loop model of respiratory control that can account for many phenomena seen in breathing. Three feedback control loops are also used in this model: (1) a loop for the control of blood respiratory chemistry; (2) a loop for the control of the activity of the respiratory muscles; and (3) a loop for the control of airway dimensions. The three loops are assumed to be coordinated by a higher central nervous system center which relies on information fed back during previous breaths.

Although much remains to be learned about complex feedback-guided control mechanisms, certain aspects of the speech system can be described which illustrate its multiple-feedback-loop characteristics. Perhaps the most prominent example is the case of the individual who completely loses his hearing sometime after he has become a fluent speaker of his language. It is observed that in such an individual speech quality is not immediately and totally degraded. However, with the passage of time it is usual to witness increasing articulatory sloppiness, rate and loudness deviations, and a general overall deterioration of speech quality to some low asymptotic level. The gradual deterioration seen in such a case suggests that the auditory feedback channel is an important contributor to speech control but is not its sole determinant. It is clear that other sources of feedback are also being used in speech guidance. And, in fact, the occurrence of this type of phenomenon requires that other feedback loops be used for control of speech. The cues provided through somesthetic feedback obviously are increasingly important in this instance.

The quality of performance in a multiple-feedback-loop system can be reduced either by eliminating a specific feedback loop or by producing interference in a loop. In the model described here, stuttering is assumed to result *only from perturbations* in the auditory feedback loop. It would be predicted that removal of the auditory feedback loop in stutterers should reduce stuttering. The low incidence of stuttering seen in deaf and hard-of-hearing populations supports this interpretation. It should also be pointed out that there is no reason to predict that elimination of auditory feedback would result in stuttering. Instead, the observed types of speech quality degradation would be expected. It has been demonstrated in a series of experiments by Taub and Berman (1968) that when monkeys are deafferented, movement can occur in the absence of the usual sources of sensory feedback. However, the movements which are observed lack the precision seen in the movements of normal monkeys. It seems in the cases of the deafened speakers and the deafferented monkeys that sensory feedback is used for "fine tuning" or timing the detailed, precise movements involved in skilled motor sequences.

Additional data support the suggestion that during instances of stuttering the speech apparatus functions as a servosystem experiencing feedback disturbances. Zinkin (1968) presented a report on a series of x-ray motion pictures taken during moments of stuttering. In general, the photographs show discoordinations between pharyngeal movements and other gestures involved in articulation. At times the pharynx was seen to retain one shape for abnormally long time periods, while other articulatory gestures continued. At other times, movements of articulation remained static while pharyngeal modulation occurred. These types of disruption in speech output seen during stuttering are very much analogous to what is observed in servosystems that are underdamped (Bayliss, 1966). Such systems show a characteristic "overshooting" of the output beyond prescribed levels. A momentary underdamping could be produced by auditory feedback delay, cancellation of the early portion of auditory feedback, or loss of the error rate control information that would be derived in some way from auditory feedback. These findings are also consistent with the report of Agnello (1966) as summarized in Van Riper (1971), which show that there may be failure in the coarticulation characteristics of stuttered speech. Stromsta (1965) also showed that the usual formant transitions seen in the spectrograms of normal speakers are not seen in some of the spectrograms from stuttered speech. The failure of coarticulation in speech production, if indeed it is a reliable characteristic of stuttering, is consistent with a servosystem interpretation.

POSSIBLE INVOLVEMENT OF THE MIDDLE EAR MUSCLES IN STUTTERING

If there is a physically specifiable mechanism that could be involved in mediating auditory feedback interference, then that mechanism seems most likely to involve the transmission characteristics of the auditory system. The auditory system is extremely complex, and much remains to be learned about its functioning in stutterers. As a first step, it appears useful to examine the characteristics of the middle ear. The middle ear system is of potential importance because the ossicular chain—the malleus, incus, and stapes—has attached to it two small muscles, the tensor tympani and the stapedius. The tensor tympani is attached to the upper portion of the manubrium of the malleus (Gulick, 1971), crosses the tympanum, and goes into the tensor canal, which is just superior to the Eustachian tube. The tensor tympani is supplied from a branch of the trigeminal nerve. The average reflex latency of the tensor tympani to an auditory stimulus is approximately 150 milliseconds. The tendon of stapedius is attached to the head of stapes and travels posteriorly where it bends to enter a vertical canal posterior to the stapes. The muscle is approximately 6 to 7 millimeters long and lies in this canal. The average reflex latency of the stapedius to an auditory stimulus is approximately 60 milliseconds.

The muscles apparently have several functions. First, they may help maintain the position of the ossicular chain. Second, contractions of the stapedius muscles serve to shield the inner ear from excessive transmission of energy into that system (Jepsen, 1963; Simmons, 1964). There are two apparent contributions to the protective function. The contraction of the tensor tympani directly attenuates sound transmission by increasing frictional loading, and contraction of the stapedius rotates the stapes footplate, thereby damping any large-amplitude waves carried to it from other members of the ossicular chain. The major contribution seems to come from the stapedius (Jepsen, 1963).

Bilateral contractions of the middle ear muscles can be elicited by at least two conditions: (1) when loud sounds are presented to the ear; and (2) as part of the complex of behaviors associated with the initiation of speech. The acoustic reflex is thought to consist of the contractions of both the stapedius and the tensor tympani, with the stapedius preceding. The reflex elicitation of the middle ear muscles by an external auditory stimulus requires a sound intensity approximately 85 decibels above the threshold of hearing (Jerger, 1970).

Shearer and Simmons (1965) have shown that middle ear muscle contractions occur in association with speech. In the speech-associated mode of elicitation, the middle ear contractions occur from 65 to 100 milliseconds before the initiation of speech. Although the Shearer and Simmons study is important because it calls attention to the involvement of the middle ear muscles as part of the speech act, the study, which examined five normal speakers and five stutterers, reported that there were no differences found between these groups in terms of the time interval between middle ear muscle activity and speech output. It is not clear from this study whether Shearer and Simmons examined the time intervals between middle ear muscle activity and instances of stuttering which preceded what might be identified as speech output.

A later report (Shearer, 1966) dealt with behavior of the middle ear muscles during speech in five stutterers. Shearer indicated that middle ear muscle contractions occurred with stuttering and fluent speech in all subjects. Of particular importance is the observation by Shearer that the "impedance changes during several stuttering blocks on initial P sounds did not always parallel the sound level of speech in a precise manner" (p. 1280). A careful examination of the strip chart record presented in Shearer's report shows that middle ear muscle contractions apparently occurred at approximately the same time *as*, rather than *before*, the instances of stuttering. The first three instances of stuttering in his figure show that where the initiation of the speech attempt is indicated the middle ear muscle contractions occur roughly coincident with the initiation attempts, rather than before. This observation suggests that the middle ear muscle activity during stuttering may well be different from that seen during fluent speech in stutterers.

Simmons (1964) indicated that the speech-associated middle ear muscle contractions do not seem to habituate and that their magnitude is roughly proportional to the intensity of the vocal response which is anticipated. Simmons also pointed out that contractions of middle ear muscles in cats can attenuate sound transmission through the ossicular chain by as much as 20 to 25 decibels. Neergaard, Andersen, Harsen, and Jepsen (1964) indicated that in human temporal bones, middle ear muscle contractions attenuate sound transmission by up to 20 decibels. Galambos (1956) measured the cochlear microphonic in cats during auditory stimulation using a series of clicks. During movements of the stapedius muscle, the responses of the cochlea which corresponded to auditory stimulus inputs were suppressed. Hugelin, Dumont, and Paillas (1960), also using cats, showed that the cochlear microphonic was reduced only in ears in which the middle ear muscles were not removed. These investigators concluded that attenuation of the cochlear response was directly controlled by middle ear muscle contractions.

Recently, clinical information from a nearby hospital has come to our attention which suggests the potential value for further exploration of middle ear muscle functions in stuttering. A 25-year-old male stutterer required an operation for chronic otitis media in his left ear. The stapedius and tensor tympani muscles of the left ear were excised during the course of the operation. Audio tapes were made of the stutterer during conversation and oral reading before and immediately following the operation. No improvements in speech fluency were observed immediately after the operation. However, in a follow-up examination six months later, the subject, without the benefit of any form of speech therapy, displayed substantial improvements in speech fluency. The preoperation and immediate postoperation disfluent word rates in conversation ranged from approximately 8 to 12 percent. Disfluent word rates in conversation at six months after the operation were in the range from 1 to 3 percent. The subject reported that his speech blockage had shown progressive reductions in frequency and duration. Postoperatively, a moderate conductive hearing loss was observed in the operated ear (averaging approximately 57 decibels in the speech frequencies). Excellent word discrimination was observed. The subject was fitted with a hearing aid eight months after the operation. Disfluent word frequencies have remained in the 1 to 3 percent level in conversation. The fact that there is still some stuttering could be attributed to the presence of faulty middle ear muscle function in the right ear. Although this one case does not confirm the concept that the middle ear system is a determinant of stuttering, it does provide support for the suggestion that the relationship between stuttering and middle ear functions deserves further careful study.

The first hypothesis to merit investigation regarding the possible role of middle ear muscles and stuttering is that there is a direct attenuation of auditory feedback produced by late, asynchronous, or possible unstable contractions of the intratympanic muscles during speech initiation (and possibly even during transitions from one sound to another). The attenuation function conceivably could produce sufficient interference in the auditory feedback signal to halt the initiation of vocalization. The specific form of interference is not known. The phenomenon of backward masking may be involved (Raab, 1963). Backward masking occurs when a signal is masked by the presentation of a later signal. Elliott (1962) found that there was about 60 decibels of masking when the second signal began 1 millisecond after the first, and about 20 decibels of masking when the interval between signals was increased to 10 milliseconds.

In stutterers, bone-conducted feedback could serve as the first signal in the masking paradigm. Attenuation of the first part of the air-conducted feedback signal by slightly delayed middle ear muscle action could result in a clipping of the early part of the signal. The interval between the first and second signal would be well within the early part of the 10-millisecond range explored by Elliot.

Additional evidence for this specific hypothesis comes from a study by Stuttert-Kennedy, Shankweiler, and Schulman (1970), who found that when pairs of 250-millisecond consonant-vowel syllables were presented to opposite ears the introduction of a delay between syllables led to increases in the accuracy of identification of the lagging syllable. Identification favored the lagging syllable, even when the lag exceeded 50 milliseconds, the time normally required to extract enough information to identify the initial consonant. The lag effect occurred across a range of from 5 to 120 milliseconds. Berlin, Willett,

Thompson, Cullen, and Lowe (1970), Lowe, Cullen, Thompson, Berlin, Kirkpatrick, and Ryan (1970), and Darwin (1971) have confirmed the backward masking effects with dichotically presented speech stimuli. Of particular interest was the finding that the "lag" effect occurred only for the dichotic presentation of stimuli. During monaural tests with the same stimuli, the leading syllable was correctly identified with the greatest accuracy.

The tympanic muscle-speech onset hypothesis stated here also provides a relatively straightforward means of accounting for the fluent speech shown by stutterers who complete the fluency shaping program. By slowing movements and reducing the magnitude of the physical forces in speech it is conceivable that the temporal relationship between middle ear muscle contractions and speech onset could be realigned. The logical inference would be that after fluency shaping the middle ear muscles would contract prior to speech initiation. If the middle ear muscle contractions are cued by contractions of the facial musculature as has been suggested by Djupesland (1964, 1965) instead of by centrally originated commands, then the early deliberate assumption of articulatory positions prior to the onset of voicing produced by fluency shaping could result in earlier activity in the middle ear muscles.

A second hypothesis, somewhat more complex than the first, is that the contractions of the middle ear muscles may not be temporally displaced in stutterers. Their action may mediate a potential interaction between air- and bone-conducted auditory feedback. Stromsta (1956) manipulated phase relationships between air- and bone-conducted auditory feedback in stutterers and normally fluent speakers. He found significant differences between stutterers and nonstutterers in phase angle shifts and amplitude adjustments required to produce cancellation between air- and bone-conducted pure tone signals. Later, Stromsta (1959) reported that manipulation of air-conducted side tone could result in phonetory blockage in normal speakers. Thus it is also possible that the mechanism of auditory feedback interference could involve the mediation of air- and bone-conducted auditory feedback signal phase relationships. A possible third hypothesis is that there is momentary inhibition of electrical activity in the cochlea during activation of the stapedius.

Other hypotheses could be advanced; however, they would require considering the more central characteristics of the nervous system. For example, it is conceivable that the perceptual processing of speech may be involved. If speech perception occurs by reference to production (Ladefoged, 1959; Ladefoged and McKinney, 1963; Lane, 1965; Liberman, Cooper, Shankweiler, and Studdert-Kennedy, 1967), then a defect in the cues used in speech guidance may occur at any one of several different loci or combinations of these loci. For example, if the basic articulatory skills involved in sequences of phonemes have been mislearned (i.e., if there is a lack of parallel transmission of information regarding both consonants and vowels), then acoustic information needed for speech guidance may be missing from the auditory signal and the conditions may be met for a halt in speech production. It is also possible that an intervening mechanism like that of the middle ear system could distort or eliminate a critical portion of the auditory cue that is referred to the production system in perception.

If the middle ear muscles are involved in stuttering, there is probably a genetically determined difference in this characteristic function in stutterers. The relatively high familial incidence of stuttering (Jameson, 1955; Andrews and Harris, 1964), showing that approximately 30 percent of stutterers had relatives who stuttered versus the less than 0.5 percent in fluent control subjects, supports such a hypothesis. In addition, the general preponderance of males who stutter compared with females (from 2.5:1 to 5:1, as reported in various studies) supports such an interpretation.

Although the discussion pertaining to the probable role of the middle ear muscles in stuttering is somewhat speculative, the hypothesis deals with a directly observable physical mechanism. We maintain that this type of approach provides the most meaningful potential direction for the conduct of future research on the problem of stuttering. There is sufficient evidence to stimulate the careful investigation of middle ear systems as they pertain to stuttered speech.

THE ROLE OF LEARNING IN THE ACQUISITION AND MAINTENANCE OF STUTTERING

Learning could be involved in stuttering in a variety of ways. First, after a few instances of blockage early in the development of speech, the automatic, compensatory response of the speech system may be to increase the degree of effort involved in sound initiation. The intensity and rate of articulatory gestures may increase. This would be an expected form of response in a servosystem experiencing some form of initial feedback delay; that is, the system shows a tendency to overshoot. Thus the subject might learn that initial increases in effort with speech initiation may at first be helpful in overcoming the blockage. The repetitions seen in stuttering may also represent another form of response to feedback disturbance. If auditory feedback is interfered with, one form of response in a feedback-governed system would be to restart the response. In general, it should be noted that these two behaviors seen in stuttering, blockage and repetitions, may well represent unconditioned responses to interference in auditory feedback processing.

After a number of occasions in which blocking and repetitions occur, one might expect to find the stutterer developing a variety of anticipatory responses. For example, the use of "starters" (a characteristic word or phrase used before different sentences in order to get them started) may develop in an attempt to initiate speech flow. Other symptoms of stuttering, such as the eye blinks, sound initiation prior to attempting to say an intended word, head turning, and changes in posture that occur with speech initiation could also become anticipatory responses. These behaviors might well represent various forms of avoidance and/or escape responses that are used in an attempt to avoid or reduce the noxious properties of speech blockage. In addition to the specific motoric forms of anticipation that have been observed in stuttering, one would also expect that the more comprehensive "psychological" problems would also begin to occur. The stutterer would begin to experience fear in those situations in which he had difficulty in speaking, would begin to avoid speech situations, and would possibly develop a variety of protective behaviors designed to reduce the discomfort in being a stutterer.

There is substantial evidence to suggest that there is, indeed, a specific stimulus for stuttering which is directly involved in the speech act. The immediate improvements in fluency seen in stutterers under conditions of delayed feedback, auditory masking, and the use of unusual speech patterns suggest that properties of auditory cues are directly implicated. In addition, perhaps the most meaningful demonstration may be seen in the fluency shaping program itself. We have observed with the initiation of the fluency shaping activities that stuttering-associated behaviors drop out immediately. The fact that stuttering-associated behaviors reliably disappear with the beginning of the fluency shaping activities suggests that they are cued by specific stimulus events within the speech process.

THE CONTRIBUTION OF ANXIETY TO STUTTERING

Although we do not consider anxiety to be a primary determinant to stuttering, we do feel that its mode of action is important and may be described in a fairly straightforward manner. The primary contribution of anxiety, or other forms of emotional arousal, is to increase muscle tonus (Damste, 1970). The direct effects of emotionality upon most skeletal muscle groups is to accelerate their rate of movement. Thus, with the speech mechanism, emotional arousal is hypothesized to produce direct increases in the rate and amplitude of the gestures involved in speech production. The acceleration of these movements induced by anxiety causes the speech mechanism to exceed the movements and forces which are "permissible" for that type of system. That is, the effect of the acceleration of articulatory gestures results in further temporal disarrangement between the action of the middle ear muscles and the onset of speech.

The effects of desensitization therapy, if manifested in the improved speech fluency of the stutterer, are probably produced because of the reduction in the velocity and amplitude of the specific gestures in speech. It seems unlikely to us that there are any deeper or more profound emotional implications as fundamental contributing factors to stuttering. Thus it seems reasonable to predict that any disturbances of personality that may be related to stuttering stem directly from the fact that the stutterer is a disfluent speaker. It seems improbable that the stutterer is a disfluent speaker because of a continuing emotional disturbance.

SUMMARY

Stuttering is a form of behavior that has proven resistant to treatment by traditional therapies. Most therapies derived from contemporary theories attempt to treat the assumed emotional basis for stuttering, even though there is little but subjective, impressionistic data to support such a view. Researchers and clinicians have not directed sufficient attention toward (1) measuring the observable aspects of stuttered speech and (2) the determination of lawful relationships between various stimulus dimensions and the observed speech characteristics of stutterers.

The efficacy of the direct manipulation of stuttered speech as a form of therapy is illustrated by the fluency shaping program described in this chapter. Careful, systematic reconstruction of the articulatory gestures in speech can lead to the establishment of markedly improved speech fluency in even severe stutterers. After systematic retraining, lasting approximately 40 to 60 hours, it has been observed that approximately seven out of ten stutterers can retain improved speech fluency. The relative ease with which most stutterers can acquire these skills and the absolute lack of any other so-called neurotic symptoms lead us to suggest that stuttering is caused by variables other than those of an emotional nature.

A multiple-feedback-loop servosystem model is described in this chapter. The model is based on similarities between the speech behavior of the stutterer and characteristics of known servosystems. It appears as if perturbations in auditory feedback, caused by faulty action of the middle ear muscles, are responsible for the disfluencies in the speech of the stutterer.

REFERENCES

Agnello, J. G. Some acoustic and pause characteristics of nonfluencies in the speech of stutterers. Technical Report, National Institute of Mental Health, 1966.

Albright, M. A. H., and Malone, J. Y. The relationship of hearing acuity to stammering. *Journal of Exceptional Children*, 1942, **8,** 186–190.

Andrews, G., and Harris, M. *The Syndrome of Stuttering.* London: Heinemann, 1964.

Backus, O. Incidence of stuttering among the deaf. *Annals of Otology, Rhinology, and Laryngology*, 1938, **XLVII**, 632–635.

Barber, V. Studies in the psychology of stuttering. XV. Chorus reading as a distraction in stuttering. *Journal of Speech Disorders*, 1939, **4**, 371–383.

Barber V. Studies in the psychology of stuttering. XVI. Rhythm as a distraction in stuttering. *Journal of Speech Disorders*, 1940, **5**, 29–42.

Bayliss, L. E. *Living Control Systems*. San Francisco: Freeman, 1966.

Beech, H. R., and Fransella, F. *Research and Experiment in Stuttering*. Oxford: Pergamon Press, 1968.

Berlin, C. I., Willett, M. E., Thompson, C., Cullen, J. K., and Lowe, S. S. Voiceless versus voiced CV perception in dichotic and monotic listening. *Journal of the Acoustical Society of America*, 1970, **47**, 75(a).

Black, J. W. Systematic research in experimental phonetics. 2. Signal reception: Intelligibility and side-tone. *Journal of Speech and Hearing Disorders*, 1954, **19**, 140–146.

Black, J. W. The persistence of effects of delayed side-tone. *Journal of Speech and Hearing Disorders*, 1955, **20**, 65–68.

Bloodstein, O. Hypothetical conditions under which stuttering is reduced or absent. *Journal of Speech and Hearing Disorders*, 1950, **15**, 142–153.

Bloodstein, O. Stuttering as anticipatory struggle reaction. In J. Eisenson (Ed.), *Stuttering: A Symposium*. New York: Harper and Row, 1958.

Bloodstein, O., *A Handbook on Stuttering*. Chicago: Easter Seal Society, 1969.

Bloodstein, O., Alper, J., and Zisk, P. K. Stuttering as an outgrowth of normal disfluency. In D. A. Barbara (Ed.), *New Directions in Stuttering*. Springfield, Ill.: Thomas, 1965.

Bluemel, C. S. Concepts of stammering: A century in review. *Journal of Speech and Hearing Disorders*, 1960, **25**, 24–32.

Brady, J. P. Studies on the metronome effect on stuttering. *Behavior Research and Therapy*, 1969, **7**, 1–8.

Brady, J. P. Studies on the metronome effect on stuttering. *Behaviour Research and Therapy*, 1969, **7**, 1–8.

Brutten, E. J., and Shoemaker, D. J. *The Modification of Stuttering*. Englewood Cliffs, N. J.: Prentice-Hall, 1967.

Bryngelson, B. The stuttering personality and development. *Nervous Child*, 1943, **2**, 162–171.

Chase, R. A., Sutton, S., First, D., and Zubin, J. A developmental study of changes in behavior under delayed auditory feedback. *Journal of Genetic Psychology*, 1961, **99**, 101–112.

Chase, R. A., Sutton, S., and Rapin, I. Sensory feedback influences on motor performance. *Journal of Auditory Research*, 1961, **3**, 212–223.

Cherry, C., and Sayers, B. McA. Experiments upon the total inhibition of stammering by external control, and some clinical results. *Journal of Psychosomatic Research*, 1956, **1**, 233–246.

Cullinan, W. I., Prather, E. M., and Williams, D. E. Comparison of procedures for scaling severity of stuttering. *Journal of Speech and Hearing Research*, 1963, **6**, 187–194.

Damste, P. H. A behavioral analysis of a stuttering therapy. In M. Fraser (Ed.), *Conditioning in Stuttering Therapy: Applications and Limitations*. Memphis, Tenn.: Speech Foundation of America, 1970.

Darwin, C. J. Dichotic backward masking of complex sounds. *The Quarterly Journal of Experimental Psychology*, 1971, **23**, 386–398.

Davidson, G. D. Sidetone delay and reading rate, articulation, and pitch. *Journal of Speech and Hearing Research*, 1959, **2**, 266–270.

Djupesland, G. Middle ear muscle reflexes elicited by acoustic and nonacoustic stimulation. *Acta Oto-Laryngologica* (Supplement), 1964, **188**, 287–292.

Djupesland, G. Electromyography of the tympanic muscles in man. *International Audiology*, 1965, **4**, 34–41.

Eisenson, J. A perseverative theory of stuttering. In J. Eisenson (Ed.), *Stuttering: A Symposium*. New York: Harper and Row, 1958.

Elliott, L. I. Backward and forward masking of probe tones of different frequencies. *Journal of the Acoustical Society of America*, 1962, **34**, 1116–1117.

Fairbanks, G. Systematic research in experimental phonetics. I. A theory of the speech mechanism as a servosystem. *Journal of Speech and Hearing Disorders*, 1954, **19**, 133–139.

Fairbanks, G. Selective vocal effects of delayed auditory feedback. *Journal of Speech and Hearing Disorders*, 1955, **20**, 333–346.

Fairbanks, G., and Guttman, N. Effects of delayed auditory feedback upon articulation. *Journal of Speech and Hearing Research*, 1958, **1**, 12–22.

Fender, D. H. Control mechanisms of the eye. *Scientific American*, 1964, **211**, 24–33.

Fender, D. H., and Nye, P. W. An investigation of the mechanisms of eye movement control. *Kybernetik*, 1961, **1**, 81.

Fenichel, O. *The Psychoanalytic Theory of Neurosis*. New York: Norton, 1945.

Flanagan, B., Goldiamond, I., and Azrin, N. Operant stuttering: The control of stuttering behavior through response-contingent consequences. *Journal of the Experimental Analysis of Behavior*, 1958, **1**, 173–177.

Galambos, R. Suppression of auditory nerve activity by stimulation of efferent fibers to cochlea. *Journal of Neurophysiology*, 1956, **19**, 424–437.

Goldiamond, I. Stuttering and fluency as manipulatable operant response classes. In L. Krasner and L. P. Ullmann (Eds.), *Research in Behavior Modification: New Developments and Implications*. New York: Holt, Rinehart and Winston, 1965.

Goldiamond, I., Atkinson, C. J., and Bilger, R. C. Stabilization of behavior and prolonged exposure to delayed auditory feedback. *Science*, 1962, **135**, 437–438.

Gulick, W. L. *Hearing: Physiology and Psychophysics*. New York: Oxford University Press, 1971.

Harms, M. A., and Malone, J. Y. The relationship of hearing acuity to stammering. *Journal of Speech and Hearing Disorders*, 1939, **4**, 363–370.

Hugelin, A., Dumont, S., and Paillas, N. Tympanic muscles and control of auditory input during arousal. *Science*, 1960, **131**, 1371–1372.

Jacobson, E. *Progressive Relaxation*. Chicago, Ill.: University of Chicago Press, 1938.

James, K. Alterations in speech characteristics as a function of delayed auditory feedback. Unpublished M.A. thesis, Hollins College, 1971.

James, W. N. Characteristics of oral reading as a function of different practice procedures and delayed auditory feedback. Unpublished M.A. thesis, Hollins College, 1972.

Jameson, A. Stammering in children. *Speech*, 1955, **19**, 60–67.

Jepsen, O. Middle-ear muscle reflexes in man. In J. Jerger (Ed.), *Modern Developments in Audiology*. New York: Academic Press, 1963.

Jerger, J. F. Clinical experience with impedance audiometry. *Archives of Otolaryngology*, 1970, **92**, 311–324.

Johnson, W. *Stuttering in Children and Adults*. Minneapolis: University of Minnesota Press, 1955.

Johnson, W., and Rosen, L. Studies in the psychology of stuttering. VII. Effects of certain changes in speech pattern upon frequency of stuttering. *Journal of Speech and Hearing Disorders*, 1937, **2**, 105–109.

Ladefoged, P. The perception of speech. In *Mechanization of Thought Processes*. London: H. M. Stationery Office, 1959.

Ladefoged, P., and McKinney, N. P. Loudness, sound pressure and subglottal pressure in speech. *Journal of the Acoustical Society of America*, 1963, **35**, 454–460.

Lane, H. Motor theory of speech perception: A critical review. *Psychological Review*, 1965, **72**, 275–309.

Lee, B. S. Effects of delayed speech feedback. *Journal of the Acoustical Society of America*, 1950, **22**, 824–826. (a)

Lee, B. S. Some effects of side-tone delay. *Journal of the Acoustical Society of America*, 1950, **22**, 639–640. (b)

Lee, B. S. Artificial stutter. *Journal of Speech and Hearing Disorders*, 1951, **16**, 53–55.

Liberman, A. M., Cooper, F. S., Shankweiler, D. P., and Studdert-Kennedy, M. Perception of the speech code. *Psychological Review*, 1967, **74**, 431–461.

Lowe, S. S., Cullen, J. K., Thompson, C., Berlin, C. I., Kirkpatrick, L. L., and Ryan, J. T. Dichotic and monotic simultaneous and time-staggered speech. *Journal of the Acoustical Society of America*, 1970, **47**, 76(a).

Maraist, J. A., and Hutton, C. Effects of auditory masking upon the speech of stutterers. *Journal of Speech and Hearing Disorders*, 1957, **22**, 385–389.

Marx, M. M. The general nature of theory constructions. In M. Marx (Ed.), *Theories in Contemporary Psychology*. New York: Macmillan, 1963.

Mysak, E. D. *Speech Pathology and Feedback Theory*. Springfield, Ill.: Thomas, 1966.

Mysak, E. D. A servo model for speech therapy. *Journal of Speech and Hearing Disorders*, 1954, **24**, 144–149.

Mysak, E. D. Servo theory and stuttering. *Journal of Speech and Hearing Disorders*, 1960, **25**, 188–195.

Neergaard, E. B., Andersen, H. C., Hansen, C. C., and Jepsen, O. Experimental studies on sound transmissions in the human ear. III. Influence of the stapedius and tensor tympani muscles. *Acta Oto-laryngology Supplement*, 1964, **188**, 280–286.

Newman, P. W. A study of adaptation and recovery of the stuttering response in self-formulated speech. *Journal of Speech and Hearing Disorders*, 1954, **19**, 450–458.

Peters, R. W. The effect of changes in side-tone delay and level upon rate of oral reading of normal speakers. *Journal of Speech and Hearing Disorders*, 1954, **19**, 483–490.

Priban, I. P. Self-adaptive control of respiration. In A. R. Meethan (Ed.), *Encylopedia of Linguistics, Information and Control*. Oxford: Pergamon Press, 1969.

Priban, I. P., and Fincham, W. F. Self-adaptive control and the respiratory system. *Nature*, 1965, **208**, 339–345.

Raab, D. Backward masking. *Psychological Bulletin*, 1963, **60**, 118–129.

Rothenberg, L. P. An exploratory study of adult stutterers' perceptions of stuttering. Unpublished research, Pennsylvania State University, 1963.

Rousey, C. L. Stuttering severity during prolonged spontaneous speech. *Journal of Speech and Hearing Research*, 1958, **1**, 40–47.

St. Onge, K. R., and Calvert, J. J. Stuttering research. *Quarterly Journal of Speech*, 1964, **50**, 159–165.

Shames, G. H., and Sherrick, C. E. A discussion of nonfluency and stuttering as operant behavior. *Journal of Speech and Hearing Disorders*, 1963, **28**, 3–18.

Shcarer, W. M. Speech: Behavior of middle ear muscle during stuttering. *Science*, 1966, **152**, 1280.

Shearer, W. M., and Simmons, F. B. Middle ear activity during speech in normal speakers and stutterers. *Journal of Speech and Hearing Research*, 1965, **8**, 203–207.

Shearer, W. M., and William, J. D. Self-recovery from stuttering. *Journal of Speech and Hearing Disorders*, 1965, **30**, 288–290.

Sheehan, J. Conflict theory of stuttering. In J. Eisenson (Ed.), *Stuttering: A Symposium*. New York: Harper and Row, 1958.

Sheehan, J. Stuttering as a self-role conflict. In H. Gregory (Ed.), *Learning Theory and Stuttering Therapy*. Evanston, Ill.: Northwestern University Press, 1968.

Sheehan, J. G., and Martyn, M. Spontaneous recovery from stuttering. *Journal of Speech and Hearing Research*, 1966, **9**, 121–135.

Simmons, F. B. Perceptual theories of middle ear muscle function. *Annals of Otology*, 1964, **73**, 724–739.

Stromsta, C. P. A methodology related to the determination of the phase angle of bone-conducted speech sound energy of stutterers and non-stutterers. Unpublished doctoral thesis, Ohio State University, 1956.

Stromsta, C. P. Experimental blockage of phonation by distorted sidetone. *Journal of Speech and Hearing Research*, 1959, **2**, 286–301.

Stromsta, C. P. A spectrographic study of dysfluencies labeled as stuttering by parents. *De Therapie Vocis et Loquellae*, 1965, **1**, 317–320.

Studdert-Kennedy, M., Shankweiler, D., and Schulman, S. Opposed effects of a delayed channel on perception of dichotically and monotically presented CV syllables. *Journal of the Acoustical Society of America*, 1970, **48**, 599–602.

Sutton, S., and Chase, R. A. White noise and stuttering. *Journal of Speech and Hearing Research*, 1961, **4**, 72.

Tate, M. W., Cullinan, W. L., and Ahlstrand, A. Measurement of adaptation in stuttering. *Journal of Speech and Hearing Research*, 1961, **4**, 321–339.

Taub, E., and Berman, A. J. Movement and learning in the absence of sensory feedback. In S. J. Freeman (Ed.). *The Neuropsychology of Spatially Oriented Behavior*. Homewood, Ill.: Dorsey Press, 1968.

Travis, L. E. *Speech Pathology*. New York: Appleton, 1931.

Trotter, W. D. The severity of stuttering during successive readings of the same material. *Journal of Speech and Hearing Disorders*, 1955, **20**, 17–25.

Van Dantzig, M. Syllable-tapping, a new method for the help of stammerers. *Journal of Speech and Hearing Disorders*, 1940, **5**, 127–131.

Van Riper, C. The preparatory set in stuttering. *Journal of Speech Disorders*, 1937, **2**, 149–154.

Van Riper, C. *Speech Correction: Principles and Methods*. Englewood Cliffs, N. J.: Prentice-Hall, 1954.

Van Riper, C. Symptomatic therapy for stuttering. In L. E. Travis (Ed.), *Handbook of Speech Pathology*. New York: Appleton, 1957.

Van Riper, C. Experiments in stuttering therapy. In J. Eisenson (Ed.), *Stuttering: A Symposium*. New York: Harper and Row, 1958.

Van Riper, C. Historical approaches. In J. G. Sheehan (Ed.), *Stuttering: Research and Therapy*. New York: Harper and Row, 1970.

Van Riper, C. *The Nature of Stuttering*. Englewood Cliffs, N. J.: Prentice-Hall, 1971.

Webster, R. L., and Dorman, M. R. Decreases in stuttering frequency as a function of continuous and contingent forms of auditory masking. *Journal of Speech and Hearing Research*, 1970, **13**, 82–86.

Webster, R. L., and Dorman, M. R. Changes in reliance on auditory feedback cues as a function of oral practice. *Journal of Speech and Hearing Research*, 1971, **14**, 307–311.

Webster, R. L., and Lubker, B. B. Interrelationships among fluency producing variables in stuttered speech. *Journal of Speech and Hearing Research*, 1968, **11**, 754–766.

Webster, R. L., Schumacher, S. J., and Lubker, B. B. Changes in stuttering frequency as a function of various intervals of delayed auditory feedback. *Journal of Abnormal Psychology*, 1970, **75**, 45–49.

West, R. Is stuttering abnormal? *Journal of Abnormal Psychology*, 1936, **31**, 76–86.

West, R. An agnostic's speculations about stuttering. In J. Eisenson (Ed.), *Stuttering: A Symposium*. New York: Harper and Row, 1958.

Williams, E. D. Stuttering therapy: An overview. In H. H. Gregory (Ed.), *Learning Theory and Stuttering Therapy*. Evanston, Ill.: Northwestern University Press, 1968.

Wingate, M. E. A standard definition of stuttering. *Journal of Speech and Hearing Disorders*, 1964, **29**, 484–489.

Wingate, M. E. Prosody in stuttering adaptation. *Journal of Speech and Hearing Research*, 1966, **9**, 550–556.

Wischner, G. J. Stuttering behavior and learning: A preliminary theoretical formulation. *Journal of Speech and Hearing Disorders*, 1950, **15**, 324–335.

Woolf, G. The assessment of stuttering as struggle, avoidance, and expectancy. *The British Journal of Disorders of Communication*, 1967, **2**, 158–171.

Zinkin, N. I. *Mechanisms of Speech*. The Hague: Mouton, 1968.

CHAPTER 3

Clinical and Theoretical
Aspects of Depression*

PETER M. LEWINSOHN

The clinical manifestations of depression have been recognized for at least 3000 years and probably much longer than that. The current importance of depression is suggested through its rank as the second most frequent mental disorder and by its association with suicide. Despite its long history and the important contributions made by Freud (1957) and by Karl Abraham (1911) a half-century ago, one can agree with Beck (1967), Grinker (1961), and Silverman (1969), the authors of recent books on this topic, that our empirical and theoretical knowledge and understanding of depression is remarkably limited. Most of the important issues regarding etiology and treatment are still unresolved.

The term "depression" itself is ubiquitous and is often poorly defined. It is sometimes used to refer to a normal mood state, an abnormal mood state, a symptom, a symptom syndrome, as well as to a disease process, and possibly to a series of disease processes. It has been traditional to distinguish between neurotic and psychotic depressions, as if these represented different kinds of disorder rather than representing different intensities of the same disorder. Distinctions have also been made between endogenous and reactive depressions, between retarded depressions and agitated depressions, between involutional melancholia, postpartum depressions, various combinations of manic-depressive psychosis, and other depressions.

In their search for the causes of depression, theorists have tended to stress several classes of etiological factors. The attribution of depression to physiological or constitutional causes has perhaps the longest history, going back to the ancient Greeks, who believed that depression was the result of an overabundance of black bile in the body fluids. The search for the causes of depression

*The preparation of this paper was supported in part by United States Public Health Service Grant MH19784 from the National Institute of Mental Health. This paper draws heavily on material appearing in Friedman and Katz (1972) and Lewinsohn, Shaffer, and Libet (1969).

in the heredity and in the biochemistry and physiology of the individual has continued to the present.

The second important class of etiological factors has been emphasized by theorists who are interested in internal psychological mechanisms (e.g., Gaylin, 1968). The psychoanalytic position compares depression to grief reactions, suggesting that depression may occur following the loss of a real or fantasied love object in conjunction with certain intrapsychic processes. The person who is likely to become depressed is said to have identified narcissistically with the love object and hence to be unable to differentiate an external loss from a loss within the ego. Loss of love object thus leads to loss of self-esteem. Later theorists such as Bibring have broadened this conception by adding that not only can frustration of the need for love and affection lead to depression, but so can the frustration of other aspirations of the individual. In addition to the importance of a loss of some sort in the etiology of depression, dynamic theorists have also assumed that internalized hostility plays an important part in the development of depression. To the extent that the relationship with the love object was ambivalent, hostility is assumed to be introjected and to manifest itself as self-blame and a tendency toward self-destruction. The emphasis within traditional approaches, then, is upon a loss which is translated into a loss of self-esteem and into the internalization of hostility with a consequent further loss of self-esteem.

Other theorists, including Aaron Beck, have emphasized the cognitive aspects of depression. Beck (1967) assigns a primary position to a cognitive triad consisting of a very negative view of the self, of the outside world, and of the future. This triad is seen as the key to the consequences of depression, such as the lack of motivation, the affective state, and other ideational and behavioral manifestations. The depressed person's cognitions lead to misinterpretations of experiences and hence many of the secondary responses are logical consequences of such misinterpretations. The depressed person is locked in an insoluble situation, the result of which is further despair.

The interpersonal aspects of depression have been relatively neglected, although Bonime (1966) and others have noted that depressive behaviors are frequently used to manipulate others. It was Ferster (1965) who first noted that the loss of a close friend or relative constitutes a sudden shift or reduction in the schedule of reinforcements maintaining many of an individual's behaviors, and that a reduction in the rate of the person's behavior would be a logical consequence following the death of a close relative. Ferster noted that some depressed individuals are strikingly restricted in the range of persons with whom they interact, in some cases there being only one person. This makes the depressed person especially vulnerable, since the absence of that person or drastic changes in his behavior brings about drastic changes in the depressed person's behavior. More recently, Arnold Lazarus (1968) conceptualized depression as a response to "inadequate or insufficient reinforcers."

For the past six years, my associates and I have been developing and testing a behaviorally oriented theory of depression. The general goals of the research have been (a) to test hypotheses about the socioenvironmental reinforcement conditions associated with depression, (b) to develop systematic and replicable treatment strategies for depressed individuals, and (c) to provide tools to assess and to evaluate behavior change.

The purpose of this chapter is threefold: (1) to explicate the major theoretical assumptions and premises which have been guiding the design of our research; (2) to present empirical findings obtained by us which are consistent with these assumptions; and (3) to describe intervention strategies that have been found useful in the treatment of depressed individuals.

Operational Definition of Depression and a Methodological Point

The term "depression" is used to refer to the syndrome of behaviors which have been identified in descriptive studies of depressed individuals (e.g., Grinker et al., 1961), including verbal statements of dysphoria, self-depreciation, guilt, material burden, social isolation, and somatic complaints; it also involves a reduced rate for many behaviors. We assume depression to be a continuous variable which can be conceptualized as a "state" (which fluctuates over time) but also as a "trait" (some people, "depressives," are more prone to becoming depressed than others). Being depressed is not mutually exclusive with other psychopathological conditions such as schizophrenia, psychosis, sexual deviation, alcoholism. For research purposes a patient (subject) is defined as "depressed" if he meets certain experimental criteria (e.g., Lewinsohn and Libet, 1972) based on selected MMPI scales and on the interview factors identified by Grinker (1961). The criteria are presented in Table 1. The selection procedures are intended to yield a sample of "pure" depressives, individuals in whom depression (state) is present to a clinically significant degree, constituting the major presenting psychopathology. This strategy presupposes the availability of a large pool of subjects. Only 40 percent of those selected to be interviewed are included as subjects. Many patients who are referred for the treatment of depression manifest a rather mixed symptomatology. Patients who are "merely" depressed are relatively rare. We have also learned that patients sometimes use the term depression to refer to states which are better labeled as anxiety, turmoil, and confusion. We have also found it to be difficult to find older male depressed subjects. This may be a function of the generally reported higher incidence of depression in females, but it may reflect a reluctance of males in our society to emit those verbal behaviors that allow one to label them as being depressed.

It seems important that any study relying on differences between depressed and nondepressed groups for its conclusions have a normal control group as well as a "psychiatric control" group (i.e., patients for whom anxiety or other neu-

Table 1. Classification Procedure for Selecting Depressed and Nondepressed Subjects

Group	Classification Criteria	
	Step 1: MMPI (Byrne Scale)	Step 2: Grinker Interview Ratings
Depressed	(a) D $\geqslant$ 70T	(a) One or more factor scores > 1.0
	(b) D > Pt	(b) Mean factor score > .70
	(c) D > Hy	
Psychiatric control	(a) Hy $\geqslant$ 70T or Pt $\geqslant$ 70T	(a) Factor one < .70
	(b) D < 70T	(b) S rated as manifesting emotional difficulties other than depression
	(c) D < Pt−10T or D < HY−10T	
Normal control	(a) L < 60T	(a) Mean factor score $\leqslant$ .35
	(b) Clinical scales < 70T	(b) No factor score > .70

rotic symptoms but not depression constitutes the major psychopathology) if any observed group differences are to be attributed to depression (depressed $\neq$ psychiatric control, normal control) and not to the deviation hypothesis (depressed, psychiatric control $\neq$ normal control).

The Major Assumptions of the Behavioral Theory of Depression

This theory is based on three major assumptions:

1. A low rate of response-contingent positive reinforcement (resconposre) acts as an eliciting (unconditioned) stimulus for some depressive behaviors, such as feelings of dysphoria, fatigue, and other somatic symptoms.

2. A low rate of resconposre constitutes a sufficient explanation for other parts of the depressive syndrome such as the low rate of behavior. For the latter the depressed person is considered to be on a prolonged extinction schedule.

3. The total amount of resconposre received by an individual is presumed to be a function of three sets of variables: (1) the number of events (including activities) which are potentially reinforcing (PotRe) for the individual. PotRe is assumed to be a variable subject to individual differences, influenced by biological (e.g., sex and age) and experiential variables; (2) the number of potentially reinforcing events that can be provided by the environment, that is, the availability of reinforcement in the environment (AvaiRe); and (3) the instrumental behavior of the individual, that is, the extent to which he possesses the skills and emits those behaviors which will elicit reinforcement for him from his environment.

A schematic representation of the theory is presented in Figure 1.

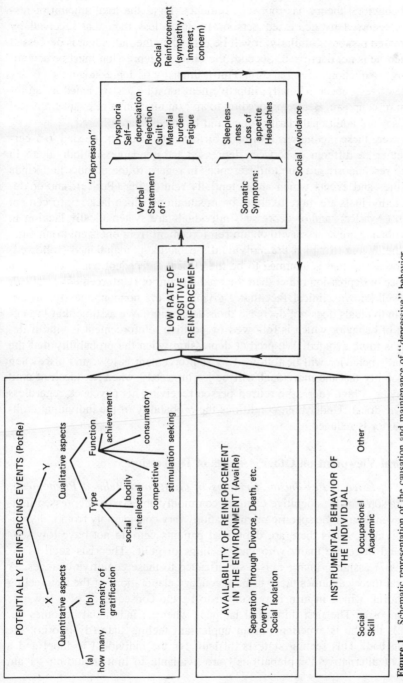

Figure 1. Schematic representation of the causation and maintenance of "depressive" behavior.

The behavioral theory has four requirements. First, the total amount of resconposre received by depressed persons must be less than that received by nondepressed persons. Similarly, it will be less when the individual is depressed than when he is not depressed. Second, the onset of depression must be accompanied by a reduction in resconposre. Third, intensity of depression must covary with rate of resconposre. Finally, improvement must be accompanied by an increase in resconposre. Before proceeding to an examination of relevant empirical studies, several additional clarifications and hypotheses are offered.

Even were these predictions affirmed, further data would be needed to ascertain whether the differences between depressed and nondepressed individuals in regard to resconposre are due to differences in regard to the number and kinds of activities and events which are potentially reinforcing (PotRe), and/or depressed individuals are more likely to be in situations which lack reinforcement for them (AvaiRe), and/or depressed individuals are systematically lacking in those skills that are necessary to obtain reinforcement from one's environment.

It is the degree to which the individual's behavior is maintained (followed) by reinforcement that is assumed to be the critical antecedent condition for the occurrence of depression rather than the total amount of reinforcement received. It is a well-known clinical fact that "giving" (i.e., noncontingently) to depressed individuals does not decrease their depression. We assume that the occurrence of behavior which is followed by positive reinforcement is vital if depression is to be avoided. We predict depression when the probability that the individual's behavior will be followed by reinforcement is low, and also when the probability that the individual will be "reinforced" when he does not emit the behavior is high (e.g., the retired person receiving his paycheck regardless of what he does). Under both conditions the probability of the individual emitting behavior is reduced.

Behavioral Viewpoint on Other Aspects of Depression

Low Self-Esteem, Pessimism, Feelings of Guilt, and Related Phenomena. These are some of the cognitive changes commonly observed in depressed individuals even though the specific manifestations vary considerably from individual to individual. Thus there are depressed patients who do not have low self-esteem and there are many who lack feelings of guilt. Theorists such as A. Beck (1967) assign primary causal significance to these cognitive changes. A behavioral theory assumes these to be secondary elaborations of the low feeling of dysphoria, which in turn is presumed to be the consequence of a low rate of resconposre. The first thing that happens when an individual becomes depressed is that he is experiencing an unpleasant feeling state (dysphoria). He *is* feeling bad. This feeling state is difficult for the individual to label and a number of alternative "explanations" are available to him including "I am sick" (somatic symptoms), "I am weak or otherwise inadequate" (low self-esteem), "I am bad" (feelings of guilt), "I am not likeable" (feelings of social isolation). The research of Stanley Schachter (Schachter and Singer, 1962) may contain important implications for this aspect of the behavior of depressed individuals and for treatment as well (cognitive relabeling). If the depressed individual can be helped to relabel his emotion (e.g., "I am worthless" into "I am feeling bad because I am lacking something that is important to my welfare"), he may be in a much better position to do something about his predicament.

Relationship between Hostility and Depression. The role of hostility which is so central to psychodynamically oriented theories of depression (i.e., depression is caused by internalized hostility) is hypothesized to be secondary to the low rate of resconposre. In a manner analogous to the way in which aggressive behavior is elicited by an aversive stimulus in Azrin's (1966) studies, aggressive behavior may be assumed to be elicited by a low rate of resconposre in the depressed individual. When these aggressive responses are expressed, they serve to alienate other people and therefore contribute even further to the social isolation of the depressed individual. He therefore learns to avoid expressing hostile tendencies by suppressing (or repressing) them.

Role of Precipitating Factors in Occurrence of Depression. In a substantial number of depressed patients the depression can be shown to have begun after certain environmental events (e.g., Paykel et al., 1969). Many of these events involve a serious reduction of positive reinforcement in that the event deprives the individual of an important source of reinforcement (e.g., death of spouse) or of an important set of skills (e.g., spinal cord injuries, brain disease, and other somatic diseases). The relationship between the occurrence of such events and depression is consistent with the behavioral theory of depression. There are, however, also instances of depression following "success" experiences (e.g., promotions, professional success). It is also not at all uncommon for an individual to become depressed following the attainment of some important and long-sought goal (e.g., award of Ph.D. degree). The existence of such precipitating factors would seem at first glance to contradict the notion of a relation between a reduction in positive reinforcement and depression. Two considerations seem relevant. First, the fact that the individual is judged to be a "success" by external criteria (e.g., is promoted) does not necessarily mean that the number of potentially reinforcing events available to him has increased. Thus for example a promotion may *actually* involve a serious reduction in the amount of social reinforcement obtained by the individual. Second, the behavioral theory would predict depression for an individual who attains a goal for which he has worked long and hard *if* the reward (e.g., award of degree) turns out to be a weak reinforcer for him. In that case he has worked hard for little, that is, his rate of resconposre is low.

EMPIRICAL FINDINGS CONSISTENT WITH THE THEORY AND STUDIES IN PROGRESS

Relationship Between Rate of Positive Reinforcement and Depression

A critical test of the major hypothesis requires a two-step strategy. First one must identify, functionally, events that act as reinforcement for individuals who may be characterized as either depressed, psychiatric controls, or normal controls. Second, one must compute the rate of response-contingent reinforcement for these subjects. The theory predicts a lower rate of positive reinforcement for depressed individuals. This crucial test has not been performed so far, but data from a study currently in progress in collaboration with Julian Libet based on home observation and group interaction will do just that. To date we have completed several studies which are *consistent* with the major tenet of the behavioral theory of depression, that there is an association between positive reinforcement and depression.

Depressed Individuals Elicit Fewer Behaviors from Other People Than Do Control Subjects (Shaffer and Lewinsohn, 1971; Libet and Lewinsohn, 1971). Assuming that it is reinforcing to be the object of attention and interest, this finding suggests that depressed persons receive less social reinforcement. The studies forming the basis for this conclusion are discussed in greater detail below.

There Is a Significant Association between Mood and the Number of "Pleasant" Activities Engaged In (Lewinsohn and Libet, 1972). In this study three groups of ten subjects, (depressed, psychiatric controls, and normal controls) were used. An activity schedule was generated for each subject from his responses on the Pleasant Events Schedule (MacPhillamy and Lewinsohn, 1971). This is an instrument consisting of 320 events and activities which were generated after a very extensive search of the universe of "pleasant events." The subjects were asked to rate each item on the schedule on a 5-point scale of pleasantness. An activity schedule, consisting of the 160 items judged by the subject to be most pleasant, was then constructed for each subject. The schedules were duplicated, and each subject was asked to indicate at the end of each day in which of the activities he engaged. In addition, subjects were asked to fill out the Depression Adjective Check List at about the same time of day. Each completed set was mailed to the experimenters for 30 consecutive days. Three groups of ten subjects each were started in the experimental procedure two weeks apart. The entire experiment ran from February 1, 1971, to April 1, 1971.

Three scores were computed for the Depression Adjective Check List: score 3 is the standard score (Lubin, 1965) and is based on the number of unhappy items checked plus the number of happy items not checked. The number of happy items not checked (score 1) and the number of unhappy items checked (score 2) were also analyzed separately.

Two scores were calculated for the activity schedules: (a) a raw activity score defined as the total number of activities checked and (b) a weighted activity score defined as the sum of the activities checked with each item weighted for its original pleasantness rating. Since there was no a priori reason to choose between the raw and weighted activity score, or among depression scores 1, 2, and 3, it was decided to compute product-moment correlation coefficients for all six combinations. The correlations between the mood and pleasant activity scores were computed over days ($N = 30$) for individual subjects. To obtain evidence pertinent to the issue of the direction of causation, additional correlations, using a variant of autocorrelation, were computed. The two sets of ratings were displaced so that in one case the depression score member of each pair was from an earlier date (-2 and -1 days, respectively), whereas in the other case the depression score member came from a later date ($+1$ and $+2$ days, respectively). The condition in which the correlation is based on pairs of ratings obtained on the same day is referred to as 0 displacement. If mood causes activity level, then one would expect the negative displacement to yield larger correlation coefficients than the positive displacements, while the reverse should obtain if activity level determines mood. The general relationship between mood and pleasant activities is graphed in Figure 2. The null hypothesis ($r = 0$) was strongly rejected ($t = 9.3$, $df = 29$, $p < .001$, one-tailed). The relation between mood and pleasant activity based on the same day (0 displacement) is also significantly greater than the correlation obtained for all displacements from zero ($F = 53.8$, $df = 1/96$, $p < .001$).

To clarify the direction of causality, it was of interest to compare the magnitude of association between mood and activity with the mood data displaced by -2 and -1 days (mood preceding activity), and by $+2$ and $+1$ days (activity preceding mood), respectively. The correlations calculated for displacements in one direction from zero are not significantly different from those based on displacements in the other direction ($F = .2$, $df = 1/96$, ns). The empirical question whether an individual's mood is more strongly associated with involvement in prior activities as opposed to subsequent activities awaits further experimental investigation.

Inspection of Figure 2 also reveals the existence of large individual differences with respect to the magnitude of the correlation between mood and pleasant activities. For example, for 10 of the 30 subjects, the correlation between mood and activity is not significantly different from zero. Mood can be more accurately predicted from activities (depression score data displaced by $+1$ and $+2$ days) for 10 subjects, but the reverse is the case for 5 subjects. Future research might address itself to the hypothesis that there are important individual

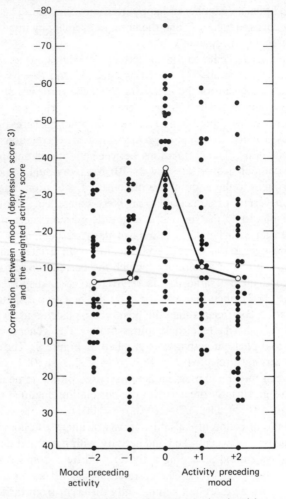

Figure 2. Association between mood and "pleasant" activity level. (Each point represents one subject.) (From P. M. Lewinsohn and J. Libet, Pleasant events, activity schedules and depressions. *Journal of Abnormal Psychology*, **79**:291-295, 1972. Copyright (1972) by tne American Psychological Association. Reproduced by permission.)

difference variables *moderating* the relationship between mood and activity.

The data were also examined for systematic differences in the magnitude of the correlation coefficients between the depressed, psychiatric, and normal control groups. Means of the correlation coefficients between mood and activity scores with the groups are presented in Table 2. Neither the differences between groups nor the differences between male and female subjects attain statistical significance.

To determine whether the degree of association between mood and activity varies as a function of a particular mood and activity score (depression scores 1, 2, and 3; raw and weighted activity scores), correlations were computed for all six combinations, and these are also shown in Table 2. It is apparent that the number of happy items not checked (depression score 1) was found to yield significantly higher correlations than either depression score 2 ($F = 30.7$, $df = 2/54$, $p < .001$) or depression score 3 ($F = 19.3$, $df = 2/54$, $p < .001$) with the activity scores. Although the difference between the magnitude of the correlations for the raw and weighted activity scores is slight, the greater association obtained from the weighted score is statistically significant ($F = 7.4$, $df = 1/27$, $p < .05$).

A post hoc examination of the data was made to determine whether there were some activities whose occurrence was associated with changes in mood for a substantial number of subjects. Only correlation coefficients greater than .30, which would be significant at the .01 level under conditions of independence of observation, were considered.* The number of subjects for whom each item was so correlated with mood was tabulated. Those items that were found to be associated with mood for at least four subjects are listed in Table 3. An important qualitative aspect of this list appears to be the fact that many of the items involve social interaction. It remains for future studies to determine the generalizability of the nature of the items associated with mood to other subject populations. A study currently in progress evaluates the nature of the activities associated with mood in three different age groups.

Another post hoc comparison involved the number of "significant" items for the depressed, psychiatric, and normal control groups. As can be seen in Table 4, the depressed and the psychiatric control groups have a larger number of "significant" items than the normal control subjects ($F = 7.7$, $df = 2/24$, $p < .05$). The finding that both deviant groups have a significantly larger number of items associated with their mood deserves further study. Ever since Freud pointed to "loss of love object" as an etiological factor in depression, the general hypothesis of a greater vulnerability of the depressed individual to the vicissitudes of everyday experiences has been central to a great deal of theorizing about depression. The present finding suggests that the hypothesis may need to be extended to other pathological groups as well.

"Total Amount of Positive Reinforcement Obtained" Is Less in Depressed than in Nondepressed Persons (MacPhillamy and Lewinsohn, 1972). Any attempt to study positive reinforcement with human subjects (e.g., determination of the amount of positive reinforcement received by the individual, identification of what are potentially reinforcing events for him) is handicapped by the fact that there is no psychometrically sound instrument for the assessment of

---

*There were a small number of items that occurred only one or two, or 28 or 29, times out of the 30 possible pairings. It was decided to select for analysis only items occurring with a frequency of $> .125$ and $< .875$.

Table 2. Means and Standard Deviations of Product-Moment Correlation Coefficients (Transformed to Z Scores) between Mood and Activity Scores for the Groups

Group	Raw activity score						Weighted activity score					
	Depression Score 1		Depression Score 2		Depression Score 3		Depression Score 1		Depression Score 2		Depression Score 3	
	$\bar{X}$	σ	$\bar{X}$	σ	$\bar{X}$	σ	$\bar{X}$	σ	$\bar{X}$	σ	$\bar{X}$	σ
Depressed	−.444	.254	−.189	.253	−.368	.279	−.457	.238	−.191	.257	−.373	.270
Psychiatric control	−.398	.227	−.229	.237	−.375	.227	−.411	.219	−.235	.237	−.388	.218
Normal control	−.320	.181	−.168	.271	−.297	.167	−.339	.187	−.202	.242	−.329	.153

Source. P. M. Lewinsohn and J. Libet, Pleasant events, activity schedules and depressions. Journal of Abnormal Psychology, **79**:291-295, 1972. Copyright (1972) by the American Psychological Association. Reproduced by permission.

Table 3. Rank-Order List of Items Correlating More Than .30 with the Mood Ratings for at Least Four Persons

Item	No. "Good" Out of 30
Being with happy people	12
Being relaxed	10
Having spare time	9
Having people show interest in what you have said	8
Laughing	8
Looking at the sky or clouds	7
Saying something clearly	6
Talking about philosophy or religion	6
Meeting someone new (opposite sex)	6
Watching attractive girls or men	6
Reading stories or novels	5
Taking a walk	5
Seeing beautiful scenery	5
Sleeping soundly at night	5
Amusing people	5
Having coffee or a coke with friends	5
Having someone agree with you	4
Petting	4
Being with someone you love	4
Traveling	4
Breathing clean air	4
Having a frank and open conversation	4
Having sexual relations with a partner of the opposite sex	4
Watching people	4

Source. P. M. Lewinsohn and J. Libet, Pleasant events, activity schedules and depressions. *Journal of Abnormal Psychology,* **79**:291-295, 1972. Copyright (1972) by the American Psychological Association. Reproduced by permission.

Table 4. Means and Standard Deviations of Number of Items Correlating More Than .30 with the Mood Ratings for the Groups

Group	Males X	Males SD	Females X	Females SD
Depressed	13.40	7.89	13.00	8.09
Psychiatric controls	10.20	3.49	12.80	6.02
Normal controls	5.60	5.41	6.40	2.19

Source. P. M. Lewinsohn and J. Libet, Pleasant events, activity schedules and depres. s. *Journal of Abnormal Psychology,* **79**:291-295, 1972. Copyright (1972) by the American Psychological Association. Reproduced by permission.

Note. $N = 5$ per cell. Frequency of occurrence for the items: $.125 \leqslant$ frequency $\leqslant .875$.

responses to potentially reinforcing events. Direct observation of behavior is very expensive and often practically impossible. The closest equivalent, the Reinforcement Survey Schedule (Cautela and Kastenbaum, 1967) was designed primarily to assess the valence of reinforcers potentially available for clinical or laboratory manipulation rather than to provide a systematic survey of the potentially reinforcing events for a given individual. The Pleasant Events Schedule (MacPhillamy and Lewinsohn, 1971) was constructed for the purpose of providing quantitative and qualitative information about what is potentially reinforcing for a given individual. Normative data about the instrument and its psychometric properties and dimensional structure are presented elsewhere (MacPhillamy and Lewinsohn, 1971).

Sample size for this study (MacPhillamy and Lewinsohn, 1972) was 120, evenly divided between the three diagnostic groups. Demographic characteristics of these subjects are presented in Table 5. As can be seen, the three groups were closely matched on all demographic variables. The depressed group was composed primarily of mildly and moderately depressed individuals: 15 of these subjects were currently in therapy for depression and 7 subjects were receiving antidepressant medications. The psychiatric control group was composed primarily of individuals manifesting anxiety states, obsessive-compulsive neuroses, schizoid personality, hysteria, and hypomania. This group must not be regarded as a random sample of psychiatric patients but rather as a group of people carefully selected on the basis of their manifesting psychological disorders in the absence of significant depression.

Table 5.   Demographic Characteristics of the Diagnostic Groups

Characteristic	Group		
	Depressed	Psychiatric Control	Normal Control
Number men	16	16	16
Number women	24	24	24
Mean age (years)	30.0	29.7	30.0
Mean social class[a]	3.0	3.0	2.9
Mean MMPI[b]D score	85.1	59.0	49.2

[a]Hollingshead (1965) two-factor index.
[b]T score units.

Each subject who successfully met the classification criteria described earlier was administered the Pleasant Events Schedule, Form III-S. Subjects were instructed to respond to each item twice, first rating the frequency with which the event (activity) occurred during the past month, and second rating its subjective enjoyability. A 3-point scale was used for both ratings. The *obtained reinforcement* for any event was defined as the product of the frequency and enjoyability ratings for that event. A multiplicative function was chosen so that an activity of zero frequency or no enjoyability would yield a zero product score. Since an attempt had been made to sample exhaustively from the domain of "pleasant events," the average of the obtained reinforcement product scores was defined as the measure of *net obtained reinforcement*.

In a series of extensive studies on the validity of the Pleasant Events Schedule (MacPhillamy and Lewinsohn, 1972), 86 items had been identified which demonstrated both convergent and discriminative validity when placed in a multitrait-multimethod matrix (Campbell and Fiske, 1959) with ratings made about the subject by a peer. Only these items were used in the statistical analysis. Three scores were completed for each subject: the sum of his frequency ratings, the sum of his enjoyability ratings, and the sum of the products of the two sets of ratings. These scales are assumed to be measures of general activity level, reinforcement potential, and obtained reinforcement. The results are presented in Table 6. As can be seen, the depressed had a lower activities score, rated fewer items as pleasant, and had a lower net obtained reinforcement value than either of the two control groups. Mean scores for the normal and psychiatric control groups were virtually identical, suggesting that the observed effect was associated uniquely with depression. Mean differences between male and female subsamples of the depressed group were small, indicating that the effect was present in both sexes. The results of this study provide strong support for the behavioral theory of depression.

Table 6. Comparison of Depressed and Nondepressed Groups on the PES Variables

Variable	Mean Depressed	Mean Combined Controls	t	p (two-tailed)
Activity level	.503	.610	4.33	<.001
Potential reinforcement	.695	.763	2.47	<.01
Obtained reinforcement	.419	.538	4.34	<.001

"Sensitivity" of Depressed Individuals to Aversive Stimuli (Lewinsohn, Lobitz, and Wilson, 1973)

In addition to being interested in possible differences between depressed and nondepressed groups in regard to events that are potentially positively reinforcing, we have also been interested in collecting data relative to the general hypothesis that depressed individuals are more sensitive to aversive stimuli (i.e., negative reinforcers) than are nondepressed subjects.

Many studies have been concerned with the autonomic reaction pattern of "neurotics" (e.g., Rubin, 1964). However, relatively few studies have focused on the subset of depressed individuals (Greenfield et al., 1963; Zuckerman et al., 1968). These studies have generated contradictory findings.

A relevant study was conducted by Stewart (1968), who hypothesized that "the behavior of depressed subjects is more influenced by the quality (positive or negative) of social reinforcement elicited than is the behavior of nondepressed subjects" (p. 2). Stewart found that depressed individuals generally had a longer latency of response, operationally defined as the amount of time between the reaction by another person to the subject's verbalization and a subsequent action by that subject in a group situation. The largest differences between depressed and nondepressed subjects occurred following the incidence of a negative social reaction (e.g., being ignored, criticized, disagreed with). The subjects in Stewart's study were also asked to rate their liking or disliking for various kinds of positive and negative social reactions on a 6-point scale. The depressed subjects reported disliking negative reactions more than did nondepressed subjects. However, these results did not attain statistical significance.

The present investigation was undertaken to test the general hypothesis that depressed individuals are more sensitive to aversive stimuli than are nondepressed control subjects. Specifically the following predictions were made:

H_1. Aversive stimuli elicit a greater autonomic response in depressed subjects.

H_2. Aversive stimuli elicit a greater autonomic anticipatory response in depressed subjects.

H_3. Return to base level following an aversive stimulus is less complete in depressed subjects.

H_4. The autonomic responses of depressed subjects show less adaptation over repeated trials.

Since most "real-life" situations contain both positive (approach) and negative (avoidance) components, confirmation of the hypotheses would predict greater avoidance on the part of the depressed individual in many social situations. The short-term consequence would be greater isolation, with the long-term consequence of less skill acquisition for the depressed individual. The hypothesis about the autonomic reactivity of depressed persons postulates a reaction pattern opposite to that described by Hare (1965) for the psychopath. Psychopaths and depressed individuals are conceptualized as being located at opposite ends of an autonomic response continuum; one is thought to be overresponsive, whereas the other is considered underresponsive to aversive stimuli.

The experimental subjects were classified, using the previously described two-stage selection procedure, into three groups: depressed (D), psychiatric controls (PC), and normal controls (NC). The subjects included 12 D, 12 PC, and 12 NC, with an equal number of males and females in each group.

Data were collected during one experimental session which lasted approximately 45 minutes with the subject seated in a comfortable chair. The procedure consisted of the following eight standardized steps:

1. The Depression Adjective Check List (DACL) (Lubin, 1965) was administered.

2. The GSR electrodes were attached.

3. Partially to allow time for hydration, the subjects were administered the Subjective Interpretation of Reinforcement Scale (Stewart, 1968). The statements from the Subjective Interpretation of Reinforcement Scale had been tape recorded, and the subjects were asked to rate their reaction to each one on an 11-point scale with +5 indicating the most pleasant and −5 indicating the most negative reaction.

4. The threshold for electric shock delivered to the finger was determined for each subject. The intensity of the shock was controlled by the experimenter by means of a calibrated dial which had 10 positions. The Method of Ascending Limits was used to determine each subject's threshold.

5. The shock level for the subject was set at one arbitrary unit above the threshold. The shock apparatus delivered a shock of short duration (approximately 2 milliseconds) with a spike of approximately 500 volts. Shock was delivered by means of electrodes attached to the index and ring fingers.

6. The subjects on this and all subsequent shock administrations rated their reactions on an 11-point scale. The mean shock level and the mean subjective shock ratings for the three groups were comparable.

7. In this next phase the subject was told that the experimenter would be counting along with an automatic printout mechanism which was set to print every 3 seconds. The subject was told that the experimenter would start with 5 and count down 4-3-2-1-0 and then count up 1-2-3-4-5 and that the subject would receive one shock when the experimenter said "zero." This constituted one trial.

8. The procedure was repeated five times.

Skin resistance was measured by passing a constant 7-microamp current through the subject's hand, using zinc zinc-sulfate electrodes. The resistance was measured directly in kilohms on a digital volt meter and with a printout occurring every 3 seconds. Following standard psychophysiologic procedure, the scores were converted into log conductance units.

The autonomic data can be thought of as comprising a $36 \times 5 \times 11$-element three-dimensional matrix where one dimension consists of 36 subjects, the second consists of 5 trials, and the third consists of 11 countdown measures within each trial. The 36 subjects are nested within two orthogonal factors, groups (D,

PC, NC) and sex (male, female). The study can be conceptualized as a four-factor experiment with repeated measures on two of the four factors, trials *(T)* and countdown measures *(M)* (Winer, 1962).

The entire experiment, using identical procedures and *N*s, was repeated with another group of subjects (Study 2).

Figures 3 and 4 show the groups' mean log skin conductance levels, averaged across all five trials. Points -5 through -2 reflect the anticipatory phase, points -1 through $+1$ indicate the subject's response to the occurrence of the shock, and points $+2$ through $+5$ reflect recovery. Results of the ANOVAs for the two studies are presented in Table 7.

Table 7.   Results of ANOVAs of Skin Conductance Data for Studies 1 and 2

Source of Variance	df	F		p	
		Study 1	Study 2	Study 1	Study 2
Groups (G)	2	0.5	0.6	NS	NS
Sex (S)	1	0.0	0.1	NS	NS
Trials (T)	4	7.2	23.6	.01	.001
Measurements (M)	10	69.5	51.0	.001	.001
G × S	2	0.0	0.1	NS	NS
G × T	8	2.3	1.6	.05	.20
S × T	4	3.0	8.5	.05	.01
G × M	20	1.7	2.2	.05	.01
S × M	10	2.4	3.5	.01	.01
T × M	40	1.9	2.4	.01	.01
G × S × T	8	3.2	0.6	.01	NS
G × S × M	20	0.6	0.4	NS	NS
G × T × M	80	0.6	0.9	NS	NS
S × T × M	40	1.3	1.2	NS	NS
G × S × T × M	80	0.6	0.8	NS	NS

Our first concern is with the effectiveness of the aversive stimulus in producing *change* in skin conductance. The main effect due to *measurements* is highly significant in both studies. There is also a significant decrease in skin conductance level as a function of the repeated administration of the experimental procedure *(trials)*. It may thus be concluded that the experimental manipulations were successful in eliciting an autonomic response and that adaptation occurred as a function of repeated exposure to the shock.

In both studies the overall skin conductance level is highest (suggesting greater arousal) for the depressed subjects. However, due to large differences in conductance level between subjects within the groups, the differences between groups do not attain statistical significance.

Hypotheses 1, 2, and 3 demand greater *change* on the part of the depressed

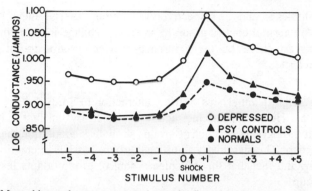

Figure 3. Mean skin conductance, averaged over the five trials, for male and female subjects in (Study 1). (From P. M. Lewinsohn, W. C. Lobitz, and S. Wilson, Sensitivity of depressed individuals to aversive stimuli. *Journal of Abnormal Psychology*, **81**:259-263, 1973. Copyright (1973) by the American Psychological Association. Reproduced by permission.)

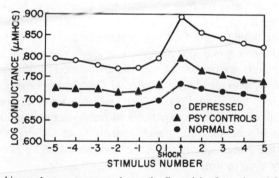

Figure 4. Mean skin conductance, averaged over the five trials, for male and female subjects in (Study 2). (From P. M. Lewinsohn, W. C. Lobitz, and S. Wilson, Sensitivity of depressed individuals to aversive stimuli. *Journal of Abnormal Psychology*, **81**:259-263, 1973. Copyright (1973) by the American Psychological Association. Reproduced by permission.)

group during the anticipatory phase, in response to the shock, and during the recovery phase. The interaction of groups × measurements is statistically significant in both studies. To explicate the basis for this interaction, the three time segments, anticipatory phase (-5 through -2), response to shock (-1 through $+1$), and recovery phase ($+2$ through $+5$), were subjected to separate AN-OVAs. The results suggest that, contrary to H_2, the depressed subjects do not show a greater anticipatory response in Study 1 ($F < 1$) and actually decrease slightly in skin conductance during this period in Study 2 ($F = 2.7$, $df = 6$, 90, $p < .02$). Consistent with H_1, depressed subjects show a greater increase in skin conductance in response to the shock ($F = 1.8$, $p < .2$; $F = 2.9$, p

< .05, for Studies 1 and 2, respectively). Contrary to H3, there is a slight tendency for the normal control group to show less change in skin conductance during the recovery phase, but the differences between groups do not attain statistical significance.

There was a significant groups × trials interaction in Study 1 ($F = 2.3$, $df = 8$, 120, $p<.05$). However, this interaction is caused by the fact that both the depressed and the psychiatric control groups show less adaptation than the normal control group. The marginally significant groups × trials interaction in Study 2 is caused by the fact that the psychiatric control group adapts less than the other two groups.

The statistically significant groups × sex × trials interaction in Study 1 is also relevant to H4. Inspection of the data indicates that the female depressed subjects adapt less than the psychiatric and normal control subjects but this effect is not present in the data for males. This triple interaction, however, is not replicated in Study 2.

Taken in their totality, the findings provide strong support for H1. In both studies the depressed group was found to be more responsive to the aversive stimulus. Our results are consistent with those obtained by Zuckerman, Persky, and Curtis (1968), who also found greater autonomic responsivity to a different aversive situation, the Cold Pressor Test, to be associated with depression. Within the limits of the present experimental manipulations and measurements, the results also suggest that the greater sensitivity of the depressed individual is restricted to the actual occurrence of the aversive stimuli and does not extend backward or forward in time.

Even though three of the four predictions were not confirmed, the fact that the depressed individuals respond more to an aversive stimulus would still lead one to expect them to show a greater tendency to avoid and to withdraw from unpleasant situations. Hence desensitization to aversive situations may be therapeutically useful with depressed individuals. The findings also suggest the hypothesis that the increased latency of response following the incidence of a negative social reaction from another person found in Stewart's (1968) study may be due to the emotional disruption experienced by the depressed individual in situations involving negative consequences.

Relationship Between Social Skill and Depression

In testing the hypothesis about the instrumental behavior of depressed individuals we tended to focus on social skill. The general hypothesis is that depressed persons as a group are less socially skillful than nondepressed individuals. It is conceivable and not incompatible with this hypothesis that depression further reduces the person's social skill.

The first study of the social skill hypothesis was conducted by Rosenberry et al. (1969). The hypothesis being tested was that the depressed person's *timing* of social responses is deviant. The experimental subjects listened to tape-recorded speeches and responded by pressing a button whenever they would normally say or do something to maintain rapport with the speaker. The depressed subjects, as a group, responded less predictably and less homogeneously than did the control group.

Another unpublished study (Lewinsohn, Golding, Johannson, and Stewart, 1968) had subjects talking to each other via teletypewriters. Pairs of subjects took turns talking to each other and each subject could say as much or as little as he wanted to before ending his turn. Subjects from two groups, depressed and nondepressed, were randomly assigned to one of three types of diadic pairing—depressed-depressed, depressed-normal, or normal-normal. Each pair of subjects was tested in front of the teletype machines The subjects were able to communicate with each other through the teletypewriters, which were connected through a wall between two rooms in which the subjects were seated. There was thus no visual contact between the subjects and they were unable to talk to each other except via the teletypewriters. For all subjects the number of words typed per person increased over the 45-minute session, but for depressed subjects the increase in output was much less than for nondepressed subjects ($F = 3.86$, $df = 1,26$, $p < .10$). Figure 5 is a graph of the data.

We have since then been concerned with more systematic comparisons between the interpersonal behavior of depressed and nondepressed individuals in small-group situations and in the home.

Operational Measures of Social Skill

Social skill is defined as the ability to emit behaviors which are positively reinforced by others. This definition involves sequences of behavior consisting of actions emitted by an individual together with the reactions he elicits from the social environment. An individual is considered to be skillful to the extent that he elicits positive (and avoids negative) consequences from the social environment. A behavior sequence may elicit positive reactions in situation A but not in situation B. A second behavior sequence may elicit positive reactions in situation B but not in situation A. The socially skillful individual is the one who emits sequence 1 in situation A and sequence 2 in situation B. By definition lack of social skill is associated with a low rate of positive reinforcement.

As a result of investigating the behavior of depressed and nondepressed persons in group therapy situations (Lewinsohn, Weinstein, and Alper, 1970; Libet

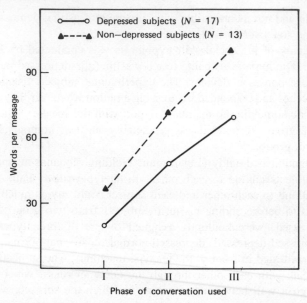

Figure 5.   Mean number of words used for the initial, middle, and final two messages by depressed and nondepressed subjects.

and Lewinsohn, 1973) and in their home environment (Lewinsohn and Shaffer, 1971; Shaffer and Lewinsohn, 1971) a number of different measures of social skill have evolved. The measures differ in that they focus on various aspects of an individual's interpersonal behavior. Nevertheless, they embody a common rationale. Consistent with the definition of social skill, each measure of social skill is assumed to be related to the amount of positive reinforcement an individual elicits from the environment.

A system for coding the interactional behavior of people serves as an operational basis for the measures of social skill. The system is shown schematically in Figure 6. Behavior interactions are seen as having a "source" and an "object." "Actions" are followed by "reactions," which can be coded as either positive (i.e., expressions of affection, approval, interest) or negative (criticism, disapproval, ignore, etc.). A simplified illustration of an interaction involving four people might be as follows: A makes a statement (an action) which is responded to by B (a reaction). B continues talking (an action) and this is followed by a reaction on the part of C, which in turn is followed by some new action on the part of D, and so on. Data so generated allow one to focus on any one individual in terms of the actions he emits and the kinds of reaction he elicits. Two observers code all interactional behaviors. The observers pace themselves with an automatic timer which delivers an auditory and visual signal

Action

Interactional Categories

Psychological complaint	PsyC
Somatic complaint	SomC
Criticism	Crit.
Praise	Pr
Information request	I−
Information giving	I+
Personal problem	PP
Instrument problem	IP
Other People's problems	OP
Talking about abstract impersonal, general, etc.	Ta

Reaction

Positive		Negative	
Affection	Aff	Criticism	Crit
Approval	App	Disapproval	Disapp
Agree	Agr	Disagree	Disagree
Laughter	L+	Ignore	Ign
Interest	Int	Change topic	ChT
Continues talking about topic	ConT	Interrupts	Inter
Physical affection	PhysAff	Physical punishment	Pun

Content—Topics

School	Sch
Self	X, Y, Z
Other people (group, family)	X, Y, Z
Treatment	Rx
Therapist	T
Sex	Sx

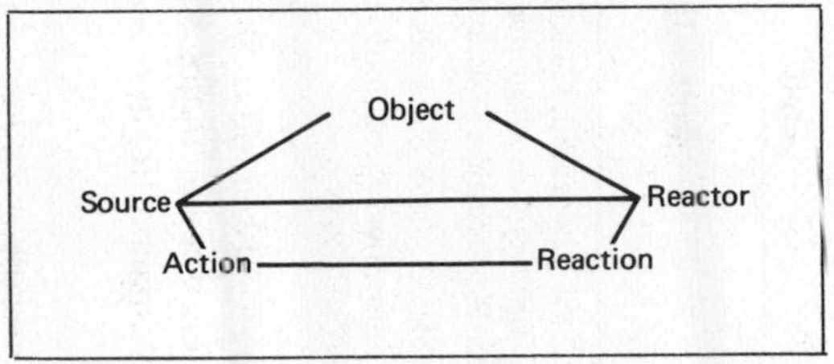

Figure 6. Behavior rating schedule.

85

Table 8. Estimated Spearman-Brown Reliability Coefficients for One Conferenced Rating Based on Three-Way ANOVAs[a] (Ten Persons, Categories, Two Conferenced Ratings)

	Actions		Reactions	
Source	Emit	Elicit	Emit	Elicit
(A) Persons	.995	.774	.956	.973
(B) Categories	.800	.763	.890	.893
(AB) Profiles	.851	.634	.956	.914

Source. J. Libet and P. M. Lewinsohn, Concept of social skill with special reference to the behavior of depressed persons. *Journal of Consulting and Clinical Psychology*, **40**:304-312, 1973. Copyright (1973) by the American Psychological Association. Reproduced by permission.

aWiner (1962, pp. 124-132, 289) discusses the statistical basis of and outlines the computational procedures for estimation of reliability using an analysis of variance model.

simultaneously every 30 seconds. Differences between raters are conferenced. Interjudge agreement for the major scoring categories has been quite high, as seen in Table 8. A manual for the coding system has been developed (Lewinsohn et al., 1968).

The amount of behavior emitted by the individual. A very simple but very important aspect of social skill is represented by the activity level of the individual, defined as the total number of actions emitted by him (expressed as a rate per hour). We have found (Libet and Lewinsohn, 1973; Shaffer and Lewinsohn, 1971) that depressed individuals emit interpersonal behaviors at about half of the rate of nondepressed control subjects.

Interpersonal efficiency. One can conceptualize the "efficiency" with which an individual interacts with other people in two different ways. First, the *interpersonal efficiency-actor* is represented by the ratio of the number of behaviors directed toward the individual (return, income) divided by the number of behaviors he emits toward other people (work, effort). If individuals X and Y each emit 100 actions during a session and X is the object of 80 actions while Y is the object of 120 actions, then Y gets more for what he does than X. Interpersonal efficiency-actor looks at the individual's efficiency from the point of view of what he has to do relative to what he gets. A low interpersonal efficiency-actor ratio would imply that the individual is on a low schedule of reinforcement.

Another way of looking at interpersonal efficiency is from the vantage point of the other person, wondering what he "gets" for interacting with our subject (e.g., a depressed individual). For example, if B (the other person) emits 10 actions to A (a nondepressed person) and 10 actions to C (a depressed patient), and if he elicits 20 actions from A but only 5 from C, then clearly it is more "efficient" for B to interact with A than it is for him to interact with C. C might be said to be less reciprocal (his *interpersonal efficiency-other* ratio is lower) and holding other things constant, one would over a period of time expect B to reduce his interactions with A and to increase his interactions toward C. We have not been able to find systematic differences between depressed and nondepressed individuals in either interpersonal efficiency-actor or in interpersonal efficiency-other (Libet and Lewinsohn, 1973; Shaffer and Lewinsohn, 1971).

However, a post hoc analysis (Shaffer and Lewinsohn, 1971) indicated that, although it was impossible to predict the direction of lack of reciprocity, the relationships of depressed individuals tended to be less reciprocal overall, that is, the depressed individual either did much more for the other person than the other person did for him or vice versa. We intend to examine this emergent (or revised) hypothesis again with new data. One might hypothesize that to the extent that relationships lack reciprocity, they would tend to be less stable over longer periods of time.

Interpersonal Range. Another aspect of social skill, interpersonal range, concerns the number of individuals with whom a person interacts—those to whom he emits behaviors and from whom he elicits behaviors.

To quantify the degree to which an individual distributes his actions equally to other members, a measure was derived from information theory (Attneave, 1959). The interpersonal range measure (relative uncertainty value R) varies from 0 to 1. If an individual emits actions to one other group member, $R = 0$, which indicates minimum unpredictability and minimum interpersonal range. Conversely, if a person distributes his actions equally among his peers, $R = 1$, which indicates maximum unpredictability of the targets of his actions or maximum interpersonal range. Procedural details on how to compute R have been provided elsewhere (Libet and Lewinsohn, 1973). On the basis of small-group interaction data the prediction that depressed individuals have a restricted interpersonal range is supported for males but not for females (Libet and Lewinsohn, 1973).

Use of Positive Reactions. Another aspect of social skill involves reinforcing the behavior of others which is directed toward the subject. The number of positive reactions emitted per session (holding activity level constant) is used to measure this aspect of social skill. The depressed subjects emitted a smaller proportion of positive reactions than did the nondepressed persons (Libet and Lewinsohn, 1973).

Action Latency. Another operational measure of social skill is represented by action latency, which is defined as the lapse of time between the reaction of another person to the subject's verbalization and another subsequent action by that subject. To maintain the behavior of others, it is not merely sufficient to reinforce their behavior, but this has to be done at the appropriate time, namely, in close temporal proximity to the other person's behavior. Also, the individual who delays (has a long action latency) is more likely to "lose the floor." We have found (Stewart, 1968; Libet and Lewinsohn, 1973) significant differences reflecting a 3–1 ratio in latency for depressed and nondepressed.

General Comments about Social Skill and Depression. Although the data support the hypothesis that measures of social skill discriminate between depressed and nondepressed groups, there remain many unanswered questions. For example, does the social skill of an individual when he is depressed differ systematically from when he is not depressed? Clinically one can find individuals who show extreme manifestations of one or more of the foregoing measures of social skill. The advantage of the social skill measures is that they are quantitative and that they can easily be used to define goals for behavior change (Killian, 1971; Lewinsohn, Weinstein, and Alper, 1970). New hypotheses that have suggested themselves to us and that can be tested empirically but for which we have as yet no data are as follows:

H-1. The social skill of depressed persons is more adversely affected by size of group than that of nondepressed persons.

H-2. Being unfamiliar to others in the group has a more negative effect on social skill of depressed than of nondepressed persons.

The Relevance of the Behavioral Theory of Depression to the Phenomena of Aging

Within a behavioral framework depression is conceptualized as an extinction phenomenon. On reading the gerontological literature one is struck by the many behavioral similarities between the depressed and the elderly person. One of the most striking features of both old age and depression is a progressive reduction in the rate of behavior. The concept of "disengagement" has been advanced to account for this reduction of behavior. It is assumed to be a natural process which the elderly person accepts and desires, and which is thought to have intrinsic determinants (Cumming and Henry, 1961). From a behavioral framework, the elderly person's reduced rate of behavior suggests that his behavior is no longer being reinforced by his environment, that is, he, like the depressed person, is on an extinction schedule. Other aspects of the depressive syndrome (feeling rejected, loss of self-esteem, loss of interest, psychophysiological symptoms, etc.) are quite common among the elderly (Wolf, 1959). Motivation is a critical problem in the elderly as it is in the depressed patient. It is hard to find effective reinforcers for either. The number of potentially reinforcing events seems reduced. Finally, the elderly person and the depressed person are turned inward, focused on themselves, their memories, fantasies, and the past.

The hypothesis that a reduction in the response-contingent rate of positive reinforcement is a critical antecedent condition for many of the behavioral changes described in the elderly person immediately suggests itself.

BEHAVIORAL APPROACH TO THE TREATMENT OF DEPRESSED INDIVIDUALS

The behavioral theory has a number of clear implications for the treatment of depressed persons. The guiding principle is to restore an adequate schedule of positive reinforcement for the individual through altering the level, the quality, and the range of the patient's activities and interactions.

Over the past five years a number of case reports describing the application of learning theory to the treatment of depression have appeared in the literature (Badri, 1967; Lazarus, 1968; Lewinsohn and Atwood, 1969: Lewinsohn and Shaw, 1969; Lewinsohn, Weinstein, and Alper, 1970; Lewinsohn and Shaffer, 1971; Liberman and Raskin, 1971; Seitz, 1971; Wolpe, 1971). However, a systematic study of the efficacy of the behavioral techniques which have been proposed for the treatment of depression, with appropriate control groups and follow-up data, has yet to be done. Such a study is vitally needed because, as is well known, depressions are cyclical and usually self-limiting (Beck, 1967). Moreover, there is no generally acceptable criterion for improvement in depressed patients. Case studies have tended to rely on self-report, clinical judgment, depression inventories (Beck, 1967; Hamilton, 1960; Zung, 1965) and on the MMPI. Since the major treatment goal is an increase in the emission of behaviors which are followed by positive consequences, the measure of improvement should be behavioral.

Treatment Strategies

The treatment strategies which have been proposed for depression seem to fall into five categories.

Techniques Aimed at Increasing the Patient's Activity Level

Historically the oldest approach with this goal in mind is the *antidepression milieu-therapy* program developed at the Menninger Foundation during the 1950s. The approach involved making patients perform menial tasks with the staff insisting on a high level of performance. One might speculatively compare the implied use of coercion in this program with the use of force found efficacious by Seligman (1967, 1968, 1971) in the treatment of "conditioned helplessness" in dogs. In his efforts to overcome the passive and helpless behavior shown by his dogs subsequent to inescapable shock, Seligman found that the only intervention which was successful was physically compelling the animal to walk across the electrified side of the cage to the safe side.

Since the use of such strong measures is often impractical, therapists have devised other means to get patients to increase their rate of behavior. Burgess (1969) used a *graded task assignment* procedure whereby the patient was first told to emit some simple behavior like making a telephone call. The task requirements were then increased. The patient was reinforced by the attention and interest of the therapist for successfully completing the tasks. The goal was to reinforce active and constructive behaviors. Beck (1970) uses simple cognitive tasks, in which minimal responding is successful, as part of the treatment of depression.

A more subtle approach to increasing the patient's rate for certain behaviors makes use of the *Premack principle:* the occurrence of high-frequency behaviors can be used to reinforce low-frequency behaviors. The potential utility of the Premack principle for the treatment of behavior disorders was first pointed out by Homme (1965). Homme used high-frequency behaviors such as smoking and drinking coffee to reinforce low-frequency behaviors such as thinking self-confident thoughts. Similarly, Seitz (1971) had his patient generate a list of positive thoughts and then instructed him to think about one or more items on the list before lighting a cigarette (which was a high-frequency behavior). Lewinsohn; Weinstein, and Shaw (1969) and Johansson, Lewinsohn, and Flippo (1969) have made use of high-frequency verbal behavior categories (e.g., talking depression) to reinforce low-frequency verbal behaviors in therapy as well as extratherapy behavior.

Activity schedules (Lewinsohn, Weinstein, and Shaw, 1969; Lewinsohn and Graf, 1973)—having the patient keep a daily record of his behaviors—have also been employed to get patients to increase their activity level.

Techniques Aimed at the Identification of Potential Reinforcers for the Patient

An increase in activity level on the part of the depressed individual cannot be sustained unless the behaviors are followed by positive reinforcement, that is, by consequences which serve to strengthen the behaviors. Hence the therapist must be able to identify reinforcing stimuli for his patient. Since reinforcing stimuli are highly idiosyncratic (MacPhillamy and Lewinsohn, 1971), particular activities, persons, events, objects, and situations which can serve as reinforcers need to be established for each patient. This type of information is typically elicited by interviewing the patient and his spouse or relatives (Kanfer and Saslow, 1965). A quantitative approach to the identification of potential reinforcers is used by Lewinsohn and Libet (1972) and Lewinsohn and Graf (1972). Base level data are collected for 30 days on the patient's activities and on his mood level. By using a correlational approach, specific activities which are associated with the patient's mood are identified. The patient is then reinforced for increasing his rate for these particular activities.

Techniques Aimed at the Induction of Affects Incompatible with Depression

In the same way that anxiety can be reduced by associating an incompatible response such as muscle relaxation with the anxiety-provoking stimulus, it might be suggested that there are affects which are incompatible with feeling depressed. This hypothesis has indeed been proposed by Lazarus (1968) and his use of *affective expression* is based on the premise that "the deliberate stimulation of feelings of amusement, affection, sexual excitement or anxiety tends to break the depressive cycle" (p. 88). *Relaxation training* has been found useful by Seitz (1971) and by us with several cases, perhaps because it induces an affect which is incompatible with depression.

Another technique aimed at the induction of positive affect is Lazarus' *time projection with positive reinforcement* (1968). With the use of hypnosis, the patient is asked to imagine herself engaged in rewarding experiences and activities six months in the future. The patient is then "brought back" to the present with the suggestion that she feels now what she had imagined herself feeling six months in the future.

Techniques Aimed at Enhancing the Patient's Instrumental Skill

A frequent goal of therapy is to train the patient in those skills that are necessary for him to deal effectively with his environment, thus reinforcing him for his efforts. Under this heading come such techniques as *assertive training* (Wolpe and Lazarus, 1966), *social skill training* (Lewinsohn, Weinstein, and Alper, 1970), and *desensitization* (Seitz, 1971; Wolpe, 1971). Where the patient has lost some important set of skills due to physical illness, more extended occupational and academic training may be indicated.

The use of systematic desensitization with depressives seems especially useful in cases where the patient is avoiding fear-arousing situations (e.g., social interactions) that might otherwise be rewarding for him. The suggestion that desensitization to aversive situations may be therapeutically useful with depressed individuals is strengthened by the finding of a heightened sensitivity to aversive stimuli in depressed persons (Stewart, 1968; Lewinsohn, Lobitz, and Wilson, 1973).

Since many depressed patients have few friends, live by themselves, and emit very few social behaviors when they are with people, the use of social skill training as part of the treatment of depression is often suggested. Lewinsohn, Weinstein, and Alper (1970) attempted to create a social environment, in the form of a therapy group, for the depressed person where his behavioral difficulties could be identified and where he could acquire a new and more efficient pattern of interpersonal behavior. The main therapeutic strategy was to provide each patient with information about his own behavior and its consequences, to define behavioral goals with him, and to use the peer group and the therapist to reinforce behavior consistent with these goals, in the group interaction.

Techniques Aimed at Increasing the Drive Level of Depressed Individuals

Depressed individuals are said to be insensitive to stimuli and to respond inadequately to reinforcers (Lazarus, 1968). One way to remedy this deficit is to heighten their drive level. This is the goal of the technique of *behavioral deprivation*, which, as used by Lazarus, involves a period of bed rest without access to external stimuli. The intent is to make the depressed individual more susceptible to incoming stimuli. The technique is an adaption of the Morita therapy (Kora, 1965). Some of the drugs used to treat depression probably enhance the person's drive level.

General Treatment Paradigm

We have found several treatment strategies useful in the treatment of depressed individuals. The first is the general treatment paradigm. We think it is important to do a great deal of "structuring" in the treatment of depressed individuals so that there is a clear mutual understanding of expectations, goals, time commitments, and other conditions.

Three-Month Time Limit

Originally instituted for practical reasons, it quickly became apparent that the inclusion of a time limit of three months had a facilitative effect on the behavior of the client and the therapist. As the end of the three-month time limit approaches, both seem to increase their efforts. We have found the time limit to be effective in both individual and group treatment. One might speculate that the provision of a definite period within which behavior change is to occur can serve as a discriminative stimulus to avoid the aversive consequences of terminating treatment without improvement. The three-month time limit makes it essential for both therapist and client to define and to accept reasonable treatment goals that can be accomplished in three months.

The beginning phase of treatment is clearly defined for the patient as a diagnostic phase. During this phase the patient is told that he and the therapist(s) will try to obtain as much information as possible about him and his behavior so that we may sit down with him, at the end of the diagnostic phase, share our findings with him, and arrive at some mutually acceptable treatment recommendations with him. During this initial phase, the necessity of observing him in his own home is emphasized, as is the possibility of observing him interact with other people. The importance of all kinds of data, such as his filling out mood ratings, his monitoring his activity level, finding out about his interests and obtaining relevant medical information, is emphasized.

Ideally, the initial phase involves two therapists or a therapist and a cotherapist. The interest we are showing, the demands we are making, as in going into the home, are probably important in reversing the downhill cycle within which the depressed patient finds himself at the point where he asks for help. In other words, we put a lot of positive reinforcement into the system in the beginning phase of treatment, and this is especially important in very depressed or suicidal patients. An intensive involvement with the patient is a very important aspect of beginning treatment, especially with the very depressed and suicidal type of patient. If a therapist does not have the time, which some of these patients demand initially, then he probably should not have accepted them.

During the initial diagnostic phase, the therapist forms his hypotheses about what is maintaining the depression and about the kinds of changes in the patient's behavior and in his life situation that are likely to result in a reduction of the depression. The therapist gradually introduces these hypotheses into his sessions with the client and in this the therapist has to be very closely in tune to the patient's level of functioning. There is nothing more useless than to try to present the patient with hypotheses or ideas or data about himself which he is not ready to absorb. This process has been described more carefully and in a detailed way in a number of case histories which have been presented elsewhere (Lewinsohn and Atwood, 1969; Lewinsohn and Shaw, 1969; Martin, Weinstein, and Lewinsohn, 1968).

The diagnostic phase usually ends within two weeks of the beginning of treatment. During the diagnostic phase, base level information is obtained with which to define treatment goals and with which to measure behavior change. The diagnostic phase is followed by one or more review sessions, which are scheduled ahead of time. The patient is told that we will meet with him on a certain date to try to pull everything together and to make our recommendations to him. At these review sessions, the conclusions are presented to the patient. Behavioral terms, graphs, and other visual aids are used to present the "behavioral diagnosis" as clearly as possible. Several sessions, individual and joint, are sometimes required to present the information and to agree upon treatment goals. This process requires a great deal of skill and sensitivity on the part of the therapist and cannot be rushed. It involves considerable interaction between patient and therapist. The end product is a *mutually acceptable* "contract" (understanding) as to the nature of the client's difficulties and as to desirable treatment goals and procedures. For example, in one case our recommendations focused on the patient's relationship with her daughter, her activities, and her many concerns. We felt that it would be beneficial for the patient to increase her activity level. This recommendation was made and accepted by her very readily. We also pointed out to her that we wanted to make her talking about her numerous concerns (which was very high-frequency verbal behavior for her, and which we agreed was very important for her to do) contingent upon her increasing her activity level; that we were going to use a rather complicated procedure involving a green light and other devices in such a way that she could talk about her depression only while the green light was on. In other words, we explicate goals of treatment using terminology that the patient can comprehend as well as any reinforcement schemes and other aspects of treatment. We don't believe in deceiving patients. Following the review sessions, "treatment" begins and tries to accomplish the goals that have been agreed upon.

The main aim of treatment is to restore an adequate schedule of positive reinforcement for the individual. This is the guiding principle for the therapist. In other words, the diagnostic phase is intended to find ways and means of increasing the level of positive reinforcement for the patient. The goal is to alter the level, the quality, the range of interactions, and other activities in order to increase the amount of positive reinforcement which follows from these behaviors.

Use of Home Observations as an Integral Part of the Treatment of Depression

The home observation probably constitutes our most powerful procedure. In addition to providing the therapist with very important diagnostic information, the home visits appear to have two beneficial consequences. First, they immediately focus the therapist-client interaction on behavioral and interpersonal problems. This is especially important since many depressed persons start by defining themselves in a medical way, as having some kind of disease that they expect you to treat. This notion has often been reinforced by previous professional contacts and is quite consistent with the depressed person's tendency to assume a passive role. In a very powerful manner, the home observation communicates to the patient that we see his problem as being interactional, as being intimately related to his relationships with other people. Second, the home observations constitute an easy way of involving a significant part of the client's environment in the treatment process. The necessity of arranging for the home observations gives us a natural opening to relate to the spouse, children, and others close to the client, in ways that are potentially more constructive than the usual information-gathering oriented kind of social history interview with the relative.

The necessity of observing the depressed individual's interaction with his family in his own home is stressed in the intake interview. Initially this ran into a considerable amount of resistance. It was a relatively unexpected and novel request for the patient, we ourselves felt uncertain about it, and the local professional community thought we were engaged in some research project for which we needed subjects. At this time, however, we feel very comfortable about what we are doing, and referring agencies are also becoming increasingly convinced of the value of going into the patient's home. As a matter of fact, they are interested in having us show them how to do it. The home visits typically become the focal point for discussion between therapist and patient and requires the patient to communicate or to plan with members of his family. The manner in which this is accomplished usually results in important diagnostic information such as the patient's resistance to seeing his problem in terms of disturbed interpersonal relationships, wishes, and often attempts to dissociate the significant others from the therapy process and difficulties in communicating with spouse and children. The therapist needs to handle these and related concerns (e.g., feelings about being observed) *before* the home visit. Home visits lasting about an hour each are scheduled around mealtimes (usually dinner) when all members of the family are present. If at all possible, home observations are done for two or three times in succession to gather a more representative sample of interactions. The interactions are coded every 30 seconds using the system for coding interactional behavior which was described earlier.

The primary objective of the home observation is to obtain base level information with which to define treatment goals and to measure behavior change. On the basis of the home observations, the therapist identifies those interpersonal behavior patterns which he assumes to be causally related to the depression. These conclusions are presented to the patient and his spouse at the review session at which treatment goals are defined and agreed upon.

Interpersonal patterns that have emerged as critical vary from case to case and range from the complete absence of any interaction between patient and spouse to very one-sided interactions. There are those patterns where the patient does not reinforce behavior which is directed toward him, as well as where a small portion of the time is devoted to topics of interest to the client, or where his only topic of conversation is depression talk. Three case illustrations demonstrate these procedures.

THE CASE OF MRS. K. (Lewinsohn and Shaw, 1969)

The client, Mary K., was an attractive, 24-year-old female. She was referred to the Psychology Clinic following a fainting spell. Prior to this she had been depressed for several months. In addition to feelings of dysphoria, she also complained of a stiff neck, a urinary infection, a constant preoccupation with having a brain tumor. Except for the urinary infection, medical examinations had not revealed any physical basis for the other symptoms or complaints. Mary K. had been married to Bill, who is about her age, for three years and both were employed as teachers since their graduation from college. During the preceding spring, however, Mary resigned her job "because the pressure was too much." She had obtained employment as a retail clerk. During the summer of 1967, Bill was taking graduate courses and was preparing for a new position to begin in the fall.

The K.'s were seen for a total of 10 sessions, including the intake interview extending over a period of less than six weeks. The results of the home observations, or rather what appeared to us as the salient features, are presented in Table 9. The table shows the proportion of time spent on topics of interest to her, to him, and to both of them. It is clear that more topics of interest to him than to her were being discussed, and that more time was devoted to the former than to the latter. Table 10 shows the number of positive and negative reactions for the case. As can be seen, she "dispenses" a greater number of positive reactions than he does. The immediate effect of the home observations was to shift the focus of the interviews away from somatic concerns to everyday, concrete happenings at work and home. The home observations and other data that had been collected in this case also stimulated a great deal of interaction between the K.'s, both in and out of subsequent joint interviews. She expressed dissatisfaction with the small number of affectionate interactions between them. The therapy sessions subsequently evolved primarily around very concrete, down-to-earth kinds of interaction between the two, the general goal of the therapist being to increase the number of positive interactions between them. At the end of treatment, the K.'s reported that things were definitely better between them, and they both seemed wholeheartedly committed to the idea that most of their problems lay in the interactions between them.

Table 9.   Percentage of Total Time Spent on Each Conversation Topic during Initial (July 14 and 15, 1967) and Final (July 28 and 29; August 7, 1967) Home Observations

Topic	Initial (%)	Final (%)
"His" (e.g., music, school)	36	14
"Hers" (e.g., work, somatic complaints, cat, etc.)	12	23
"Mutual" (new home, going out, etc.)	36	45
Not talking	16	12

THE CASE OF MRS. G. (Lewinsohn and Atwood, 1969)

Mrs. G. was born in 1930. In the intake interview, she reported herself to be on the brink of total despair, finding it increasingly difficult to keep going, spending large amounts of time in bed; generally she appeared to be confused and very upset. She complained of having difficulty sleeping because of obsessive ruminations about incidents in which she believed she had been rejected by other people. She also mentioned recurring fantasies in which she saw her children killed by wild animals or in an automobile accident or by drowning. She also complained about the absence of close friends, blaming the situation on her husband, who professed no need for people. She said that she no longer

Table 10.   Incidences Expressed as Rate per Minute of Behavioral Categories
During Initial and Final Home Observations

Category	Mr. K.		Mrs. K	
	Initial	Final	Initial	Final
Laughs	.07	.06	.33	.13
Listens attentively to other				
conversations	.45	.33	.63	.20
Shows affection	.03	.02	.00	.02
Complies with other request	.01	.02	.05	.01
Shows sympathy	.10	.03	.05	.02
Continues topic	.30	.52	.41	.23
Total	.96	.98	1.47	.61
Interrupts	.11	.04	.06	.05
Nonsympathetic	.06	.03	.02	.00
Shows boredom	.06	.09	.00	.02
Misses chance to reinforce other	.02	.01	.03	.00
Changes topic	.28	.32	.31	.48
Ignores	.10	.10	.15	.01
Total	.63	.59	.57	.56
Initiates conversation	.24	.12	.23	.33

had any feeling for her husband and that she had neither the capacity nor the desire to love him. She indicated an interest in discussing past experiences about which she felt a great deal of guilt.

Two home observations were conducted during the diagnostic phase. During the first visit, the family was moderately defensive, whispering to each other, at least initially, and generally giving the appearance of not wanting the two observers to see or hear very much. The family's defensiveness diminished during the second observation period. The main finding which emerged from the data was that Mrs. G. initiated many interchanges with others, but that they initiated very few with her. This is graphically shown in Figure 7. Others in the family would continue talking about a topic introduced by her, but the data showed that Mr. G. rarely took an active role in his interactions with Mrs. G. The lack of any positive interaction categories was also very striking, as was the absence of topics of conversation that might have been of interest to the adults. Most of the conversation centered around the food, the children, school, and other topics such as the dog, the Christmas tree, the children's clothing, which appeared to be of very little intrinsic interest to Mr. and Mrs. G.

On the basis of the diagnostic information, one of the treatment goals was to change and improve the nature of the marital relationship. Initially, Mrs. G.

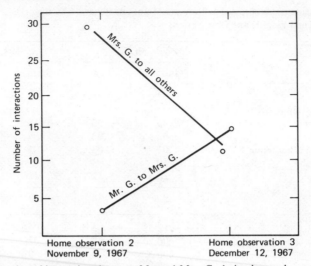

Figure 7.   Number of interactions between Mr. and Mrs. G. during home observations 2 and 3. (From P. M. Lewinsohn and G. E. Atwood, Depression: A clinical-research approach. The case of Mrs. G. *Psychotherapy: Theory, Research and Practice,* **6**:166-171, 1969. Copyright (1969) by *Psychotherapy.* Reproduced by permission.)

expressed dissatisfaction with Mr. G.'s passivity and expressed the wish that he be more active and demanding, particularly in sex. Detailed discussion of Mr. G.'s passivity, however, revealed that she simultaneously demanded and rejected the attention of Mr. G. For example, she related one incident in which she and Mr. G. had been in bed and he had made tentative gestures toward sex. Mrs. G. immediately turned her back on him, repulsed. But when Mr. G. ceased his advances, she resented his lack of interest and accused him of not loving her. This general pattern described an immense number of interchanges between them. Mrs. G. reported making concerted efforts to break through the contradictory pattern in their relationship and by the end of several weeks of treatment, she and her husband reported themselves as feeling much closer again. At about the same time, her mood ratings indicated that she was feeling very good. This seemed like an opportune time to make another home observation with the expectation that the positive changes that were being reported would be reflected and correlated with changes in the nature of the interactions in the home.

A third home observation was conducted on December 12, 1967. Comparison of the data in Table 11 for the second and third home observations reflect changes generally consistent with expectations. In the third observation, Mr. G. initiated a great many more communications to Mrs. G. He had moved from

Table 11. Interactions during Home Observations on November 9, 1967 (6:00-6:40 pm) and December 12, 1967 (5:30-6:00 pm)

Content of Communications Initiated	November 9			December 12		
	Mrs. G.	Mr. G	Children	Mrs. G.	Mr. G.	Children
Food	8[a]	2	0	8	2	3
School	1	0	0	0	0	0
Finances	0	0	0	0	0	0
Children	2	0	0	0	1	0
In-laws	1	0	0	0	0	0
Other people	1	0	0	0	1	1
Somatic complaints	2	1	0	1	1	0
Psychological complaints	1	0	0	0	0	0
Mutual outside activities	4	0	0	0	2	0
His work	0	0	0	0	3	0
Other	9	0	1	2	3	0
Total	29	3	1	11	13	4

Verbal behaviors						
Continues topic	13	13	13	26	15	6
Listens	4	0	0	1	0	0
Approval	0	0	0	0	0	0
Command	3	0	0	2	0	0
Affection	0	0	0	0	0	0
Sympathy	0	0	0	0	0	0
Ignore	0	2	1	0	0	0
Criticism	0	0	1	0	0	1
Disapproval	1	0	1	0	0	0
Changes topic	0	0	0	0	0	0

Nonverbal Behaviors						
Social activity	12	0	0	2	0	0
Help	1	0	0	0	0	0
Compliance	0	0	1	0	0	1
Affection	0	0	0	0	0	0
Laugh, smile	0	1	0	2	1	0
Noncompliance	0	0	2	0	0	1
Aggression	0	0	0	0	0	0
Self-stimulation[b]	17	0	0	7	0	0

[a]The numbers in this table reflect the number of 30-second intervals during which the behavior was observed.
[b]Periods during which the subject is not interacting with another member of the family. Only interactions involving Mrs. G. were counted. Interaction between the children and those between Mr. G. and the children are not included.

99

the passive position indicated in the original observation to a much more active one.

THE CASE OF MRS. B. (Martin, Weinstein, and Lewinsohn, 1968)

Mrs. B., a 28-year-old, married mother of two presented herself as tearful, at the end of the line, afraid of losing control, and crying most of the time. She appeared lethargic and somewhat confused and bewildered. She said she "had little to go on," that she was devoid of feeling for her family, although at times she felt extremely angry with them. She recognized that she "used" headaches and sleep to avoid interacting with the family and that this was no solution. She complained that she and her husband lived in separate worlds, communicating very little, and then only in anger. She said that she did not know whether she wanted to continue the marriage. Shortly after the initial interview, the client was hospitalized following a suicidal gesture. After one week of hospitalization, she was released from the hospital and treatment began.

When Mrs. B. was informed that part of the diagnostic process would include home observations, she expressed some concern that the home observations would not reflect the type of environment she had described and that the picture she had painted of a very discouraging and uncooperative husband would not come through. However, she agreed to ask her husband to give his permission for such home observation, even though she expected that he would not agree. Contrary to her expectations he agreed to this procedure. During the first week of therapy, three home observations were carried out. The major finding was the paucity of interactional behavior between any of the B.'s and especially between Mr. and Mrs. B. (Figure 8). Following the home observations, the therapists saw the marital situation as critical and Mrs. B.'s depression as secondary to the lack of social reinforcement in her family life. In the second week of interviews, this conclusion was presented to Mrs. B., who agreed that she had to reach a decision about whether to remain in the marriage.

It was agreed that defining the problem in this way made it necessary to involve Mr. B. in the treatment program as well. Mrs. B.'s initial reaction to this suggestion was that he would not agree to it. He had ridiculed the idea of psychological help in the past and had been reluctant to pursue it. However, Mr. B. did agree and it was arranged that Mr. and Mrs. B. would be seen jointly once a week. Mrs. B. was also seen individually once a week. In the joint interviews, Mr. and Mrs. B. were as uncommunicative as they had been at home. To summarize, the therapists in the ensuing interviews emphasized the importance of the B.s' communicating with each other, attending to each other's behavior, being more sensitive to each other's feelings, and being able to engage in more open discussions of important aspects of their relationship.

In the last interview the B.'s talked about how well things were going, their ability to express their feelings toward each other more directly, their awareness

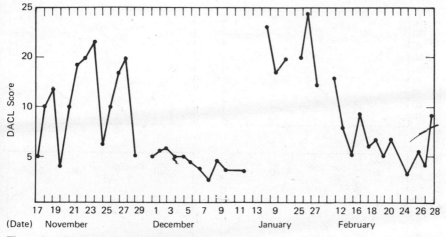

Figure 8. Changes in interactional behavior in the family of Mr. and Mrs. B. from the beginning (October 1967) to the end of the three-month period (January 1968).

of how their behavior influenced the behavior of each other, and their recognition of how they had changed their own behavior. They recognized that their relationship was far from ideal, but they felt better able to work at this on their own. They had decided not to separate, even though Mrs. B. held out the possibility that she might decide to separate at some point. She said that it would be a rational decision rather than a response to anger and frustration. The final home observation was made at the end of therapy to assess change in family interaction. The results are also shown in Figure 8. They reflect change in the direction of more interaction among all members of the family.

Observation of the patient's behavior in his home is not offered as a panacea for the treatment of depression. Rather, it is offered as a valuable adjunct to the assessment of the interpersonal aspects of the depressed person's environment which can provide powerful diagnostic information. We have been especially impressed with the amount of clinical information generated by these home observations and by their utility in the definition and evaluation of treatment goals and of behavior change (Lewinsohn and Shaffer, 1971).

Daily Mood Ratings

Another strategy consists of having the patient rate his mood at the end of each day on one of the alternate forms of the Depression Adjective Check List (DACL) developed by Lubin (1965). The objective is to sensitize the patient and the therapist to correlations of environmental change and shifts in reinforcement contingencies with changes in the client's depression. Figure 9 illustrates several points that can be made about these mood ratings.

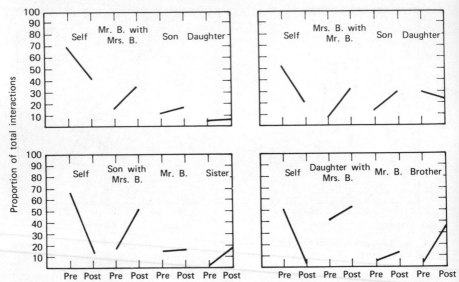

Figure 9.   DACL scores over the course of treatment for Mrs. G (From P. M. Lewinsohn and G. E. Atwood, Depression: A clinical-research approach. The case of Mrs. G. *Psychotherapy: Theory, Research and Practice,* **6**:166-171, 1969. Copyright (1969) by *Psychotherapy;* reproduced by permission.)

With most depressed patients, the daily mood ratings tend to be extremely variable, fluctuating between very depressed levels and levels that are within the range one would expect from a random sample of people. This in itself is interesting, but it also helps the therapist and the patient to identify environmental events that seem to be correlated with how the patient feels. For example, in the case of Mr. B., it was discovered that he tended to feel most depressed on Sundays. This was taken up with him, as it was very clear that he had little to do on Sundays. He then took up coaching a basketball team on which his son was one of the players and this was accompanied by a reduction in his DACL ratings. In the case of Mrs. G., after an initial period of treatment during which her DACL ratings had come down, they then shot up rather dramatically at a point where her relationship with her husband had again deteriorated. The obvious correlation helped to reinforce for her the association between her relationship with her husband and her depression. What sometimes seems to happen is that as therapy progresses, the patient's mood ratings become not only lower in overall level, but also much less variable.

Monitoring the Patient's Activity Level

Other requirements used include having the patient keep a detailed record of his daily activities, and the administration of Vocational Interest tests. The infor-

Table 12.   Activity Schedule

Name _____ Date _____ Raw Score _____Weighted Score _____

Instructions: Place check marks in the frequency column to correspond to the number of times an activity takes place during the day. For example, if you go for a walk two times during the day, place two check marks in the frequency column. Only activities that were at least a little pleasant during the day being considered should be checked. If an activity differs in pleasantness from your initial ratings, write in how pleasant the activity was for that particular day, using the following rating system: 2 means a little, 3 means a fair amount, 4 means much, and 5 means very much.

Activity	How Pleasant		
	Initially	Today	Frequency
Talking with other teachers	3		
Developing own teaching materials	4		
Talking with students			
Teaching students	4		
Cleaning house	3		
Carrying on conversation with daughter	4		
Taking a trip (to)	5		
Going on a date			
Hearing a lecture	3		
Attending class	3		
Going to a play	4		
Going to a concert	2		
Attending a church discussion group	4		
Playing a game	2		
Eating at home	2		
Dining out	3		
Having a drink with a friend			
Solving mathematical problems	4		
Solving crossword puzzles	2		
Listening to music	3		
Watching animals	3		
Watching sports	1		
Reading for teaching purposes	3		
Reading for entertainment	4		
Looking at interesting buildings	2		
Looking at beautiful scenery	4		
Watching TV	2		
Singing alone			
Singing with others	3		
Dancing	2		
Performing on a musical instrument	1		

mation provided by such records emphasizes the small amount of time the depressed patient spends on activities he considers to be enjoyable and meaningful. By means of such data, the therapist can pinpoint behavioral goals (e.g., spending more time outside the home, learning new skills, attending lectures, concerts, sports, making career decisions) as well as identify and reinforce desirable behavior change when it occurs.

To accomplish this, we constructed lists for patients with their help. Table 12 is part of a list used with Mrs. W. (Flippo and Lewinsohn, 1969). In the treatment of this lady, a schoolteacher, it quickly became apparent that she was engaging in very few activities beyond those absolutely required of her. With her help, we constructed a list of activities she considered to be enjoyable, pleasant, meaningful, and interesting. This resulted in a fairly long list and we had her indicate how pleasant these activities were on a 5-point scale. As part of our treatment recommendations, we strongly urged her to engage in more activities, with which she heartily agreed. She would then check off all the activities she had engaged in during each day and bring those in for her treatment hour. The list was then used by the therapist to determine how many minutes of "depression-talk time" she would get. Her activity level increased markedly as treatment progressed.

More recently we have been relying on the Pleasant Events Schedule to generate tailor-made activity schedules for each patient. The patient takes the Pleasant Events Schedule early during the diagnostic phase, rating each activity on a 3- or 5-point scale of pleasantness. On the basis of the patient's ratings, 160 pleasant (for him) activities are identified; these in turn become the basis for his activity schedule, which is then duplicated. The patient then is asked to check off at the end of each day which of these activities he engaged in. Table 13 is a sample Activity Schedule. The patient also rates his mood on the Depression Adjective Check Lists for 30 days. At the end of the base level period (30 days) it is possible to compute the correlation between the patient's mood and his total activity level and to identify individual activities that seem to be especially important (correlated) to how he feels. The patient continues to monitor his activity level and his mood throughout the rest of the treatment.

The patient is provided with feedback about the extent to which how he feels is associated with what he does. Specific activities which are correlated with mood are brought to his attention.

We have completed a pilot study with 10 depressed subjects who were reinforced with therapy time for increasing their activity level (Lewinsohn and Graf, 1973). The subjects for this study were assigned to graduate student therapists who saw the patients between one and three times per week for 10 weeks. Frequency of sessions varied across patients but was determined early by the patient and his therapist. The patients were informed that they were participating in an experimental treatment project and that the activity schedules would play an important part in the treatment. They were told that the purpose of the base level period was to identify activities especially important for them, and that in order to motivate them to increase their activity level, therapy time would be made contingent on how many activities they engaged in after the base level period (30 days). Patients were told that they should feel free to use

Table 13. Activity Schedule

Name **Mr. S.W.** Date _____ (R) Score _____ (W)3 Score _____

Make check mark(s) in the columns to correspond to the activities of this day. Only activities that were at least a little pleasant should be checked.

Activities	Frequency Check
1. Wearing expensive or formal clothes (2c)	
2. Making contributions to religious, charitable, or other groups (3c)	
3. Talking about sports (4c)	
4. Meeting someone new of the same sex (5c)	
5. Taking tests when well prepared (6c)	
6. Playing baseball or softball (8c)	
7. Planning trips or vacations (9c)	
8. Buying things for myself (10c)	
9. Being at the beach (11c)	
10. Going to a sports event (19c)	
11. Pleasing my parents (31c)	
12. Watching TV (33c)	
13. Shaving (45c)	
14. Having lunch with friends or associates (46c)	
15. Taking a shower (49c)	
16. Being with friends (74c)	
17. Being with my grandchildren (83c)	
18. Wearing new clothes (99c)	
19. Seeing good things happen to my family or friends (105c)	
20. Wearing clean clothes (133c)	
21. Getting a job advancement (being promoted, given a raise or offered a better job, accepted into a better school, etc.) (137c)	
22. Wrestling or boxing (148c)	
23. Doing a job well (154c)	
24. Having spare time (155c)	
25. Going to a health club, sauna bath, etc. (1d)	
26. Being with my parents (9d)	
27. Being at a family reunion or get-together (30d)	
28. Being with someone I love (83d)	
29. Playing handball, paddleball, squash, etc. (125d)	
30. Being with my children (136d)	
31. Being in the country (1c)	
32. Going to a rock concert (7c)	
33. Reading the Scriptures or other sacred works (14c)	
34. Playing golf (15c)	
35. Re-arranging or redecorating my room or house (17c)	
36. Reading a "How To Do It" book or article (20c)	
37. Going to the races (horse, car, boat, etc.) (21c)	
38. Reading stories, novels, poems, or plays (22c)	

their time with the therapist in whatever way seemed most useful to them. The therapists were instructed to be good, nondirective client-centered therapists, and some training was provided for this purpose. They were told to adhere to the framework which is referred to in the literature by terms like empathy, unconditional positive regard, and congruence. The therapists were also asked not to engage in any active interventions. The rationale for the first instruction was that a good nondirective therapist, by completely focusing on the patient—his verbalizations, his feelings, and the like—is an effective reinforcer. That is, we wanted the patients to have a positive attitude toward their therapist and to be motivated to talk with him. The rationale for the second instruction was to minimize individual differences between therapists.

At the end of the base level period the patient's activity scores and mood ratings were submitted to the computer. The 10 most highly correlated activities were selected. A formula was developed for each patient whereby the patient would get some minutes of therapy time as a function of how many activities he engaged in. The patients were told which activities would earn therapy time. At the beginning of each subsequent therapy hour, the patient would return his completed activity schedules and mood ratings to a research assistant. She would then score the forms, compute the amount of therapy time to which the patient was entitled, and inform the therapist about the amount of time the patient was to be seen on this session. With very few exceptions, the therapists adhered closely to the time limits.

Table 14 consists of a sample list and time formula. Figure 10 presents the

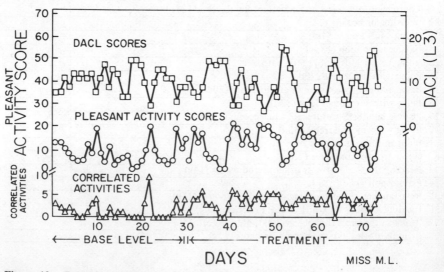

Figure 10. Depression Adjective Check List, Pleasant Activity, and correlated activities scores during base level and treatment (Case M. L.).

Table 14. Sample of Critical Activities and Reinforcement Schedule for Two Patients

Case 70 ♀ Age 58

Ten Most Highly Correlated Activities
Laughing
Solving problems, puzzles, etc.
Being with friends
Hiking
Learning to do something new
Being praised by people you admire
Doing physical fitness exercises
Planning something
Just sitting and thinking
Having a drink

Reinforcement Schedule	
Number of Activities/Day	Minutes of R_x Time
0-1	10
2	20
3	30
4	40
5 or more	50

Case 86 ♀ Age 20

Ten Most Highly Correlated Activities
Doing favors for people
Talking about sports
Breathing clean air
Driving skillfully
Driving fast
Looking at sky or clouds
Making snacks
Visiting friends
Seeing old friends
Going to a restaurant

Reinforcement Schedule	
Number of Activities/Day	Minutes of R_x Time
0-1	10
2-3	20
4	30
5	40
6 or more	50

data for a patient, illustrating the correlation between activity level and mood which can be demonstrated for most patients.

We were interested in a number of questions. First, does the total procedure produce a significant increase in the patient's engaging in the pinpointed (pleasant) activities? To provide a basis for comparison, 10 "control" activities were selected for each patient. These were comparable in frequency of occurrence to the correlated activities but they had not been found to be correlated with mood. The results are seen in Figure 11. As can be seen, there was a significant increase in frequency for the correlated activities ($F = 3.4; df = 1/71; p$ .01), which was not accompanied by a corresponding increase in either the control activities or in the total activities score. It may thus be concluded that the procedure as a whole was successful in producing a significant change (increase) in the pinpointed activities. The results, of course, do not allow one to identify the critical components of the procedure which were responsible for the behavior change. The critical control groups are lacking. "Telling" patients to do more might have been equally effective.

The second question we asked is how stable are the correlations between mood and the individual's activity scores (pinpointed and total)? Since the whole procedure capitalizes heavily on chance, a certain amount of "shrinkage" was

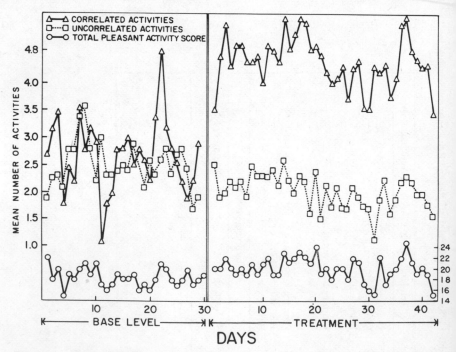

Figure 11.   Mean correlated, uncorrelated, and total pleasant activity scores for group of 10 patients.

Table 15. Correlation between the Depression Adjective List Scores and the Pleasant Activities (PA) and Raw Activity Scores (RA) for 14 Subjects Computed Separately for Base Level (30 Days) and Treatment (42 Days)

Subject Code Number	Pleasant Activities				Raw Activities			
	Base Level	p	Treatment	p	Base Level	p	Treatment	p
62	-.57	.001	-.31	.05	-.36	.05	-.43	.01
63	-.62	.001	-.45	.01	-.26	.10	-.51	.001
70	-.62	.001	-.75	.001	-.25	.10	-.71	.001
72	-.64	.001	-.13	NS	-.53	.01	-.10	NS
74	-.43	.001	-.28	.05	-.08	NS	-.44	.01
78	-.59	.001	.00	NS	-.46	.01	-.08	NS
86	-.67	.001	-.50	.001	-.80	.001	-.82	.001
108	-.68	.001	-.19	NS	-.52	.001	-.32	.02
113	-.63	.001	-.09	NS	-.20	NS	-.36	.01
248	-.84	.001	-.29	.05	-.26	.10	-.36	.02
840	-.66	.001	-.31	.05	-.44	.01	-.25	.10
069	-.63	.001	-.44	.01	-.35	.02	-.36	.02
082	-.72	.001	-.43	.02	-.35	.02	-.33	.05
114	-.79	.001	-.73	.001	-.66	.001	-.81	.001
Mean	-.65		-.36		-.39		-.42	

to be expected. Base level and treatment data on 14 patients (four additional patients had not been included in the time contingency study) were available and the results are presented in Table 15. As can be seen, although there is a drop from base level to treatment in the magnitude of the correlations between mood and the "correlated" activities, the correlation continues to be above chance for 10 of 14 patients. On the other hand, the magnitude of the correlation between mood and total activity level remains stable. We interpret these results as justifying the use of *either* a small number of selected activities or the patient's total activity level as legitimate treatment goals for the purpose of modifying mood level.

There are several procedural changes we intend to make. The use of the 10 most highly correlated activities seems, in retrospect, to have been too rigid. A considerably larger but variable number of correlated activities, selected in cooperation with the patient, might have been better.

A question can be raised about the honesty with which people fill out these activity schedules, especially when therapy time is made contingent on activity level. Like other self-report measures they are completely under the subject's control. In our experience with about 30 patients we have questioned the truthfulness of three. Two of these were poorly motivated, missing many sessions, and were generally critical of the approach. The third patient immediately increased her activity level substantially when the contingency program was instituted to where she was earning fifty minutes of therapy time every session. However, the majority of depressed individuals seem to be quite conscientious about filling out these schedules. In another context (MacPhillamy and Lewinsohn, 1972) we found the frequency ratings of the PES to possess good reliability when compared with ratings made by independent observers.

Application of the Premack Principle in the Treatment of the Depressed Individual

A commonly recognized difficulty in the treatment of depressed persons is that they are often poorly motivated. Even though it may be possible to define desirable changes in the patient's behavior or in his life situation, the depressed patient often does not follow through. The Premack Principle states that the occurrence of a high-frequency behavior can be used to reinforce a low-frequency behavior by making the occurrence of the high-frequency behavior contingent upon the emission of the low-frequency behavior. In many depressed patients, certain behaviors (e.g., verbal statements of dysphoria, guilt, self-depreciation, rejection, material burden) are emitted at a consistently high rate. Hence, according to Premack's Principle, the occurrence of these high-frequency behaviors would have reinforcing value for low-frequency behaviors. In other words, it should be possible to reinforce low-frequency behaviors in the depressed individual (e.g., self-assertive, realistic, constructive behaviors) by making high-frequency (self-depreciatory statements, for example) behaviors contingent upon them. We have tried using this with several cases so far, and preliminary results look very promising indeed.

The case of Mrs. W. can be used to illustrate this. As mentioned earlier, it was the impression of her therapist that an increase in her activity level would constitute desirable behavior change. This recommendation was readily accepted by her. The therapist then reviewed the many concerns and anxieties which she had spent a great deal of her time telling him about. He indicated that these were important and that he was interested in helping her with them, but since it seemed so much easier for her to talk about them than for her to increase her activity level, he would accomplish two goals and make her talk about her psychological complaints contingent upon her increasing her activity level. The amount of psychological complaint time that she was going to get would be proportional to the number of activities she engaged in. She would be able to talk about her concerns only when a certain light in the therapy room was on; the rest of the time her verbal behavior would be restricted to any category other than psychological complaint. It took very little to explain her high-frequency verbal category to her, and it usually is very easy to do this with other patients as well.

The initial reaction of Mrs. W. to all this was one of angry indignation. She angrily declared that she was coming here to talk about her concerns and that she was going to complain as much as she wanted for as long as she wanted. Upon the therapist's accepting and reflecting upon her feelings of anger, she indicated that she was willing to give it a try. For the rest of the session, we trained her with two minutes of green light on and two minutes of green light off to make sure she understood what her high-frequency category was. Subsequently, her activity level increased substantially and her depression level went down and has remained down. She feels that the method was a very useful one and she attributes its utility to its having helped her to control her feelings, so that now when she feels herself suddenly obsessing and worrying about something, she reminds herself that the green light is not on. During the course of treatment, she also coped with a number of reality problems that she was facing, such as getting a divorce from her husband and dealing with questions about the custody of her children.

More recently we have been able to produce increases in specific low-rate verbal behaviors in depressed individuals by using their own high-rate verbal behaviors as a reinforcer (Johansson, Lewinsohn, and Flippo, 1969; Robinson and Lewinsohn, 1973).

A Behaviorally Oriented Approach to the Group Treatment of Persons with Depression

Since many depressed patients have very few friends, live by themselves, and emit very few social behaviors when they are with people, the possibilities for the observation of the patient's behavior with others are often quite limited. In these cases, the therapist is dependent on verbal reports by the patient of his own behavior with people. Such reports are usually imprecise and difficult to evaluate and generally not too helpful. To overcome these common difficulties in the treatment of depressed persons, we have attempted to create a social environment for the depressed patient in the form of psychotherapy groups where his behavioral difficulties can be identified and where he can acquire new and more efficient patterns of interpersonal behavior. The principal therapeutic strategy is to provide the patient with information about his own behavior and its consequences. His behavior in the group is used to define behavioral goals with him, and the therapist can then be programmed to reinforce behaviors consistent with these goals in the group interaction. These groups have been described in greater detail elsewhere (Lewinsohn, Weinstein, and Alper, 1970).

We called the first group Self-Study Group I and the second one Self-Study Group II, both consisting of eight to ten people. In the first group, all subjects were depressed, whereas the second had four depressed and four nondepressed subjects. The groups have met for 16 and 18 sessions, respectively, and the subjects were seen individually as well. The groups were structured as "self-study" groups where members would be able to learn about their own behavior and its consequences upon others. Group I was run along fairly traditional group therapy lines; however, instead of focusing primarily on the attitudes, feelings, and content of the communications, the therapists focused on the quantitative and qualitative aspects of the interactions among members in the group setting. In other words, it was process oriented. In Self-Study Group II, a series of structured exercises, borrowed from and adapted from the training group-sensitivity people, was used to facilitate and to expedite interpersonal communication.

Several individual cases illustrate the kinds of behavioral goals that can be set for clients in the group situation. The ultimate objective is the attainment of a higher rate of positive (social) reinforcement. With a single exception, it has been possible to obtain a verbal statement on the part of the subject as to what specific changes in his behavior would be desirable for him. Figure 12 shows the activity level of a very passive subject. This subject was provided with an explanation of the reciprocity concept: if one wishes for people to attend and respond to one, one has to be more active in responding to them. She acknowledged that she wished to become more actively engaged with people and her subsequent increased activity level was met with a great deal of approval and

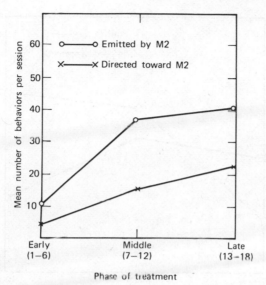

Figure 12. Changes in activity level of M2 and corresponding changes in amount of behavior directed toward M2 during group sessions.

attention by the peer group. The figure also shows the consequent increase in the number of behaviors that were directed toward her.

Figure 13 shows an individual who emits very few positive reactions. In spite of this, he was the object of many actions on the part of the other members. Inspection of his data revealed that he emitted many critical and challenging statements which resulted in defensive reactions on the part of the others (e.g., he informed another member of the group that her problem was trivial and easily soluble, whereupon she tried to convince him that this was not so). When presented with this information, M3 expressed his concern over the fact that he had very few friends in spite of his concerted efforts. He was encouraged, whenever possible, to emit positive reactions and to cut down on the use of negative reactions. The degree to which he was able to accomplish this is seen in Figure 13.

Figure 14 illustrates a case with a very limited range of interactions. The social isolation of F3 was quantitatively represented by the proportion of the total group with whom she interacted. She initially directed most of her behavior toward the therapist and interacted minimally with less than one-third of the members of the group. This and her consequent vulnerability were focused on with her and she was encouraged to direct her behavior toward the larger number of individuals in the group. The success with which she was able to accomplish this is seen in Figure 14.

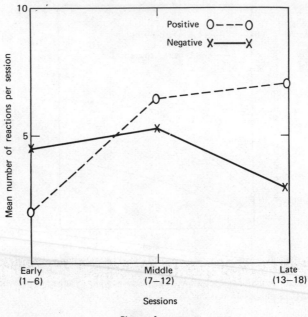

Figure 13. Changes in rate of positive and negative reactions for M3 during group sessions.

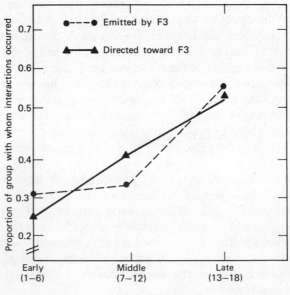

Figure 14. Changes in rate of interaction for F3 during group sessions.

114

In Self-Study Group II, beginning with session 9, the subjects wore a single earphone, thus making it possible for their therapists to communicate with them while the group therapy session was in progress. The patient's own therapist thus was able to provide him with instant reinforcement. The therapists in Self-Study Group II met regularly with each client once a week between the two group sessions. Sessions 1 through 4 were essentially used to identify base level rates. Between sessions 5 and 8, the therapist had to have agreement with the client on some behavioral goal for himself. Each therapist carried two subjects, one depressed and one nondepressed. Since we had some practical problems of getting all four therapists into the observation room at the same time, along with the two coders, along with several experimenters, and others, we decided to stagger the reinforcement sessions so that four subjects would be reinforced during one session and the other half of the group would be at the next session, the two groups alternating places. Part of the group was thus on a one-zero, one-zero, one-zero, zero-zero sequence while the other half was on a zero-one, zero-one, zero-one, zero-zero sequence. In presenting these data (Figure 15), we have combined the two groups so that there is some confounding between the reinforcement scheme and the number of sessions for half of the subjects. These data are extremely tentative and we see this as a very, very crude beginning. It is clear that between sessions 6 and 10 when the subjects were identifying some behavioral goal for themselves, there was a substantial increase in the rate with which they were emitting the behavior that was being reinforced compared with the baseline level. After this, some of the subjects seemed to actually cut down on the reinforced behavior category and there were large individual differences. We are generally encouraged with the total treatment package, so to speak, even though we feel that there is much room for improvement.

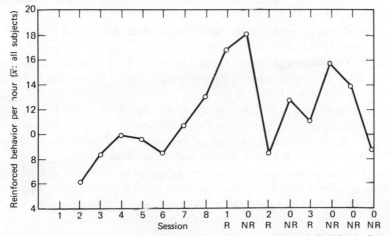

Figure 15.   Change in rate of reinforced behavior emitted across sessions in Self-Study Group 2.

The data, hypotheses, and treatment methods we have tried to present are meant to be very tentative. Our conceptualization of depression, our ways of dealing with it, are in a continuous state of flux. New possibilities suggest themselves continuously. There is no doubt that our framework is an oversimplification and that some of the hypotheses will have to be revised and new ones developed. We do think that we are developing some methods for studying depression. Perhaps this constitutes progress.

ACKNOWLEDGMENT

The author wishes to express his appreciation to the many members of the "Depression Team" at the University of Oregon. Their contributions to this research have been very substantial.

REFERENCES

Abraham, K. (1911) Notes on the psychoanalytic investigation and treatment of manic-depressive insanity and allied conditions. *Selected Papers on Psychoanalysis*. New York: Basic Books, 1960.

Attneave, F. *Application of Information Theory to Psychology*. New York: Holt, Rinehart and Winston, 1959.

Azrin, N. H., Hutchinson, R. R., and Hake, D. F. Extinction-induced agression. *Journal of the Experimental Analysis of Behavior*, 1966, **9**, 191–204.

Badri, M. B. A new technique for the systematic desensitization of pervasive anxiety and phobic reaction. *Journal of Psychology*, 1967, **65**, 201–208.

Beck, A. T. *Depression: Clinical, Experimental, and Theoretical Aspects*. New York: Harper and Row, 1967.

Beck, A. T. Cognitive therapy: Nature and relation to behavior therapy. *Behavior Therapy*, 1970, **1**, 184–200.

Beck, A. T. The phenomena of depression: A synthesis. In D. Offer and D. X. Freedman (Eds.), *Clinical Research in Perspective: Essays in Honor of Roy R. Grinker, Sr.* New York: Basic Books, 1970.

Bibring, E. The mechanism of depression. In D. Greenacre (Ed.), *Affective Disorders*. New York: International University Press, 1953.

Bonime, T. The psychodynamics of neurotic depression. In S. Arieti (Ed.), *American Handbook of Psychiatry*, Vol. 3. New York: Basic Books, 1966.

Burgess, E. The modification of depressive behavior. In R. Rubin and C. Franks (Eds.), *Advances in Behavior Therapy*. New York: Academic Press, 1968.

Campbell, D. T., and Fiske, D. W. Convergent and discriminant validation by the multi-trait multi-method matrix. *Psychological Bulletin*, 1959, **56**, 81–105.

Cautela, J., and Kastenbaum, R. A reinforcement survey schedule for use in therapy, training, and research. *Psychological Reports,* 1967, **20,** 1115–1130.

Cumming, E., and Henry, W. *Growing Old: The Process of Disengagement.* New York: Basic Books, 1961.

Fenichel, O. *The Psychoanalytic Theory of Neurosis.* New York: Norton, 1945.

Ferster, C. B. Classification of behavior pathology. In L. Krasner and L. P. Ullman (Eds.), *Research in Behavior Modification.* New York: Holt, Rinehart and Winston, 1965.

Flippo, J. and Lewinsohn, P.M. Unpublished manuscript, University of Oregon, 1969.

Freud, S. Mourning and melancholia. In *Collected Papers,* Vol. 4. London: Hogarth Press, 1957, pp. 152–170.

Friedman, R. J., and Katz, M. M. (Eds.) *The Psychology of Depression: Contemporary Theory and Research.* (In Press)

Gaylin, W. *The Meaning of Despair.* New York: Science House, 1968.

Greenfield, N. S., Kate, D., Alexander, A. A., and Roessler, R. The relationship between physiological and psychological responsivity: Depression and galvanic skin response. *Journal of Nervous and Mental Disease,* 1963, **136,** 535–539.

Grinker, R. R., Miller, J., Sabshin, M., Nunn, J., and Nunnally, J. D. *The Phenomena of Depression.* New York: Hoeber, 1961.

Hamilton, M. A rating scale for depression. *Journal of Neurology, Neurosurgery and Psychiatry,* 1960, **23,** 56–61.

Hare, R. D. A conflict and learning theory analysis of psychopathic behavior. *Journal of Research in Crime and Delinquency,* 1965, **2,** 12–19.

Homme, L. E. Perspectives in psychology. XXIV. Control of coverants, the operants of the mind. *Psychological Record,* 1965, **15,** 501–511.

Johansson, S., Lewinsohn, P. M., and Flippo, J. R. An application of the Premack principle to the verbal behavior of depressed subjects. Paper presented at the meeting of the Association for Advancement of Behavior Therapy, 1969. University of Oregon, 1969. (mimeo)

Kanfer, F. H. Self-monitoring: Methodological limitations and clinical applications. *Journal of Consulting and Clinical Psychology,* 1970, **35,** 148–152.

Kanfer, F. H., and Saslow, G. Behavioral analysis, an alternative to diagnostic classification. *Archives of General Psychiatry,* 1965, **12,** 529–538.

Killian, D. H. The effect of instructions and social reinforcement on selected categories of behavior emitted by depressed persons in a small group setting. Unpublished doctoral dissertation. University of Oregon, 1971.

Kora, T. Morita therapy. *International Journal of Psychiatry,* 1965, **1,** 611–640.

Lazarus, A. A. Learning theory and the treatment of depression. *Behaviour Research and Therapy,* 1968, **6,** 83–89.

Lewinsohn, P. M. Manual of instruction for the behavior rating used for the observation of interpersonal behavior. Unpublished manuscript, University of Oregon, 1968. Revised, 1971.

Lewinsohn, P. M., and Atwood, G. E. Depression: A clinical-research approach. *Psychotherapy: Theory, Research, and Practice*, 1969, **6**, 166–171.

Lewinsohn, P. M., Golding, S. L., Johansson, S. L., and Stewart, R. Patterns of communication in depressed and nondepressed subjects. Unpublished manuscript, University of Oregon, 1968.

Lewinsohn, P. M., and Graf, M. Pleasant activities and depression. *Journal of Consulting and Clinical Psychology*, 1973, **41**, 261–268.

Lewinsohn, P. M., and Libet, J. Pleasant events, activity schedules, and depression. *Journal of Abnormal Psychology*, 1972, **79**, 291–295.

Lewinsohn, P. M., Lobitz, C., and Wilson, S. "Sensitivity" of depressed individuals to aversive stimuli. *Journal of Abnormal Psychology*, 1973, **81**, 259–263.

Lewinsohn, P. M., and Shaffer, M. The use of home observations as an integral part of the treatment of depression: Preliminary report and case studies. *Journal of Consulting and Clinical Psychology*, 1971, **37**, 87–94.

Lewinsohn, P. M., Shaffer, M., and Libet, J. Depression: A clinical-research approach. Paper presented at the meeting of the Western Psychological Association, 1969. University of Oregon, 1969. (mimeo)

Lewinsohn, P. M., and Shaw, D. A. Feedback about interpersonal behavior as an agent of behavior change: A case study in the treatment of depression. *Psychotherapy and Psychosomatics*, 1969, **17**, 82–88.

Lewinsohn, P. M., Weinstein, M. S., and Alper, T. A behaviorally oriented approach to the group treatment of depressed persons: A methodological contribution. *Journal of Clinical Psychology*, 1970, **4**, 525–532.

Lewinsohn P. M., Weinstein, M. S., and Shaw, D. Depression: A clinical-research approach. In R. D. Rubin and C. M. Franks (Eds.), *Advances in Behavior Therapy, 1968*. New York: Academic Press, 1969.

Liberman, R. P., and Raskin, D. E. Depression: A behavioral formulation. *Archives of General Psychiatry*, 1971, **24**, 515–523.

Libet, J., and Lewinsohn, P. M. The concept of social skill with special references to the behavior of depressed persons. *Journal of Consulting and Clinical Psychology*, 1973, **40**, 304–312.

Lubin, B. Adjective checklists for the measurement of depression. *Archives of General Psychology*, 1965, **12**, 57–62.

MacPhillamy, D. J., and Lewinsohn, P. M. Pleasant events schedule. University of Oregon, 1971. (mimeo)

MacPhillamy, D. J., and Lewinsohn, P. M. The structure of reported reinforcement. University of Oregon, 1972. (mimeo)

MacPhillamy, D. J., and Lewinsohn, P. M. Studies on the measurement of human reinforcement. University of Oregon, 1972. (mimeo)

MacPhillamy, D. J., and Lewinsohn, P. M. Relationship between positive reinforcement and depression. University of Oregon, 1972. (mimeo)

Maier, S. F., Seligman, M. E. P., and Solomon, R. L. Pavlovian fear conditioning and learned helplessness. In B. A. Campbell and R. M. Church (Eds.), *Punishment*. New York: Appleton-Century Crofts, 1969.

Martin, M. L., Weinstein, M., and Lewinsohn, P. M. The use of home observations as an integral part of the treatment of depression: The case of Mrs. B. Unpublished manuscript, University of Oregon, 1968.

Patterson, G. R. Manual for the behavior check list. Unpublished manuscript, University of Oregon, 1967.

Patterson, G. R., and Reid, J. B. Reciprocity and coercion: Two facets of social systems. In C. Neuringer and J. Michaels (Eds.), *Behavior Modification for Clinical Psychology* New York. McGraw-Hill, 1969.

Paykel, E. S., Myers, J. K., Dicnett, M. N., Klerman, G. L., Lindenthal, J. J., and Pepper, M. D. Life events and depression: A controlled study. Yale University, 1969. (mimeo)

Premack, D. Toward empirical behavior laws. I. Positive reinforcement. *Psychological Review,* 1959, **66,** 219–233.

Robinson, J., and Lewinsohn, P. M. Experimental analyses of a technique based on the Premack principle for changing the verbal behavior of depressed individuals. *Perceptual and Motor Skills,* 1973, **32,** 199–210.

Rosenberry, C., Weiss, R. L., and Lewinsohn, P. M. Frequency and skill of emitted social reinforcement in depressed and non-depressed subjects. Paper presented at meeting of Western Psychological Association, 1969. University of Oregon, 1969. (mimeo)

Rubin, L. S. Autonomic dysfunction as a concomitant of neurotic behavior. *Journal of Nervous and Mental Disease,* 1964, **138,** 558–574.

Schachter, S., and Singer, J. E. Cognitive, social, and physiological determinants of emotional state. *Psychological Review,* 1962, **69,** 379–399.

Seitz, F. C. Behavior modification of depression. Proceedings, 79th Annual Convention, American Psychological Association, 1971, 425–426.

Seitz, F. C. A behavior modification approach to depression: A case study. *Psychology,* 1971, **8,** 58–63.

Seligman, M. E. P. Depression and learned helplessness. University of Pennsylvania, 1971. (mimeo)

Seligman, M. E. P., and Groves, D. P. Non-transient learned helplessness. *Psychonomic Science,* 1970, **19,** 191.

Seligman, M. E. P., and Maier, S. F. Failure to escape traumatic shock. *Journal of Experimental Psychology,* 1967, **74,** 1–9.

Seligman, M. E. P., Maier, S. F., and Greer, J. H. Alleviation of learned helplessness in the dog. *Journal of Abnormal Psychology,* 1968, **73,** 256–262.

Shaffer, M., and Lewinsohn, P. M. Interpersonal behaviors in the home of depressed versus non-depressed psychiatric and normal controls: A test of several hypotheses. Paper presented at meeting of the Western Psychological Association, 1971. University of Oregon, 1971. (mimeo)

Silverman, D. *The Epidemiology of Depression.* Baltimore: Johns Hopkins Press, 1968.

Stewart, R. C. The differential effects of positive and negative social reinforcement upon depressed and nondepressed subjects. Unpublished master's thesis. University of Oregon, 1968.

Winer, B. J. *Statistical Principles in Experimental Design.* New York: McGraw-Hill, 1962.

Wolf, K. *The Biological, Sociological and Physiological Aspects of Aging.* Springfield, Ill.: Thomas, 1959.

Wolpe, J. Neurotic depression: Experimental analog, clinical syndromes, and treatment. *American Journal of Psychotherapy,* 1971, **25,** 362–368.

Wolpe, J., and Lazarus, A. A. *Behavior Therapy Techniques.* New York: Pergamon Press, 1966.

Zuckerman, M., Persky, H., and Curtis, G. C. Relationship among anxiety, depression and autonomic variables. *Journal of Nervous and Mental Disease.* 1968, **146,** 481–*487.*

Zung, W. W. K. A self-rating depression scale. *Archives of General Psychiatry,* 1965, **12,** 63–70.

CHAPTER 4

The Treatment of Sexual Deviation: Toward a Comprehensive Behavioral Approach *

DAVID H. BARLOW

Sexual deviation encompasses a number of behavioral excesses and deficits. The most notable behavior is sexual arousal to non-normal or deviant persons, objects, or activities. In fact, deviant sexual arousal has come to define sexual deviation in textbooks of psychopathology and in the *Diagnostic and Statistical Manual* of the American Psychiatric Association (DSM II). In the clinic this emphasis on deviant arousal is misleading. It is very seldom indeed that a client who complains of deviant sexual arousal does not present associated behavioral deficits or excesses. Yet, as we shall see, treatment is often aimed exclusively at eliminating deviant arousal and success is defined as its absence.

There are at least three associated problems that may accompany deviant arousal. Excluded are temporary emotional reactions such as "anxiety" or "depression" which result from life circumstances of the client and not from deviant arousal per se, and personality disorders which are patterns of interpersonal behavior not directly connected with deviant sexual arousal.

1. Deficiencies in Heterosexual Arousal Deviant arousal may or may not be associated with absence or minimal levels of heterosexual arousal. Occasionally a client may have frequent heterosexual arousal and behavior with a wife or girlfriend and still engage in deviant sexual behavior. The "true" bisexual and some fetishistic clients are included here. Often, however, deviant sexual arousal is accompanied by diminished heterosexual arousal.

2. Deficiencies in Heterosocial Skills. Deviant arousal may or may not be

*Preparation of this manuscript and some of the research herein was supported by National Institute of Mental Health Grant MH-20258.

accompanied by deficiencies in heterosocial skills necessary for meeting, dating, and relating to persons of the opposite sex. Clients who complain of deviant arousal also have adequate heterosexual arousal but may be unable to "act on" this arousal due to inadequate heterosocial skills. On the other hand, a client with deviant arousal may have adequate heterosocial skills but experience no sexual arousal to the opposite sex.

3. Gender Role Deviation. Finally, a client with deviant arousal may have some degree of gender role deviation in which opposite sex role behaviors are present and some preference for the opposite sex role is verbalized. This is most common in some homosexuals and transvestites. When opposite sex role behavior is completely adopted and the client consistently thinks, feels, and behaves in the opposite sex role, this "mistaken gender identity" is called transsexualism (Green and Money, 1969). These clients usually request sex reassignment surgery.

In some cases of exclusive homosexuality there is recent evidence that deviant sexual arousal is associated with biochemical excesses or deficits (Kolodny, Masters, Hendryx, and Toro, 1971; Loraine, Ismail, Adamopoulos, and Dove, 1970). However, these investigations are in a preliminary stage and do not as yet have treatment implications.

The three problems often associated with deviant sexual arousal are relatively independent of each other. Deviant arousal may be associated with one, some, all, or none of the problems as outlined in the accompanying diagram.

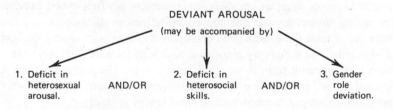

DEVIANT AROUSAL
(may be accompanied by)

1. Deficit in   AND/OR   2. Deficit in   AND/OR   3. Gender
heterosexual   heterosocial   role
arousal.   skills.   deviation.

Various treatment approaches to sexual deviation have not been remarkably successful. Traditional psychotherapy has had little success in eliminating deviant arousal in homosexuals (Curran and Parr, 1957; Woodward, 1958; Bieber et al., 1963). Results from a widely used treatment, aversion therapy, are generally more encouraging (Barlow, 1973) but vary a great deal from series to series and deviation to deviation. One difficulty seems to be the narrow focus of treatment. Although the exact procedures of psychotherapy are seldom described, when they are specified, the focus is clearly on decreasing heterosexual anxiety and teaching appropriate heterosocial skills (e.g., Ovesey, Gaylin, and Hendin, 1963). Deviant arousal is not dealt with in any direct way and problems of heterosexual arousal and sex role reversal are also ignored. Aversion therapy, on the other hand, focuses directly on deviant arousal but leaves to chance associated deficits in heterosexual arousal or social skills and sex role behavior. As Bond and Evans (1967) put it, "It is probable that if they can abstain from their deviant behavior for a sufficient period of time, normal outlets for the control of sexual arousal will develop" (p. 1162).

The notion of applying one treatment, such as aversion therapy or psychotherapy, to every type of disorder is a traditional one in clinical psychology and psychiatry which is now giving way to development of specific treatments for specific problems (Bergin and Strupp, 1972). In sexual deviation, no client is the same. Each has some combination of the excesses or deficits noted above. A recurring theme in this chapter is the need for individualized assessment of each client and the construction of specific treatment packages based on an analysis of behavioral excesses and deficits found in sexual deviation.

This chapter briefly reviews the latest evidence for effectiveness of various treatments on each specific behavioral component of sexual deviation.

DEVIANT SEXUAL AROUSAL

The one treatment with an explicit goal of reducing deviant arousal is aversion therapy. As early as 1935 (Max, 1935) aversion therapy was applied to sexual deviation, but this approach did not receive wide attention until the decade of the 1960s concurrent with the emergence of behavior modification. Aversion therapy is a relatively broad term. Several types of aversive stimulus have been used. The most frequently used are emetic drugs, electrical shock, and covert sensitization (Cautela, 1967), in which the stimulus is a description of an aversive scene. These aversive stimuli have been applied in several learning paradigms such as classical fear conditioning, punishment, escape, and avoidance. See Barlow (1972) for a review and description of aversive techniques. When applied to sexual deviation, the purpose is to suppress deviant sexual arousal and behavior, and there is some evidence that this occurs.

In two single-case A-B-A reversal designs covert sensitization, specifically pairing descriptions of sexually arousing scenes with descriptions of scenes aversive to the client, was tested to determine its responsibility for decreases in deviant sexual arousal (Barlow, Leitenberg, and Agras, 1969). In the first phase, one pedophilic client and one homosexual client were administered covert sensitization consisting of vivid descriptions of their deviant behavior paired with noxious scenes of nausea and vomiting. In a second phase the noxious scenes were removed but the clients were told to expect continued improvement. In the last phase the noxious scenes were reintroduced. Reports of deviant urges and fantasies and deviant arousal, as measured by an attitudinal scale, decreased during covert sensitization, increased during the middle phase, and decreased once again when covert sensitization was reintroduced. In one case, GSR to vivid images of the deviant behavior also decreased, increased again, and then decreased. These results suggested that aversion therapy was responsible for the decrease in reports of deviant behavior.

To test further the notion that the pairing procedure in aversion therapy is critical in reducing deviant arousal, the preceding study was replicated with two important changes (Barlow, Agras, Leitenberg, Callahan, and Moore, 1972). First, an objective measure of sexual arousal, penile circumference change, was added (Barlow, Becker, Leitenberg, and Agras, 1970). Second, the instructions were changed. Four homosexuals were told that covert sensitization would temporarily make them worse but that a phase where the noxious scene was absent would result in improvement, that is, decreases in sexual arousal.

The experiment began with the placebo phase in which vivid descriptions of the client's homosexual behavior were presented while the subject was deeply relaxed. The instructions stated, "Sexual arousal is characterized by a certain

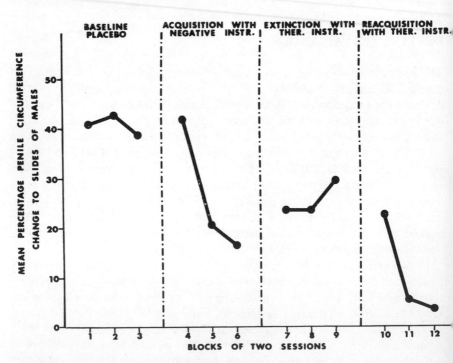

Figure 1.   Mean penile circumference change to male slides for the four subjects, expressed as a percentage of full erection. In each phase, data from the first, middle, and last pair of sessions are shown. (From D. H. Barlow, H. Leitenberg, W. S. Agras, E. J. Callahan, and R. C. Moore. The contribution of therapeutic instruction to covert sensitization. *Behaviour Research and Therapy* **10:**411–415, 1972. Copyright (1972) by Pergamon Press Ltd. Reproduced by permission.)

pleasurable tension which is difficult to control. This sexual arousal to males has been learned and we're going to get rid of the tension by substituting a relaxed response for the tension state and, in this way, eliminate sexual arousal to males.'' Although all clients reported that they were getting better, this procedure did not result in any decreases in deviant arousal.

During the next phase the noxious scene, in this case vivid descriptions of nausea and vomiting, was introduced and paired with descriptions of homosexual scenes in a covert sensitization paradigm. The instructions stated, "To obtain the best effects we are going to heighten the tension by pairing the sexually arousing scenes with images of vomiting. You will probably notice an increase in your sexual arousal to males and in your homosexual urges but don't be alarmed, this is part of the treatment." Despite these instructions, deviant arousal decreased sharply during this phase, which is labeled "Acquisition with negative instructions" in Figure 1. Interestingly, most clients believed they were getting worse, that is, that their homosexual arousal was increasing, in line with the instructions.

When the noxious scene was removed again but therapeutic instructions reintroduced, deviant arousal increased somewhat, on the average, but decreased again when covert sensitization was reintroduced, this time with therapeutic instructions. A statistical analysis indicated that differences between the two covert sensitization phases and extinction were significant in both instances.

This study clearly demonstrates that aversion therapy, rather than nonspecific placebo factors, was responsible for decreases in deviant sexual arousal. This study, of course, was not designed to determine whether aversion therapy was effective in producing broad-based clinical improvement in sexual deviation. The purpose was to ascertain the specific effects of aversion therapy on deviant sexual arousal and the mechanism of action in aversion therapy that produced these results.

The question of clinical effectiveness must be answered by application of this procedure to large numbers of sexual deviates whether in comparison with control groups or in a systematic replication series (Sidman, 1960; Barlow and Hersen, 1973). Several reports have attempted to answer these questions. The most ambitious clinical outcome study to date was recently reported by Feldman and MacCulloch (1971). In this controlled experiment, three groups of 10 homosexuals each were treated. The first group received electrical aversion in a complex paradigm called anticipatory avoidance learning, which had been described and applied by the authors in an earlier series of cases (Feldman and MacCulloch, 1965). In brief, the client can occasionally avoid shock by switching off the homosexual stimulus. The purpose of the technique is to prolong the effect of the procedure after treatment is terminated, in that clients will develop a habit of avoiding homosexual stimuli. This notion is based on well-established principles of learning from the laboratories of experimental psychology.

A second group also received electrical aversion but in a straight classical fear conditioning paradigm without any avoidance components. A third group received traditional psychotherapy. Interviews and a rating scale measure of homosexual responsiveness after treatment demonstrated the aversive procedure to be significantly more effective than psychotherapy but no difference emerged between the two aversive techniques, each of which produced significant decreases in homosexual responsiveness in 60 percent of the clients as opposed to a 20 percent decrease rate for the psychotherapy group. These results held up at a one-year follow-up.

Three other controlled studies have examined the clinical effectiveness of aversion therapy in decreasing deviant responsiveness, each reporting less impressive results. McConaghy (1969) compared a group of homosexuals receiving chemical aversion and a group receiving electrical aversion with a no-treatment control group. Again, no difference emerged between treatment groups but the combined treatment group evidenced a significantly greater "change in sexual orientation" than the control group, based on penile circumference scores and subjective reports. The percentage of success is not impressive, however, since only 6 of 18 clients changed their sexual orientation. In addition, these findings are difficult to interpret due to a complex system of presenting the results that makes it impossible to determine whether a "change" was produced by a drop in homosexual arousal, an increase in heterosexual arousal, or some combination. Furthermore, in some cases a very small difference in arousal patterns could produce a "change."

Birk, Huddleston, Miller, and Cohler (1971) also found decreased homosexual responsiveness in a group of eight homosexuals receiving group therapy, psychotherapy, and electrical aversion compared to a control group which did not receive the electrical aversion. Immediately after treatment, five clients in the aversion group and none of the clients in the control group were significantly improved based on reports of behavior. At a two-year follow-up, two clients were exclusively heterosexual but three clients had relapsed somewhat, due to "inability to establish a good object relationship with a woman."

These studies indicate that aversion therapy is a statistically effective treatment when compared to no treatment or psychotherapy, but the results are far from impressive clinically. With the exception of the 60 percent success rate in Feldman and MacCulloch's study, the percentage of success, even if it is narrowly defined as diminution of deviant arousal and/or behavior, is quite low.

An obvious and important question is what client characteristics or behaviors predict success in aversion therapy and, conversely, are there any client behaviors that predict failure? Based on the analysis at the beginning of the chapter, it is not surprising to find that lack of associated problems in heterosexual responsiveness or sex role behavior is the best predictor of success in treatment by aversion procedures. In Feldman and MacCulloch's study (1971), 80 percent of those clients with prior heterosexual experience improved, whereas only 20 percent of those with no prior heterosexual experience improved. Thus it seems that focusing on deviant interest through aversion therapy does not diminish deviant interest significantly (Feldman and MacCulloch's definition of improvement was a drop in deviant interest on an attitude scale) if deficits in other areas exist. In other words, access to alternative behaviors, in this case heterosexual behavior, is necessary before deviant behavior can be permanently suppressed.

Results from other series of cases also bear directly on this issue. It was previously noted that successful suppression of deviant homosexual arousal by aversion therapy ranged from 30 percent (McConaghy, 1969; Bancroft, 1969) to approximately 60 percent (Feldman and MacCulloch, 1971). However, results from the application of aversion therapy to other sexual deviations have been better.

Marks and Gelder (1967; Gelder and Marks, 1969) report that a series of "uncomplicated transvestites" did very well when treated by electrical aversion. All ten clients treated were improved and nine were "much improved." Of seven clients who were followed for six months, six maintained their gains. It is interesting to note that nine of the ten clients reported some past heterosexual experience. Five other transvestites, however, had some degree of sex role disturbance or "transsexual" feelings. Of four who were followed, only one was improved after six months and this client relapsed at one year. The one client who would be diagnosed as transsexual by more rigorous standards (Stoller, 1969; Green, 1969) did not improve at all. Despite this lack of improvement, all "transsexual" clients reported past heterosexual experience. In another series, Evans (1967) reported cessation of exhibitionistic behavior and urges in ten out of ten exhibitionists six months after beginning of treatment.

The better results with transvestites and exhibitionists may be due to procedural differences (e.g., Gelder and Marks, in a well-designed program, shocked actual cross-dressing). It is noteworthy, however, that presence or absence of additional problems correlated highly with outcome in the Gelder and Marks series. Those transvestites with some heterosexual experience and no gender identity problems did quite well. In clinical experience, clients with transvestite, fetishistic, or exhibitionistic behavior are, on the whole, less likely to have associated deficits than some other deviations; that is, many are married and have ample heterosexual behavior. If further research bears this out, it may account for the greater percentage of success with aversion alone in these cases. Nevertheless, deviant arousal seldom exists in the absence of other problems and the failure of aversion in those cases with no heterosexual responsiveness suggests that instigating heterosexual responsiveness is an important aspect of treatment.

HETEROSEXUAL RESPONSIVENESS

Unlike deviant arousal, several procedures have been devised to increase heterosexual responsiveness. However, due to the emphasis on aversion during the 1960s, most techniques are still in a preliminary stage of development (Barlow, 1973. This is surprising when one examines the prevailing theories on the etiology of homosexuality and, to some extent, deviant sexual behavior in general. Both psychoanalytic and behavioral theories emphasize the importance of avoidance of heterosexuality in the genesis and maintenance of deviant behavior (e.g., Rado, 1949; Wolpe, 1969). This notion finds some support in two surveys. Bieber et al. (1963) noted that 70 of the 106 clients in their survey reported fear of or aversion to female genitalia. Ramsey and Van Velzen (1968), in a survey of homosexuals, heterosexuals, and bisexuals, found that both homosexuals and heterosexuals had strong negative emotional feelings concerning sexual practices with the nonpreferred sex. Freund, Langevin, Cibiri, and Zajac (1973) obtained similar results in homosexuals and heterosexuals on attitudinal and penile response measures.

Interestingly, one of the procedures that recently has been found to increase heterosexual arousal is aversion! Although the increase is often small, several independent investigations (e.g., Gelder and Marks, 1969; Barlow, Leitenberg, and Agras, 1969) have noticed increases in heterosexual arousal or behavior during aversion therapy, although no attempt was made to accomplish this in treatment.

This effect is illustrated in one homosexual whose data are presented in Figure 2. Preliminary placebo phases produced no effect on either heterosexual or homosexual arousal as measured by penile circumference changes to slides of nude males and females. Introduction of aversion therapy produced expected decreases in homosexual arousal. Correlated with this drop, however, was a sharp increase in heterosexual arousal. This paradoxical finding is also present in a study by Bancroft (1970), who treated a group of 15 homosexuals by electrical aversion. This group was then compared to another group who received systematic desensitization. The results of treatment in the aversion group, as measured by penile circumference change to homosexual and heterosexual stimuli, demonstrated that on the average homosexual arousal dropped but heterosexual arousal simultaneously increased. Six months after treatment, Bancroft divided his clients into improved and unimproved based on reports of behavior. When Bancroft reexamined results during treatment, from the perspective of the six-month follow-up, he found that reduction in homosexual arousal occurred in both the improved and unimproved groups during treatment but that increases in heterosexual arousal during treatment were found only in the improved group. Once again this suggests that for lasting clinical changes the reduction of deviant arousal is not enough and alternative behavior must be instigated.

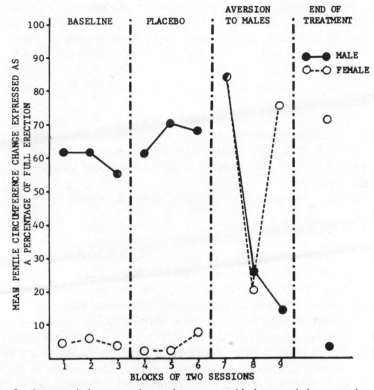

Figure 2.   Increases in heterosexual arousal concurrent with decreases in homosexual arousal during covert sensitization.

The perplexing question here, however, is why increases in heterosexual arousal and behavior occurred without any attempt to accomplish this.

A similar observation has been reported during application of aversive techniques to disruptive behavior in children and psychotic adults. In these cases, socially appropriate behaviors begin to appear as disruptive behavior decreases, and in the absence of any positive contingencies (e.g., Sajwaj and Risley, 1974; Wahler, Sperling, Thomas, Teeter, and Luper, 1970).

Although these examples of response-response relationships deserve further investigation, the overall results in Bancroft's aversion group were not impressive as only five out of twelve clients who finished treatment (three dropped out) were rated as improved. Thus the instigation of heterosexual arousal as a "side effect" of aversion does not occur in all clients and is weak in others, necessitating the development of stronger, more reliable procedures.

Several techniques have been employed which do not seem particularly effective. One procedure, aversion relief, which involves introducing a heterosexual stimulus after the aversive stimulus in aversion therapy, has been frequently utilized, probably because it is convenient to apply in conjunction with aversion therapy. The notion here is that the pleasant sensation of relief from shock will become associated with heterosexuality, replacing any maladaptive emotional response such as anxiety. There is no evidence, however, that this occurs (Barlow, 1973).

Another procedure, classical conditioning of heterosexual arousal using deviant stimuli as unconditioned stimuli, was recently experimentally analyzed (Herman. Barlow, and Agras, 1974). Although this procedure proved capable of increasing heterosexual arousal, procedural difficulties would seem to rule out widespread application.

Four techniques show promise and deserve further investigation.

Systematic Desensitization

When applied to sexual deviation, the goal of systematic desensitization is to reduce anxiety or avoidance of heterosexuality. Several case histories (e.g., Kraft, 1967; Huff, 1970; LoPiccolo, 1971) report that systematic desensitization in imagination was successful in increasing heterosexual behavior in the absence of other therapeutic techniques such as aversion therapy. It is interesting to note that in some instances (e.g., Kraft, 1967) the client reported decreased deviant interest concurrent with establishment of heterosexual behavior.

Other case reports describe the use of systematic desensitization in the real situation in which heterosexual behavior leading to and including intercourse is actually attempted in a stepwise fashion. This allows the client to learn the intricacies of sexual approach behavior from a cooperative partner and has been successful in treating homosexuality (DiScipio, 1968) and exhibitionism (Wickramasekera, 1968), although DiScipio's client later relapsed.

The only attempt to evaluate the efficacy of systematic desensitization in treating sexual deviation was reported by Bancroft (1970) in the study mentioned previously. A group of 15 homosexuals was treated by systematic desensitization in imagination to heterosexual themes and compared to the group which received electrical aversion. At a six-month follow-up, only five of eleven who finished treatment (four dropped out) were rated as improved or much improved, based on reports of behavior. These results did not differ significantly from the aversion group. Furthermore, it is difficult to assess the significance of the changes that did occur since a placebo or no-treatment control group was not included. Thus there is no experimental evidence that systematic desensitization is effective in increasing heterosexual responsiveness, but the numerous instances of clinical success and the consistency of the approach with data showing a high incidence of fear and avoidance of heterosexuality in sexual deviates would justify further experimental investigation.

Exposure to Explicit Heterosexual Themes

A second procedure, recently experimentally evaluated, is exposure to explicit heterosexual themes (Herman, Barlow, and Agras, 1971; Herman, 1971). The procedure is straightforward. One pedophilic and two homosexual clients with little or no heterosexual arousal were shown movies depicting nude, seductive females assuming various sexual postures, 10 minutes per day. The effect of this procedure was evaluated in single-case, A-B-A experimental designs. During the control phase the client continued to see erotic movies for 10 minutes a day, accompanied by therapeutic instructions, but the stimuli were deviant. The third phase consisted of a return to the female exposure condition. Measures of sexual arousal and attitudes were taken in separate measurement sessions.

The results from one case are presented in Figure 3. This client was a 24-year-old, male, exclusive homosexual who had recently attempted suicide. Homosexuality began at age 13. For the last year the frequency of homosexual encounters had been one to three per day. During this period he was arrested twice and mugged once. He had two heterosexual contacts in college but these were initiated by the females and he was not able to maintain an erection or ejaculate.

During a baseline phase, arousal to females averaged 30 percent of a full erection. The subjective report of arousal to females, as obtained in a daily card sort, averaged 40 percent of a score representing "much arousal."

During the first phase, objective and subjective heterosexual arousal rose. The client reported that masturbatory fantasies were increasingly heterosexual and he began to date. During the control phase heterosexual arousal dropped, but his attitude scale continued to rise, consistent with therapeutic instructions. Masturbatory fantasies, however, became exclusively homosexual once more and heterosexual dating stopped. When the female film was reintroduced, heterosexual arousal returned as did reports of female masturbatory fantasies and dating. These findings were replicated on the remaining two clients. Despite these increases in heterosexual responsiveness, this approach had little effect on deviant arousal, which remained high.

The mechanism of action in this procedure is unclear. One possibility is that avoidance of heterosexuality is extinguished. If this is the case, this procedure would be analogous to "flooding" (Marks, 1972) in that the client is confronted with representatives of heterosexual stimuli in such a way that neither the avoidance response nor the aversive consequences can occur. The client whose data are presented here remarked toward the end of treatment that seeing the girl in the film was like being with an old friend, in front of whom he was not embarrassed. Another possibility is that viewing explicit visual stimuli provides the client with novel or intense fantasies which are then paired with masturbation outside of treatment.

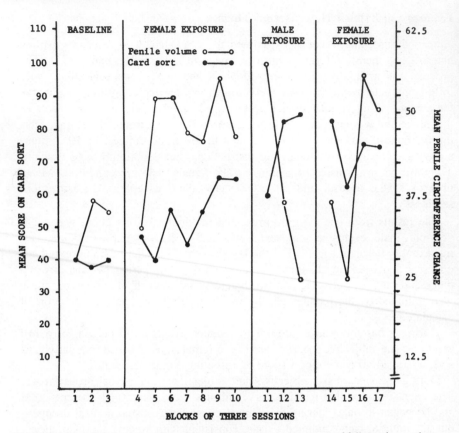

Figure 3.   Mean penile circumference change expressed as a percentage of full erection, and mean female card sort averaged over three experimental days. Lower score indicates less sexual arousal. (From S. H. Herman, D. H. Barlow, and W. S. Agras, Exposure to heterosexual stimuli: An effective variable in treating homosexuality? *Proceedings of the 79th Annual Convention of the American Psychological Association,* American Psychological Association, 1971, pp. 699–700. Copyright (1971) by the American Psychological Association. Reproduced by permission.)

Masturbatory Conditioning

The suggestion that masturbatory behavior plays a role in increasing heterosexual responsiveness is not new. Several case studies have reported pairing sexual arousal produced by masturbation with heterosexual stimuli in the treatment of various deviations such as homosexuality (Marquis, 1970), sadomasochism (Davison, 1968; Mees, 1966), voyeurism (Jackson, 1969), and heterosexual pedophilia (Annon, 1971).

There is no evidence for the efficacy of masturbatory conditioning beyond the case study level. However, it is interesting to note that pairing masturbatory arousal with various fantasies has been hypothesized to play an important role in the etiology of specific deviant sexual preferences. McGuire, Carlisle, and Young (1965) suggested that deviates have some critical first sexual experience with a person or object which need not be sexually arousing at the time, but later provides a fantasy for masturbation. Historical evidence for the process is presented in a series of 45 deviates by McGuire et al. (1965), and in a second series reported by Evans (1968). Thus altering masturbatory fantasy may be the most direct and efficient method of changing sexual preferences and deserves further investigation.

Fading

A final technique for increasing heterosexual responsiveness concentrates on introducing or "fading in" heterosexual stimuli during periods of sexual arousal in an effort to change stimulus control of sexual responsiveness. This technique has been investigated in a series of three controlled, single-case experiments with homosexuals (Barlow and Agras, 1973). In this procedure, one male and one female slide were superimposed on one another. Through the use of an adjustable transformer, an increase in the brightness of the female slide resulted in a simultaneous decrease in the brightness of the male slide. During treatment the female stimulus was faded in, contingent on the subject maintaining 75 percent of a full erection as measured by a strain gauge device through a series of 20 steps ranging from 100 percent male brightness to 100 percent female brightness. The experimental design consisted of fading, a control procedure where fading was reversed or stopped, followed by a return to fading.

Data from one case are presented in Figure 4. The client was a 29-year-old, male, exclusive homosexual with a 14-year history of homosexual behavior. Although he had never engaged in heterosexual behavior, he reported dating girls on important social occasions despite the fact that it made him uneasy and anxious. He had engaged in psychotherapy on three prior occasions, for a total of three years, without benefit. He referred himself for treatment after reading that aversion treatment might help homosexuality. Upon referral he was mildly depressed, moderately anxious, and was regularly taking minor tranquilizers.

During a baseline phase, sexual arousal to females, as measured by penile circumference, was near zero. Homosexual arousal was extremely high, averaging near 80 percent of a full erection. Heterosexual arousal, in the separate measurement sessions, rose when fading was introduced. When the client was emitting the criterion arousal to the 50 percent male, 50 percent female image, fading was stopped and the two slides were shown side by side on the screen. During the control phase, heterosexual arousal in separate test sessions dropped. Fading was begun once again and continued until the client was emitting the

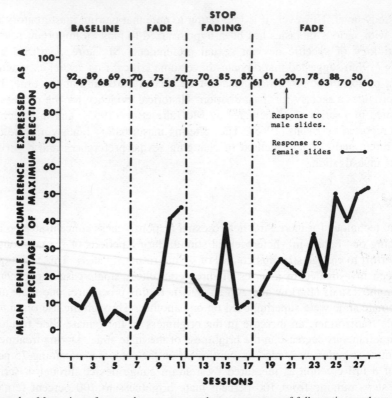

Figure 4. Mean circumference change, expressed as a percentage of full erection, and presented in blocks of two sessions (circumference change to males averaged over each phase), and total heterosexual urges and fantasies collected from four days surrounding each session. Lower scores indicate less sexual arousal. Note: The last circumference change point in Phase 2 (Fade) represents data from only one session. (From D. H. Barlow, and W. S. Agras, Fading to increase heterosexual responsiveness in homosexuals. *Journal of Applied Behavior Analysis,* **6:**355-366, 1973. Copyright (1973) by the Society for the Experimental Analysis of Behavior, Inc. Reproduced by permission).

criterion arousal to the female slide alone. In separate test sessions, heterosexual arousal increased once more. Homosexual arousal remained high, averaging approximately 65 percent of a full erection. The newly instigated heterosexual arousal generalized to the environment and the client began to engage in heterosexual intercourse for the first time. These findings were replicated on two additional clients.

Clinical reports from some cases mentioned earlier (e.g., Kraft, 1967) noted decreases in homosexual responsiveness after instigation of heterosexual arousal. Increases in heterosexual responsiveness in the exposure series and fading series described above, however, had no effect on homosexual arousal. In these cases homosexual arousal remained strong, although it later dropped in the client who received the fading procedure, without any therapeutic attempt to accomplish this. Once again it is not clear why deviant responsiveness drops in some cases after increases in heterosexual arousal but not in others. The relation between deviant and heterosexual arousal requires more investigation.

Another clinical finding from our laboratories and from others (Herman, Barlow and Agras, 1971, 1974; Barlow and Argas, 1973; Annon, 1971) is that an increase in heterosexual arousal does not always lead to heterosexual behavior. Many clients report that they have never experienced heterosocial relationships and do not know how to meet, date, or make sexual advances. Without these social skills, acquisition of heterosexual arousal is functionally of limited utility.

HETEROSOCIAL TRAINING

Treating sexual deviation by teaching new heterosocial skills is not a new idea. From descriptions of case reports, this approach often constitutes a major part of the psychoanalytic-oriented psychotherapeutic treatment of sexual deviation, with individuals or groups. Although procedures are seldom specified, several case reports illustrate this process.

Ovesey, Gaylin, and Hendin (1963), in approaching homosexuality from the analytic viewpoint of heterosexual phobia, state: "psychotherapy of homosexuality is essentially that of any phobia. Sooner or later the homosexual patient must make the necessary attempts and he must make them again and again." Insight in the approach is "a means to an end." They then describe successful treatment of three homosexuals, each of whom seemed to gradually learn more effective heterosexual approach behavior. Ovesey et al. also state that "the patient must become more masculine by learning appropriate patterns of assertion and increasing his self-sufficiency. In some cases merely an increase in nonsexual assertion may prove sufficient to initiate and maintain heterosexual behavior" (p. 22).

It is interesting to note that this is precisely the approach advocated by Wolpe (1969), working within a behavioral framework. Several cases of sexual deviation have been successfully treated by assertive training (Stevenson and Wolpe, 1960; Edwards, 1972) where clients were taught nonsexual assertion which presumably enabled them to be more successful in heterosocial situations, which, in turn, led to heterosexual relations. In many of these cases it seems that deviant responsiveness dropped out once heterosexual behavior was established.

In a group psychotherapy approach, Birk, Miller, and Cohler (1970) report that a female cotherapist was most useful during therapy in that homosexuals had opportunities to learn to relate to the female in a heterosocial way. Their newly learned feelings and behavior then generalized to other heterosocial situations based on reports of the clients.

A similar procedure within a behavioral framework is reported by Cautela and Wisocki (1969), who actually rehearsed such heterosocial behaviors as asking for a date with a young female therapist before sending homosexual clients out to attempt these steps.

A strong advocate of direct heterosocial and sexual retraining in the treatment of sexual deviation is Ellis (1964). In one early series (Ellis, 1956), he reported 75 percent of 40 homosexuals increased heterosocial and heterosexual behavior. Descriptions of changes in homosexual behavior are not reported, since decreasing this behavior was not a goal in therapy.

Controlled research on the effectiveness of various techniques for teaching heterosocial behavior is entirely lacking despite the importance of these skills for effective heterosexual functioning. Furthermore, the relation of these social skills to other factors, such as heterosexual and deviant arousal, is not clear. Some case studies (e.g., Stevenson and Wolpe, 1960) report elimination of deviant arousal after instigation of "assertive" behavior. On the other hand, many clients are found in the clinics who have seemingly adequate social skills but report no heterosexual arousal and strong deviant arousal.

GENDER ROLE DEVIATION

A problem often overlooked in the treatment of sexual deviation is the presence of opposite sex role behavior. Although the development of gender identity has always been a topic of some interest (e.g., Brown, 1958), its relationship to deviant arousal patterns has not been examined. The transsexual client, whose mistaken gender identity is so complete that he requests sex reassignment surgery, presents the most striking example of opposite sex role behavior. As noted, the transsexual consistently thinks, feels, and behaves in the opposite sex role. To date, surgery has been the only effective treatment since all attempts at changing the transsexual's gender identity through psychotherapy or behavior modification have failed (Pauly, 1965; Gelder and Marks, 1969).

A major problem in the literature on transsexuals, however, is diagnosis (Stoller, 1969). This problem arises because several other diagnostic classifications also include opposite sex role behavior and occasionally requests for sex reassignment surgery. Most often this occurs in homosexuals and transvestites. An extremely effeminate male homosexual or transvestite is very difficult to distinguish from a transsexual. Stoller (1969) reports that true transsexuals emit certain behaviors early in childhood, such as spontaneous cross dressing, which differentiate them from other classifications.

More recently, Freund, Nagler, Langevin, and Steiner (1974) devised a questionnaire for gender role which was administered to a group of male transsexuals, homosexuals, and normals and found that for homosexuals gender role is on a continuum. That is, some homosexuals had male gender identities and overlapped with the normals, some had female gender identities and overlapped with the transsexuals, and many fell somewhere between. This correlates with clinical observation of homosexuals, who may emit varying degrees of effeminate motor behavior.

It was also noted previously that presence of gender role problems correlated negatively with treatment of deviant arousal. Gelder and Marks (1969) observed that unlike "simple" transvestites who did well when treated by aversion, transvestites with opposite sex role interests did poorly. The one client who fit Stoller's (1971) definition of a true transsexual did not improve at all. Bieber et al. (1963) also noted that homosexuals with gender role problems in childhood responded more poorly to psychoanalytic intervention than those without such problems. This suggests that modification of gender role problems is necessary in the treatment of these cases.

Recently, some measures and procedures have been devised in a preliminary attempt to modify opposite sex role behaviors and interests (Barlow, Reynolds, and Agras, 1973). Application of this procedure to one transsexual client will be described in some detail.

The client was a 17-year-old male and the last of five children. He was a keen disappointment to his mother since she desired a girl. Nevertheless, he became her favorite child. His father worked long hours and had little contact with the boy. For as long as the patient could remember, he had thought of himself as a girl. Spontaneous cross-dressing, as reported by the client and confirmed by his parents, began before the age of five years and continued into junior high school. During this period his mother reported that he developed an interest in cooking, knitting, crocheting, and embroidering, skills which he acquired by reading an encyclopedia. His older brother often scorned him for his distaste of "masculine" activities such as hunting. The client reported associating mostly with girls during this period, although he remembered being strongly attracted to a "boyfriend" in the first grade. In his sexual fantasies, which developed at about 12 years of age, he pictured himself as a female having intercourse with a male.

Upon referral he was moderately depressed, withdrawn, and attending secretarial school where he was the only boy in the class. He reported a strong desire to change his sex. Since surgery was not possible at his age, he agreed to enter a treatment program designed to change his gender identity on the premise that it might at least make him more comfortable and that surgery was always possible at a later date.

Measures of patterns of sexual arousal and interest as well as transsexual interest were recorded. Attempts to suppress deviant arousal and transsexual interest through aversion therapy failed, as did early attempts to increase heterosexual arousal. At this point an attempt was made to modify the client's extremely effeminate motor behavior, which was causing much scorn and ridicule. To this end, a behavioral checklist of gender-specific motor behaviors was developed. Males and females were observed over a period of time in the natural environment, and characteristic ways of sitting, walking, and standing were chosen on the basis of uniqueness to sex. Four male characteristics and four female characteristics of sitting, walking, and standing were chosen to form the scale. For example, one of the behavioral components characteristic of sitting in males is crossing the legs with one ankle resting on the opposite knee. One of the female behaviors is legs crossed, closely together, with one knee on top of the other.

Direct modification of sitting, standing, and walking was then attempted by modeling and videotape feedback. The effect of modeling and videotape feedback was experimentally analyzed in a multiple baseline design in which the modification of only one category of behavior was attempted while measures of all three categories were collected. After completion of work on the first category, modification of the second category was attempted, and so on.

In the experimental treatment phase, daily measures of masculine and feminine components of sitting, standing, and walking were taken as the patient came into the waiting room before his session, by a rater who was not aware of changes in the treatment program. One 30-minute session was held daily. After five days of baseline procedures in which no treatment was given, modification of sitting behavior was begun. In each session the constellation of appropriate behavior was broken down and taught piece by piece. Each behavior was modeled by a male therapist and then attempted by the subject. Praise for success and verbal feedback of errors was administered. The last trial of the day was videotaped and shown at the beginning of the following session. When the subject was sitting appropriately in the session and reported feeling comfortable, treatment was begun on walking.

The data are presented in Figure 5. During the no-treatment baseline period, the patient showed a feminine manner of sitting, with no masculine characteristics in the surreptitious setting. Walking was more variable, with male and female walking behaviors approximately equal. Standing was mostly feminine. In the first phase of treatment, in which sitting behavior was worked on, male sitting behaviors increased and female behaviors decreased in the separate surreptitious measurement situation. There was little simultaneous change in male and female walking behaviors other than a slight drop in female components. A similar slight drop in female standing behavior was noticeable.

When treatment of walking behavior began, male walking behavior increased and female walking behavior dropped considerably. Female behavior continued to drop in sitting and standing. When standing behavior was treated, although changes occurred *within* the sessions, these did not generalize to the surreptitious situation as other behaviors did. In fact, female standing behavior lessened gradually across all phases with little change in male standing behavior.

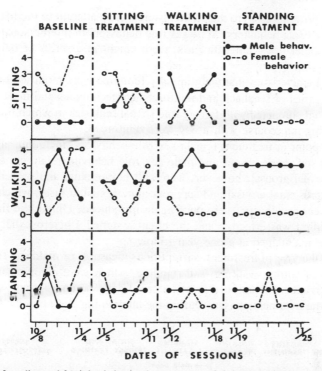

Figure 5. Masculine and feminine behavioral components of sitting, walking, and standing during therapeutic attempts to increase masculine behavior in each of the three categories. (From D. H. Barlow, E. J. Reynolds, and W. S. Agras, Gender identity change in a transsexual. *Archives of General Psychiatry,* **28**:569–576, 1973. Copyright (1973) by the American Medical Association. Reproduced by permission.)

These data indicate that the patient learned to behave in a more masculine manner while sitting, standing, and walking. Furthermore, there is evidence that the treatment, modeling and videotape feedback, was responsible for these changes since male and female behaviors comprising sitting and walking did not change appreciably until treated. Once treated, however, improvement in the surreptitious setting continued. It seems, in this case, that changes in sitting and walking also generalized to standing, with the biggest change in standing occurring during the walking treatment. This is not very surprising, since walking and standing are closely related and share many of the same behavioral components.

After completion of this phase the client reported enjoying his masculine behavior since people did not stare at him quite so much, but these changes in motor behavior had no effect on patterns of sexual arousal, which remained homosexual.

Several procedures were then administered in an attempt to modify additional feminine sex role behaviors. Male sex role behaviors in interpersonal situations, both with other boys and with girls, were taught in a series of behavioral rehearsal sessions.

Vocal characteristics that were initially feminine were modified to masculine through a series of feedback and reinforcement techniques and male role sexual fantasies that competed with female role sexual fantasies in which the client was a girl having intercourse with a boy were reinforced.

At this point in treatment female sex role behaviors, including all desire for change of sex, were absent and male sex role behavior relatively strong. Patterns of sexual arousal, however, were still homosexual and procedures to increase heterosexual arousal and suppress homosexual arousal, which had failed nearly a year previously, were once again introduced. Unlike the first attempt, this procedure was effective and the client assumed a heterosexual orientation which was maintained at a one-year follow-up.

During the year of treatment, surreptitious measures of male and female characteristics of sitting, walking, and standing, which were modified in an earlier phase of treatment, continued to be recorded daily by an assistant who was not aware of the treatment phases. During the intervening eight months between the

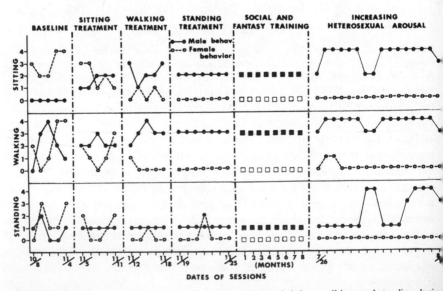

Figure 6. Masculine and feminine behavioral components of sitting, walking, and standing during therapeutic attempts to increase masculine behavior in each of three categories, and later during investigation of heterosexual arousal. (From D. H. Barlow, E. J. Reynolds, and W. S. Agras, Gender identity change in a transsexual. *Archives of General Psychiatry*, **28**:569–576, 1973. Copyright (1973) by the American Medical Association. Reproduced by permission.)

end of the motor retraining phase and the initiation of the procedure to increase heterosexual arousal, no changes were noted in these behaviors. This lack of change is represented in Figure 6 under the section labeled social and fantasy training.

During instigation of heterosexual arousal, however, masculine components of sitting, standing, and walking showed a sharp increase, despite no therapeutic attempts to accomplish this goal at this time. These unexpected changes are represented in the last column of Figure 6.

This case does not demonstrate that these procedures constitute a treatment for transsexuals, since this would require systematic replication on a large series of transsexuals. But these data do suggest the importance of modifying sex role behaviors that are gender inappropriate in the treatment of sexual deviation, since increases in heterosexual arousal and suppression of deviant arousal occurred only after changes in sex role behavior.

Furthermore, an interesting relationship between gender specific motor behavior and sexual arousal emerged when increases in heterosexual arousal unexpectedly produced increases in masculine motor behaviors, although increases in masculine motor behaviors did not increase heterosexual arousal. The relationship between sex role behaviors and patterns of sexual arousal deserve further investigation.

CONCLUDING COMMENTS

The central theme of this chapter is that sexual deviation is not a unitary concept, amenable to a single treatment approach. Increasingly sophisticated measurement procedures are pinpointing numerous behavioral excesses and deficits associated with deviant sexual arousal. In addition to the three broad categories outlined—patterns of sexual arousal, heterosexual skills, and gender role deviations—the area of biochemical variables and their relation to deviant sexual behavior is just beginning to be investigated.

What is needed now is a more precise delineation of the various behavioral components constituting sexual deviation and further development of reliable and valid assessment devices, particularly in the area of heterosocial skills and gender-specific behavior. These precise behavioral assessment procedures will, in turn, stimulate further research into treatments that are effective on one component or another of sexual deviation.

A valid and precise behavioral assessment of a sexually deviant client would also indicate what treatment or combination of treatments is required. Clinical evidence cited in this chapter (e.g., Gelder and Marks, 1969) indicates that in clients with deviant arousal and no other apparent problems, aversion therapy may be a sufficient treatment. On the other hand, the assessment of a transsexual such as the one described in Barlow, Reynolds, and Agras (1973) would presumably reveal numerous excesses and deficits, both behavioral and in some cases biochemical, which would require intervention. The development of a comprehensive assessment procedure, then, would do much to eliminate the tendency to attack all sexual deviates with a single, narrow treatment approach such as psychotherapy or aversion therapy.

It is apparent, however, that although there is preliminary evidence that some of the specific treatment approaches described here are effective, most are in a preliminary stage of development. Thus, following the development of comprehensive assessment procedures, a second important goal is the development of more efficient and effective treatment procedures for the various components of sexual deviation. Even in aversion therapy, which was used extensively in the 1960s, the mechanism of action is not clear. Particularly puzzling is the question of why aversion therapy continues to suppress deviant arousal in some clients long after treatment is terminated (Bandura, 1969; Rachman and Teasdale, 1969; Barlow, Agras, and Leitenberg, 1970). If variables responsible for this effect can be discovered, then they can be systematically applied to all clients, making aversion therapy a more effective procedure.

Discovery of techniques to increase heterosexual responsiveness is in an even more preliminary stage of development. Several promising approaches have been described in this chapter. Future research should distill those variables in each procedure that are responsible for success so that these variables can be combined in a single, powerful procedure for increasing heterosexual responsiveness.

Although important treatments are being developed for assertive components of heterosocial behavior (e.g., Serber, 1972), a systematic look at procedures effective in modifying social and sex role behaviors relevant to sexual deviation must await development of assessment procedures such as the gender-specific motor behavior scale mentioned in Barlow, Reynolds, and Agras (1973) which is currently under further development.

When more effective treatments are developed, an important and intriguing question will be the relationship among the various behavioral and biochemical components of sexual deviation. Preliminary clinical evidence suggests that in some cases deviant arousal drops out after either increases in heterosexual arousal (Barlow and Agras, 1971) or increases in heterosocial skills (Stevenson and Wolpe, 1960). Another interesting relationship is the increase in masculine motor behavior after the instigation of heterosexual arousal in the transsexual case (Barlow, Reynolds, and Agras, 1973). It is possible that, at least in some clients, intervening in a key area such as heterosexual arousal will be sufficient, thus saving the time and expense of additional treatment. The relation between behavioral change and biochemical change has yet to be investigated, although preliminary evidence from our laboratory suggests that changes in sexual behavior of sexual deviates may lead to changes in hormonal levels. As effective assessment procedures and treatments are developed, nonsexual client characteristics which may predict patterns of response to treatment must be observed, pinpointed, and considered when choosing appropriate treatment procedures.

Finally, when valid assessment procedures and efficient treatments are developed for each component of sexual deviation, this treatment package must be tested on a large series of clients in either a systematic replication series (Sidman, 1960; Barlow and Hersen, 1973) or a large controlled study.

It is clear that these problems will not be solved overnight, or even in several years. Diligent, rigorous, step-by-step research is required to arrive at meaningful solutions. Although this laborious process is not always reinforcing in the face of demands by society for instant clinical benefit, it is the only way.

REFERENCES

Annon, J. S. The extension of learning principles to the analysis and treatment of sexual problems. Unpublished doctoral dissertation, University of Hawaii, 1971.

Bancroft, J. Aversion therapy of homosexuality: A pilot study of 10 cases. *British Journal of Psychiatry,* 1969, **115,** 1417–1431.

Bancroft, J. A comparative study of aversion and desensitization in the treatment of homosexuality. In L.E. Burns and J. L. Worsley (Eds.), *Behavior Therapy in the 1970's.* Wright, Bristol, 1970.

Bandura, A. *Principles of Behavior Modification.* New York: Holt, Rinehart and Winston, 1969.

Barlow, D.H. Increasing heterosocial responsiveness in the treatment of sexual deviation: A review of the clinical and experimental evidence. *Behavior Therapy,* 1973, **4,** 655–671.

Barlow, D.H. Aversive procedures. In W.S. Agras (Ed.), *Behavior Modification: Principles and Clinical Applications.* Boston: Little, Brown, 1972.

Barlow, D.H., and Agras, W. S. Fading to increase heterosexual responsiveness in homosexuals. *Journal of Applied Behavior Analysis,* 1973, **6,** 355–367.

Barlow, D. H., Agras, W. S., and Leitenberg, H. A preliminary report on the contribution of therapeutic instructions to covert sensitization. Paper read at Association for the Advancement of Behavior Therapy, Miami Beach, Florida, September 1970.

Barlow, D. H., Agras, W. S., Leitenberg, H., Callahan, E. J., and Moore, R. C. The contribution of therapeutic instruction to covert sensitization. *Behaviour Research and Therapy,* 1972, **10,** 411–415.

Barlow, D. H., Becker, R., Leitenberg, H., and Agras, W. S. A mechanical strain gauge for recording penile circumference change. *Journal of Applied Behavior Analysis,* 1970, **3,** 73–76.

Barlow, D. H., and Hersen, M. Single case experimental designs: Uses in applied clinical research. *Archives of General Psychiatry,* 1973, **29,** 319–325.

Barlow, D. H., Leitenberg, H., and Agras, W. S. The experimental control of sexual deviation through manipulation of the noxious scene in covert sensitization. *Journal of Abnormal Psychology,* 1969, **74,** 596–601.

Barlow, D. H., Reynolds, E. J., and Agras, W. S. Gender identity change in a transsexual. *Archives of General Psychiatry,* 1973, **29,** 569–579.

Bergin, A., and Strupp, H. H. *Changing Frontiers in the Science of Psychotherapy.* Chicago: Aldine-Atherton, 1972.

Bieber, B., Bieber, I., Dain, H. J., Dince, P. R., Drellich, M. G., Grand, H. G., Frundlach, R. H., Kremer, M. W., Wilber, C. B., and Bieber, T. D. *Homosexuality.* New York: Basic Books, 1963.

Birk, L., Huddleston, W., Miller, E., and Cohler, B. Avoidance conditioning for homosexuality. *Archives of General Psychiatry,* 1971, **25,** 314–323.

Birk, L., Miller, E., and Cohler, B. Group psychotherapy for homosexual men by male-female cotherapists. *Acta Psychiatrica Scandinavica, Supplementum,* **218,** 1970, 5–36.

Bond, I. K., and Evans, D. R. Avoidance therapy: Its use in two cases of underwear fetishism. *Canadian Medical Association Journal,* 1967, **96,** 1160–1162.

Brown, D. G. Sex-role development in a changing culture. *Psychological Bulletin,* 1958, **55,** 232–242.

Cautela, J. R. Covert sensitization. *Psychological Record,* 1967, **20,** 459–468.

Cautela, J. R., and Wisocki, P. A. The use of male and female therapists in the treatment of homosexual behavior. In R. Rubin and C. Franks (Eds.), *Advances in Behavior Therapy, 1968.* New York: Academic Press, 1969.

Curran, D., and Parr, D. Homosexuality: An analysis of 100 male cases seen in private practice. *British Medical Journal,* 1957, **1,** 797–801.

Davison, G. Elimination of a sadistic fantasy by a client-controlled counterconditioning technique: A case study. *Journal of Abnormal Psychology,* 1968, **73,** 84–90.

Diagnostic and Statistical Manual of Mental Disorders, 2nd ed. Washington, D.C.: American Psychiatric Association, 1968.

DiScipio, W. Modified progressive desensitization and homosexuality. *British Journal of Medical Psychology,* 1968, **41,** 267–272.

Edwards, N. B. Case conference: Assertive training in a case of homosexual pedophilia. *Journal of Behavior Therapy and Experimental Psychiatry,* 1972, **3,** 55–63.

Ellis, A. The effectiveness of psychotherapy with individuals who have severe homosexual problems. *Journal of Consulting Psychology,* 1956, **20,** 191–195.

Ellis, A. A homosexual treated with rational psychotherapy. In H. J. Eysenck (Ed.), *Experiments in Behaviour Therapy.* New York: Macmillan, 1964, pp. 300–308.

Evans, D. R. An exploratory study into the treatment of exhibitionism by means of emotive imagery and aversive conditioning. *Canadian Psychologist,* 1967, **8,** 162.

Evans, D. R. Masturbatory fantasy and sexual deviation. *Behaviour Research and Therapy,* 1968, **6,** 17–19.

Feldman, M. P., and MacCulloch, M. J. The application of anticipatory avoidance learning to the treatment of homosexuality. I. Theory, technique, and preliminary results. *Behaviour Research and Therapy,* 1965, **2,** 165.

Feldman, M. P., and MacCulloch, M. J. *Homosexual Behavior: Therapy and Assessment.* Oxford: Pergamon Press, 1971.

Feldman, M. P., and MacCulloch, M. J. Personal communication, 1971.

Freund, K., Langevin, R., Cibiri, S., and Zajac, Y. Heterosexual aversion in homosexual males. *British Journal of Psychiatry,* 1973, **122,** 163–169.

Freund, K., Nagler, E., Langevin, R., and Steiner, B. Measuring feminine gender identity in homosexual males. *Archives of Sexual Behavior,* 1974.

Gelder, M. G., and Marks, I. M. Aversion treatment in transvestism and transsexualism. In R. Green and J. Money (Eds.), *Transsexualism and Sex Reassignment.* Baltimore: Johns Hopkins Press, 1969.

Green, R. Attitudes toward transsexualism and sex-reassignment surgery. In R. Green and J. Money (Eds.), *Transsexualism and Sex Reassignment.* Baltimore: Johns Hopkins Press, 1969.

Green, R., and Money, J. (Eds.) *Transsexualism and Sex Reassignment.* Baltimore: Johns Hopkins Press, 1969.

Herman, S. H. An experimental analysis of two methods of increasing heterosexual arousal in homosexuals. Unpublished doctoral dissertation, University of Mississippi, 1971.

Herman, S. H., Barlow, D. H., and Agras, W. S. Exposure to heterosexual stimuli: An effective variable in treating homosexuality? *Proceedings of the 79th Annual Convention of the American Psychological Association,* American Psychological Association, 1971, pp. 699–700.

Herman, S. H., Barlow, D. H., and Agras, W. S. An experimental analysis of classical conditioning as a method of increasing heterosexual arousal in homosexuals. *Behavior Therapy,* 1974, **5,** in press.

Huff, F. The desensitization of a homosexual. *Behaviour Research and Therapy,* 1970, **8,** 99–102.

Jackson, B. A case of voyeurism treated by counter-conditioning. *Behaviour Research and Therapy,* 1969, **7,** 133–134.

Kolodny, R. C., Masters, W. H., Hendryx, J., and Toro, G. Plasma testosterone and semen analysis in male homosexuals. *New England Journal of Medicine,* 1971, **285,** 1170–1174.

Kraft, T. A case of homosexuality treated by systematic desensitization. *American Journal of Psychotherapy,* 1967, **21,** 815–821.

LoPiccolo, J. Case study: Systematic desensitization of homosexuality. *Behavior Therapy,* 1971, **2,** 394–399.

Loraine, J. A., Ismail, A. A. A., Adamopoulos, D. A., and Dove, G. A. Endocrine function in male and female homosexuals. *British Medical Journal,* 1970, **4,** 406–408.

Marks, I. M. Flooding (implosion) and allied treatments. In W. S. Agras (Ed.), *Behavior Modification: Principles and Clinical Applications*. Boston: Little, Brown, 1972.

Marks, I. M., and Gelder, M. G. Transvestism and fetishism: Clinical and psychological changes during faradic aversion. *British Journal of Psychiatry*, 1967, **113**, 711–729

Marquis, J. N. Orgasmic reconditioning: Changing sexual choice through controlling masturbatory fantasies. *The Journal of Behavior Therapy and Experimental Psychiatry*, 1970, **1**, 263–271.

Max, L. W. Breaking up a homosexual fixation by the conditioned reaction technique: A case study. *Psychological Bulletin*, 1935, **32**, 734. (Abstract)

McConaghy, N. Subjective and penile plethysmograph responses following aversion relief and apomorphine aversion therapy for homosexual impulses. *British Journal of Psychiatry*, 1969, **115**, 723–730.

McGuire, R., Carlisle, J., and Young, B. Sexual deviations as conditioned behavior: A hypothesis. *Behaviour Research and Therapy*, 1965, **2**, 185–190.

Mees, H. L. Sadistic fantasies modified by aversion conditioning and substitution: A case study. *Behaviour Research and Therapy*, 1966, **4**, 317–320.

Ovesey, L., Gaylin, W., and Hendin, H. Psychotherapy in male homosexuality. *Archives of General Psychiatry*, 1963, **9**, 19–31.

Pauly, I. Male psychosexual inversion: Transsexualism. *Archives of General Psychiatry*, 1965, **13**, 172–181.

Rachman, S., and Teasdale, J. *Aversion Therapy and Behavior Disorders: An Analysis*. Coral Gables, Fl.: University of Miami Press, 1969.

Rado, S. An adaptational view of sexual behavior. In P. Hoch and J. Zubin (Eds.), *Psychosexual Development in Health and Disease*. New York: Grune and Stratton, 1949.

Ramsey, R. W., and Van Velzen, V. Behaviour therapy for sexual perversions. *Behaviour Research and Therapy*, 1968, **6**, 17–19.

Sajwaj, T. E., and Risley, T. Some punishment procedures in behavior modification. *Journal of Applied Behavior Analysis*, 1974, in press.

Serber, M. Teaching the nonverbal components of assertive training. *Journal of Behavior Therapy and Experimental Psychiatry*, 1972, **3**, 179–183.

Sidman, M. *Tactics of Scientific Research*. New York: Basic Books, 1960.

Stevenson, I., and Wolpe, J. Recovery from sexual deviations through overcoming nonsexual neurotic responses. *American Journal of Psychiatry*, 1960, **116**, 739–742.

Stoller, R. J. Parental influences in male transsexualism. In R. Green and J. Money (Eds.), *Transsexualism and Sex Reassignment*. Baltimore: Johns Hopkins Press, 1969.

Stoller, R. J. Personal communication, 1971.

Wahler, R. G., Sperling, K. A., Thomas, M. R., Teeter, N. C., and Luper, H. L. Modification of childhood stuttering: Some response-response relationships. *Journal of Experimental Child Psychology*, 1970, **9**, 411–428.

Wickramasekera, I. The application of learning theory to the treatment of a case of sexual exhibitionism. *Psychotherapy: Theory, Research, and Practice*, 1968, **5**, 108–112.

Wolpe, J. *The Practice of Behavior Therapy.* Oxford: Pergamon Press, 1969.

Woodward, M. The diagnosis and treatment of homosexual offenders. *British Journal of Delinquency*, 1958, **9**, 44–59.

CHAPTER 5

Alcoholism: Experimental Analyses of Etiology and Modification*

ROBERT S. DAVIDSON

Several investigators in recent years have devoted major research programs to the experimental analysis of clinical phenomena (Sandler and Davidson, 1971, 1972; Franks, 1967; Mendelson and Mello, 1966; Nathan and O'Brien, 1971). These programs are frequently broad in coverage and designed to isolate the major variables responsible for the etiology as well as the modification of the pathological behavior in question. One of the common assumptions at the heart of such large-scale projects is that most such pathological behaviors are learned, and therefore capable of modification by learning variables, procedures, or operations.

One of the goals in such experimental analyses is to generate information relevant to the etiology or formation of pathological behaviors of various sorts. Because such an undertaking may create ethical problems (e.g., initiating of drinking problems in humans), studies in this area are frequently done with animal subjects. Once a model or analog of a particular pathological behavior has been generated in an animal subject, it might be possible to further screen experimental treatment techniques with this model, as has been done in experimental surgery and pharmacology.

When an effective treatment or modification technique has been demonstrated with the animal analog, frequently it can be applied directly to the human pathological behavior. This was roughly the way in which penicillin, the heart transplant, and pacemaker technologies developed.

In light of the vast number of disciplines investigating various facets of alcoholism and the extensive literature generated by such involvement, one might conclude that a great deal must be known about alcoholism. However, the fact

*The composition of most of this chapter, and the conduct of the research reported therein, has been supported by Grant #9-69 from the Veterans Administration and a small grant from the Licensed Beverage Industries.

149

that no very reliable experimental model of alcoholism exists as well as the feeble outcome reports of most programs designed to treat and modify alcoholism give the lie to this supposition.

Without denying the importance of physiological, biochemical, metabolic, and genetic aspects of alcoholism, the current model analyzes the contribution of learning variables pertinent to alcoholism. Three important assumptions are an explicit part of the model: (1) alcoholism is a set of behaviors which can be learned, potentially, by anyone; and (2) alcoholism is most likely learned according to the same principles and under the control of the same variables that govern the learning of other pathological behaviors; and (3) alcoholic behavior, being learned in this fashion, is amenable to treatment or modification by techniques or procedures that are, in principle, the same procedures that have proven effective with other learned pathological behaviors.

From the learning point of view, alcoholism consists essentially of excessive rates of drinking of alcoholic beverages which may also meet the physiological criteria of tolerance and withdrawal and which are usually maintained over extensive periods of time (Franks, 1963, 1966; Jaffe, 1970; Mello and Mendelson, 1965; Mendelson and Mello, 1966). Behavioral tolerance, in which a higher blood alcohol concentration is necessary to produce a given degree of intoxication in tolerant than in intolerant subjects, has been demonstrated in animals (Chen, 1968; Cicero et al., 1971; LeBlanc et al., 1969) as well as in humans (Goldberg, 1943; Isbell et al., 1955). Chronic use of alcohol has also been observed to result in more rapid metabolism or degradation in humans (Isbell et al., 1955; Mendelson et al., 1965). Similarly, states of physical dependence on alcohol which regularly produce withdrawal symptoms on removal of alcohol have also been observed in both animal (Cicero et al., 1971; Ellis and Pick, 1970; Freund, 1970) and human subjects (Isbell et al., 1955; Mello and Mendelson, 1965; Victor and Adams, 1953). It now appears that regular intoxication over any sustained period of time may produce withdrawal symptoms, ranging from mild hangover after a few hours of intoxication to alcoholic hallucinosis and delirium tremens, which may appear only after chronic, long-term intoxication (Isbell et al., 1955; Mello and Mendelson, 1965, 1970; Mendelson and Mello, 1964, 1966; Victor and Adams, 1953).

ETIOLOGICAL CONSIDERATIONS

As mentioned earlier, it is only in fairly recent years that serious approaches to the experimental analysis of the learning components of alcoholism have taken place. For example, Conger (1956), Franks (1958, 1963, 1966), Kepner (1964), and Kingham (1958) all suggested that alcoholism could be learned according to the general principles of acquisition and modification of behavior, but several years passed before direct experimental tests of these proposals were reported. The research that finally emerged began to explode many popular myths or stereotypes which had existed. One of these myths, which arose out of earlier experimentation by Pavlov (1927) and Masserman and Yum (1946) in the context of experimental neurosis, was that the primary mechanism of alcoholism is the reduction of anxiety. Congruent with this model, alcoholism was interpreted as behavior acquired to reduce states of tension or fear or to escape or avoid states of anxiety (however that may be defined). However, the research conducted within this framework revealed that although rates of alcoholic drinking might increase temporarily during periods of conflict, for example, avoidance or fear, it did not usually persist beyond such periods (Clark and Polish, 1960; Conger, 1951; Freed, 1968, 1969; Masserman and Yum, 1946; Moskowitz and Asato, 1966; Pawloski et al., 1961; Perensky et al., 1969; Reynolds and van Sommers, 1960; Scarborough, 1957; Smart, 1965). Thus the anxiety reduction model in general has not appeared maximally productive of alcoholic analogs, particularly if maintained drinking is a required part of the model.

One of the favored paradigms for testing the anxiety reduction hypothesis used the shock avoidance situation as a model of anxiety production. Aside from the question of the appropriateness of this model, many studies were designed to determine whether alcoholic intake would increase during such avoidance conditioning (Clark and Polish, 1960; Pawloski et al., 1961; Perensky et al., 1969). Most of these studies reported some increase in the intake of alcohol during such avoidance conditioning sessions, which was not maintained following the termination of avoidance training.

Of course, there are several other aversive states that might lead people to drink alcohol in order to avoid or escape from them. These may include states of disequilibrium, discrimination, social ostracism or punishment, depression, loss of a job or loved one, or states of physiological upset, such as hunger, illness, or hangover from previous drinking. Any one of these states, in addition to anxious states, might conceivably lead one to drink. Negative reinforcement (Skinner, 1953) is the term that may best characterize the behavior common to avoidance of or escape from any or all of these aversive states. However, several recent studies (Baum, 1969, 1970; Moskowitz and Asato, 1966; Perensky et al., 1969) have reported equivocal and often opposing results regarding the negative reinforcement hypothesis in connection with drinking alcohol.

In addition, some investigators, working directly with alcoholic patients given the opportunity to drink *ad libitum*, observed that several indicators of anxiety or discomfort rose rather than fell during and after prolonged drinking (McNamee et al., 1968; Mendelson and Mello, 1966; Mendelson et al., 1968; Nathan et al., 1970; Nathan and O'Brien, 1971). This evidence again seems directly opposed to what one would predict from the negative reinforcement hypothesis. Thus it seems that negative reinforcement, although it may sometimes be involved in excessive drinking, may not be the only factor, or the major factor involved in etiological configurations.

Thus the question of why some people increase their rates of drinking past the point of qualifying as alcoholics while others maintain a low or "social" rate of drinking remains mysterious. Recent research and several anecdotal reports, however, have begun to implicate more strongly models of positive reinforcement. The natural drinking history of an alcoholic, to the extent that it demonstrates increasing rates of alcoholic intake, seems to suggest that alcohol may function as a positive reinforcer, that is, it may increase the probability of future drinking.

In a few operant analyses of the function of alcohol in chronic alcoholic patients, it has been demonstrated that such patients will engage in operant behaviors that produce alcohol (Davidson and Wallach, 1972; Mello and Mendelson, 1965, 1966; Mendelson et al., 1968; Nathan et al., 1970; Nathan and O'Brien, 1971), will choose alcohol over other reinforcers such as money (Mello and Mendelson, 1965; Mello et al., 1968), and will engage in behaviors ranging from simple to complex under the control of various schedules of alcohol reinforcement (Mello and Mendelson, 1965; Mendelson and Mello, 1966; Mendelson et al., 1968). These data indicate clearly that alcohol may function as a potent reinforcer for alcoholic patients, but the case for the reinforcing properties of alcohol in nonalcoholic populations is not as well established (Cutter, 1969; Cutter et al., 1970; Nathan and O'Brien, 1971).

The reinforcing function of alcohol in animals has been studied through the use of a wide range of techniques and procedures, not all of which have been equally productive. Most investigators have found it difficult or impossible to arrange the conditions sufficient to produce maintained voluntary drinking of alcoholic solutions to the point of intoxication in animals (Cicero and Myers, 1968; Goodrick, 1967; Keehn, 1969; Myers, 1966; Myers and Carey, 1961; Richter and Campbell, 1940; Senter et al., 1968). If self-selection of alcohol in a free choice situation is allowed, preferences are demonstrated only for low-concentration solutions, generally ranging from 2 to 8 percent ethanol or some equivalent (Freund, 1969; Myers, 1966; Myers and Carey, 1961; Richter and Campbell, 1940; Senter et al., 1968). Outside these ranges, animals usually show preferences for water, saccharin, or other, perhaps more palatable, solutions. With 24-hour access to alcohol solutions, not enough is usually consumed to suggest that intoxication has been produced. Thus many of these preference tests have suggested that alcohol solutions are positive reinforcers to naive animal subjects only at lower concentrations. At higher concentrations alcoholic solutions may have aversive properties perhaps due to taste, smell, and local tissue irritation (Woods et al., 1971).

In some situations in which alcoholic solutions of low concentrations were the only liquids provided to animals, subsequent deprivation led to an increase in drinking of the same or slightly higher concentration alcoholic solutions (Senter and Richman, 1969; Sinclair and Senter, 1968). This again suggests a positive reinforcement function. In a few paradigms involving forced choice exposure to alcoholic solutions, animals have been induced to drink enough to show symptoms of intoxication (Cicero et al., 1971; Freund, 1969, 1970). As will be mentioned later, one of the more effective ways to accomplish this may be to mask the orosensory properties of alcohol by dissolving or mixing it in a preferred solution or diet. Otherwise, it may be difficult to demonstrate positive reinforcement functions.

Two indirect procedures have demonstrated ways in which alcohol drinking may be increased, after which alcohol may function as a reinforcer. The first of these uses the polydipsic model of Falk (1961, 1964, 1966), which brings drinking to a high frequency as a schedule-adjunctive behavior. Several investigators have used this model, which allows subjects free access to water or other solutions while being trained on a schedule of food reinforcement. Some reports have indicated that when alcohol in low concentrations is added to the water, animals may drink to the point of self-intoxication, after which alcohol may be ingested independent of the original learning conditions (Freed et al., 1970; Freed and Lester, 1970; Lester, 1961; Meisch, 1969; Meisch and Thompson, 1971; Woods and Winger, 1971). At present, the parallel between schedule-adjunctive polydipsia and human alcoholism is obscure.

Alcohol drinking has also been increased by reinforcing this response with other stimuli (such as food or drink for deprived subjects). Although this paradigm has often demonstrated increases in alcoholic intake, self-intoxication has been observed only rarely (Keehn, 1969; Keehn and Coulson, 1970; Mendelson and Mello, 1964; Mello and Mendelson, 1965, 1966; Perensky et al., 1968; Senter et al., 1967).

Some recent experiments using intravenous injection of alcohol directly into the bloodstream have demonstrated that monkeys will press a bar to self-inject alcohol at rates high enough to maintain regular intoxication (Deneau et al., 1969; Woods et al., 1971). This is one of the most powerful demonstrations of the reinforcing function of alcohol to date. Animals in these studies have been observed to maintain regular self-intoxication and to abruptly terminate periods of self-intoxication, much as human alcoholics have been observed to do (Mello and Mendelson, 1970; Mendelson and Mello, 1966). Such abrupt termination has produced the abstinence syndrome with associated withdrawal symptoms (Deneau et al., 1969; Woods et al., 1971). The observed effectiveness of the self-injection model suggests the following: (1) a parallel between behavioral effects of alcohol and other addictive drugs, such as morphine, which animals also self-inject; (2) the reinforcing function; and (3) animal-human analogs.

Another effective device has been to mask the orosensory properties of alcohol by introducing it in conjunction with palatable solutions. Fitzgerald et al. (1968) introduced vodka and ethanol in fruit juice solutions to chimpanzees, observing occasional intoxication as a result. Freund (1969, 1970) has maintained deprived mice on Metrecal with 8 percent ethanol added, observing regular high levels of intoxication, followed by withdrawal, convulsions, and sometimes death as a result of removal of alcohol from the diet. Davidson (1971) has observed that rats will emit bar press responses reinforced by alcohol of increasing concentrations in Sustagen (Pfizer, a dietary supplement).

In a systematic replication of this study, Davidson and Alvarez (1972) introduced a slight variation by allowing subjects to work to deliver themselves as much reinforcer as they wanted, to a criterion of satiation. Four rats were food deprived to 80 percent of their normal body weights, then trained to press a bar to produce 0.3 cubic centimeter of Sustagen following each tenth response (FR 10). The animals were allowed to continue responding to the point of satiation (the point at which they stopped responding for three minutes). After they stabilized in response rate (three consecutive sessions with less than 10 percent variability between them), alcohol (80 proof vodka) was introduced into the sucrose reinforcer and increased through the following concentrations: 10, 20, and 30 percent (volume/volume).

The results of this study indicated that alcohol, in these concentrations, can serve as a positive reinforcer, although it may not maintain behavior at as high a rate as sucrose alone. Figure 1 depicts the results of this study in one animal who showed decreasing response rates and numbers of reinforcements following the introduction of each successively higher concentration of alcohol. However, the response rate recovered almost to the operant or base rate following longer exposure to each alcohol concentration. As indicated by the graph, the number of reinforcements consumed also increased following exposure to each concentration, although not proportionately as high. It is also of interest to note that, although the total number of reinforcements increased much more within than between each concentration, the maximum absolute amount of alcohol consumed increased from 1.5 milliliters at 10 percent to 4.5 at 30 percent. This amounted to dose levels of 4.5 to 13.5 grams per kilogram of body weight for this subject. Increases in both response rate and number of reinforcements consumed suggest that behavioral tolerance to alcohol had developed. In addition, there were increasing indications of intoxication as the concentration increased, until, at 30 percent, it often appeared that the animal was physically unable to continue responding.

Thus several procedures have demonstrated the positive reinforcing capabilities of alcoholic solutions, in addition to providing occasional evidence of negative reinforcing functions. In the natural history of the alcoholic, both functions as well as complex combinations of these and other learning variables may occur. Some discussion of these possible conditions follows.

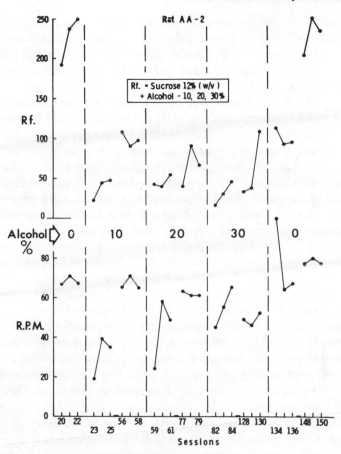

Figure 1.   Number of reinforcements delivered (upper graph) and rate of response (lower graph) by subject AA-2 in control conditions (no alcohol) and in first and last three sessions of exposure to 10, 20, and 30 percent alcohol (vodka). Reinforcement schedule was FR10, available until the subject paused for 3 minutes. Sessions 80, 81, and 131-133 are not depicted due to apparatus failure.

THE NATURAL HISTORY OF ALCOHOLISM

Recent estimates of the extent of the problem of alcoholism in the United States, although somewhat variable, indicate that at least 5 million Americans meet the pharmacological and psychological criteria of alcoholism (Boyle, 1962; Jaffe, 1970; Keller and Efron, 1955; Mensh, 1965). This rate of alcoholism is higher for the United States than for any other country (Boyle, 1962), and it places alcoholism among the four major medical problems in the United States (the other three being mental illnesses, heart disease, and cancer).

In addition to the number of alcoholics, other estimates and surveys suggest that two-thirds of the adult American population drink alcoholic beverages, and it has been noted (Jaffe, 1970) that the annual expenditure in this country for alcoholic beverages exceeds the entire national expenditure for education (over 10 billion dollars).

It is likely that the prominent advertising done by the liquor industry and the number of social situations involving drinking play reinforcing functions in the lives of individuals on the road to alcoholism. Drinking is so common in many areas of industry that it is regularly correlated with patterns of absenteeism, abuse of sick leave, and loss of productivity after "liquid lunch." Many salesmen claim that they would find it difficult to close a sale without drinking.

In addition to frequently being prescribed by physicians as a relaxant, alcohol may be the most commonly abused drug used in the effort at self-medication. Because of its CNS depressant properties, it is often used to suppress physical symptoms such as headache, hangover symptoms, psychosomatic symptoms, and psychophysiologic symptoms including anxiety and tension. Alcohol often serves negative reinforcing functions in these cases.

As mentioned earlier, several procedures have demonstrated experimentally how alcohol may serve positive reinforcing functions, in addition to its negative reinforcing capabilities. In the natural history of the alcoholic, both functions in combination with complex stimulus control are likely to occur. For example, many potential alcoholics first drink under the primary control of positive or negative reinforcement (e.g., they drink because they like the taste or the experience, or to escape or avoid aversive states such as physical tension or other physical symptoms).

Similarly, stimuli associated with alcohol may set the occasion for drinking. In this way, a person may be introduced to alcoholic beverages at an enjoyable party, and, since alcoholic beverages are typically more abundantly available at parties, such social events may set the occasion for future drinking behavior. This, then, is another way in which drinking is learned, that is, as a function of the presence and/or absence of stimuli which set the occasion for the availability of liquor. These stimuli may then become discriminative for the drinking response. The frequency of drinking could be expected to increase in the presence of such S^D's (discriminative stimuli) and to decrease in their absence. In just such ways, Italian families may associate drinking with meals, and Jewish, Catholic, or Polish people may drink at religious or sacramental affairs such as weddings, Bar Mitzvahs, and funerals. In these ethnic cases the stimulus control may be so well developed that it produces the observed lower rates of alcoholism in such groups.

In a slightly modified variation on the party theme, social reinforcement may be of primary importance in the learning to drink sequence. For example, in our own culture, social conviviality and intercommunication frequently become more available contingent on drinking or the behavioral by-products of drinking. Those who refuse drinks at parties, for instance, may be partially socially ostracized or at least mildly punished by reproof and criticism (or perhaps inattention), whereas those who indulge and "loosen up" may become the "life of the party," with the consequent social reinforcement normally implied by such regard.

Obviously, from within this framework, many stimuli set the occasion for drinking and many other stimuli, by virtue of their association with liquor consumption itself, function as conditioned reinforcers to increase the future probability of drinking. The approach of a pretty barmaid with a drink, for example, may lead a (male) person to order more drinks than he normally would had they been delivered by a male bartender. The presence of the understanding bartender of popular lore, however, would most likely function as a setting event (S^D) for drinking, rather than as the conditioned reinforcer of the previous example, since he might be present for longer periods during which behaviors other than drinking might occur.

As discussed earlier, alcoholic drinking may also be acquired and maintained on the basis of negative reinforcement. Thus, escape from aversive states of any kind may function to increase the probability of alcohol drinking in the future. For example, a person chronically suffering from headaches may find that intake of alcohol diminishes or removes this symptom. To the extent and degree to which this occurs, it might be expected to increase the future probability of drinking alcoholic beverages. The case may be extended to any other physical or psychosomatic symptom or other sort of aversive state. Any of the several behaviors related to anxiety, particularly when it is defined as involving increased heart rate, blood pressure, GSR, or other autonomic indications of stress, may be instrumental in motivating alcoholic behavior, since alcohol as a suppressant drug decreases the rates of most of these behaviors in direct proportion to the dose level.

Avoidance of many of these aversive symptoms or tension states may be learned on a similar basis. For example, stimuli previously associated with such states may now set the occasion for drinking, which helps to avoid the symptoms. Even when such symptoms have not been forthcoming, drinking may be maintained on a superstitious basis (the individual now drinks to avoid symptoms that might not have occurred in the absence of drinking). This extends the stimulus control over the behavior and increases the number and range of situations in which drinking might occur. The superstitious paradigm based on negative reinforcement is much more complex than that based on positive reinforcement, partly because the latter is so much better understood and more thoroughly investigated, but also because the mechanism underlying negative reinforcement may be more complex. It has been much easier for theorists to explain the acquisition and maintenance of behaviors that occur only in the *presence* of a particular set of stimuli, as in the case of positive reinforcement, than in their absence. This applies particularly to avoidance conditioning, where behavior may be generated by a series of aversive stimuli, after which the behavior may occur at high frequency over indeterminate lengths of time in the absence of apparent maintaining stimuli. When adventitious correlations of aversive with previously neutral stimuli are suspected, the conditioning paradigm and its controlling factors become even more complex and are largely conjectural.

Some research has been done, however, on conditioned negative reinforcers. These reports, too, support the possibility of long-term maintenance of behavior on the basis of such reinforcers. In a real-life situation, a person may drink, as in the previous example, initially because drinking reduced the severity of headache. At the next stage, the person may drink in the presence of stimuli previously associated with the headache (perhaps the "uptight" state which produced the headache or was present when he felt the headache "coming on"). This would exemplify conditioned negative reinforcement of drinking by the associated stimuli. At the next stage beyond this, the stimuli may generalize to include any other situation presenting similar stimuli (e.g., any other anxiety-arousing situations, tension states, or perhaps any other physical symptoms).

At the end of a long history of alcoholic drinking, it seems entirely conceivable that any or all of the preceding variables contribute to the maintenance of a particular individual's drinking behavior. Thus a woman may first drink at parties because everyone else does and it is "the thing to do" (illustrating social S^D's and, perhaps, modeling). At the next stage, our illustrative woman may find she likes the taste of what she drinks (positive reinforcement), but then begins to drink more because it makes her feel better (combined negative and positive reinforcement). Later, she may drink whenever she feels bad and then to avoid feeling bad (negative and conditioned negative reinforcement). Of course, as she drinks more, she begins to find that she also feels worse later (withdrawal symptoms, which may then become new negative reinforcers controlling a fresh burst of drinking), and so on, in a vicious cycle.

On the other hand, many people first drink to escape or avoid an unpleasant state of affairs. For example, members of the Air Force may be offered a drink to help calm them or help them forget dangerous bombing missions (negative reinforcement). Such a person may find that he likes the state produced by such drinking so much that he begins to drink more, simply to reproduce it (positive reinforcement). The stimuli may then generalize so that our hypothetical man now begins to drink in many more situations when he does not feel calm, for example, following a fight with his buddies (conditioned negative reinforcement). He may also begin to drink more simply because his buddies do (social S^D's or modeling), or because "there's nothing else to do" (perhaps conditioned negative reinforcement based on escape from boredom). In addition to sometimes making him feel more aggressive and masculine (positive reinforcement), the increased drinking may produce more physical symptoms and aversive withdrawal states, which then may initiate new cycles of negatively reinforced drinking. These vicious cycles may be the main factor responsible for alcoholism's apparent self-maintaining capability as well as the off-and-on "binge" pattern.

After a long history of increasing rates of alcoholic drinking (which alone may substantiate some positive and/or negative reinforcing functions), any stimulus or any conceivable state of the organism may potentially set the occasion for further drinking. From the negative reinforcement viewpoint alone, this may well account for much of what previous writers have described as the low "frustration tolerance" of alcoholic persons. Finally, the chronic long-term alcoholic may begin most days suffering the aversive consequences of the previous day's drinking (e.g., withdrawal, hangover symptoms), which very often are selfmedicated with more alcohol, following which much of the rest of the day is spent in alcohol-seeking and drinking behaviors maintained by avoidance or superstitious avoidance of withdrawal states.

Alcohol-seeking behaviors may extend into a long behavioral chain of several individual responses linked together by their common termination in and maintenance by alcoholic drinking. Alcohol-seeking behaviors may include thinking about a drink, desiring a drink, searching for a drink, seeking out friends or acquaintances who may have money or liquor, going to bars or liquor stores if money is available, procuring alcohol, and, finally, drinking it. All of these and more related behaviors may occur in the same or varying stimulus contexts (in bars, with friends, in cars, at home alone, or in the gutter).

This analysis has only begun to suggest and to catalog the many and various immediate consequences of alcoholic drinking that may function as negative and/or positive reinforcers to maintain the behavior. In addition, like most other excessive or addictive behaviors (e.g., smoking, overeating, or drug addiction), moderate or low rates of occurrence of the behavior may not be harmful, whereas high-rate emission of the behavior may generate hazardous, but long-delayed, consequences. Chronic alcoholic drinking, for example, may produce two classes of such delayed consequences: first, symptoms of intoxication (slurring of speech, gradual loss of physical coordination, vertigo, blackout, nausea, and eventual loss of consciousness, convulsions, and death) and, second, symptoms of withdrawal which occur only after alcohol has been removed for a period of time (nausea, blackouts, headache, gastrointestinal symptoms, pancreatitis, cirrhosis of the liver, delirium tremens, Korsakoff's psychosis, convulsions, and death). Both sets of consequences, which would be aversive to most people, probably occur so long after the initial alcohol-seeking and drinking behaviors that they have little effect on them. But if many of these ultimate aversive consequences (Ferster et al., 1962) occurred immediately following each drink, there might be fewer alcoholics in the world today. As will be indicated later, aversive conditioning treatment models seek to make the immediate consequences of drinking proportionately more aversive than primarily reinforcing.

To the extent that the foregoing experimental as well as programmatic and hypothetical analysis of alcoholic drinking is heuristic and workable, a similar logic should apply to the modification as well as the formation or acquisition of such behavior. That is, no experimental analysis of such pathological behavior is complete with a demonstration of the factors responsible for the formation or etiology of the behavior, but should be able to demonstrate as well factors or variables that might serve to modify or eliminate such behaviors. Thus, if alcoholism can be acquired through conditioning and learning mechanisms (e.g., positive and negative reinforcement), then it should also be possible to modify drinking by manipulation of the same or similar variables. In addition, to the extent that alcoholic drinking is learned and maintained in accordance with general behavioral principles, then it should be modifiable by behavioral techniques, as are many other pathological behaviors (Bandura, 1969; Kanfer and Phillips, 1970; Ullmann and Krasner, 1966). The remainder of this chapter reviews past and current attempts to modify previously existing alcoholic behavior in human patients.

ANALYSIS OF POTENTIAL MODIFICATION (TREATMENT) VARIABLES

Few treatment techniques of any kind have been very effective in alleviating or preventing alcoholism. In 1962, Gerard, Saenger, and Wile followed up some 300 patients treated in a variety of clinics and found that less than 19 percent were abstinent for one year following treatment. This may not vary greatly from the base rate of change in this population, which has been reported in the range from 1 to 10 percent (Kendall and Staton, 1965; Lemere, 1953).

According to reports in the literature, verbal psychotherapy has been relatively ineffective in modifying alcoholic behavior. Tillotson and Fleming (1937), for example, found that 15 percent of 124 patients treated with psychotherapy for an average of six months were still abstinent eighteen months after treatment. Wall and Allen (1944) reported that 24 percent of 1000 patients treated similarly for an average of four months maintained abstinence for three to eight years.

Other nonlearning approaches which have been popularly used with alcoholic patients include Antabuse regimens and Alcoholics Anonymous. AA groups are distributed throughout this and other countries and seem to rely on a combination of religious exhortation, confession, catharsis, persuasion, and social reinforcement for their effect. Although there have been no well-controlled studies on the success of AA, some reports indicate maintained abstinence in a high proportion of subjects who regularly attend meetings over long periods of time (perhaps a year or more), while AA is relatively ineffective with those who attend only a short period of time (Bill W., 1949, 1968). The reasons underlying the lack of universal appeal of AA programs might be worth investigating.

Antabuse regimens, on the other hand, have been found more effective than psychotherapeutic approaches (Wallerstein, 1957) and have sometimes been found as effective as aversive conditioning procedures, though little or no attempt at direct comparison has been made (Bourne et al., 1966). Antabuse is not a conditioning agent, but serves only to make nauseous and ill the person who consumes alcohol while Antabuse is active in his biological system. Consequently, many patients quickly learn that they must wait only three to five days after taking the Antabuse before they can again drink without dangerous consequence. As some authors have suggested (Billet, 1968), Antabuse programs might be improved if a monitoring agent could be assigned the task of reminding the patient to take the drug on a daily basis and to warn the therapist of anticipated or actual discontinuance. Antabuse might also be incorporated into a contingency management system whereby the alcoholic person would be allowed access to privileges or other reinforcement contingent on consuming a standard dose of the drug.

Many learning-oriented studies have produced more effective and long-lasting results than other reported programs. However, many of the reported outcomes are difficult to compare, due to differing criteria and stated goals. Most of the medical, Antabuse, and AA programs, for example, accept and report abstinence as the only desirable outcome of effective treatment, whereas most learning programs accept reduction in rate of drinking or rates consistent with social or controlled, subintoxicating rates of drinking as effective or improved outcomes. In addition, several reports indicate that it is altogether possible to generate reduced rates of drinking, even when this is not a stated goal of treatment (Davies, 1962; Kendell, 1965).

As mentioned previously, no experimental analysis of pathological alcoholic behavior is complete with a demonstration of the factors responsible for the formation or etiology of such behavior alone; any analysis should also be able to demonstrate factors or variables that might serve to modify or eliminate such behavior. Thus, if it is conceivable that the behaviors subsumed under the label of alcoholism might be learned responses, they should be capable of modification, as well as acquisition, by manipulation of the same or similar variables serving these functions in other behaviors. In this way, removal of positive or negative reinforcers should result in decrements and eventual extinction of responses maintained by these reinforcers. Similarly, extinction of alcohol-maintained responses and reinforcement of incompatible responses should make new behaviors available through the counterconditioning model. Stimulus control, token economy, and contingency management programs should also offer possibilities. And, as has been found with other learned behaviors. effective punishment contingencies should suppress behaviors maintained by alcohol as a reinforcer. Escape and avoidance training may offer effective variations of the punishment paradigm and function in a way similar to counterconditioning to provide new behaviors alternative to drinking.

Removal of alcohol from alcoholic patients is a routine accompaniment of hospitalization of most of these patients. However, this "drying-out" process differs from experimental extinction in several respects. First, many alcohol-maintained behaviors (visits to bars, liquor stores, and taverns as well as other precursors to drinking) are prevented from occurring within the confines of the hospital. Typically, many other contingencies are applied to other behaviors, as well, which might affect drinking behavior in as yet unknown ways. At any rate, the typical drying-out period seems to have little effect on the behavior, as demonstrated by the recidivism rates for alcoholics, which appear to be higher than for any other single patient group. For example, most of the patients who are treated in this manner (medical detoxification) at the Miami VA Hospital return to the hospital two to six times per year (Davidson and Greenwald, 1972).

Experimental programs designed to gradually fade out liquor reinforcements and approach experimental extinction may have some merit, but they have as yet received little or no attention. Some ways in which this might be done include gradually increasing the required number of responses per reinforcement to infinity, fading out reinforcement along temporal dimensions (increasing fixed intervals between reinforcement or decreasing maximal rates of response required per reinforcement), and increasing the required magnitude of response for reinforcement until responding is beyond the physical capacity of the subject.

Another model which has demonstrated its utility and power in the modification of many other pathological behaviors is the counterconditioning procedure. This model offers the joint possibilities of extinction of the pathological or undesirable behavior while presenting other, perhaps new and incompatible, behaviors. This procedure should be particularly useful with long-term chronic alcoholic subjects who may show impoverished behavioral repertoires, most of which are under the control of alcohol or related stimuli (e.g., money, alcoholic friends or environments supporting alcohol-related behaviors). The counterconditioning procedure, like the straight extinction model, has received little attention.

One notable exception is the report of Narrol (1967), who set up a token economy for alcoholic patients in which points were paid to the subjects for work behavior. These points could then be exchanged for room and board, ground privileges, canteen purchases, passes, medication, attendance at Alcoholics Anonymous meetings, and/or group therapy. Contingent upon proper behavior, patients could also work their way from a closed, confined ward environment with little freedom and comfort to an open ward with ground and leave privileges. Though this was only a pilot study, all but 3 of the 17 patients remained in the project for 9 weeks or more and their work behavior increased to higher rates and longer days (8 hours average) than other patients at the same hospital, who worked an average of 4 hours per day. Some difficulties were reported with the complexities of alcoholic behavior, although the procedures used seemed to have effectively modified the behavior and greatly increased the probability of constructive alternative behaviors. When facilities are available for long-term contact with alcoholic patients and contingencies can be reliably scheduled, this sort of approach seems to be the most powerful and potentially long-lasting form of modification.

In a more recent experimental ward program, alcoholic patients at Baltimore City Hospital were allowed to earn money by maintaining abstinence or moderation in the presence of alcoholic beverages offered after a priming dose (Cohen, Liebson, Faillace, and Allen, 1971). These experimenters found the success of this program depended upon the size of the priming dose and the delay of reinforcement (money). In another variation (Cohen, Liebson, Faillace, and Speers, 1971), these investigators found that arranging an enriched environment (including privileges such as access to a job and money, use of a private telephone, reading material, recreation, good meals, and a bedside chair) contingent upon moderate rather than heavy drinking established effective control of drinking behavior. This contingency controlled drinking to less than 6 ounces of 95-proof ethanol per day when up to 24 ounces was available. If one of the six subjects drank more than 5 ounces in one day, he was denied access to the privileges mentioned for the rest of that day and for 24 hours thereafter. In the 30 periods in which this contingency management program was compared to noncontingent access to either "enriched" or "impoverished" environments, there were only 11 occasions on which more than 5 ounces were consumed.

Very clearly, these reports indicate the powerful control token economy and contingency management programs may exert over pathological behaviors such as excessive drinking. In addition, the reports of the Baltimore City group support the position advanced previously that rates of alcoholic consumption, like other behaviors, should be capable of modulation, regulation, and reduction, in addition to simple elimination (abstinence). This theme will again arise as aversive models of modification are discussed.

Before 1950, most of the conditioning studies of alcoholic treatment used classical conditioning models of drug-induced nausea (Franks, 1963; Lemere and Voegtlin, 1950). In these studies the patient is given injected or oral doses of emetic drug (usually emetine or apomorphine), which produces nausea and often (but not always) vomiting, just prior to which the patient is given liquor to drink. One alcoholic beverage may be used or, to enhance stimulus generalization, many can be used. Lemere and Voegtlin (1950) report 50 percent abstinence over follow-up periods ranging from one to ten years in over 4000 patients. This seems to be the best large-scale success ratio reported thus far. However, these data represent selected patients who usually pay a sizable bill ($600) for treatment and, in addition, may be exposed to unspecified amounts of psychotherapy in addition to aversive conditioning. DeMorsier and Feldmann (1950), using a variant of the foregoing procedure, extended sessions until subjects developed aversion to several varieties of alcoholic beverage (two to four 1-hour sessions) and reported about the same level of obtained abstinence in their European population (46 percent of 150 cases) over 8 to 31 months.

One difficulty with these procedures is that both patients and staff frequently find them very disagreeable (Rachman and Teasdale, 1969). As Franks (1963), Rachman (1965), and Rachman and Teasdale (1969) pointed out, it is impossible to precisely control the parameters of the drug aversive conditioning procedure, due to individual differences in time from injection to nausea and whether or not vomiting occurs. Also, if the paradigm is a classical conditioning one, as Lemere and Voegtlin (1950) claim, then alcohol is the CS, and the drug injection which it follows is the UCS. This defines the backward classical conditioning procedure, which is perhaps the weakest form of such conditioning. Other disadvantages of the drug aversive conditioning procedure have to do with side effects of the drug, the fact that it is inappropriate to use with patients who have gastric ailments or cardiac histories, and that its unpleasant nature may produce hostility on the part of some patients. However, since this form of therapy has been reportedly more effective than most other treatment procedures, with the largest reported groups of patients, it should be considered seriously and analyzed carefully in the hope of improvement. In terms of an experimental analysis, it may be that the most powerful function of the program is to rearrange the normal consequences of drinking behavior so that the patient suffers aversive consequences immediately or soon after drinking.

Even more disagreeable and objectionable from several points of view is the traumatic aversive conditioning proposed originally by Sanderson, Campbell, and Laverty (1963). This procedure uses succinycholine chloride, which produces 60 to 90 seconds of paralysis of the respiratory musculature. Patients who were not fully informed reported that they felt as if they were dying. Ethical objections and lack of clinical efficacy suggest that less extreme measures may be more appropriate (Bandura, 1969; Kanfer and Phillips, 1970; Laverty, 1966).

In recent years electric shock has been used as the aversive stimulus in an increasing number of studies. The use of electric shock has much to recommend it, including both clinical and experimental advantages. As Azrin and Holz (1966) point out, shock can be precisely controlled over its major parameters (intensity, duration, frequency, etc.), makes constant contact with the subject, can be varied over a wide range of values to produce differential effects, and produces similar effects (though perhaps at different intensities) in most subjects. This is not true of drugs or other previously used aversive stimuli. In addition, several studies have reported lasting or permanent effects of aversion paradigms using shock with animals (Boe and Church, 1967; Walters and Rogers, 1963).

An early reported Russian study (Kantorovich, 1928) applied shock to the sight of cards containing the names of drinks and the sight, smell, and taste of alcoholic beverages. Of the subjects treated, 70 percent remained abstinent at 3-week to 20-month follow-ups, whereas all but one of a control group treated with medication and hypnotic suggestion drank within a few days of discharge from the hospital.

Blake (1965, 1967) compared electrical aversion treatment with aversion combined with relaxation, finding a slight but nonsignificant advantage for the combination in follow-up. Follow-ups, done at 6- and 12-month intervals, found 25 to 48 percent abstinence.

In a variation which combined shock punishment with avoidance, Hsu (1965) applied pulsing electric shock of 2 to 5-milliamp intensity and 30-second duration to the head of patients 0.5 to 5 seconds following a drink of alcohol. The patient often had a choice of drinking nonalcoholic or alcoholic beverages, the former enabling shock avoidance. Hsu reported reduction in alcoholic consumption over 6 months in 7 of 20 patients who completed this procedure. However, the dropout rate was high and all patients reacted anxiously or disagreeably to the procedure.

Morosko and Baer (1970) used a procedure similar to that of Hsu with 2-second shock to the leg and shock avoidance following drinking of nonalcoholic beverages. Each subject was exposed to this procedure until he demonstrated consistent avoidance. Follow-up at six months reported reduction in drinking rate in each of three treated patients.

More recently, Vogler et al. (1970) conducted a well-designed study in which subjects were given shock escape conditioning in a simulated bar setting. Subjects could order drinks of their choice, but each drink was followed by shock which stayed on until the liquor was spit out. Control groups got pseudo-conditioning (random shock), sham conditioning (no shock), or routine hospital ward treatment. Conditioning produced increased days to relapse and a lower percentage of relapse at eight-month follow-up than found in controls, with 70 percent of subjects receiving conditioning plus later booster sessions unrelapsed at eight months. No differences were found between control groups.

In two interesting variations on aversive conditioning, chronic alcoholic patients have been trained in voluntary programs to become moderate, controlled drinkers of alcoholic beverages. In the first study (Lovibond and Caddy, 1970), 31 chronic alcoholic patients volunteered for treatment; 28 completed the treatment, and 21 appeared to have successfully learned patterns of controlled, low-rate drinking. The first step in this procedure was discrimination training, in which the patients were trained to use their own behaviors and direct feedback of their blood alcohol levels to discriminate between levels above and below a cutoff point (0.08 percent blood alcohol). Once discrimination training was accomplished, each patient was allowed to freely drink alcoholic beverages at blood alcohol levels below the cutoff point but was shocked at unpredictable times when the blood alcohol level was higher. In addition, various responses in the drinking chain might be followed by shock of increasing duration and intensities, and the shock electrodes might be moved about the face and neck.

Follow-up reports from this study indicate that conditioned subjects consumed significantly less alcohol over a 16- to 60-week posttreatment period than did control subjects who received random shock. Of the 28 subjects who completed treatment, 21 continued drinking moderately, rarely raising their blood alcohol levels higher than 0.07 percent. The remaining seven subjects were only partially successful.

In another study (Mills et al., 1971) chronic alcoholic patients at a California state hospital were trained to behave more like social drinkers than their own previous drinking topography. That is, they were trained to order more mixed drinks and to sip, rather than gulp, their drinks. The contingencies were explained to the patients at the outset of treatment, during which they received painful shock to the fingers when the contingencies were violated. Each time liquor was made available in a mock bar setting, each subject could avoid shock by ordering a mixed drink or a nonalcoholic beverage and sipping it. If, however, he ordered a straight drink, or ordered and gulped a mixed drink, or ordered more than three drinks, mild or strong shock was delivered.

Of 13 subjects who initiated treatment, 9 approximated the contingencies over 12 to 14 sessions, while 4 showed exaggerated, rapid acquisition of shock avoidance behavior then left the hospital AWOL before completion. Follow-up at six weeks found the following results when experimental subjects were compared with untreated control subjects: social drinkers—experimental 2, control 0; abstinent—experimental 3, control 2; drunk—experimental 0, control 4.

These two studies indicate the clear possibility of training chronic, long-term alcoholic patients to drink in moderation. This challenges the beliefs of the medical disease orientation and of Alcoholics Anonymous that alcoholics cannot learn to drink in moderation, but instead must become entirely abstinent of alcohol in order to show lasting improvement.

THE MIAMI VA ALCOHOLIC MODIFICATION PROJECT

In pilot projects begun at the Miami VA Hospital by Sandler (1969) and Davidson (1969), alcoholic patients have been presented with an array of five shot glasses each of six different alcoholic beverages and instructed to engage in various drinking and related behaviors. For example, each patient was instructed to pick up a bottle behind one of the columns of drinks, smell one of the drinks, take a drink, imagine getting up in the morning needing a shot to get a fresh start on the day or imagine passing a liquor store after a hot and tiring day and buying a bottle of his favorite beverage. When each of these responses was completed, the subject received an electric shock which was adjusted to as high an intensity as each individual could take.

In later variations of the same treatment paradigm, shock was delivered automatically by the experimenter, or a switch was given to the patient, who could then deliver shock to himself, or selection of an added nonalcoholic beverage made shock avoidance possible.

This program produced some striking successes, but it also produced an extremely high dropout rate (over 50 percent during treatment and up to 90 percent during follow-up). In addition, there was no good measure allowing evaluation of changes during treatment, measures which have been lacking in most programs. Lack of precise measures of treatment progress not only made assessment of treatment effectiveness difficult but also rendered difficult or impossible the prediction of the point of maximum therapeutic benefit.

In later programmatic approaches (Davidson, 1969, 1972b, 1972c), these defects have been corrected by providing the patient with a simple, easily repeatable response (pulling a Lindsley manipulandum similar to the popular candy vendor plunger) which could be reinforced with very small amounts (2 cubic centimeters) of alcoholic beverage, diluted 50 percent with water. Alcoholic subjects have been observed to work at high and stable rates of response for alcohol offered as reinforcement under these conditions, when they are required to respond a fixed number of times (e.g., 30) to secure each reinforcement. This technology extends the experimental analysis of alcoholic behavior, in addition to bringing it in line with the experimental analysis of many other pathological behaviors (Ferster, 1958; Sandler and Davidson, 1971; Skinner, 1953). This technology also makes contact with the long history of experimental analysis which began in the 1930s and has shown steady progress in the controlled environments offered by animal laboratories (Ferster and Skinner, 1957; Honig, 1966).

Davidson and Wallach (1972) made both cola and alcoholic beverages available to three patients in an apparatus similar to that described above. After training each patient to work for only one reinforcer at a time under stimulus control (a light flash signalled when one, but not the other reinforcer was available), both were made available and the patient was given free choice of either reinforcer. Electric shock of gradually increasing intensity was then applied contingent upon the alcohol-reinforced (or thirtieth) response. In two of the three cases, this produced little or no change at first, then an increase in response rates, followed by a decrease and a switch to the other, less preferred reinforcer. Later presentation of a red light which had been paired with each shock delivery produced a switch away from the plunger currently manipulated prior to the delivery of shock. This was one of the few examples of control of human responding by a conditioned aversive stimulus or conditioned punishment. This study further extended the experimental analysis of alcoholic behavior and suggested some control procedures that may have possibilities for clinical treatment or long-term modification as well. Although this study was not designed to be a clinical trial, all three treated patients showed abstinence or low and controlled rates of alcoholic drinking through a three-year follow-up.

The Miami VA Alcoholic Treatment Program currently is conducted as a combined research and clinical effort, with patients randomly assigned to treatment programs designed to be maximally effective. The control groups have been largely statistical groups collected while they were undergoing medical or psychiatric treatment programs, or groups receiving different forms of conditioning. A sham conditioning group which is being collected will receive alcohol reinforcement but no shock.

Assessment

In each of the studies subjects are selected on the basis of information gathered from hospital records, objective reports, and a questionnaire designed to aid in evaluation. Patients are seen for initial interview on a referral basis from any of the wards in the hospital, or on an outpatient basis. Once the patient is evaluated as acceptable for treatment, he may be treated on a medical ward or transferred to one of the psychiatric wards, where the majority of patients are treated.

Each patient was given a structured interview and administered a 55-item questionnaire designed to assess the areas of chronicity and severity of alcoholism, drinking rate, and topography. The type(s) of alcoholic beverages consumed, pattern of consumption, and resulting symptoms of intoxication and withdrawal were carefully established, as were the associated social, marital, and occupational functioning of each patient. Objective reports, hospital reports, and current staff observations on the ward were all assessed as well.

Each subject was selected according to the following criteria: (1) primary or secondary diagnosis of alcoholism by a physician; (2) a history of chronic alcoholism or high-rate drinking based on hospital and staff reports corroborating questionnaire responses; (3) absence of cardiovascular, neurological, or physical disorder that would preclude operant responding or electrical stimulation; and (4) residence in or near the greater Miami area.

Once selected, each patient signed a voluntary informed consent form (VA form 10-1086), was told that treatment would occupy a four- to six-week period of time, and was told of the experimental nature of the program. If the patient did not sign the form or would not otherwise agree to participate, treatment was not initiated. Once the patient was selected, medically released, and informed, he was scheduled for treatment for two half-hour periods each weekday.

Each patient was randomly assigned to a treatment group until a full complement of 12 to 15 had completed treatment. There was some attempt to roughly match the groups on the basis of age, sex, chronicity, and severity of alcoholism, as well as marital and social status.

In general, the design of each of the studies in the program was a single-subject ABA design, with pretreatment and posttreatment baseline measurements of operant rates under the control of alcoholic reinforcement. This supplied maximal information regarding the immediate treatment effect in each individual case, with each new subject providing a further replication.

In addition, follow-up information was gathered periodically on each subject over a two-year period. Rates of drinking and associated behaviors were assessed behaviorally through self-reports and corroborated objectively at each of the follow-up visits.

Experimental Treatment Environment

The human treatment laboratory consisted of a series of interconnecting rooms containing offices and experimental space. The experimental space consisted of three adjacent rooms intercommunicating by closed-circuit television. Two rooms contained Industrial Acoustical Chambers (IAC 402A and IAC 403A), which served to isolate the subject from environmental and equipment noise. Each chamber contained a wooden console (Figure 2) on a table in front of which each patient was seated. The console contained two plungers (Lindsley manipulanda, Gerbands), above which appeared recessed magazines containing 1-ounce shot glasses. Remotely controlled solenoid liquid valves (Lehigh Valley Electronics 1527) automatically dispensed 2 cubic centimeters of alcoholic beverage into the glass in one of the magazines. The beverage dispensed corresponded to that most frequently consumed in the recent past by each subject. Wine and beer were dispensed undiluted; liquor was diluted 50 percent with water.

Red and white lights which could be programmed as discriminative stimuli (S^{D}s) appeared above each magazine and each plunger, respectively. In addition, a 4- × 5-inch cutout centered above the liquid magazines contained a rear projection screen on which could be projected slides, for example, one reading "I want a drink."

Closed circuit television allowed observation of each subject's behavior from the adjoining control room. Standard 6-foot relay racks contained electromechanical and solid-state control components which automatically scheduled experimental events and recorded the data on cumulative recorders and counters.

Figure 2.   Photograph of the operant conditioning console, 31 inches wide × 32 inches high, of plywood with the face angled 15 degrees from vertical. Manipulanda (lower left and right) were Lindsley plungers. Stimulus lights were 25 watt white (just above each plunger) and red (just above each magazine). Beverages were dispensed into a 1-ounce shot glass placed in either 6 inch square cutout magazine. Slides illuminated from the rear could be presented on the screen above and between the magazines.

Shock sources were commercially available units (Grason-Stadler 6070B) which remotely delivered constant current shock over a wide range of available intensities (0 to 40 milliamps) to two electrodes mounted on the subject's arm. The shock sources were carefully grounded and isolated to protect the patient from other than preset output. The electrodes (Nu-Way snaps) were attached to an elastic armband and mounted over a light coat of electrode paste (Sanborn Redux) on a cleaned portion of the ventral forearm about 2 inches below the elbow of the nonpreferred (usually left) hand.

EXPERIMENT I

Twenty-two male and one female veterans volunteered for the first study. The patients were all selected according to the criteria listed in the assessment section. Of the initial 23 subjects, 13 completed treatment (a dropout rate of 43 percent). The patients who completed treatment, 12 male and 1 female, had a mean age of 46 years (range, 31 to 62), reported chronic alcoholic drinking for a mean of 11.3 years (range, 5 to 25), which had led to a mean of 3.8 hospitalizations. The patients reported drinking a mean of 29.5 ounces of liquor per day for most of the previous three years (one reported 75 ounces of beer per day), over which they reported abstinent periods of 1 to 3 months duration. All but one of the patients had attended up to 100 meetings of Alcoholics Anonymous. Of the 13 subjects, 2 were employed at the time of current hospital admission.

Following intake evaluation, selection, and informed consent, each patient was ushered into the acoustical chamber and seated before the console; shock electrodes were mounted and the patient was instructed that he would receive a series of short shocks (0.5 seconds duration). The patient was administered a series of increasing intensities of shock at the outset of the first five sessions. He was told to react by raising his hand when he first felt shock and when it was as much as he could take. Both thresholds were recorded.

The patient was next instructed that pulling the plunger (only the right one was available) a certain number of times would produce a small shot of his favorite beverage. The procedure was demonstrated (the schedule of reinforcement was FR30, which required 30 plunger pulls per reinforcement), and the patient was allowed to drink the delivered beverage. The patient was then instructed that he could begin when signaled and work at his own rate until told to stop. The latter portion of these instructions was repeated to the patient at the outset of each remaining session. Half-hour sessions were scheduled twice each weekday per patient.

During the first, or baseline phase of the study, each patient was allowed to continue responding on the FR30 schedule until response rate stabilized. Stability was defined as consistent responding throughout each session with no long postreinforcement pauses and less than 10 percent variability in overall response rate for five consecutive sessions.

Once stability was obtained, treatment was initiated. Attainment of stability allowed precise analysis of treatment effects, since gross variability as well as increasing and decreasing trends were eliminated. Treatment consisted of delivery of electric shock of 0.5 seconds duration contingent on each reinforced (or thirtieth) response. Electric shock was introduced at an intensity at or slightly below the subject's lower threshold and increased logarithmically. The intensity was increased following each session unless a change in response rate of more than 10 percent occurred, in which case the same intensity was delivered for two consecutive sessions. The intensity was increased until each subject showed complete behavioral suppression through two consecutive sessions. Behavioral suppression was defined as cessation of responding or less than enough responses to produce the first reinforcement. Following behavioral suppression, shock electrodes were removed for two consecutive sessions in order to evaluate the immediate, intraexperimental effects of treatment. This phase consisted of a return to the baseline condition, with the absence of shock clearly indicated by the removal of electrodes. If a subject responded enough to produce reinforcement in the first 15 minutes of either of these sessions, shock electrodes were remounted and shock of suppressive intensity was delivered as in previous treatment during the last 15 minutes. Discharge was recommended if the patient stopped responding under these conditions, providing that the patient had a home and job to return to.

Before discharge, each patient was assigned to return to the hospital for follow-up visits 1, 2, 4, 8, 12, 24, 52, and 104 weeks following the termination of treatment. A follow-up visit schedule indicating each of the dates was given to each patient as a reminder. On each return visit, the patient was interviewed regarding his drinking (if any) since treatment and his marital, social, and occupational status. These reports were corroborated whenever possible by an objective reporter such as a spouse, friend, or employer.

In addition, another session in the chamber, like the final baseline (Generalization Test) sessions, was conducted at each follow-up visit. Each patient was escorted into one of the chambers and allowed once again to respond at his own rate for alcohol reinforcement if he chose. This allowed a further estimate of the patient's current probability of drinking. As in the Generalization sessions, if the patient delivered alcohol to himself in the first 15 minutes, shock electrodes were attached and shock was delivered during the last 15 minutes.

Results and Discussion. Of the 23 patients who volunteered for treatment, 13 completed the program in a mean of 40.5 sessions (range, 28 to 65); those who dropped out did so after a mean of 14 sessions (range, 1 to 41). A larger proportion of these dropouts had also been unemployed for longer periods (mean, 15.5 months) than completers (10 months).

The remainder of the results concerns only those 13 patients who completed the program. Clinical follow-up, completed two years after treatment, revealed that 5 (38 percent) of the completers reported abstinence from all alcohol with rare exceptions. Three of these patients maintained abstinence—corroborated by outside sources—for the entire period, while two patients remained abstinent for 7 and 13 months, then drank for periods of a week, after which they returned and requested retreatment. Following retreatment, one of these patients returned to abstinence, whereas the other drank in three binges of 2 to 5 days.

Three (23 percent) of the patients completing treatment showed changes in patterns of drinking, drinking beer or mixed drinks, but at low, apparently controlled rates. One of these patients remained abstinent for 5 months after treatment, then began drinking beer (up to 72 ounces per day) periodically, when he became depressed. Another showed periods of abstinence alternating with moderate, subintoxicating rates until he left the state 14 months after treatment and has not been contacted since. The third showed periods of sobriety, some of which were spent in the hospital for treatment of nonalcoholic problems, alternating with periods of moderate drinking. After 7 months he was apprehended for stealing federal property and jailed, and he later committed suicide.

Three (23 percent) more patients continued to drink in binges or sprees that still represent reduction from their pretreatment rates. These patients, who were high daily rate drinkers before treatment, drank an average of two to six binges of 1 to 5 days duration per year. Although this represents some improvement, their periodic drinking still presents problems.

No follow-up information is available on two patients who could not be contacted following treatment. Eight of the patients report maintaining gainful employment during most of the follow-up period, five full-time and three part-time.

Individual response to treatment fell into four modes, each of which will be reported and represented by an individual behavioral profile. Each of these behavioral profiles depicts an individual subject's rate of manipulating the plunger on the operant console under baseline, treatment, and generalization conditions.

The first group of four subjects all responded with high base rates (132 to 195 responses per minute), a moderate amount of variability between sessions, increases above the base rate during treatment sessions 1 to 29, and sudden reduction to suppression or cessation. The first graph (Figure 3) illustrates a typical patient's response to treatment. This patient, a 42-year-old printer, had drunk approximately 28 ounces of rum or bourbon per day for most of the previous 10 years, had been hospitalized five times previously for alcoholism, and had attended Alcoholics Anonymous. This subject responded at an operant rate of 131 responses per minute, increased above this rate over eight sessions, with great variability, suppressed to zero six sessions later at 40 milliamps, and did not respond in Generalization, when the electrodes were removed. This was typical of the other three subjects, only one of whom responded in Generalization. This subject reported taking six drinks two months after treatment, getting sick, and then maintaining abstinence for most of the following two years.

Five subjects in the second group stabilized at intermediate base rates (80 to 125 responses per minute), responded to treatment with less variability, showed no increases beyond base rates, and gradually decreased to the point of total suppression. Figure 4 is a typical behavioral profile, in this case of a 55-year-old male copyreader who had drunk 26 to 32 ounces of Scotch per day for 11 months of the year for the previous 10 years. He responded for Scotch at a base rate of 86 responses per minute, showed little or no increase, and regular suppression beyond 0.2 milliamps, until cessation occurred at 6 milliamps. In the first Generalization Test session, this subject emitted 125 responses but did not drink, thus the rate was recorded as zero. Neither this subject nor any other in this group made any other responses in Generalization.

Near the end of treatment, this subject reported feeling nauseous and sometimes vomiting following treatment sessions. Two weeks after treatment, he reported drinking two Scotches, but said they did not taste good and he did not drink again after that. Since he worked in the V A Hospital daily for one year following discharge, it was easy to corroborate his reports. During most of the second year he was a patient, due to double leg amputation.

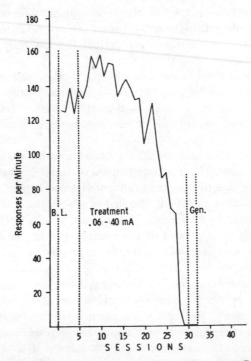

Figure 3.   Behavioral profile of response to treatment of subject from Group 1, Experiment 1. Graph depicts rate of plunger pulling per half-hour session over 5 baseline, 25 treatment, and 2 generalization sessions. Reinforcement (2 cubic centimeters 100 proof bourbon diluted 50 percent with water) was delivered on FR30 schedule. During treatment, each reinforced (thirtieth) response produced a 0.5-second shock which increased in log steps from 0.06 to 40 milliamps. Mean base rate was 131 responses per minute. Note later increases and systematic decline. No responses occurred in generalization.

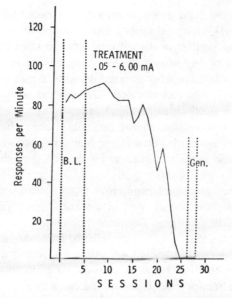

Figure 4. Graph of response to treatment of subject from Group 2, Experiment 1. Rate of plunger pulling over 5 baseline, 20 treatment and 2 generalization sessions are depicted. Each reinforced (thirtieth) response produced a 0.5-second shock of 0.05 to 6 milliamp intensity, followed by 2 cubic centimeters 80 proof Scotch diluted 50 percent with water. Mean base rate was 86 responses per minute, followed by little or no increase and gradual suppression. Some responses, but no reinforcements, occurred in generalization (see text).

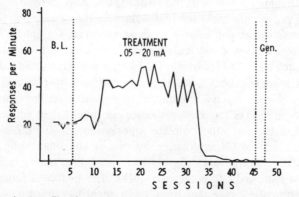

Figure 5. Behavioral profile of response rate during treatment of subject from Group 3, Experiment 1. Reinforcement (2 cubic centimeters 100 proof bourbon diluted 50 percent with water) followed each thirtieth response, which also produced a 0.5-second shock of 0.05 to 20 milliamp intensity during 40 sessions of treatment. Mean base rate was 20 responses per minute, followed by increases to 53 responses per minute in session 23 at 2 milliamps, then sharp suppression and cessation at 20 milliamps. No responses occurred in generalization.

175

Two subjects in the third group responded at lower base rates (18 and 47 responses per minute), followed by precipitous drops to suppression or cessation. The behavioral profile for the subject with the lowest initial rate (18 responses per minute) of any subject in this study is seen in Figure 5. This patient was a 47-year-old male who reported drinking a pint or more of bourbon per day for five years, who had attended AA, and had been hospitalized previously three times for alcoholism. As shock intensity increased, this patient's response rate rose to the greatest relative facilitation above base rates (over 250 percent) observed in this study, then fell at 6 and stopped at 20 milliamps. No responses were made in Generalization by this or the other subject in this group.

Figure 6 presents segments of cumulative records made during this patient's treatment. Responses stepped the pen in a vertical direction, whereas pauses were recorded as horizontal lines. Diagonal hatch marks indicate reinforcement deliveries. The numbered segments were selected from various sessions (see figure legend). Note how this technique enables a fine-grain analysis of the patient's moment-by-moment behavior in response to treatment. For example, the duration of postreinforcement pauses indicates that the primary effect of treatment in this patient was to lengthen such pauses rather than decrease the rate between reinforcements, which remained relatively constant following segment 2.

This patient had a few short binges within 6 months following treatment, but he was apprehended robbing a VA display case, a federal offense, for which he was jailed. He later committed suicide in prison.

The two remaining subjects in the fourth group also showed low base rates (36 responses per minute each) but less variability than group 3 and no facilitation. Response to treatment of one of these subjects is graphed in Figure 7. This patient was a 50-year-old male veteran who had been drinking 16 to 28 ounces of Scotch each day for most of a 10-year period, had attended approximately 100 Alcoholics Anonymous meetings, had been hospitalized seven times for drinking problems, and had contracted emphysema. As the figure indicates, this patient began responding at 36 responses per minute then gradually decelerated, somewhat variably, to complete suppression at 40 milliamps. No responses were made in Generalization by this or the other subject, who responded similarly, though with slightly less variability, during treatment. The follow-up data indicated one binge two weeks after treatment followed by five months of abstinence. Since that time, this patient has drunk in binges about three times per year. Operant responses during a binge have ranged from 30 to 160 responses per minute.

These data support the effectiveness of this aversive conditioning paradigm in the modification of rates of alcoholic drinking. Each of the patients in this study showed extensive modification of his operant rates of response to produce

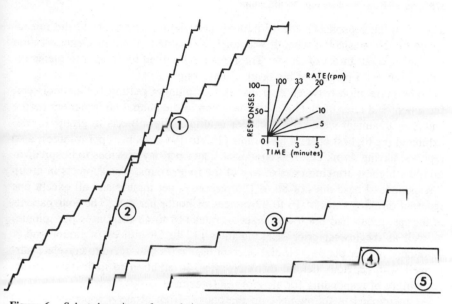

Figure 6. Selected portions of cumulative records from the same subject's last baseline session (20 responses per minute, no shock, segment 1), session 23 (53 responses per minute at 2 milliamps, segment 2), session 33 (7 responses per minute at 6 milliamps, segment 3), session 36 (3 responses per minute at 10 milliamps, segment 4) and cessation in session 45. Responses moved the recording pen upward, downward hatch marks indicate reinforcement, and horizontal portions indicate pauses. Note that the main effect of treatment was to increase the length of these pauses.

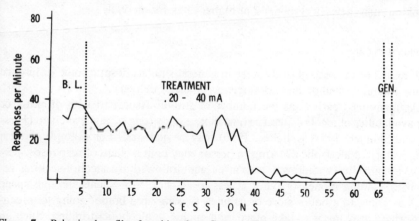

Figure 7. Behavioral profile of a subject from Group 4, Experiment 1, who responded to produce 2 cubic centimeters 100 proof Scotch diluted 50 percent with water. During treatment each reinforced response also produced a 0.20 to 40 milliamp shock of 0.05 second duration. Mean base rate was 36 responses per minute. Most rapid deceleration occurred in session 38 at 13 milliamps. Note low base rate, gradual suppression, and variability.

177

alcohol in the console. Of the 13 patients completing treatment, 12 did not respond to deliver alcohol when it was made available to them in Generalization sessions without threat of shock. The remaining patient responded in Generalization, but at 25 percent of his original base rate.

Some correlation between operant rates of plunger pulling for alcohol reinforcement and rates of alcoholic consumption in the natural environment before and after treatment were observed. For example, the subjects in group 1, who exhibited the highest operant base rates (132 to 195 responses per minute), also reported having drunk 28 to 64 ounces of liquor per day previous to hospitalization, the highest drinking rates of any of the four groups. The subjects in group 2 responded at base rates of 80 to 125 responses per minute and all except one reported drinking rates of 16 to 32 ounces of liquor per day. The four patients in the last group had the lowest operant rates (18 to 48 responses per minute) as well as the lowest prior drinking rates (12 to 28 ounces of liquor and/or 72 ounces of beer per day). Initial operant base rates thus seem to correlate fairly well with previous natural drinking rates, in addition to indicating current probability of responding for alcohol reinforcement.

As mentioned in follow-up with the patient from group 4, operant rates of plunger pulling during posttreatment periods also correlated well with drinking following treatment. For example, most of the patients who reported corroborated abstinent periods did not respond to produce alcohol on follow-up visits, frequently pushing away from the console, sometimes turning away from it or reading a magazine. The patients who reported moderate drinking occasionally showed low rates of response on the console; patients who had been recently drinking more heavily responded at higher rates for alcohol.

EXPERIMENT II

The results of the second study were in general similar, despite some difference in the training schedule and contingency of shock delivery.

As mentioned earlier, as the number of stimuli associated with drinking or the availability of alcohol increases, an increasingly long behavioral chain (Ferster and Skinner, 1957; Kelleher, 1966) may be acquired. For example, after a long history of alcoholic drinking, a person may emit a chain of responses, perhaps initiated by withdrawal responses and followed by alcohol-seeking responses, finding money or other access to alcohol, movements through space such as going to a liquor store or cabinet, picking up a bottle, going to a location where drinking is to take place, and ending in alcoholic drinking. Such an entire chain is assumed to be under the control of alcohol reinforcement, but it may be complicated by delayed aversive consequences such as slurring of speech, loss of coordination, vertigo, blackout, nausea, hangover, and delirium tremens. Such ultimate aversive consequences (Ferster et al., 1962), which might suppress drinking should they immediately follow drinking responses, may be delayed too long to have much effect on them (Vogel-Sprott and Banks, 1965). If strong aversive events were to occur immediately following early responses in the alcoholic chain, early suppression of the behavior might occur. If, for example, the early responses in the chain could be more easily suppressed than those more temporally proximate to reinforcement, the latter might also be suppressed or eliminated. This was the rationale of this study, which sought, like the first study, to compare punishment of an early response in the alcohol-maintained chain with punishment of the reinforced response.

Twenty chronic alcoholic patients volunteered to participate in this study and were selected according to the criteria reviewed earlier. These patients were similar in most respects to the first group treated. They ranged from 24 to 62 in age (mean, 45), reported chronic alcoholic problems for 3 to 41 years, had previously attended 0 to 288 Alcoholics Anonymous meetings, had been exposed to an average of four other treatment programs for alcoholism, and had been hospitalized an average of six previous times for alcoholism. The patients reported drinking an average of 32.9 ounces of liquor or 138 ounces of beer per day (10 patients) or in binges averaging 7 days duration every 70 days (10 patients). Fourteen of the subjects had not been employed for an average of 42 days, and the remaining 6 had maintained full-time employment.

Following intake, evaluation, informed consent, and selection, each subject was scheduled as before for two half-hour sessions each weekday. In the first session, the patient was ushered into one of the acoustical chambers, was seated, and shock electrodes were mounted. Upper and lower shock thresholds were taken, using the same procedure as in Experiment I.

After shock thresholds were recorded, the patient was instructed in the rest of the procedure. The subject was told that one response on the left plunger in the presence of the left white light followed by a number of responses on the right plunger signaled by the right white light would deliver a small shot of his favorite beverage. The first response on the left plunger also illuminated a slide reading "I want a drink" on the screen for 1 second. The procedure was demonstrated and the patient was allowed to drink the liquid. The patient was then told that he could begin and work at his own rate until asked to stop. The latter portion of the instructions was delivered at the outset of each session thereafter.

The first or baseline phase was conducted as in Experiment I. The reinforcement schedule remained as described until the subject's response rate stabilized. Stability was again defined as consistent responding throughout each of five consecutive sessions with no long postreinforcement pauses and less than 10 percent variability in overall response rates.

Once stability was obtained, treatment consisting of 0.50 seconds duration shock contingent on the first (left plunger) response in the chain was initiated.

Again, the intensity of the shock was initially at or below the subject's lower threshold and increased in logarithmic steps thereafter until the subject stopped responding. That is, shock contingent on the first (rather than the last, as in Experiment I) operant response in the chain of alcohol-reinforced behaviors was introduced at subthreshold levels, then increased logarithmically until the subject stopped responding for two consecutive sessions.

To determine whether the effects of treatment might generalize to the same environment in the absence of shock, the electrodes were removed for the last two sessions. If, in the first 15 minutes of either session, the subject responded enough to produce reinforcement, the experimenter entered the chamber and put the electrodes back on, and shock was again delivered at suppressive intensity for the remaining 15 minutes. As before, the Generalization Test sessions represent a return to the baseline condition, conducted as a test of the intraexperimental effects of the treatment procedure.

As before, discharge from the hospital was recommended as soon after the completion of treatment as living accommodations and vocational arrangements had been made. A follow-up visit schedule card was again given to each patient, with instructions to return to the hospital 1, 2, 4, 8, 12, 24, 52, and 104 weeks following treatment termination. The procedure on each follow-up visit was the same as in the Generalization Test sessions. That is, each patient was again ushered into the acoustical chamber and allowed to respond for alcohol without threat of shock for 15 minutes, after which electrodes were remounted and shock was delivered if responding occurred. Structured interviews and questionnaires again provided information on amount and kind of drinking and occupational, marital, and social adjustment in the home environment.

Results and Discussion. At the termination of treatment, 5 of the original 20 patients had left the hospital against medical advice (a dropout rate of 25 percent, as opposed to 43 percent in Experiment I). These differences may be due primarily to the launching of a behaviorally oriented psychiatric ward on which five beds were set aside for the alcoholic treatment program.

Follow-up data are not yet complete for the subjects in this experiment, but they can be reported over a 6- to 18-month period. Of the 15 patients who completed treatment, 5 (33 percent) have remained abstinent of all alcoholic beverages, according to their own report, their operant performance, and objective reports. These patients have also most frequently reported maintaining gainful employment.

Three (20 percent) of the subjects have reduced their rate of alcoholic consumption to low and apparently controlled levels. Two of these subjects have switched from liquor to beer, which they now drink at the rate of one to three bottles per day.

Five (33 percent) of the subjects have drunk in at least one binge, often responding on the operant console during a binge but not during sober periods. One of these patients drank after treatment in three short binges, once when his mother stopped living with him and moved to New York, and twice later when he was turned down for jobs for which he had applied. He has been employed and abstinent for 8 months since.

Little or no information was available on three (20 percent) of the subjects.

Changes in operant rate during treatment were similar to those in Experiment I. During the baseline phase, individual subjects responded at stability with means ranging from 25 to 173 responses per minute, which earned them an average of 1.5 ounces of liquor per session.

Again, there were four characteristic modes of response to treatment. Six subjects responded with high initial base rates (90 to 110 responses per minute), pronounced variability, consistent increases in rate prior to suppression, which was usually abrupt. Representative of this group is the behavioral profile in Figure 8, of a 46-year-old male veteran who reported having drunk 28 ounces of vodka plus 12 to 64 ounces of beer per day whenever he could afford it over the previous 13 years, for which he had been hospitalized three times and attended Alcoholics Anonymous. This subject responded for vodka at a base rate of 91 responses per minute, showed variability thereafter, increases over 20 sessions, followed by abrupt suppression at 10 and cessation at 13 milliamps. This subject did not respond during Generalization, nor did any of the other subjects in this group.

After treatment, this patient showed controlled, low-rate beer drinking (up to 32 ounces per day) and occasional vodka binges usually lasting about three days for the first year, after which he returned to the hospital and requested retreatment.

The second group, represented by Figure 9, began at intermediate base rates (45 to 60 responses per minute), showed less variable rates during treatment, regular increases, and abrupt suppression. The four subjects in this group finished treatment in fewer sessions (mean, 27) and at lower shock intensities (mean 10.5 milliamps) than average. The subject whose profile is seen in Figure 9 was a 56-year-old male former copywriter who had drunk 32 ounces of whiskey per day in binges of 7 to 14 days duration two to four times per year for 25 years, had been hospitalized nine times for alcoholism, and attended Alcoholics Anonymous meetings nine times. This patient began responding at a mean base rate of 53 responses per minute, then accelerated beyond this rate for eight treatment sessions, finally decelerating precipitously at 13 milliamps. This subject, like the other three in this group, made no responses in Generalization.

In clinical follow-up over a one-year period, this patient drank in one heavy binge lasting eight days after being rejected from a monastery in New Mexico. The patient got a job as a desk clerk at a local hotel after this binge. He held this job for most of a year and recently married a teetotaler. He has been abstinent of all alcoholic beverages for one year since his binge.

Figure 10 demonstrates that the same pattern was also characteristic of his drinking behavior during treatment. The selected cumulative records are samples taken from sessions during baseline, treatment, and first suppression in session 16. As these cumulative records clearly demonstrate, and Figure 9 suggested, this patient either responded at a high response rate to produce whiskey or tended not to respond at all.

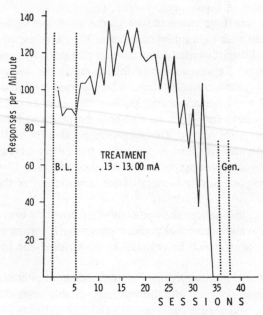

Figure 8.   Profile of response to treatment of a subject from Group 1, Experiment 2, in which reinforcement was delivered on Chain FR1 FR30 (one response on the left plunger followed by 30 on the right produced 2 cubic centimeters 80 proof vodka diluted 50 percent with water for this subject). Shock of 0.13 to 13 milliamps was delivered following the first (left plunger) response. Base rate averaged 90 responses per minute, followed by increases and abrupt suppression at 10 and 13 milliamps. No responding was observed in generalization.

Two subjects responded at low initial base rates (24 and 66 responses per minute), accelerated to high rates during treatment, then rapidly decelerated and stopped responding after 41 and 39 sessions, respectively. Figure 11 summarizes the treatment data for one subject, a 46-year-old male veteran who had drunk up to 28 ounces of gin per day or gin plus beer in binges for 28 years, had been hospitalized four times, attended Alcoholics Anonymous, and had been arrested many times. This subject began at a base rate of 24 responses

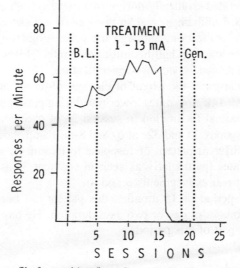

Figure 9. Treatment profile for a subject from Group 2, Experiment 2. This patient responded for dilute bourbon at a mean base rate of 52 responses per minute, then increased in rate from 3 to 13 milliamp intensity, after which rapid suppression occurred. No responses occurred in generalization.

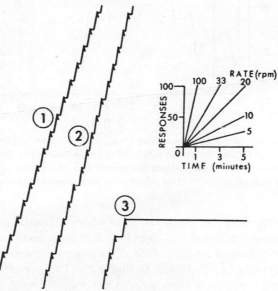

Figure 10. Portions of cumulative records from baseline, treatment, and suppression phases of the same subject. Segment 1 shows representative baseline responding (49 responses per minute, no shock), segment 2 shows increases to 65 responses per minute at 10 milliamps, and segment 3 is from session 16 (4 responses per minute at 13 milliamps shock), pattern of responding at high rate or not at all.

183

per minute, accelerated erratically during treatment as high as 55 responses per minute, slowed at 5 milliamps, and stopped at 16 milliamps. This subject did not respond in Generalization, although the other subject in this group did respond, but at a rate less than half his initial base rate. This was the only subject in this study who responded during Generalization.

Figure 12 demonstrates the extent of changes observed during this patient's treatment. Segment 1 demonstrates lower rate during pretreatment baseline, segment 2 shows maximal facilitation in session 25 of treatment, and segments 3 and 4 are from sessions 29 and 32, at 6- and 8-milliamp shock intensity. These records show a different pattern of response to treatment, which involved reduced response rates (particularly as seen in segment 3) as well as increased postreinforcement pauses (segments 3 and 4).

In a follow-up period of 15 months, this patient has been abstinent except for five reported binges of one or two days duration. He has held a job as night watchman during part of this period.

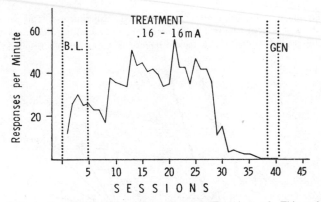

Figure 11. Behavioral profile for subject from Group 3, Experiment 2. This patient responded to produce 80 proof gin diluted 50 percent with water at a mean base rate of 24 responses per minute. Shock of 0.16 to 16 milliamps produced acceleration over 20 sessions, suppression at 5 milliamps and cessation at 16 milliamps. This subject made no responses in generalization.

In the last group were three subjects, all of whom responded at low base rates (18 to 63 responses per minute), showed little variability and slowly accelerated suppression, with little or no facilitation. This group is represented by the subject whose behavioral profile is seen in Figure 13. This patient was a 56-year-old male diabetic former jazz drummer who had drunk 12 to 16 ounces of bourbon per day for most of 41 years, for which he had been hospitalized seven times and had attended Alcoholics Anonymous. This subject responded at 18 responses per minute base rate, showed no acceleration, and stopped responding at 13 milliamps, after 30 sessions.

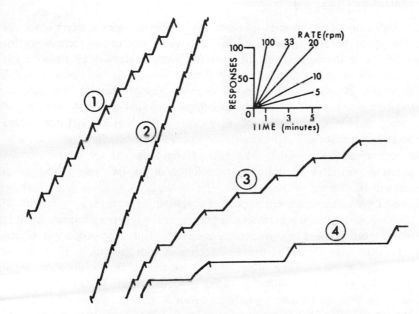

Figure 12. Segments of cumulative records from representative baseline and treatment sessions for the same subject. Segment 1 shows 26 responses per minute in the last baseline session, segment 2 shows 47 responses per minute at 2.5 milliamps in session 25, segment 3 shows suppression to 11 responses per minute at 6 milliamps in session 29, and segment 4 shows 4 responses per minute at 8 milliamps shock intensity. Note declining rate between reinforcements, in addition to postreinforcement pauses.

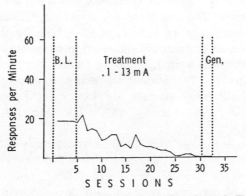

Figure 13. Treatment profile of a subject from Group 4, Experiment 2. This subject responded to produce bourbon at a rate of 19 responses per minute during baseline, showed no acceleration and gradual suppression to cessation at 13 milliamps. No responding was observed in generalization.

In a follow-up period over 11 months, this patient has been entirely abstinent of all alcoholic beverages. He lived in a halfway house in the community for some time after discharge from the hospital. During his stay he found a job as a cook, which he has retained on a full-time basis.

The results of Experiments I and II were surprisingly similar. The proportions falling into each of the follow-up categories found abstinent, drinking at low rates, and binge drinking were all within limits close enough not to lead one to expect statistically significant differences. Thus both programs seem to have been clinically effective, but not differentially so. Of course precise comparisons will have to await the completion of the two-year follow-up in Experiment II.

Some of the within-treatment data have suggested advantages for Experiment II. The dropout rate during treatment has decreased, suggesting improvement in either the intratreatment or extratreatment environment. The proportion of patients responding in Generalization has decreased with this study, suggesting a slight advantage in generalizability beyond treatment. In addition, treatment seems to have been accomplished in fewer sessions (mean, 38.4) than previous treatment models, which have sometimes taken 50 to 60 sessions. The patients may also have reached the end of treatment at lower shock intensities (mean, 23 milliamps) than in previous studies, which suggests increased effectiveness. Further analysis and comparison with initial thresholds is under way.

Further variations on this chain schedule are being investigated in the hope of developing even more effective treatment techniques.

EXPERIMENT III

Several variations on these aversive conditioning techniques have been or are being designed, but two remaining techniques which did not use electric shock will now be described. The first of these is covert sensitization (Cautela, 1966, 1970). This is a punishment procedure, in which both the response to be punished and the aversive stimulus are presented in imagination. For example, a patient may be instructed to imagine taking a drink, but then getting nauseous and vomiting afterward. This is done repeatedly, sometimes producing actual nausea and vomiting. Some efficacy has been reported (Anant, 1967, 1968; Ashem and Donner, 1968; Cautela, 1970), but controlled clinical trials are lacking.

Six patients ranging in age from 29 to 51 were treated with covert sensitization. They were similar to other treated groups in that they had suffered chronic alcoholic problems for 7 to 28 years, drunk 16 to 52 ounces of liquor and/or 96 to 288 ounces of beer per day either daily or in frequent binges, had been hospitalized up to 10 previous times (except for one patient), and had suffered blackouts, shakes, seizures, and/or delirium tremens.

Each patient was treated in a half-hour session each weekday, which was followed by a half-hour assessment session in which the patient had free access to alcohol delivered as reinforcement on an FR30 schedule. During the first few treatment sessions, each patient was given a general orientation to covert sensitization in which they were told, for example, that aversive consequences of their drinking had probably occurred and may have led up to their hospitalization, but may not have been effective in controlling their previous drinking habits, due to the delay between drinking (especially the first few drinks) and these consequences. It was suggested that if these aversive consequences had more closely followed after their drinking, they might not have drunk as much, if they drank at all. The goal of therapy was described as reducing or eliminating their drinking behavior by making the immediate consequences of drinking aversive (at least in fantasy). They were told that the technique had been found effective with some other patients, but it was still in the experimental stage.

Each patient was also asked to describe his typical drinking pattern from the time he got the first urge to drink to swallowing the first drink. The patient was informed that he would later be instructed to imagine engaging in the steps leading up to and including taking a drink. The importance of providing specific details was emphasized so that the scenes could be as realistic as possible.

After a thorough description of the chain (or chains) of drinking behaviors was obtained, the patient was asked to describe any unpleasant things that had happened to him as a result of drinking. The patient was told that this information would also be used in treatment.

In the first or second session, each patient was trained in a brief variant of Jacobson's (1938) deep muscle relaxation procedure. Each subject was instructed to practice the technique on his own at least once or twice a day for the next few days and to report on his progress.

The third session and each session thereafter began with relaxation induction. After the patient was relaxed, he was asked to imagine as vividly as possible the scenes gathered from his own report. At various times the patient was instructed to describe his fantasies to the therapist in order to check or probe the degree of detail and involvement of the patient in the scenes.

During covert sensitization, subjects were instructed to imagine the drinking scenes they had earlier described, after which they were instructed to imagine aversive consequences which their own drinking had produced, or which they stated would be disturbing or upsetting to them. Items varied greatly but typical aversive scenes included descriptions of nausea and vomiting, financial crises, being fired from a job, suffering a heart attack or other physical symptoms, being rejected socially or by a family member for drunkenness, getting arrested, or having an auto accident. An attempt was made to make the aversive stimulus appropriate to the drinking sequence; for example, accident scenes might follow drinking while driving, being fired followed drinking while on the job. Thus the natural consequences of drinking were utilized when possible.

The basic design of the experiment was an ABAB format, with drinking scenes presented alone in the control (A) condition and drinking scenes paired with aversive scenes in the treatment (B) phase. A minimum of four sessions was devoted to each condition, with the exception that if the treatment condition was introduced and no reduction or maintained low rate was produced, another technique would be introduced. This was done with two cases, who showed little or no reduction in operant rates after eight treatment sessions, after which electric shock was introduced. Shock was introduced and increased gradually, much as in Experiment I, until each subject stopped responding.

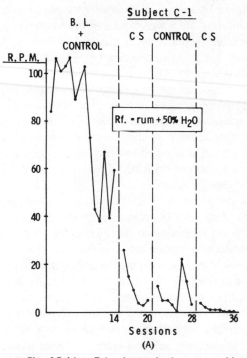

Figure 14.   Treatment profile of Subject C-1, who received covert sensitization in Experiment 3. The profile illustrates rate of responding to produce dilute rum on an FR30 schedule through two control and two treatment conditions (see text).

Figures 14 to 16 are behavioral profiles of three of the patients who showed favorable response to this form of treatment. The profile in Figure 14 is from the youngest of this group, a 29-year-old male veteran who had drunk 28 ounces of rum and/or vodka per day for most of 7 years, which led to delirium tremens and two previous hospitalizations. This patient began responding for rum at a high base rate (85 to 105 responses per minute), but he then fell to 40 to 60 responses while drinking scenes were being presented. During treatment his rate fell to less than 5 responses per minute, showed slight recovery following removal of the aversive scenes, and fell to zero during the second phase of treatment. Following treatment, this patient drank 26 ounces of rum after a family dispute and while driving hit a car, which led to his being jailed. He currently resides in jail, one month posttreatment.

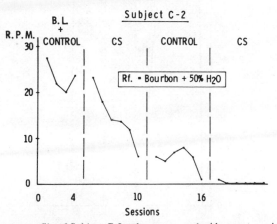

Figure 15.   Treatment profile of Subject C-2, who was treated with covert sensitization in Experiment 3. The graph plots response rate under FR30 reinforcement with dilute bourbon through two control and two treatment conditions.

The second profile (Figure 15) is from a 51-year-old male veteran who had drunk 16 to 28 ounces of bourbon and/or up to 288 ounces of beer per day for most of 15 years. This led to eight hospitalizations, frequent blackouts, seizures, and a later diagnosis of epilepsy. As indicated in the figure, this patient responded at low rates, never exceeding 30 responses per minute. His maintained downward trend throughout treatment and most of the control conditions was accompanied by verbal statements that he had vowed never to drink again. Following discharge, he remained abstinent for one month while working in the voluntary service at the VA Hospital, but then stopped taking his prescribed dilantin, drank two beers, had four seizures, and was rehospitalized. He is again abstinent but still in the hospital three months after treatment.

The profile in Figure 16 is from a 50-year-old male veteran who had been a sports fishing boat captain, had been drinking 8 to 16 ounces of bourbon plus 96 to 144 ounces of beer 11 months out of the year for 10 years, which had led to six hospitalizations, frequent blackouts, and suspected fugue states. As the profile indicates, this patient did not respond at first, saying he did not feel like drinking, but he then accelerated to 30 responses per minute, showing decreases after that, particularly during paired covert sensitization. This patient

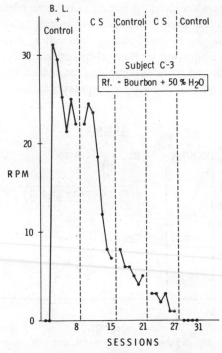

Figure 16.   Treatment profile of Subject C-3, also treated with covert sensitization in Experiment 3. This subject responded to produce dilute bourbon on FR30 through three control and two treatment conditions.

has reported abstinence from all alcoholic beverages for one month following treatment.

With these three patients, some question is raised regarding the therapeutic effectiveness of covert sensitization, since they all showed falling trends throughout control and treatment conditions.

As mentioned earlier, two other subjects did not show such trends during treatment and were later given aversive conditioning with electric shock, since covert sensitization did not noticeably affect their operant rates (and thus, it is hoped, their probability of drinking outside the hospital).

Three more subjects were accepted for treatment with covert sensitization, although two dropped out before completion. One of these showed accelerating rates during covert sensitization, whereas the other demonstrated little change. The third subject, who remained to complete treatment, announced at the outset that he would opt for one drink a day rather than the 26 to 52 ounces of Scotch per day he had been drinking, and he responded each day to produce one Scotch reinforcement, after which he stopped responding through the rest of each session. He maintained this pattern throughout control and treatment conditions, which also made it difficult to evaluate in favor of the treatment. In the two months since this patient completed treatment, he reports abstinence except for the last 15 days, on which he has had up to 3 ounces of Scotch, but no more.

Thus at this point it is very difficult to evaluate the effects of covert sensitization, at least on the sample treated so far. This form of treatment does not yet appear to be as effective as aversive conditioning with shock, although it may remain for a larger sample size and a longer follow-up period to make a fair comparison.

Even this procedure, however, may have been more effective than a nonaversive technique designed to change the preference of alcoholic patients from alcoholic to nonalcoholic beverages. In this paradigm, patients were first trained to make operant responses for either alcoholic or nonalcoholic (cola) reinforcement under stimulus control. That is, a light (S^D) indicated when either reinforcement would be forthcoming (contingent on responses on either side of the console). Once this had been accomplished, each subject was allowed free choice of alcohol or cola reinforcement. The choice wes perfectly predictable: each subject responded only for alcohol.

After the usual criterion of stability was obtained, the number of responses required per reinforcement was increased geometrically from one session to the next. That is, the number of responses required for each alcohol delivery was doubled between sessions. By the time the subject reached FR7,680, reinforcement was no longer available within a half-hour session, with the result that extinction was the procedure in effect.

It was assumed that, as has been observed in animals (Ferster and Skinner, 1957), lengthy exposure to this extinction schedule without available reinforcement would decrease the response rate, which might eventually cease. It was further assumed that a switch to the cola bar might follow behavioral extinction on the "booze" bar. However, despite 20 to 40 sessions of exposure to the extinction schedule, this did not occur. Finally, the (S^D) light on the alcohol side was extinguished, which led to every subject switching to the cola bar, where they then regularly responded with rare probing responses on the alcohol side.

To test whether there had been any lasting change in the probability of responding to produce alcohol, the following Generalization Test was programmed:

1. No S^D (light) or cola available for the first minute, cola available on FR30 for the remaining 29 minutes.

2. Ten alcohol reinforcements available on FR30, then the ratio requirement was doubled each succeeding reinforcement delivery through the first 10 minutes.

3. S^D, but no alcohol reinforcement was available through the second 10 minutes.

4. No S^D and no reinforcement for the remaining 10 minutes.

This procedure was followed in each of four sessions, after which the patient was discharged.

Each of the patients responded the same in these Generalization sessions. Each subject switched from the cola to the alcohol manipulandum very quickly, then responded without switching until the alcohol S^D went out.

On the basis of behaviors just described, which were observed during the treatment and Generalization phases of this experiment, large changes from pretreatment base rates of drinking could not be predicted and were not observed. Of the six subjects treated, four returned to heavy drinking sooner than had been observed in earlier aversive paradigms. Three of these subjects returned to the hospital requesting retreatment and reporting uncontrolled drinking within six months. Another subject was known to have resumed drinking at high rates. Only one subject continued drinking at low rate and the remaining one subject maintained abstinence for most of a year but then drank in a heavy binge resulting in sevcral blackouts.

Thus, by contrast, although this procedure took as long as aversive conditioning, it produced clearly different results, both within and following treatment. The kind of research design, then, in which one very effective treatment is compared to a much less productive treatment procedure, may be much more heuristic and provide more information to be used in further treatment development than the traditional control group design.

SUMMARY

Four treatment procedures in various stages of completion have been described and compared on the basis of the available data. It appears very clear that aversive conditioning techniques have been successful, on the basis of within-treatment as well as follow-up results. Most of the patients treated by these techniques showed little or no evidence of drinking to the point of intoxication. Moreover, 38 to 40 percent of the patients have maintained abstinence for periods up to two years. These results compare well to any of the published reports of treatment under controlled conditions (Lemere and Voegtlin, 1950; Lovibond and Caddy, 1970; Mills et al., 1971; Vogler et al., 1970).

The precision of the operant technology has been evident in providing a moment-to-moment analysis of behavioral response to treatment, a methodology that enables a precise comparison of pretreatment and posttreatment base rates of response for alcohol reinforcement, and the direct sampling of a pathological behavior to be modified. It is assumed that similar methodologies could be developed in the experimental analysis of many pathological behaviors.

As mentioned at several junctures, operant measurement of base rates of response for alcohol reinforcement has provided interesting and highly positive correlations with drinking in the natural environment. This corroborates and extends the suggestions and observations of previous studies (Mello and Mendelson, 1971, 1972; Nathan et al., 1971). In addition to showing correlations with previous drinking behavior outside the laboratory, the operant rate at which the subject responded for alcohol at the termination of treatment was a good predictor of later behavior following treatment. Most of those subjects who left treatment against medical advice while their operant rates were still high returned to drinking very soon in the natural environment, as did most of those who went through the nonaversive treatment model using concurrent cola and alcohol reinforcement and increasing the size of the FR. Those who finished shock aversive or covert sensitization treatments with their rates at or near zero, on the other hand, showed much longer maintained periods of abstinence or low-rate drinking.

These studies have also demonstrated the advantage in the use of a research design that allows one to focus on the behavior of individual subjects, as both clinicians and operant conditioners prefer to do, in addition to comparisons between experimental groups which were treated differentially. Without such a design, it might have been impossible to discover the individual behavioral profiles which identified differential patterns of response to treatment. Further analysis may reveal helpful relationships between these individual patterns of immediate response to treatment and long-range therapeutic effectiveness.

A great deal of progress has been made in the general area of assessment of alcoholic drinking and related behaviors. Within this program, a clear advantage has been demonstrated for the use of converging measures and operations. Thus, for example, self-reports from the patient as to historical rates of drinking, drinking pattern, and associated social, occupational, and marital behaviors were corroborated through objective sources, such as previous hospital records, reports of referral sources, and reports of family members or friends. Data on the questionnaires given at intake and during follow-up were corroborated in the same fashion. Studies are now under way to determine specific reliability and validity coefficients of questionnaire responses.

Perhaps a final note on the mutual contributions and interaction of animal and human, laboratory and clinical portions of the program would be helpful at this point. As indicated at the outset of this chapter, the goal of this program is the full-scale experimental analysis of alcoholic behavior, including the factors or variables responsible for its acquisition or etiology, its maintenance, and its modification or treatment. Because of ethical and other precautions, most of the etiological and maintenance work is done with animal subjects in the basic laboratory. This also has the advantage of increased experimental control, within the individual project as well as historically. That is, animal subjects raised in laboratory conditions have specifiable histories, a condition which rarely if ever pertains to human research.

The animal laboratory may also be conveniently employed to screen and develop new treatment techniques. Thus the historical antecedents of the first treatment models applied to human alcoholic patients in this program are to be found in animal research which was conducted earlier (Davidson, 1970a, 1970b). Some of the current research in this program on the positive reinforcing function of alcohol was reviewed. In addition, some of the implications and questions raised by the clinical research are now being put to the test in the animal laboratory, where increased precision and shorter, less expensive studies with smaller numbers of subjects may make the information available earlier. For example, studies are now being conducted to determine how permanent the effects of suppression by electrical shock of food-reinforced responses in pigeons are. This should help in the analysis of the long-lasting effects of shock on alcohol-maintained responses in patients.

Thus the continuous interaction and feedback loop from the basic to the applied laboratory may provide the most creative and productive method to expedite the experimental analysis of pathological behavior.

ACKNOWLEDGMENTS

Deepest thanks and gratitude are expressed to the technical staff, including Tom Sayles, Dan Doleys, Mike Messer, Eugene Crosier, Bob Bremser, and Dave Streeb, but especially to my wife, Joy, who helped create the time for writing the chapter.

REFERENCES

Anant, S. S. A note on the treatment of alcoholics by a verbal aversion technique. *The Canadian Psychologist*, 1967, **8**, 19–21.

Anant, S. S. Comment on "A follow-up of alcoholics treated by behavior therapy." *Behaviour Research and Therapy*, 1968, **6**, 133.

Ashem, B., and Donner, L. Covert sensitization with alcoholics: A controlled replication. *Behaviour Research and Therapy*, 1968, **6**, 7–12.

Azrin, N. H., and Holz, W. C. Punishment. In W. K. Honig (Ed.), *Operant Behavior: Areas of Research and Application*. New York: Appleton-Century-Crofts, 1966.

Bandura, A. *Principles of Behavior Modification*. New York: Holt, Rinehart and Winston, 1969.

Baum, M. Paradoxical effects of alcohol on the resistance to extinction of an avoidance response in rats. *Journal of Comparative and Physiological Psychology*, 1969, **69**, 238–249.

Baum, M. Effect of alcohol on the acquisition and resistance-to-extinction of avoidance responses in rats. *Psychological Reports*, 1970, **26**, 759–765.

Billet, S. L. Antabuse therapy. In R.J. Catanzaro (Ed.), *Alcoholism: The Total Treatment Approach*. Springfield, Ill.: Thomas, 1968.

Blake, B. G. The application of behavior therapy to the treatment of alcoholism. *Behaviour Research and Therapy*, 1965, **3**, 75–85.

Blake, B. G. A follow-up of alcoholics treated by behavior therapy. *Behaviour Research and Therapy*, 1967, **5**, 89–94.

Boe, E. E., and Church, R. M. Permanent effects of punishment during extinction. *Journal of Comparative and Physiological Psychology*, 1967, **63**, 486–492.

Bourne, P. G., Alford, J. A., and Bowcock, J. Z. Treatment of skid row alcoholics with disulfiram. *Quarterly Journal of Studies on Alcohol*, 1966, **27**, 42–48.

Boyle, T. J. Social effects. In W.C. Bier (Ed.), *Problems in Addiction. Alcohol and Drug Addiction*. New York: Fordham University Press, 1962.

Cautela, J. R. Treatment of compulsive behavior by covert sensitization. *Psychological Record*, 1966, **16**, 33–41.

Cautela, J. R. The treatment of alcoholism by covert sensitization. *Psychotherapy: Theory, Research and Practice*, 1970, **7**, 83–90.

Chen, C. S. A study of the alcohol-tolerance effect and an introduction of a new behavioral technique. *Psychopharmacologia*, 1968, **12**, 433–440.

Cicero, T. J., and Myers, R. D. Selection of a single ethanol test solution in free-choice studies with animals. *Quarterly Journal of Studies on Alcohol*, 1968, **29**, 446–448.

Cicero, T. J., Snider, S. R., Perez, V. J., and Swanson, L. W. Physical dependence on and tolerance to alcohol in the rat. *Physiology and Behavior*, 1971, **6**, 191–198.

Clark, R., and Polish, E. Avoidance conditioning and alcohol consumption in rhesus monkeys. *Science*, 1960, **132**, 223–224.

Cohen, M., Liebson, I. A., Faillace, L. A., and Allen, R. P. Moderate drinking by chronic alcoholics. *Journal of Nervous and Mental Disease*, 1971, **153**, 434–444.

Cohen, M., Liebson, I. A., Faillace, L. A. and Speers, W. Alcoholism: Controlled drinking and incentives for abstinence. *Psychological Reports*, 1971, **28**, 575–580.

Conger, J. J. The effects of alcohol on conflict behavior in the albino rat. *Quarterly Journal of Studies on Alcohol*, 1951, **12**, 1–29.

Conger, J. J. Alcoholism: Theory, problem and challenge. II. Reinforcement theory and the dynamics of alcoholism. *Quarterly Journal of Studies on Alcohol*, 1956, **17**, 296–305.

Cutter, H. S. G. Alcohol, drinking patterns, and the psychological probability of success. *Behavioral Science*, 1969, **14**, 19–27.

Cutter, H. S. G., Schwaab, E. L., and Nathan, P. E. Effects of alcohol on its utility for alcoholics and nonalcoholics. *Quarterly Journal of Studies on Alcohol*, 1970, **31**, 369–378.

Davidson, R. S. Research design and the aversive conditioning of alcoholic behavior. Paper presented to Southeastern Psychological Association, New Orleans, La., 1969.

Davidson, R. S. Conditioned reinforcing vs. punishing properties of electric shock. *Psychonomic Science*, 1970, **18**, 155–157.

Davidson, R. S. Conditioned punishment and conditioned negative reinforcement on a multiple schedule. *Psychonomic Science*, 1970, **20**, 163–165.

Davidson, R. S. An experimental analysis of pathological behavior. Unpublished manuscript, 1971.

Davidson, R. S. Modification of alcoholic behavior. *VA Newsletter for Research in Psychology*, 1972, **14**, 30–31. (a)

Davidson, R. S. Aversive modification of alcoholic behavior. I. Punishment of an alcohol-reinforced operant. Unpublished manuscript, 1972. (b)

Davidson, R. S. Aversive modification of alcoholic behavior. II. Punishment of an early component of a behavioral chain. Unpublished manuscript, 1972. (c)

Davidson, R. S., and Alvarez, A. Alcohol as a reinforcer for operant behavior in rats. Unpublished manuscript, 1972.

Davidson, R. S., and Greenwald, S. R. Comparison of completers and noncompleters of aversive conditioning for alcoholism. Unpublished manuscript, 1972.

Davidson, R. S., and Wallach, E. S. Shock facilitation and suppression of alcohol- and coke-maintained behavior. *Psychological Reports*, 1972, **31**, 415–424.

Davies, D. L. Normal drinking in recovered alcohol addicts. *Quarterly Journal of Studies on Alcohol*, 1962, **23**, 94–104.

Deneau, G. L., Yanagita, T., and Seevers, M. H. Self-administration of psychoactive substances by monkeys. *Psychopharmacology*, 1969, **16**, 30–48.

DeMorsier, G., and Feldmann, H. The biological treatment of chronic alcoholism with apomorphine. Study of 200 cases. *Schweizer Archiv fur Neurologie und Psychiatrie*, 1950, **65**, 472–473.

Ellis, F. W., and Pick, J. R. Experimentally induced ethanol dependence in rhesus monkeys. *Journal of Pharmacology and experimental Therapeutics*, 1970, **175**, 88–93.

Falk, J. L. Production of polydipsia in normal rats by an intermittent food schedule. *Science*, 1961, **133**, 195–196.

Falk, J. L. Studies on schedule-induced polydipsia. In M.J. Wayner (Ed.), *Thirst: First International Symposium on Thirst in the Regulation of Body Water*. New York: MacMillan, 1964.

Falk, J. L. The motivational properties of schedule-induced polydipsia. *Journal of the Experimental Analysis of Behavior*, 1966, **9**, 19–25.

Ferster, C. B. Reinforcement and punishment in the control of human behavior by social agencies. *Psychiatric Research Reports*, 1958, **10**, 101–118.

Ferster, C. B., Nurnberger, J. I., and Levitt, E. B. The control of eating. *Journal of Mathetics*, 1962, **1**, 87–109.

Ferster, C. B., and Skinner, B. F. *Schedules of Reinforcement*. New York: Appleton-Century-Crofts, 1957.

FitzGerald, F. L., Barfield, M. A., and Warrington, R. J. Voluntary alcohol consumption in chimpanzees and orangutans. *Quarterly Journal of Studies on Alcohol*, 1968, **29**, 330–336.

Franks, C. M. Alcohol, alcoholism and conditioning: A review of the literature and some theoretical considerations. *Journal of Mental Science*, 1958, **104**, 14–33.

Franks, C. M. Behavior therapy, the principles of conditioning and the treatment of the alcoholic. *Quarterly Journal of Studies on Alcohol*, **1963**, 511–529.

Franks, C. M. Conditioning and conditioned aversion therapies in the treatment of the alcoholic. *International Journal of the Addictions*, 1966, **1**, 61–98.

Franks, C. M. Behavior modification and the treatment of the alcoholic. In R. Fox (Ed.), *Alcoholism: Behavioral Research, Therapeutic Approaches*, New York: Springer, 1967.

Freed, E. X. Effect of alcohol on conflict behaviors. *Psychological Reports*, 1968, **23**, 151–159.

Freed, E. X. Metronidazole effect upon self-intoxication in the rat. *Physicians' Drug Manual*, 1969, **1**, 104–108.

Freed, E. X., Carpenter, J. A., and Hymowitz, N. Acquisition and extinction of schedule-induced polydipsic consumption of alcohol and water. *Psychological Reports*, 1970, **26**, 915–922.

Freed, E. X., and Lester, D. Schedule-induced consumption of ethanol: Calories or chemotherapy? *Physiology and Behavior*, 1970, **5**, 555–560.

Freund, G. Alcohol withdrawal syndrome in mice. *Archives of Neurology*, 1969, **21**, 315–320.

Freund, G. Impairment of shock avoidance learning after long-term alcohol ingestion in mice. *Science*, 1970, **168**, 1599–1601.

Gerard, D. L., Saenger, J., and Wile, R. The abstinent alcoholic. *Archives of General Psychiatry*, 1962, **6**, 83–95.

Goldberg, L. Quantitative studies on alcohol tolerance in man: The influence of ethyl alcohol on sensory, motor and psychological functions referred to blood alcohol in normal and habituated individuals. *Acta Physiologica Scandanavia*, 1943, **5**, Suppl. 16, 5–128.

Goodrick, C. L. Alcohol preference of the male Sprague-Dawley albino rat as a function of age. *Journal of Gerontology*, 1967, **22**, 369–371.

Hsu, J. J. Electroconditioning therapy of alcoholics: A preliminary report. *Quarterly Journal of Studies on Alcohol*, 1965, **26**, 449–459.

Honig, W. K. *Operant Behavior: Areas of Research and Application*. New York: Appleton-Century-Crofts, 1966.

Isbell, H., Fraser, H. F., Wikler, A., Belleville, R. E., and Eisenman, A. J. An experimental study of the etiology of "rum fits" and delirium tremens. *Quarterly Journal of Studies on Alcohol*, 1955, **16**, 1–28.

Jacobson, E. *Progressive Relaxation*. Chicago: University of Chicago Press, 1938.

Jaffe, J.H. Drug addiction and drug abuse. In L.S. Goodman and A. Gilman (Eds.), *The Pharmacological Basis of Therapeutics*, 4th ed. New York: Macmillan, 1970.

Kanfer, F. H., and Phillips, J. S. *Learning Foundations of Behavior Therapy*. New York: Wiley, 1970.

Kantorovich, N. V. An attempt at curing alcoholism by associated reflexes. *Novoye Refleksologii nervnoy i Fiziologii Sistemy*, 1928, **3**, 436–445.

Keehn, J. D. Voluntary consumption of alcohol in rats. *Quarterly Journal of Studies on Alcohol*, 1969, **30**, 288–292.

Keehn, J. D., and Coulson, G. E. Ethanol consumption by rats on a differential probability of reinforcement schedule. *Psychonomic Science*, 1970, **19**, 283–284.

Kelleher, R. T. Chaining and conditioned reinforcement. In W. K. Honig (Ed.), *Operant Behavior: Areas of Research and Application*. New York: Appleton-Century-Crofts, 1966.

Keller, M., and Efron, V. The prevalence of alcoholism. *Quarterly Journal of Studies on Alcoholism*, 1955, **16**, 619–644.

Kendell, R. E. Normal drinking by former alcohol addicts. *Quarterly Journal of Studies on Alcohol*, 1965, **26**, 247–257.

Kendell, R. E., and Staton, M. C. The fate of untreated alcoholics. *Quarterly Journal of Studies on Alcohol*, 1965, **27**, 30–41.

Kepner, E. Application of learning theory to the etiology and treatment of alcoholism. *Quarterly Journal of Studies on Alcohol*, 1964, **25**, 279–291.

Kingham, R. J. Alcoholism and the reinforcement theory of learning. *Quarterly Journal of Studies on Alcohol*, 1958, **19**, 320–330.

Laverty, S. G. Aversion therapies in the treatment of alcoholism. *Psychosomatic Medicine*, 1966, **28**, 651–666.

LeBlanc, A. E., Kalant, H., Gibbins, R. J., and Berman, N. D. Acquisition and loss of tolerance to ethanol by the rat. *Journal of Pharmacology and Experimental Therapeutics*, 1969, **168**, 244–250.

Lemere, F. What happens to alcoholics. *American Journal of Psychiatry*, 1953, **109**, 674–676.

Lemere, F., and Voegtlin, W. L. An evaluation of the aversion treatment of alcoholism. *Quarterly Journal of Studies on Alcohol*, 1950, **11**, 199–204.

Lester, D. Self-maintenance of intoxication in the rat. *Quarterly Journal of Studies on Alcohol*, 1961, **22**, 223–231.

Lewis, E. G., Dustman, R. E., and Beck, E. C. Sensory phenomena following ingestion of varying doses of alcohol. *Proceedings of the 77th Annual Convention of the American Psychological Association*, 1969, **4**, 887–888.

Lovibond, S. H., and Caddy, K. G. Discriminated aversive control in the moderation of alcoholics' drinking behavior. *Behavior Therapy*, 1970, **1**, 437–444.

Masserman, J., and Yum, K. S. An analysis of the influence of alcohol on experimental neuroses in cats. *Psychosomatic Medicine*, 1946, **8**, 36–52.

McNamee, H. B., Mello, N. K., and Mendelson, J. H. Experimental analysis of drinking patterns of alcoholics: Concurrent psychiatric observations. *American Journal of Psychiatry*, 1968, **124**, 1063–1069.

Meisch, R. Increased rate of ethanol self-administration as a function of experience. Report PR-69-3, Research Laboratory, Department of Psychiatry, University of Minnesota, 1969.

Meisch, R., and Thompson, T. Ethanol intake in the absence of concurrent food reinforcement. *Psychopharmacologia*, 1971, **22**, 72–79.

Mello, N. K., and Mendelson, J.H. Operant analysis of drinking patterns of chronic alcoholics. *Nature*, 1965, **206**, 43–46.

Mello, N. K., and Mendelson, J.H. Factors affecting alcohol consumption in primates. *Psychosomatic Medicine*, 1966, **28**, 529–550.

Mello, N. K., and Mendelson, J.H. Behavioral studies of sleep patterns in alcoholics during intoxication and withdrawal. *Journal of Pharmacology and Experimental Therapeutics*, 1970, **175**, 94–112.

Mello, N. K., and Mendelson, J.H. A quantitative analysis of drinking patterns in alcoholics. *Archives of General Psychiatry*, 1971, **25**, 527–539.

Mello, N. K., and Mendelson, J H. Drinking patterns during work-contingent and noncontingent alcohol acquisition. *Psychosomatic Medicine*, 1972, **34**, 139–164.

Mello, N. K., McNamee, H. B., and Mendelson, J. H. Drinking patterns of chronic alcoholics: Gambling and motivation for alcohol. In J. O. Cole (Ed.), *Clinical Research in Alcoholism*. Psychiatric Research Report No. 24, Washington D.C.: American Psychiatric Association, 1968.

Mendelson, J. H., and Mello, N. K. Ethanol and whisky drinking patterns in rats under free choice and forced choice conditions. *Quarterly Journal of Studies on Alcohol*, 1964, **25**, 1–25.

Mendelson, J.H., and Mello, N. K. Experimental analysis of drinking behavior of chronic alcoholics. *Annals of the New York Academy of Sciences*, 1966, **133**, 838–845.

Mendelson, J.H., Mello, N. K., and Solomon, P. Small group drinking behavior: An experimental study of chronic alcoholics. In *The Addictive States. Proceedings of the Association for Research in Nervous and Mental Disease*, 1968, **46**, 399–430.

Mendelson, J.H., Stein, S., and Mello, N. K. Effects of experimentally induced intoxication on metabolism of ethanol 1-C^{14} in alcoholic subjects. *Metabolism*, 1965, **14**, 1255–1266.

Mensh, I. N. Psychopathic condition, addictions, and sexual deviations. In B.B. Wolman (Ed.), *Handbook of Clinical Psychology*, New York: McGraw-Hill, 1965.

Mills, K. C., Sobell, M. B., and Schaefer, H. H. Training social drinking as an alternative to abstinence for alcoholics. *Behavior Therapy*, 1971, **2**, 18–27.

Morosko, T. E., and Baer, P. E. Avoidance conditioning of alcoholics. In R. Ulrich, T. Stachnik, and J. Mabry (Eds.), *Control of Human Behavior*, Vol, II. Glenview, Ill.: Scott, Foresman, 1970.

Moskowitz, H., and Asato, H. Effect of alcohol upon the latency of responses learned with positive and negative reinforcers. *Quarterly Journal of Studies on Alcohol,* 1966, **27,** 604–611.

Myers, R. D. Voluntary alcohol consumption in animals: Peripheral and intracerebral factors. *Psychosomatic Medicine,* 1966, **28,** 484–497.

Myers, R. D., and Carey, R. Preference factors in experimental alcoholism. *Science,* 1961, **134,** 469–470.

Narrol, H. G. Experimental application of reinforcement principles to the analysis and treatment of hospitalized alcoholics. *Quarterly Journal of Studies on Alcohol,* 1967, **28,** 104–115.

Nathan, P. E., and O'Brien, J. S. An experimental analysis of the behavior of alcoholics and non-alcoholics during prolonged experimental drinking: A necessary precursor of behavior therapy? *Behavior Therapy,* 1971, **2,** 455–476.

Nathan, P. E., O'Brien, J. S., and Lowenstein, L. M. Operant studies of chronic alcoholism: Interaction of alcohol and alcoholics. In M. K. Roach, W. M. McIsaac, and P. J. Creaven (Eds.), *Biological Aspects of Alcohol.* Austin: University of Texas Press, 1971.

Nathan, P. E., Titler, N. A., Lowenstein, L. M., Solomon, P., and Rossi, M. A. Behavioral analysis of chronic alcoholism. *Archives of General Psychiatry,* 1970, **22,** 419–430.

Pavlov, I. P. *Conditioned Reflexes: An Investigation of the Physiological Activity of the Cerebral Cortex.* London: Oxford University Press, 1927.

Pawloski, A. A., Dennenberg, V. H., and Zarrow, M. X. Prolonged alcohol consumption in the rat. II. Acquisition and extinction of an escape response. *Quarterly Journal of Studies on Alcohol,* 1961, **22,** 232–240.

Perensky, J. J., Senter, R. J., and Jones, R. B. Induced alcohol consumption through positive reinforcement. *Psychonomic Science,* 1968, **11,** 109–110.

Perensky, J. J., Senter, R. J., and Jones, R. B. Alcohol consumption in rats after experimentally induced neurosis. *Psychonomic Science,* 1969, **15,** 159–160.

Rachman, S. Aversion therapy: Chemical or electrical? *Behaviour Research and Therapy,* 1965, **2,** 289–299.

Rachman, S., and Teasdale, J. *Aversion Therapy and Behaviour Disorders: An Analysis.* Coral Gables, Fla.: University of Miami Press, 1969.

Reynolds, G. S., and Van Sommers, P. Effects of ethyl alcohol on avoidance behavior. *Science,* 1960, **132,** 42–43.

Richter, C. P., and Campbell, K. H. Alcohol taste thresholds and concentrations of solution preferred by rats. *Science,* 1940, **91,** 507–508.

Sanderson, R. E., Campbell, D., and Laverty, S. G. An investigation of a new aversion conditioning treatment for alcoholics. *Quarterly Journal of Studies on Alcohol,* 1963, **24,** 261–275.

Sandler, J. Three aversive control procedures with alcoholics: A preliminary report. Paper presented at the Southeastern Psychological Association Meeting, New Orleans, La., 1969.

Sandler, J., and Davidson, R. S. Psychopathology: An analysis of response consequences. In H. D. Kimmel (Ed.), *Experimental Psychopathology: Recent Research and Theory*. New York: Academic Press, 1971.

Sandler, J., and Davidson, R. S. *Psychopathology: Learning Theory, Research and Applications*. New York: Harper and Row, 1973.

Scarborough, B. B. Lasting effects of alcohol on the reduction of anxiety in rats. *Journal of Genetic Psychology*, 1957, **91**, 173–179.

Senter, R. J., Eimer, E., and Richman, C. L. Intersubject and intrasubject variability in the consumption of alcohol. *Psychonomic Science*, 1968, **10**, 165–166.

Senter, R. J., and Richman, C. L. Induced consumption of high-concentration ethanol solution in rats. *Quarterly Journal of Studies on Alcohol*, 1969, **30**, 330–335.

Senter, R. J., Smith, F. W., and Lewin, S. Ethanol ingestion as an operant response. *Psychonomic Science*, 1967, **8**, 291–292.

Sinclair, J. D., and Senter, R. J. Development of an alcohol-deprivation effect in rats. *Quarterly Journal of Studies on Alcohol*, 1968, **29**, 863–867.

Skinner, B. F. *Science and Human Behavior*. New York: Macmillan, 1953.

Smart, R. G. Effects of alcohol on conflict and avoidance behavior. *Quarterly Journal of Studies on Alcohol*, 1965, **26**, 187–205.

Tillotson, K. J., and Fleming, R. Personality and sociologic factors in the prognosis and treatment of chronic alcoholism. *New England Journal of Medicine*, 1937, **217**, 611–615.

Ullmann, L. P., and Krasner, L. (Eds.) *Case Studies in Behavior Modification*. New York: Holt, Rinehart and Winston, 1965.

Victor, M., and Adams, R. D. On the etiology of alcoholic neurologic diseases. *American Journal of Clinical Nutrition*, 1961, **9**, 379–397.

Vogel-Sprott, M. D., and Banks, R. K. The effects of delayed punishment on an immediately rewarded response in alcoholics. *Behaviour Research and Therapy*, 1965, **3**, 69–73.

Vogler, R. E., Lunde, S. E., Johnson, G. R., and Martin, P. L. Electrical aversion conditioning with chronic alcoholics. *Journal of Consulting and Clinical Psychology*, 1970, **34**, 302–307.

W., W. The society of Alcoholics Anonymous. *American Journal of Psychiatry*, 1949, **5**, 106.

W., W. The fellowship of Alcoholics Anonymous. In R.J. Catanzaro (Ed.), *Alcoholism: The Total Treatment Approach*. Springfield, Ill.: Thomas, 1968, pp. 117–124.

Wall, J. H., and Allen, E. B. Results of hospital treatment of alcoholism. *American Journal of Psychiatry*, 1944, **100**, 474–479.

Wallerstein, R. S. *Hospital Treatment of Alcoholism: A Comparative Experimental Study*. New York: Basic Books, 1957.

Walters, G. C., and Rogers, J. V. Aversive stimulation of the rat: Long-term effects on subsequent behavior. *Science*, 1963, **142**, 70–71.

Woods, J. H., Ikomi, F., and Winger, C. D. The reinforcing property of ethanol. In M. K. Roach, W. M. McIsaac, and P. J. Creaven (Eds.), *Biological Aspects of*

Alcohol. Austin: University of Texas Press, 1971.

Woods, J. H., and Winger, C. D. A critique of methods for inducing ethanol self-intoxication in animals. In N. K. Mello and J. H. Mendelson (Eds.), *Recent Advances in Research on Alcoholism*. U.S. Government Printing Office, 1971.

CHAPTER 6

Comprehensive Behavioral Treatment in a Training School for Delinquents

W. ROBERT NAY

The application of operant principles to behavioral management strategies in the institutional setting has become increasingly popular. Recent reviews of the literature by O'Leary and Drabman (1971) and Kazdin and Bootzin (1972) on these token or point economies illustrate that an overwhelming majority of these efforts report data from a typically small and selected group of subjects within a single classroom, cottage, or ward setting. That a token program can alter a wide variety of social, academic, and task-related behaviors within a variety of institutional setting has become increasingly popular. Recent reviews of the literature by O'Leary and Drabman (1971) and Kazdin and Bootzin (1972) on in populations, settings evaluated, and procedural and observational methodology, however, have made it somewhat difficult to compare across settings. Fortunately, recent investigations have begun to evaluate the mechanics of the token approach.

The utility and length of time-out as an aversive agent (Kaufman and Baron, 1968; Burchard and Barrera, 1972), the use of response cost (Kaufman and O'Leary, 1972; Burchard and Barrera, 1972), and an evaluation of procedures useful in promoting generalization to settings outside the manipulated setting (O'Leary et al., 1969; Walker and Buckley, 1972) are among elements currently being evaluated. This research on specific program elements may lead to increased consistency of approaches within the area.

A review of studies where the child is the subject of interest shows that a clear majority of investigators have applied the token approach to elementary age populations. Most notable are the investigations of O'Leary, Becker, and their associates (O'Leary and Becker, 1967; O'Leary et al., 1969) and Walker and Buckley (1968, 1972). Few studies have been directed at the adolescent population, probably because of the increased difficulty in structuring the environment, exerting control over potentially damaging deviant behaviors, and providing effective back-up reinforcers. In addition, the locus of social reinforcement for inappropriate behavior no doubt resides more with the peer group than with the misguided teacher or staff person (Buehler et al., 1966). Thus retraining a supervisory person to administer reinforcers more appropriately may not be sufficient to bring deviant behavior under control. We currently admit ever-increasing numbers of adolescents to so-called delinquent training institutions, and yet Kazdin and Bootzin (1972) report that few investigators have attempted to apply operant technology to these populations. Of these few investigators, most report attempts to reprogram the behavior of a subgroup selected from within the delinquent training school population.

Burchard and Tyler (1965) report the reduction of antisocial behavior in one subject following introduction of tokens for appropriate social behavior and time-out for antisocial responses. An evaluation of Achievement Place, a community-based, family-style token program for predelinquent boys, is provided by Phillips (1968) and Phillips, Phillips, Fixen, and Wolf (1971). Phillips (1968) reports that all manipulated academic and social behaviors changed in the desired direction for three boys. Phillips et al. (1971) performed a series of four experiments on groups of four to six boys. The authors show that for the small subsamples of the Achievement Place population used, promptness to meals, room-cleaning behavior, money management skills, and watching the news all seemed to be under the control of point earnings or loss.

Although most of the research has attempted to manipulate the social behaviors of delinquents, Meichenbaum, Bowers, and Ross (1968) successfully increased attending behaviors in a class of female delinquent subjects. Cohen (1968) reports an increase in achievement of two grade levels following shaping with points contingent on time spent studying.

These few reported attempts to apply a token approach to behaviors within the delinquent setting involve the manipulation of a very small sample of subjects chosen by unspecified criteria from the larger population of adolescents within the institution. No investigation has been reported which attempted to apply token management techniques to all subjects residing within the institution, with the possible exception of the work of Phillips and his associates (Phillips, 1968; Phillips et al., 1971). With regard to the research reported by Phillips, no evaluation of the overall success of the token approach with the total population is reported. This is not unusual. Few investigators using token programs with any reported populations show data indicating overall program effectiveness. Instead we are presented with the data for small samples of subjects within one classroom or one cottage. In fact, only a limited number of classrooms or residences (cottages, wards, etc.) within the institution have been manipulated by most investigators (Ayllon and Azrin, 1965, 1968; O'Leary and Becker, 1967; Girardeau and Spradlin, 1964; Barrish, Saunders, and Wolf, 1969; Walker and Buckley, 1972; Burchard and Barrera, 1972).

The present chapter describes the implementation of a comprehensive behavioral treatment program within all classrooms and cottage and vocational settings of a training school for delinquent girls. The focus is on variables important in designing and effecting a total program and on overall program evaluation rather than on a presentation of data from a small subsample within the training school population.

AN OVERVIEW

Following a description of the setting and background of the delinquent institution, a demographic description of students and staff will be offered. An analysis of data collection procedures used to establish the treatment needs of the institution will be followed by a description of the program proper. Procedures used in training the staff and students in the details of the program will be discussed, as will the effectiveness of a program of continuous in-service training. When relevant, a discussion of the literature will be made in describing the rationale for a particular approach. Extensive baseline data gathered by independent observers will be compared with data collected following program implementation. Since the focus of the chapter is on a global evaluation of the program, the data from twenty classrooms and six cottages will be summarized.

SETTING AND BACKGROUND

Founded in 1915 as an industrial school for black girls, the training school consists of a school building and six living cottages, as well as cafeteria and maintenance and laundry buildings which serve as vocational placements for the students. As a result of integration in 1965, the school can now be described as racially balanced.

Since there are marked similarities in training school approaches across localities, a description of treatment before the present program may be useful. A discipline team consisting of a group of staff, selected according to undefined criteria, was the only organized staff approach to behavior management. If a student transgressed one of a multitude of rules and regulations that varied with each classroom and living cottage, a discipline sheet was forwarded to this discipline team. In many cases a student would be required to wait for her punishment a week or more until the team convened. This marked delay between offense and punishment left many students uncertain as to why they were being punished.

Among approaches to punishment were frequent use of lengthy solitary confinement, work detail, and a severe curtailment of privileges. Regarding appropriate behavior, a student was called in at irregular intervals (in some cases intervals of six months) for feedback as to her "progress" within the institution. Progress was based on uncertain criteria, consisting primarily of global, subjective staff reports. No specific behavioral goals were set for students (or staff) on an individual or collective basis except generalities such as: "Be more respectful"; "Become a nice young lady."

In summary, treatment before the present program might be described as operating within a contingent punishment, noncontingent reward paradigm. The lack of explicit, consistent criteria for staff performance across settings was perhaps the most damaging aspect of the program.

SUBJECTS

Since the staff members were a primary focus of training, both staff and students were considered subjects.

Students

Subjects were a population of 115 females ranging in age from 11 to 15 years. This number varied somewhat with admissions and releases, but 115 was the average population over the period of time encompassed by the study. All subjects were referred for a wide variety of so-called delinquent behaviors including continued truancy from school, inability to get along with parents, stealing, aggressive assaults, and destruction of property. Subjects could be described generally as coming from a low socioeconomic background. Mean age was 14.37 years. Mean level of intelligence as measured by a group test was 86.93.

Staff

Table 1 describes the position, mean age, education level, and mean number of years of experience of the 87 staff who served as subjects.

Table 1. Staff Characteristics

Staff[a]	N	Mean Age (Years)	Mean Years of Education	Mean Years of Experience
Teachers	13	34.2	16.7	4.5
Caseworkers	8	32.3	17.8	2.4
Housemothers	21	36.5	11.3	8.4
Night matrons	12	38.4	10.5	6.3
Project supervisors	14	38.6	10.7	3.4

[a]Does not include five administrative personnel.

This represents all staff within the institution. The staff who interact directly with the students are the primary agents of treatment within most behavioral treatment programs. Unfortunately, a variety of administrative problems within most institutions drastically limits the effectiveness of the staff as treatment agents, and this training school was no exception. Annual turnover among cottage staff approaches 40 percent, due to a combination of long working hours and low financial rewards. Within the cottage setting, a lack of adequate numbers of cottage personnel severely limit time available for assessment of individual needs and treatment. Thus treatment strategies must be carefully designed to provide maximum effectiveness per unit of staff time required. Observational systems, record keeping, or token administration procedures that are elaborate look good on paper but will not be supported by the staff within many institutional settings.

Observation of staff activities over the course of a full day provides one with an appreciation of the specific limitations regarding treatment design. Pilot experiments in which a proposed treatment procedure is tested by a limited number of staff in one cottage or one classroom within the institution further insure that a program may be reasonably executed by the staff.

ASSESSMENT OF PROGRAM NEEDS AND INSTITUTIONAL RESOURCES

Many investigators who use a token economy approach within an institutional setting fail to explain why certain staff and child behaviors are chosen to be manipulated from the array of possibilities (e.g., Phillips et al., 1971; Kaufman and O'Leary, 1972). In addition, the procedures used to assess the behavioral needs and resources of the institution are rarely described. Without this information, it is difficult to determine whether the token program has effectively dealt with the specific behavioral needs of that institution or has merely manipulated those behaviors which are less difficult, least costly to alter, or more suitable to a research methodology. The diagnostic methods of the present project are presented as an approach to comprehensive assessment of institutional needs.

Initial Interview with Administrative Personnel

As a first step, a meeting with the superintendent and other key administrative staff was held. An attempt was made to operationally define their goals in seeking consultation services. It was determined that the administration desired some means of exerting control over the inappropriate behavior of students as well as being provided some level of treatment. An initial contract with the administration specified that a two-month period would be required to independently assess the needs of the institution. A report to the administrative staff followed this assessment period. Various procedures were used to assess the needs of all settings of the institution—school, cottage, and vocational.

Small Group Interviews

It was the goal of the treatment consultants (the author and a team of six graduate students in clinical psychology) to train the institutional staff as primary agents of treatment, no matter what treatment goals were ultimately endorsed. It was therefore necessary to obtain information from staff regarding treatment needs within their settings. As is typical of the training school for delinquents, many staff members were inflexible in their manner of dealing with children and wary of any "new" treatment ideas. In fact, previous treatment programs had failed within the institution due to a lack of staff support. It was thought that meeting with all 87 staff in small groups of five would allow the consultants to learn about the behavioral problems, resources, and limitations of each setting and also give the institutional staff an opportunity to meet the consultants. In addition, by giving them such an opportunity over three meeting periods, the staff made an investment in the treatment program.

Thus, from the beginning, the consultants made it clear that the staff would have a part in developing the treatment program. Many staff members had never been asked their opinions about anything regarding the care of girls under their direct supervision. To say the least, these small group meetings provided the consultants with practical information about treatment possibilities as well as a keen understanding of limitations due to staff time available and staff expertise. Perhaps most important, these meetings precipitated staff interest in looking carefully at child behaviors and served to establish lines of communication that had not previously existed among institutional settings.

Behavioral Observation

A coding system was developed which included operational definitions of 13 staff and child behaviors suggested by both the small group meetings and previous experience with token programs (Nay and Legum, 1972). Table 2 presents these codes and their corresponding definitions for child behaviors.

Regarding staff behaviors presented in Table 3, the coding system emphasized not only the class of a particular behavior (e.g., a staff verbal reinforcement or a staff request) but also the quality of the communication (e.g., the clear specification of some specific child behavior by the staff).

Thirty advanced undergraduate students were trained to employ this coding system using videotaped sequences of actual classroom behaviors as training aids. An agreement level of 85 percent with at least three other coders on three consecutive occasions was the criterion level required of each coder. Most relia-

Table 2. Child Codes

Code Definitions for Child Behaviors

Behaviors	Coding Symbols	Definition of Code	Example Behavior
Attends	C⊃S; C P	C gives full-faced attention to some task S prescribes. Task is defined as any behavior S requires of C (e.g., listening, writing, etc.)	S lectures; C listens attentively. S asks C to work quietly at desk; C gives full-faced attention to desk materials
Nonattends	C⊘S; C P	C does not give full-faced attention to some task S prescribes	S lectures; C looks out window or sleeps. C plays with fingers rather than working with materials prescribed by S
Calls out	C↷; C P	C inappropriately verbalizes or makes some noise. Inappropriateness is defined by S's rules regarding speaking out	S lectures; C yells out, makes a loud noise. S requires hand recognition; C calls out without raising hand
Negative verbal interaction	C × S or C × P	An aggressive verbal interaction with the intention of hurting or harming. Must observe facial expression and gestures to determine aggressiveness	C curses at P, or name calls. C curses staff member. Facial expression indicates harm is intended
Negative physical interaction	C * S or C*P	An aggressive physical interaction with the intention of hurting or harming. Must observe facial expression, gestures, and body stance to determine aggressiveness	C hits P; a fight ensues. C pushes S into a corner. Facial expression indicates intention to harm
Inappropriate verbal interaction	C × S; C × P	C talks to P when S has specified that talking is inappropriate. Interaction is non-aggressive	S lectures; C and P carry on a conversation. No aggressive intent is observed

Note. C = Child, S = Staff, P = Peer. If C, S, or P is underlined, this indicates the initiator of the behavior.

209

Table 3. Staff Codes

| | | Code Definitions for Staff Behaviors | |
Behaviors	Coding Symbols	Definition of Code	Example Behavior
Direct command	C = S; C P	A request of C which clearly specifies the behavior required	"Joan, please <u>pick</u> up those materials immediately". "Sara, please <u>be quiet</u>."
Indirect command	C ≃ S; C P	A request of C which does not clearly specify the behavior required. In many cases it is in the form of a question or suggestion	"Joan, wouldn't it be nice if your desk were clean?" "Class, I hear a noise."
Direct verbal reward	C + S; C P	A verbal, positive communication to C (e.g., "I like ____"), which specifies clearly the positive behavior	"You did a nice job <u>cleaning up your room.</u>" "That's correct; <u>you arranged them perfectly.</u>"
Indirect verbal reward	C +̸ S; C P	A verbal, positive communication which does not clearly specify the positive behavior	"Good" (What is good?) "Okay" (What is okay?)
Direct physical reward	C + S; C P	A physical (touch) positive behavior which is offered immediately after some C behavior occurs	C picks up materials and puts them away. S immediately pats her on the back
Labeled negative	C − S; C P	S verbally labels some scorable C inappropriate behavior for C, immediately upon its occurrence	C hits another child (P). S immediately requests that C stop, carefully labeling the behavior
Staff inappropriate	C ∅ S; C P	Some C codable inappropriate behavior occurs. S fails to identify (label) the behavior	C hits another child (P). S makes no response to deal with the behavior.

Note. C = child, S = Staff, P = Peer. If C, S, or P is underlined, this indicates the initiator of the behavior.

bilities were found to be in the 90 to 95 percent range of agreement. All relia-bility checks were performed in school and cottage settings within the institu-tion.

Each coder was assigned to a school or cottage at specified times. Twenty classrooms consisting of a given teacher and her particular class of students at some specific 50-minute class period were coded (each teacher taught a different group of girls for each school period). In addition, staff and student behaviors in all six residential cottages were coded at specified times in the evening when all girls were present.

Coding was performed using a time sampling technique. Each coder carried a tape recorder programmed to emit a 6-second tone at 8-second intervals via an earjack. Coders would observe a specific girl for the 8-second interval and then record her behavior during the 6 seconds of tone. Sequentially, all girls would be sampled during these 8-second observations over the coding period. For ex-ample, a coder observing 12 girls for 1 hour would make about 38 8-second observations spaced throughout the coding period. As opposed to sampling each subject for lengthy 5-minute time periods (Patterson et al., 1968), this proce-dure insured a pattern of observations more representative of a girl's behavior over time.

Reinforcement Survey

Sixty girls randomly selected from the population at large met in small groups. A group mediator (consultant) structured this interview to assess possi-ble reinforcers within the following general areas:

1. *Privileges.* Students were asked which current privileges they valued most and what privileges they would like to see instituted at some future time.

2. *Activities.* An assessment of desired current on-campus and off-campus ac-tivities was carried out. Students again were encouraged to suggest novel activi-ties for possible future addition

3. *Material items.* Within this area, group mediators assessed valued items by name brand within each of these areas: food/snack items; recreational/game items; cosmetic/dress items; any others offered by group members.

Group mediators surveyed each of the five girls within the group for their suggestions. Following these small group meetings, a questionnaire was con-structed which listed by category all of the items suggested by the small groups. Subjects were asked to endorse a predetermined number of items within each category representing those they maximally preferred. This questionnaire was administered to all subjects within the institution during class time made avail-able by the school. To insure a valid assessment, subjects were asked not to identify their questionnaires in any fashion. These data were summarized with regard to frequently chosen items within each category.

In addition, the treatment consultants and behavioral coders reviewed their observational data and identified a number of high-rate social behaviors which proved to be valuable reinforcers.

During the second month of program development, plans were made to provide for the availability of as many of these valued items as possible. Activities with a high potential for exposure to the community (e.g., trips to off-campus dances, cultural events) were chosen from among highly endorsed items whenever possible. With many reinforcers available, it makes sense to choose those that have a high potential for promoting positive behavior. Furthermore, a reliance on reinforcers that occur in the natural environment may facilitate a generalization of behavior learned within the institution to the community upon release. An assessment of the treatment value of a reinforcer should be among important selection criteria.

Many of the privileges and activities chosen, such as off-campus trips, additional canteen allowances, and activities calling for staff supervision, required extensive planning by the institutional administration. In some cases approval at the level of state supervisory agencies was necessary. To incorporate an extensive array of highly valued reinforcers within a treatment program, sufficient time and manpower to carry out the planning necessary is an obvious requirement for success.

PROGRAM GOALS

Based on the two-month assessment of institutional needs and resources described above, a series of treatment goals was established and reported to the administrative staff. These included student behaviors for which an increase in relative frequency was desired and some for which a reduction was desired.

Desirable Behaviors

Promptness to Settings. All teaching and vocational staff complained about the high frequency of students late to classes or placements. These students created disruption of ongoing activities. Promptness was not mentioned by the cottage staff.

Appearance. Staff from all settings varied in their assessment of what constituted appropriate dress but agreed on the importance of cleanliness and appropriate clothing as important prerequisites for community adjustment. Staff agreed that the students should have some say in these appearance requirements, and meetings with the students were immediately scheduled to provide them with an investment in defining these appearance goals. It is important that any population of subjects to be included in such a program be given the opportunity to contribute to program development, since this investment promotes subject acceptance and may be more ethically sound.

Attending to School and Vocational Tasks. Data collected by the coding team supported the staff's observations that an increase in active listening and/or participation in learning activities was a highly desired goal. Initial behavioral observations indicated that students engaged in a wide variety of nonattending behaviors when working on academic or cottage task-related assignments. Increases in following instructions and completing tasks on time and some appraisal of the quality of task performance were frequently stated goals of the staff.

Compliance with Institutional Rules. As with most institutions for delinquent adolescents, the list of institutional rules was astonishing and perplexing. Over 60 rules, which varied from setting to setting within the institution, were inconsistently enforced. This aggregate of rules was in many cases poorly phrased and ill-defined. Extensive meetings with the administrative staff, coupled with the small group data on the difficulties of enforcing many of the rules, resulted in a restatement and reduction of these institutional rules. Four clearly defined rules were established. These rules prohibited running from campus, destruction of property, damage to one's physical person (i.e., by self-mutilation), and stealing.

Undesirable Behaviors

Inappropriate Verbal and Physical Behavior. This category consisted of verbal and physical interactions during class which were not related to the academic task at hand. Observational data supported teaching staff complaints that these frequent verbalizations and hand interactions were very disruptive to academic activities. Teaching staff reported an inability to deal effectively with these behaviors.

Aggressive Verbal and Physical Behavior. The staff desired to reduce the frequency of verbal and physical interactions defined by the intention to hurt or harm another. Verbal arguments and fighting were found to be extremely low-rate behaviors in observational data from both the cottage and school settings. Although of low rate, the potential of these behaviors to cause intolerable amounts of destruction to property and to physical well-being make them primary targets for reduction within the delinquent setting. Unfortunately, their low rate made abbreviated time sampling assessment of frequency a poor measure. With such low-rate behaviors, an assessment of overall daily occurrence within a particular setting or for a specific child provides a more valid indicant of frequency. Because such an investment in coding time is typically not feasible, reliance on staff observation of frequency usually takes the place of independent assessment by a trained coder.

Noncompliance. The staff reported difficulty in managing noncompliant behaviors. Observational data on the frequency of noncompliance yielded little useful information. Since noncompliance is a behavior obviously limited by varied frequency of staff requests and is usually of low rate for any one individual (staff members made few requests of a specific youngster within a standard coding hour), time-sampling observational data are poor indicants of incidence. As with aggressive verbal and physical behaviors, a reliance on data collected by the staff became necessary.

Staff Training Goals

An analysis of observations of staff made by coders in both cottage and school settings suggested a number of staff training goals. Several staff behaviors were defined for which an increase in frequency was desirable.

Social Reinforcers. Observational data revealed a low incidence of use of verbal or physical social reinforcers by staff. Verbal praise and encouragement for appropriate behavior, as well as physical expression of satisfaction (a pat on the shoulder, hug, etc.), were rarely used by some staff and never used by others. It was decided that the use of such reinforcers should be increased since these reinforcers are important motivators within the community and serve as a significant source of feedback for appropriate behavior. Few investigators, however, have emphasized the qualitative aspects of these reinforcing communications. Training staff to define or "label" clearly and immediately the behavior rewarded became an additional treatment goal. Table 3 presents the operational definition of a well-labeled direct, as opposed to indirect, reward.

Labeling of Inappropriate Behavior. Observational data indicated that staff communicated poorly to students the reason for punishment (what behavior?). A lack of information as to which specific behavior incurs punishment precludes any learning on the student's part. From such an interchange we can expect to promote a negative emotional response on the child's part, and little new behavior. Training staff to define clearly or "label" for the student the nature of any offense in simple, operational language became an important treatment goal. Table 3 presents the operational definition of this behavior.

Direct Requests. Many cases of noncompliance probably resulted from an inadequate specification on the sender's part of required receiver behavior. Observational data revealed a high incidence of staff requests which failed to specify clearly what behavior was required of the student. These indirect requests (see Table 3) were most often observed in the classroom situation, probably due to the greater frequency of making requests in the classroom as compared with the cottage. An increment in the proportion of staff requests of a direct nature became another staff training goal.

PROGRAM MECHANISM

With these goals in mind, a token economy format was developed as the first phase of the program. A token system could be readily administered by staff with limited treatment skills for the wide variety of behaviors outlined as program goals.

Overview of Token Procedures

Earning of points accompanied by staff social reinforcement (e.g., well-labeled praise, encouragement) was made contingent on clearly specified appropriate behaviors. These points could be exchanged during the day for a wide variety of reinforcers chosen from the survey of desired privileges, activities, and material items. Time-out from reinforcement or point loss (response cost) was made contingent on a limited number of inappropriate behaviors. Table 4 describes the treatment mechanism that was applied to each behavior specified within the goals of the program. Because of a lack of adequate facilities for time-out within the school setting, point loss was the primary approach to inappropriate classroom behavior.

In addition, all staff were trained to use direct or well-labeled social reinforcers and to make requests or task requirements as well defined as possible. A major goal was to drastically curtail the use of long-term isolation. A description of each of these procedures follows.

Point Earning

Each day all girls received a point earning card (Figure 1). Listed on the card were appropriate behaviors for which a girl could earn the specified number of points shown immediately following each behavior. The lower portion of the card provides space to list time-outs incurred or to specify point loss.

Each girl was provided with a well-illustrated handbook which specified precisely what she must do to earn points, as well as a specification of the rules regarding negative behaviors. Regarding point-earning, a girl was eligible to earn points in the cottage for meeting appearance requirements and arranging her room appropriately. Points also could be earned for early morning tasks if the girl began on time, followed task instructions, and performed at a specified level of quality. If she arrived promptly at the dining hall for breakfast or at the

Table 4. Program Mechanism for Each Targeted Child Behavior

Targeted Behavior	Point Earning School and Cottage Setting	Point Loss in School Setting	Time-Out in Cottage Setting
Promptness to settings	1 point per setting	None for tardiness	None for tardiness
Appearance	5 points for meeting all appearance criteria	None for a failure to meet appearance criteria	None for a failure to meet appearance criteria
Attending to school and vocational tasks	Up to 5 points for each class period, based on following instructions (0-2 points), completing tasks (0-1 point), and task quality (0-2 points)	None for nonattends	None for nonattends
Compliance with institutional rules	None overall. Dealt with by individual encouragement point earning where appropriate	Subject pays for staff time spent and/or materials replaced as a result of rule violation (in points or canteen funds)	*Only* for runs from campus. Length determined by school administration's assessment of security risk
Compliance to staff request	2 points, based on Subject's listening carefully to staff request, and initiating at designated time	3 points for failure to comply	Yes for failure to comply
Inappropriate verbal or physical	Individual point earning for control, where appropriate	3 points, following labeling of specific behavior	Not relevant to cottage setting
Aggressive verbal and physical	Individual encouragement earning for control, where appropriate	3 points, within "three-step contingency"	Yes, within "three-step contingency"

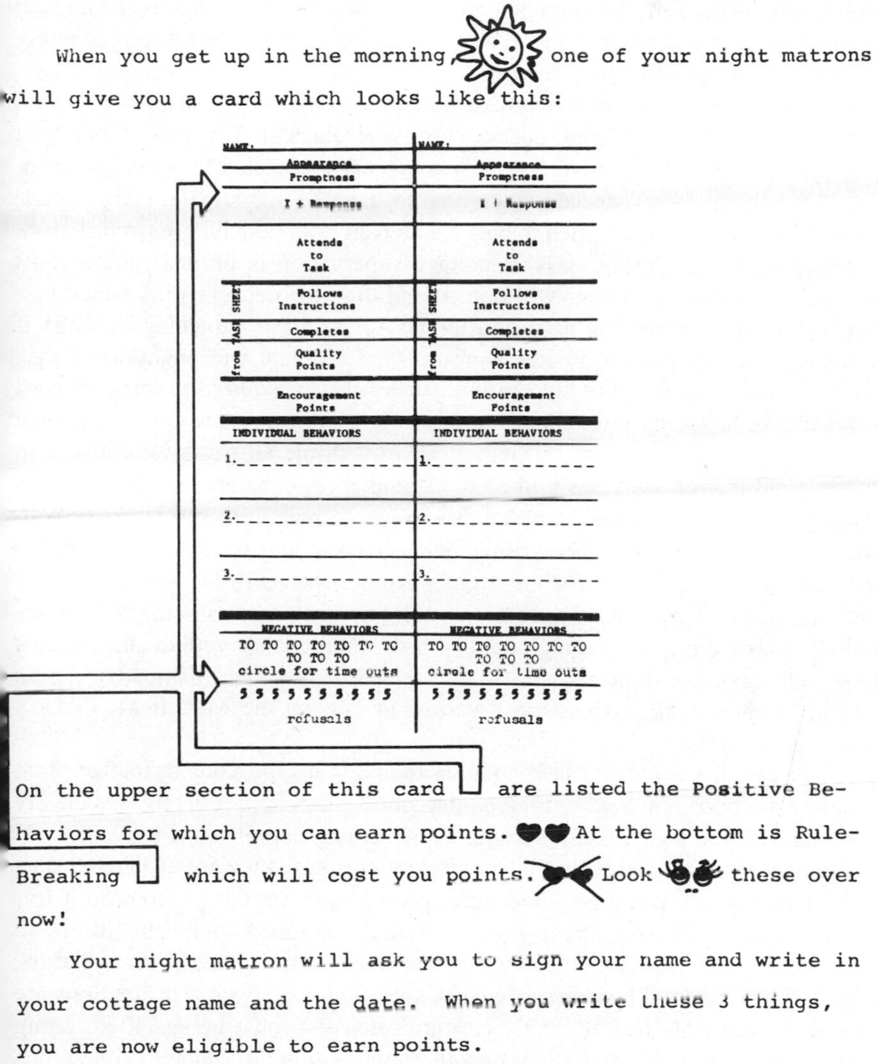

When you get up in the morning, one of your night matrons will give you a card which looks like this:

NAME:	NAME:
Appearance	Appearance
Promptness	Promptness
I + Response	I + Response
Attends to Task	Attends to Task
Follows Instructions	Follows Instructions
Completes	Completes
Quality Points	Quality Points
Encouragement Points	Encouragement Points
INDIVIDUAL BEHAVIORS	INDIVIDUAL BEHAVIORS
1. _ _ _ _ _ _ _ _ _ _ _ _ _	1. _ _ _ _ _ _ _ _ _ _ _ _ _
2. _ _ _ _ _ _ _ _ _ _ _ _ _	2. _ _ _ _ _ _ _ _ _ _ _ _ _
3. _ _ _ _ _ _ _ _ _ _ _ _ _	3. _ _ _ _ _ _ _ _ _ _ _ _ _
NEGATIVE BEHAVIORS	NEGATIVE BEHAVIORS
TO TO TO TO TO TO TO TO TO TO circle for time outs	TO TO TO TO TO TO TO TO TO TO circle for time outs
5 5 5 5 5 5 5 5 5 refusals	5 5 5 5 5 5 5 5 5 refusals

On the upper section of this card ⌐ are listed the Positive Behaviors for which you can earn points. ♥♥ At the bottom is Rule-Breaking ⌐ which will cost you points. Look these over now!

Your night matron will ask you to sign your name and write in your cottage name and the date. When you write these 3 things, you are now eligible to earn points.

Figure 1. Point earning card.

school for the beginning of each class, promptness points could be earned. Within the academic and vocational school settings she could earn additional task points within each 50-minute class period. For special nontask requests (e.g., errands, special activities) or for performing extra academic tasks above and beyond those required, she could earn additional task points. Finally, points could be earned in the dining hall and cottage in the evening for those behaviors previously mentioned. Encouragement points were used as rewards for marked improvement in a point-earning area or for recognition of some appropriate behavior not specified by the program.

Points were awarded by punching a hole in the appropriate space on the card for each point earned for some specific behavior. Each staff member was issued one punch, which, for convenience, was typically attached to a cord worn around the neck. The special punch leaves a small (about 1/8 inch), heart-shaped hole on the card, which makes counterfeit hole-punching most difficult.

Since staff time during class or cottage supervision is limited, points must be easy to administer or staff will not expend the time necessary. A punch system makes point awarding easy and allows for multiple punching of cards if cards are stacked and punched as a group. One problem with many token systems is record-keeping. For this system, each girl was required to carry her card from setting to setting throughout the day. Thus subjects transported their own record of accumulated point-earning. Prior to bedtime all cards were turned in to the night matron who was trained to expend approximately one to two hours recording point performance for the girls in her cottage in record books provided. This system required no writing or record-keeping by any staff member throughout the day except for the night matron, who had time available while the girls slept. If records of differential point earnings across settings were required, staff within each setting could be provided punches with distinctive cuts (e.g., all school staff punch hearts, all cottage staff punch diamonds). These "Gem" punches are produced in a variety of cuts by the McGill M. P. Co., Marengo, Illinois.

To insure that a cottage task such as maintaining the cottage lounge area, cleaning the restroom area, or maintaining one's room appropriately was clearly communicated to a girl, a task assignment sheet was completed (Figure 2).

Many adolescents fail within the community because they are unable to clearly formulate a behavioral goal and make preparations for completion. Staff frequently fail to clearly specify performance required and time limits in understandable behavioral language. The task assignment sheet insures that the nature of the required behavior is clearly specified and specific instructions are provided. Materials needed (e.g., cleaning utensils) must be specified, along with information as to where they may be found within the cottage. Time limits are explained clearly.

This sheet is set up as a contract which the staff member and the girl must both sign. Points earned for the various task elements are also specified on the sheet.

Task assignment sheets are most useful in prompting the cottage staff member, who is not accustomed to teaching, to specify clearly the behavior necessary for point-earning. These sheets also provide a model for problem-solving to a population of adolescents not accustomed to analyzing the behavioral requirements of a novel situation.

NAME: *Jane Smith*   DATE: *April 25, 1972*

I.   TASK DESCRIPTION: *Dust and polish furniture in the lounge*

II. TASK MATERIALS NEEDED:

1. *Clean rags*

2. *liquid wax polish*

3. _____

CIRCLE those instructions which are correctly followed

If ALL are CIRCLED, INITIAL

JS (1-2pt)

INITIAL:

JS (1 pt)

JS (1 pt)

____ (1 pt)

III. TASK INSTRUCTIONS: (If I follow these I earn 1-2 points) *(such as lamps)*

1. *remove all objects from area to be cleaned*

2. *dust surface with rag*

3. *polish surface with wax*

4. *replace objects on furniture*

5. *put all of the cleaning equipment away*

IV. TASK TIME:

1. If I LISTENED RIGHT AWAY, I earn 1 point for IMMEDIATE POSITIVE RESPONSE.

2. I must BEGIN by *1:00* o'clock to earn 1 point for IMMEDIATE POSITIVE RESPONSE.

3. I should FINISH by *2:00* o'clock to earn 1 point for COMPLETES TASK.

- -

V.   AGREEMENT: I have no further questions and agree to perform this task the best I can.

Girl: *Jane Smith*
Staff: *Miss Davis*

INITIAL:

- -

____ (1 pt)

JS (2 pt)

____ (1 pt)

VI. TASK QUALITY: If my work is:
1. Average: I do not earn a point.
2. Good: I earn 1 point.
3. Excellent: I earn 2 points.

VII. ENCOURAGEMENT POINTS for IMPROVING: If I im- and do better than my previous work, but do not qualify for points above, I can earn 1 point for this improvement ANYONE who steadely IMPROVES can earn points.

NOW TRANSFER ALL POINTS TO THE CARD WHEREVER POINTS HAVE BEEN INITIALED.

Figure 2. Task assignment sheet.

Back-Up Reinforcers

Based on the reinforcement survey previously described, a newsletter was given to all girls specifying privileges, activities, and material items that could be purchased for specified point accumulations. A newsletter format allowed point values to be altered based on demand from week to week. Subjects were allowed to bank only a limited number of points to encourage daily spending. Emphasis on daily point spending encourages immediate reinforcement for performance and discourages inflation within the program (Atthowe and Krasner, 1968). When vast numbers of points are saved, a girl can literally "retire" from point-earning for a week or two and pay herself noncontingently with banked points. These huge savings can devaluate points (inflation) since it becomes unimportant to earn one point for promptness when 1000 have been saved. Also, such saving tactics leave the program administrators open to a "run" on certain reinforcement items by subjects with enough banked points to wipe out supplies or exhaust limited numbers of passes to off-campus events.

A "night-spot" was created for the girls in the basement of one of the cottages. Representative subjects decorated the setting to suit their tastes. At specified point cost a soda counter supplied subjects with a variety of desirable food and material items. Since the provision of such material items becomes expensive, regular allotments of canteen funds provided by the state purchased many of the items—with donations and some limited program funds purchasing the remainder. Wise incorporation of existing recreational funds, training funds, and canteen allotments within a token program becomes a necessity when program funds are limited. Moreover, by requiring the program to make use of existing funds within the institution, the program is not dependent on external grants, which may vanish as state and federal budgets are altered. Since trips to the night spot were limited to two each week for each cottage, privileges, cottage activities, and off-campus events stressing social interaction and exposure to the community were emphasized.

Point Loss

Tyler and Brown (1967) described the punitive orientation of many staff within training school settings. The previous emphasis on negative behavior of the present institution suggested that staff use of point loss should be limited by the program. Therefore point loss could be incurred for only a limited number of specified behaviors suggested by the program goals. Point loss was contingent on those behaviors that must be terminated immediately because of the disruption and/or damage they may cause. Table 4 lists those behaviors for which point loss was the treatment approach.

Point loss was administered according to the following three-step contingency that all staff were required to use.

Step One: Information. Subject should be instructed in a clear communication to *stop* some specific inappropriate behavior (e.g., verbal or physical aggressiveness).

Step Two: Warning. If subject does not comply with the request, she should be told the following: "If you do not stop *(behavior clearly specified)*, you will lose three points."

Step Three: Point Loss. If subject does not respond to the warning, immediately punch three negative points on her card, carefully explaining why points were lost. Under *no circumstances* should a staff member argue, plead with, or berate the girl. Point loss should be undertaken in a calm, matter-of-fact manner, emphasizing the inappropriate behavior in question. Once points are removed, the matter is settled and no further punishment should be undertaken. Failure to give up a card for punching results in an immediate referral to the supervisor.

Steps one and two were used only on the first incidence of a negative behavior on a given day, with repeated negative behavior immediately incurring Step three. The "Three-Step Contingency" required staff to identify clearly ongoing inappropriate behavior and gave the subject an opportunity to alter her behavior or face clearly specified consequences.

Point loss is an effective means of terminating inappropriate behavior (Burchard and Barrera, 1972). Problems with response cost encountered or suggested by the present program include the following:

1. Institutional staff of modest skills and punishment-oriented backgrounds may emphasize point loss, thus providing a greater proportion of staff attention for inappropriate behavior.

2. Institutionalized subjects, particularly delinquents, may view negative point totals as a measure of status and thus work to increase negative point accumulations.

3. Negative points may reduce the value of positive point earning. A subject who is sufficiently "in the hole" with negative points gains little from positive point earning.

To effectively limit possible staff overuse of negative points, negative point earning (3 negative points for each occurrence of a specified inappropriate behavior) was limited to 15 negative points for each subject. When the fifteenth and was immediately referred to a supervisor. Thus high negative point earners were immediately brought to the attention of supervisory personnel. The supervisor would ask why the subject was losing so many points and would remove a privilege appropriate to the situation. Privileges were ordered into levels of value according to the reinforcement survey. The subject was informed that any future inappropriate behavior on that day would make her eligible for a higher level privilege loss. Thus problem girls were immediately identified and dealt with on a more flexible basis according to their individual needs.

Time-Out

Time-out from point earning was used in a fashion similar to procedures reported by Tyler and Brown (1967) and Patterson et al. (1973). When a specified inappropriate behavior occurred, the subject was sent to a boring, nonstimulating location within the cottage for 30 minutes according to a three-step contingency identical to that used for point loss, except that time-out was specified as the response cost. If she refused to participate in time-out, a supervisor was called in to deal with the girl, using a privilege loss. Thus within both the school and cottage settings the line staff were provided with effective procedures for communicating with subjects and dealing with inappropriate behavior. This was in direct contrast to the significant role played by supervisory personnel in providing punishment before program implementation.

STAFF TRAINING

Few investigators have attempted to evaluate methods commonly used in training staff in token procedures (Kazdin and Bootzin, 1972). In fact, few reports of token programs include a detailed specification of training methods or an evaluation of their relative effectiveness. Although many investigators agree that the success of a token program hinges on the effectiveness of staff training (Brierton, Garms, and Metzger, 1969; Martin, 1972), most program designers must proceed in training by a series of educated guesses (Grabowski and Thompson, 1972). Following is a detailed summary of training procedures used in the present program, as well as an informal evaluation of their effectiveness.

All staff were initially trained in groups ranging in size from five to seven participants. Each group met twice each week for two hours. Training extended over a three-week period immediately prior to program implementation. One of three graduate students or a clinical psychologist served as group trainer. A summary of the training procedures used over these six group sessions follows.

Staff Handbook

One week before the training sessions, all staff were provided with a handbook which explained the program to them and were asked to read carefully and study the material. Staff members were informed that they would be tested over the material in the training sessions. Each section within the handbook provided an operational definition of a specific child behavior (see Table 4) as well as a behavioral specification of the appropriate approach to use upon occurrence of the behavior. In all cases detailed examples illustrated the appropriate approach (e.g., award 3 points and label positive the behavior for the child) for a variety of situations typically encountered by the staff. In the case of more complex approaches, programed learning sequences provided staff with an opportunity to practice and test themselves on the material presented.

Since the demands of the cottage were somewhat different from those of the classroom, each staff member was presented with a handbook designed particularly for the setting within which he or she functioned. Setting resources and requirements proved to be so diverse that a handbook tailored for universal staff reading would have been either most limited or replete with exceptions (e.g., "You assign 3 negative points in the school; *however*, in the cottage you would send the child to time-out"). Although many investigators make use of handbooks and other written training aides (e.g., Brierton, Garms, and Metzger, 1969; Martin and Pear, 1970), no one has previously reported the use of such setting-specific materials.

A written presentation of information was found to be inferior to other commonly used methods (i.e., lectures, modeling, role playing) in training a group of 77 mothers in the use of time-out procedure (Nay, 1974). Patterson, Cobb, and Ray (1973) found a programed book to be only the first in a series of steps necessary to alter parental management techniques. In the present study, written tests over the material presented in the staff handbook were administered to all staff following their week of self-study of the handbook. These written tests indicated that an overwhelming majority of staff were unable to apply the concepts presented in the handbook to the everyday problem situations on which the test was based. Thus the written presentation alone failed to produce a significant change in staff knowledge of how to use the program. This limitation of the handbook as a training aid may have been due to the failure of many staff members to read and study the material, or to inherent limitations of the written approach. Since no well-controlled presentation and evaluation of the handbook was undertaken, these findings are only suggestive.

Pinpointing Lectures

No lectures or films presenting basic principles of reinforcement were used in training, although a number of investigators apparently favor such basic training (e.g., Haffey, 1970; Gripp and Magaro, 1971; McReynolds and Coleman, 1972). Since no well-controlled experimental investigation could be found in the literature to support the utility of training staff in basic behavioral principles, the present study focused training on the specific procedures of the program. Important basic principles were described within the presentation of aspects of the program where this was deemed helpful to promote staff understanding. It was thought that the modest abilities of many line staff, as well as the limited time available for training, called into question staff training in abstract concepts and technical language. Rather, it was decided that staff would best understand necessary underlying concepts when using procedures in the everyday situations familiar to them. It has been the experience of the present author that information can best be disseminated to community paraprofessionals in simple everyday language devoid of behavioral jargon ("reinforcement," "stimulus," "schedule," etc.). Experimental evaluation of the usefulness of training staff in basic concepts to promote behavioral change would be a welcome addition to the literature.

In presenting the appropriate staff approach to each targeted behavior, the group trainer began by verbally describing (pinpointing) each step of the procedural approach presented in the handbook. Staff were encouraged to ask questions, and in many cases the language of the handbook was reworded to make it more easily understood. Important concepts underlying a procedure were described using everyday examples relevant to the particular group of staff members.

Modeling and Role Playing

Many investigators have made use of real-life or videotape modeling of procedures in training staff (Lee and Znachko, 1968; Martin and Pear, 1970; Herzog, 1971). In addition, most trainers encourage subjects to behaviorally role play the modeled procedures to insure that information learned is successfully translated into behavioral change. Role playing enables subjects to practice, make mistakes, and (with feedback from the trainer) modify behavior on an ongoing basis. Nay (1974) has shown modeling and role playing to be more effective training methods than lecture presentation alone.

Each procedure was carefully modeled by the trainer, who verbally labeled each separate step throughout the presentation. Then staff were divided into dyads and encouraged to practice the procedure, with one staff member playing the role of a child. Role reversals enabled all staff members to practice each procedure and to experience both staff and child roles in its use. The trainer sequentially observed each dyad, providing feedback to individual staff and additional modeling of a procedure when necessary. Although many balked at the role playing as unnecessary ("This is simple; I can easily do that"), role playing revealed that most staff members were unable to translate the information presented in written, verbal, and modeled form into error-free behavior. On a first role-playing try, most staff made mistakes and, more important, were unaware of their mistakes. Without role playing and concomitant trainer feedback, most staff would have been ill prepared to use the program effectively with the students.

Student Training

Following the six training sessions, the staff were asked to implement the procedures they had learned. It should be noted that during this three-week staff training period, all of the students were also trained in the mechanics of the program. All subjects were given the student handbook described previously, which specified how to earn points in language understandable to them. Each behavior for which points could be earned or lost was defined in simple language, with illustrated examples provided. Clear descriptions of time-out, the three-step contingency and the procedures for card punching were among other topics described in the handbook.

The trainers held meetings with the students of each cottage to model each procedure and to set up role-playing situations so that subjects could behaviorally practice the elements of point earning. These meetings were conducted in an informal atmosphere (e.g., cookies and punch were served) to introduce the program on a positive basis and insure the participation of all subjects. No previously reported token program has described the training of students as well as staff before program implementation.

Follow-Up

Following program implementation, behavioral observations by coders as well as the consultation team showed that many staff members were using the program mechanism improperly. Although the six training sessions proved to be sufficient for approximately 30 percent of the staff to use the procedures in an almost error-free fashion, the remainder of the staff exhibited a varying array of significant performance errors.

Since each individual's mistakes in using the program typically occurred in one specific situation or in dealing with a certain behavior, the use of follow-up groups was limited to staff showing severe deficits in basic program procedures. In addition, 10 undergraduate students who had previously served as coders were trained as behavioral counselors. Counselors were well trained in all aspects of the program and assigned to monitor specific problem staff. These students received university course credit for their participation as counselors. By carefully observing staff use of the procedures in their specific settings, counselors were able to complete detailed evaluation sheets as well as provide immediate feedback to staff regarding inappropriate behavior. Additionally, counselors arranged individualized modeling and role-playing sessions at times convenient to staff members so that appropriate behaviors could be efficiently instituted. Within a three-month period all problem staff had shown moderate to marked improvement in their use of the program (as indicated by the evaluation sheets).

It should be noted that such personalized evaluation of staff members according to highly operationalized criteria provides training school administrators with important information useful in evaluating their staff members. Since all staff members were informed that such evaluative data would be a major criterion for pay raises and promotions, they were motivated to participate and improve in using the program. Investigators have suggested that token program success is dependent on staff reinforcement (O'Leary and Drabman, 1971; Kazdin and Bootzin, 1972). Reinforcers have ranged from beer provided at the end of the day (McNamara, 1971) to salary increases, vacations, and workshift preferences (Ayllon and Azrin, 1968). Panyon, Boozer, and Morris (1970) showed that feedback to staff regarding their performance served to reinforce more appropriate behavior.

In summary, the combination of immediate feedback as well as behaviorally contingent salary and promotion evaluation has proved to be successful in maintaining appropriate use of program procedures.

EVALUATION AND DISCUSSION

Behavioral observation data from 20 classrooms and 6 cottages were collected by the undergraduate coders for a period of eight weeks prior to program implementation at a rate of two one-hour observation sessions each week. Following implementation, data were collected for an additional period of 12 weeks at the same weekly rate. Thus a total of 20 weeks of data was collected in the initial evaluation of the program. At 32 weeks an additional 4 weeks of coding was conducted within 10 of the original 20 classrooms under the same conditions as previous coding sessions. These 10 classrooms were randomly chosen from the group of 20. No cottages were coded during this four-week follow-up interval. This reduction in settings observed at follow-up was necessary due to a decrease in the pool of reliable undergraduate coders. In summary, it should be noted that these data represent 1328 hours of observation conducted over a period of nine months.

Overview of Evaluation

The primary goal of this study was to evaluate the effectiveness of a comprehensive treatment program applied to all settings within an institution. Therefore data presentation will summarize program effectiveness across the 20 classrooms and 6 cottages evaluated rather than presenting individual subject data. In this regard, data collected during the 8 weeks of baseline will be compared to the data representing the 12 weeks following program implementation. This global assessment will be carried out for each behavior coded. Although point earning records and staff reports were plentiful, only data collected by the independent coders are presented, so that such problems as staff biases and reactive measures are precluded. Owing to a variety of potential problems to be discussed, no reversal (return to baseline) of contingencies was performed. Instead, behaviors manipulated are compared to behaviors which remained at baseline throughout the course of the program.

To provide a description of individual classroom performance, data collected within specific classrooms over the full 36 weeks of observations will be illustrated. Since no data collection took place in the cottages beyond 20 weeks, these individual presentations will rely solely on classroom performance.

Assessment of Program Effectiveness: Across Settings

Data Summarization Procedures

Data collected during each one-hour observation period were converted to proportions—ratios of each coded behavior to the total behaviors emitted (e.g., attends, .550; calling out, .120). Patterson, Cobb, and Ray (1973) suggest that proportions provide a representative appraisal of overall group (e.g., family, class) functioning.

For each classroom and cottage a mean proportion was computed for each behavior from the observation sessions during the eight weeks before program implementation (pre), as was a mean proportion from the 12 weeks of data collected following program implementation (post). For each behavior the differences between the classroom and cottage pre and post means were computed. Thus for each classroom and cottage a difference score summarizes the direction and degree of change for each behavior following program implementation. By using these difference scores and t tests, the significance of change across the 20 classrooms and across the 6 cottages was evaluated for each behavior.

Child Behavior: Classroom

Table 5 presents the difference scores for each child behavior across the 20 classrooms. At least two different class periods (C-1, C-2, etc.) were coded and are shown for each of seven teachers (T-1 through T-7). By evaluating more than one class setting for each teacher it is possible to evaluate performance across different groups of students. For example, careful evaluation of Table 5 enables the reader to assess child behavior change across different groups of students. For example, careful evaluation of Table 5 enables the reader to assess child behavior change across four classrooms (C-1, C-2, C-3, C-4) within which T-1 was contingency manager. In addition, Table 5 enables the reader to compare child behavior change in the academic classrooms to change in vocational and educable retarded classroom settings (mean IQ, 72.4).

The reader may assess behavioral change across behaviors within each classroom by viewing horizontally across the table. An assessment of change within a particular behavior across the 20 classrooms is possible by viewing vertically down the table. For each behavior the proportion of classrooms which showed

Table 5. Differences between Pretreatment and Posttreatment Means for Child Behaviors: Classroom

Teacher (T): Class (C)	Baseline Behaviors			Targeted Behaviors		
	Call Outs	Out of Seat	Attends	Nonattends	Inappropriate Verbal	Inappropriate Physical
			Academic Classroom Settings			
T-1 : C-1	−.002	−.016	+.108	+.003	+.039	+.001
T-1 : C-2	+.005	−.066	+.436	−.269	−.111	−.009
T-1 : C-3	−.220	+.007	+.220	−.151	−.049	−.004
T-1 : C-4	−.007	+.040	+.016	−.042	−.032	−.044
T-2 : C-1	−.007	−.002	+.034	−.015	.001	+.004
T-2 : C-2	−.032	+.010	+.179	−.079	+.012	−.001
T-3 : C-1	+.053	−.005	+.147	−.052	−.021	−.032
T-3 : C-2	+.022	+.037	+.095	−.092	−.029	+.021
T-3 : C-3	+.025	+.004	−.030	+.018	+.016	+.001
T-4 : C-1	−.001	+.005	+.026	−.044	−.020	−.006
T-4 : C-2	+.001	−.004	+.278	−.144	+.007	−.009
T-5 : C-1	−.002	−.035	+.038	+.041	−.012	−.008
T-5 : C-2	+.005	+.002	+.073	−.052	−.033	−.091
T-5 : C-3	−.007	+.032	+.120	−.058	+.023	+.001

	Vocational Classroom Settings			Educable Retarded Classroom Settings		
T-6 : C-1	+.008	-.001	-.157	+.001	-.016	-.006
T-6 : C-2	+.004	+.026	+.045	-.009	-.012	-.002
T-7 : C-1	-.002	+.014	-.015	+.074	-.005	-.001
T-7 : C-2	-.007	+.009	+.040	-.019	-.059	-.011
T-7 : C-3	+.001	+.003	+.133	-.081	-.019	-.001
T-7 : C-4	-.004	+.007	+.051	-.012	-.063	-.004
In desired direction[a] / total N[b]	11/20	7/20	17/20	15/20	15/20	14/20
t value	-.933	+.409	+2.94**	-3.00**	-3.34**	-1.554

Note: All numbers represent the difference between the mean proportion pretreatment and the mean proportion posttreatment. All signs indicate the actual direction of change.

[a] Number of classrooms within which a pre-postchange in the desired direction was found.
[b] Total number of classrooms reported.

**$p < .01$.

229

behavioral change in the desired direction is computed at the base of Table 5. In addition, the results of *t* tests for correlated means performed on the classroom difference scores are seen for each child behavior. One-tailed tests were used since the hypotheses were directional.

With regard to the targeted behaviors which were manipulated by the program, Table 5 illustrates that subjects showed a significant increase in attending to classroom tasks ($t = 2.94, df = 19, p < .01$), a significant decrease in nonattending ($t = -3.00, df = 19, p < .01$), and a significant decrease in inappropriate verbal behavior ($t = -3.34, df = 19, p < .01$). A decrease in child inappropriate physical behavior closely approached but did not meet an acceptable level of significance ($t = -1.55, df = 19, p < .10$).

Table 5 shows two baseline behaviors that were not directly manipulated by the program. A comparison of targeted behaviors to behaviors maintained at baseline was suggested as an alternative to reversal of contingencies by Kazdin and Bootzin (1972). Table 5 indicates that callouts and out-of-seat behaviors remained at baseline throughout the period of intervention while all manipulated behaviors showed change in the desired direction. This finding, coupled with the consistent pattern of change across a large number of settings, suggests that no idiosyncratic classroom variable (e.g., the special ability of one teacher) or institutional variable (e.g., a change in the administration) was responsible for the results obtained.

Many investigators have recently questioned a return to baseline conditions for a variety of reasons. Assuming that it is feasible to return to baseline conditions, teachers, parents, or institutional staff may be unwilling to tolerate the undesirable behaviors present at baseline. Even if willing, contingency managers may be unable to behave in the same way they behaved before intervention (O'-Leary and Drabman, 1971). Tharp and Wetzel (1969) reported on a case where a return to baseline was impossible since social reinforcers now maintained the desired behavior. In fact, the more successful the treatment effect, the more difficult it is to return to a true baseline (Browning and Stover, 1971). Moreover, successive replications may train the child to retrieve his undesired habits more quickly, as well as making them more resistant to extinction (Browning and Stover, 1971). A more thorough review of the problems associated with reversals is provided by O'Leary and Drabman (1971) and Kazdin and Bootzin (1972) in excellent review articles.

In the present case, the school administrators would not permit a return to baseline, fearing that a reversal might well provoke large-scale destructive behavior among a population of youngsters expecting to be disappointed. The predictable elevation in deviant behavior would be as much a function of subjects' anger at having their first opportunity to experience positive feedback for their efforts terminated as it would of a return to "natural" conditions. Although such a return would no doubt have produced convincing illustrations of high rate inappropriate behavior when points were removed, such data would be open to question for the reasons mentioned.

Child Behavior: Cottage

Useful observations of child behaviors within the cottage settings were limited by the low rates of many important child behaviors (e.g., noncompliance, verbal and physical aggressiveness). Moreover, since little structure was provided in the cottage, behaviors such as inappropriate verbal and physical acts have little meaning (subjects are typically permitted to talk to other peers). An assessment of attending to cottage tasks showed a significant increase ($t = 3.35$, $df = 5$, $p < .01$) when difference scores were compared across the six cottages. In summary, an evaluation of the cottage data indicated that the time-sampling, classroom-oriented approach of the coding methodology was ill suited to the cottage and must be revised before useful child data can be obtained.

Staff Behavior: Classroom

Table 6 presents the difference scores for five targeted and one baseline behavior across the 20 classrooms. Table 6 is constructed in the same fashion as Table 5. With regard to targeted behaviors, a significant increase in staff use of social rewards was observed ($t = 1.88$, $df = 19$, $p < .05$). An important finding is that the proportion of direct, well-labeled rewards to total rewards also increased significantly ($t = 2.04$, $df = 19$, $p < .05$). Thus a qualitative as well as quantitative change in staff use of social reinforcement was found. Staff use of well-labeled negative communications (e.g., carefully specifying some child inappropriate behavior) also increased significantly ($t = 1.79$, $df = 19$, $p < .05$). A significant decrement in staff inappropriate behavior ($t = -1.96$, $df = 19$, $p < .05$) illustrates an improvement in staff observation (tracking) of child inappropriate behavior.

An important goal of training was to increase the proportion of staff direct commands to total commands given the subjects. Paradoxically, a significant decrease in the proportion of direct to total commands was observed ($t = -2.23$, $df = 19$, $p < .05$). It is difficult to explain this decrease in staff use of direct commands. Training presented the use of direct commands within the context of approaches to student behaviors. Perhaps additional training sessions which specifically focus on the modeling and role playing of appropriate use of direct commands are necessary.

The use of staff physical rewards (baseline behavior) was not directly manipulated by the present study. Table 6 shows that in 10 of the 20 classrooms no physical rewards could be coded before or after program implementation. No significant change in this behavior was shown by a t test performed. It is puzzling that the staff's increased use of verbal social reinforcement did not generalize to physical expression. Kazdin and Bootzin (1972) suggest there is a need

Table 6. Differences between Pretreatment and Posttreatment Means for Staff Behaviors: Classroom

Teacher (T) : Class (C)	Baseline Behavior Physical Rewards	Total Verbal Rewards	Direct Total Rewards	Targeted Behaviors	Direct/ Total Commands	Staff Inappropriate
				Labeled Negative		
			Academic Classroom Settings			
T-1 : C-1		−.004	.000	+.010	−.150	−.001
T-1 : C-2		+.001	.000	+.001	−.690	−.079
T-1 : C-3	−.002	+.007	+.500	−.003	−.120	−.038
T-1 : C-4	+.001	+.009	+.500	+.003	+.015	−.038
T-2 : C-1	−.002	+.007	+.800	−.003	−.102	−.038
T-2 : C-2	+.011	+.063	+.011	+.013	−.183	−.001
T-3 : C-1		+.001	.000	+.001	−.633	−.114
T-3 : C-2	−.005	+.005	.000	−.008	−.385	+.135
T-3 : C-3		+.019	+.500	−.005	+.104	−.013
T-4 : C-1	−.003	+.004	+.125	+.005	+.223	−.033
T-4 : C-2	+.003	+.050	+.275	+.001	+.043	−.401
T-5 : C-1		+.001	.000	+.001	+.131	−.042
T-5 : C-2		+.006	.000	+.012	+.076	−.118
T-5 : C-3		+.002	.000	+.001	+.233	−.143

Vocational Classroom Settings

T-6 : C-1	−.004	−.031	−.333	−.003	−.305	−.065
T-6 : C-2		+.002	.000	+.004	−.176	−.001
			Educable Retarded Classroom Settings			
T-7 : C-1		+.010	.000	+.098	+.324	+.170
T-7 : C-2		+.014	−.500	+.020	−.278	−.353
T-7 : C-3	+.009	−.040	+.174	−.002	+.020	−.007
T-7 : C-4	−.011	−.017	+.456	−.003	−.225	−.031
In desired direction[a]/ total N[b]	4/10[c]	16/20	9/20	13/20	9/20	18/20
t value	+156	+1.88*	+2.04*	+1.79*	−2.23*	−1.96*

Note. All numbers represent the difference between the mean proportion pretreatment and the mean proportion posttreatment. All signs indicate the actual direction of change.

[a]Number of classrooms within which a pre-postchange in the desired direction was found.

[b]Total number of classrooms reported.

[c]Number of classrooms where some incidence of physical rewards was observed.

*$p < .05$.

233

Table 7.   Difference Between Pretreatment and Posttreatment Means for
Staff Behaviors: Cottage

Cottage	Baseline Behavior	Targeted Behaviors		
	Physical Rewards	Total Verbal Rewards	Direct/Total Rewards	Direct/Total Commands
Cottage 1	−.001	+.087	+1.000	−.211
Cottage 2	+.013	+.039	+1.000	−.060
Cottage 3	+.008	+.065	+ .050	−.054
Cottage 4	+.036	+.050	+1.000	+.169
Cottage 5	−.012	+.007	.000	+.256
In desired direction[a]/total N[b]	3/5	5/5	4/5	2/5
t value	+1.80	+6.46**	+1.29	−.015

Note. All numbers represent the difference between the mean proportion pretreatment and the mean proportion posttreatment. All signs indicate the actual
direction of change.

[a]Number of classrooms within which a pre-postchange in the desired direction
was found.

[b]Total number of classrooms reported.

**$p < .01$.

to examine response generalization within token programs. Perhaps the present
finding of little response generalization to behaviors maintained at baseline are
indicative of the highly specific effects of token contingencies.

Staff Behavior: Cottage

Table 7 presents the difference scores for three targeted and one baseline behavior across the six residence cottages. Although a highly significant increase in
total staff use of social rewards was found ($t = 6.46$, $df = 5$, $p < .01$), the
proportion of direct to total rewards showed only a nonsignificant trend of improvement. In cottages 1, 2, and 4, staff emitted no direct rewards before the
program. Following implementation it can be noted that all rewards issued were
direct in nature. This change is misleading and reflects the few rewards of any
kind that were emitted within the cottage. The lack of structured activities
(e.g., academic and vocational tasks in the school) may provide fewer opportunities for staff to make use of social rewards.

In contrast to the paradoxical classroom findings previously mentioned, no
significant change was found in the proportion of direct to total commands
across the cottages. For the baseline behavior (physical rewards) no significant
change was found. All cottage data are based on low-frequency behaviors,
which makes an analysis of proportions somewhat misleading (e.g., the extensive improvement in cottages 1, 2, and 3).

Targeted Behaviors: Staff Report

Although no independent assessment by reliable behavioral coders was feasible, staff reports of additional targeted behaviors is provided here. These data should be evaluated with caution and therefore are not emphasized in formal evaluation of the program.

An evaluation of tardy slips forwarded to the school principal showed 39 incidences of tardiness during the month before program implementation. This frequency decreased by 50 percent during the first month of the program. Tardiness continued to decrease to a low of 10 incidences during the fifth month of the program.

Rule violations decreased significantly. For example, before the program an average of 10 windows per month were willfully broken by subjects (destruction of property). Following program implementation only two windows were broken over a five-month period. Self-mutilation (pin-sticking) decreased from an average of five cases per week to less than one per week. The incidence of runs from the campus does not seem to have been significantly altered by the program, remaining at a low level. Reported stealing also remained at the very low level exhibited before program implementation. Very private acts such as stealing rarely meet with response cost, due to the difficulty in determining the initiator. In summary, school administration reports indicate that the response cost applied to rule violations has produced somewhat mixed results for the behaviors studied. A dramatic decrease in tardiness and destructive behaviors occurred following initiation of the program.

Assessment of Program Effectiveness: Within Settings

To illustrate student performance within individual settings, the data representing randomly chosen classrooms for three teachers (T-1, T-3, and T-4) are presented. Three targeted child behaviors (attends, nonattends, inappropriate verbal) as well as one nontargeted behavior (out of seat) are illustrated.

Figure 3 is a graph of the mean proportion of attending behavior for 2 week periods through the 20 weeks of initial data collection. In addition, the month of follow-up data is represented by two 2-week intervals (weeks 34 and 36). Each point on the graph represents the mean of four 1-hour observation sessions carried out over the 2-week interval. (Note that in some cases fewer than four observation sessions were conducted over a 2-week period due to classes being cancelled, coder illness, etc.) The first 8 weeks represent baseline observations and may be compared with the data collected from 10 to 36 weeks to evaluate performance following program implementation.

It may be noted that a steady increment in child attending is shown following program implementation for all three staff members. This improvement is maintained at the 34- and 36-week follow-up. Both T-1–C-1 and T-3–C-2 show

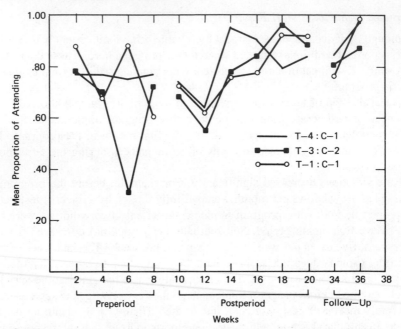

Figure 3. Three classrooms illustrate the mean proportion of child attending behavior for two-week intervals within the nine-month observation period.

considerable variability in the mean proportions of attending over the 8 weeks of baseline. This variability decreased following program implementation. This decrease in variability was found for a large number of settings evaluated, as would be expected due to the institution of a consistent approach to child behavior within and across settings.

Figure 4 shows a significant reduction in nonattending behavior for the three classrooms following the onset of the program. Again significant variability in the proportion of the behavior is shown over the 8 weeks of baseline. At 34 weeks follow-up a significant increment in nonattending is shown for T-4–C-1 and T-3–C-2. In both cases this behavior decreased to low levels at 36 weeks, suggesting increased variability at follow-up for these two classrooms. Additional follow-up observations would have clarified this trend. It should be noted that nonattending as defined by the present coding system does not include nonattentive verbal and physical interactions (these are coded as inappropriate verbal and physical interactions; see Table 2). Therefore nonattending can be at zero level while attending is less than 100 percent (due to interactive nonattending).

Figure 5 shows a significant decrease in inappropriate verbal behavior following program implementation. In fact, no inappropriate verbal interactions were coded from week 16 through week 20. At follow-up these results were main-

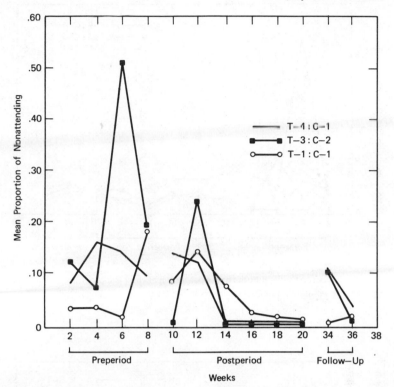

Figure 4. Three classrooms illustrate the mean proportion of child nonattending behavior for two-week intervals within the nine-month observation period.

tained for T-1–C-1 and T-4–C-1; however, a significant increment in inappropriate verbal behavior was observed for T-3–C-2. No explanation can be offered for this increment.

Figure 6 shows the mean proportions of out-of-seat behavior. It may be recalled that out-of-seat behavior was not directly manipulated by the treatment program. It is apparent that no significant change in out-of-seat behavior occurred following program implementation for any classroom presented. Out-of-seat behavior remained at baseline, whereas a consistent pattern of improvement is noted for behaviors manipulated by the program.

SUMMARY AND CONCLUSIONS

The development of a comprehensive behavioral treatment program within an institution for delinquents has been described. Following a description of the

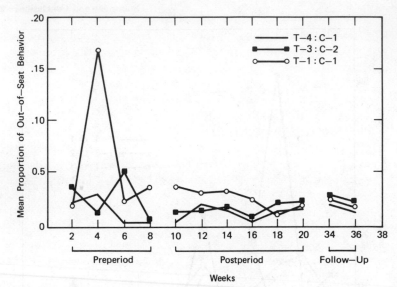

Figure 5. Three classrooms illustrate the mean proportion of child inappropriate verbal behavior for two-week intervals within the nine-month observation period.

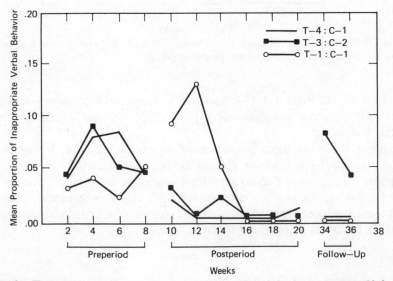

Figure 6. Three classrooms illustrate the mean proportion of seat behavior (a nontargeted behavior) for two-week intervals within the nine-month observation period.

238

setting, students, and staff, an analysis of the major steps in program development was provided. The present study illustrated an approach to assessment of institutional needs. Complex observational strategies and administration definition of problem areas within the institution were described as one important part of assessment. Inclusion of information from all staff (and students, where possible) in defining program needs and limitations was described as another important step in designing a token program. There is an advantage to developing avenues of course credit so that university students may take part in significant evaluation and treatment roles. The benefit to students of providing a community setting within which academic knowledge may be translated into behavior must also be mentioned.

Since many previous investigators have failed to provide a rationale for their choice of behaviors to manipulate, the underlying assessment data were provided, as were other criteria used to select targeted behaviors for change. A description of the treatment mechanism applied to each targeted behavior was included, along with some considerations necessary for effective use of response cost.

Regarding program evaluation, the direction and degree of behavioral change following program implementation was described for each behavior across classrooms and cottages. Significant behavioral change in the desired direction was observed for a clear majority of targeted behaviors. Significant behavioral change was not observed for any of the three behaviors that were not manipulated by the program. This finding, coupled with the extensiveness of change across a large number of settings suggests that no individual classroom or staff variable was responsible for the results. These may best be thought of as suggestive of trends of behavior change. The myriad of uncontrolled variables operating within an institution makes laboratory-level research impossible. Blind adherence to laboratory methods in the community setting when so many other variables remain uncontrolled is impractical and unrealistic.

It is apparent that no generalization from targeted to nontargeted behaviors occurred, suggesting the specificity of token program effects.

Data illustrating individual classroom performance over a period of 36 weeks showed significant behavioral change in the desired direction for three classrooms chosen randomly from the 10 classrooms observed for the full 36 weeks. In limited cases follow-up data revealed increments in undesired behavior; however, the lack of additional follow-up data made evaluation of these findings impossible. It should be noted that behavioral observations of classroom behavior are planned at regular intervals for the period of one year. These additional behavioral samples should clarify the stability of the results currently presented. Extensive follow-up within the institution is a necessary part of program evaluation, since staff and student turnover can produce significant changes in the characteristics of treatment.

Follow-up training of all staff as well as extensive training of new staff entering the institution has been necessary to insure consistent use of the program within all settings. As consultants are faded out, institutional staff must be trained to carry out program evaluation and staff training. Since many institutional staff (and administrators) rely on the consultants to see that necessary evaluation and training are performed, it is necessary to urge staff to take on new program responsibilities. Many programs fail because the staff have not been trained to administer the many aspects of the program when consultants leave.

GENERALIZATION

O'Leary and Drabman (1971) and Kazdin and Bootzin (1972) encouraged token program administrators to fade out generalized reinforcers (tokens, points) as soon as possible. Of course the main goal of any token program is to instigate new behavior with token mechanisms, then substitute social and intrinisc reinforcers to maintain the desired behavior. In point of fact, few investigators have found generalization of token-instigated behavior to nontoken environments. The fact that reversal of contingencies has produced a significant reduction in desired behavior in many studies supports this failure of token behavior to generalize. In addition, few investigators evaluate generalization to settings outside the manipulated invironment, due to the multitude of problems encountered in home, job, and school observation.

Regarding the present program, a levels approach has been implemented recently to insure a gradual fading out of token mechanisms. Within this program subjects move through a series of color-coded levels depending on their positive and negative point earning and frequency of time-outs. At each succeeding level subjects enjoy more privileges and responsibilities, as well as additional exposure to the community. The initial "green" level allows subjects to participate only in cottage activities. Subject records her weekly progress on a chart to provide her with maximal feedback of progress and encourage self-observation and reinforcement. Subject presents these charts to her treatment team (case worker, housemother, significant teachers) when she is called in for progress evaluation once each week. The treatment team may then graduate her to the next level ("yellow") or propose an individual treatment plan with subject's help, which she must carry out to earn points toward level movement.

At the two highest levels, privileges and activities are available without having to pay points. At the highest level (pre-release), subject is identified to all staff as eligible for nonsupervised community interaction (e.g., a part-time job, shopping excursions, visits home). She no longer earns points and serves as a treatment aide to assist incoming subjects in working on their individual treatment programs. Thus she has an opportunity to function in a token-free fashion within the community prior to her release. This token-free period will provide an opportunity to evaluate generalization within the institution and, with careful community follow-up, generalization outside the institution setting.

ACKNOWLEDGMENTS

The author would like to extend his appreciation to the Department of Welfare and Institutions, State of Virginia, for supporting the present research and to the many teachers, houseparents and other staff who gave of themselves. Specific thanks are offered to James C. Melvin, Frank Bishop, Louis Legum, Sam Payne, Kathy Youell, Phillip Kendall, Marion Bowyer, and to over fifty additional undergraduate and graduate students of Virginia Commonwealth University for their valuable contributions. A final thanks goes to William S. Ray for consultation provided and to Thomas Baynham for his continued interest.

REFERENCES

Atthowe, J. M., and Krasner, L. Preliminary report on the application of contingent reinforcement procedure (token economy) on a "chronic" psychiatric ward. *Journal of Abnormal Psychology*, 1968, **73**, 37–43.

Ayllon, T., and Azrin, N. H. The measurement and reinforcement of behavior of psychotics. *Journal of the Experimental Analysis of Behavior*, 1965, **8**, 357–383.

Ayllon, T., and Azrin, N. H. *The Token Economy: A Motivational System for Therapy and Rehabilitation*. New York: Appleton-Century-Crofts, 1968.

Barrish, H. H., Saunders, M., and Wolf, M. M. Good behavior game: Effects of individual contingencies for group consequences on disruptive behavior in a classroom. *Journal of Applied Behavior Analysis*, 1969, **2**, 119–124.

Brierton, S., Garms, R., and Metzger, R. Practical problems encountered in an aide administered token reward cottage program. *Mental Retardation*, 1969, **7**, 40–43.

Browning, R. M., and Stover, D. O. *Behavior Modification in Child Treatment: An Experimental and Clinical Approach*. Chicago: Aldine-Atherton, 1971.

Buehler, R. E., Patterson, G. R., and Furniss, J. M. The reinforcement of behavior in institutional settings. *Behavior Research and Therapy*, 1966, **4**, 157–167.

Burchard, J. D., and Barrera, F. An analysis of time-out and response cost in a prgorammed environment. *Journal of Applied Behavior Analysis*, 1972, **5**, 271–282.

Burchard, J. D., and Tyler, V. O. The modification of delinquent behaviour through operant conditioning. *Behaviour Research and Therapy*, 1965, **2**, 245–250.

Cohen, H. L. Educational therapy: The design of learning improvements. In J. M. Shlien (Ed.), *Research in Psychotherapy*, Vol. III. Washington, D.C.: American Psychological Association.

Girardeau, F. L., and Spradlin, J. E. Token rewards in a cottage program. *Mental Retardation*, 1964, **2**, 345–351.

Grabowski, J., and Thompson, T. A behavior modification program for behaviorally retarded institutionalized males. In J. Grabowski and T. Thompson (Ed.), *Behavior Modification of the Mentally Retarded*. New York: Oxford University Press, 1972.

Gripp, R. F., and Magaro, P. A. A token economy program evaluation with untreated control ward comparisons. *Behaviour Research and Therapy*, 1971, **9**, 137–149.

Haffey, V. Behavior modification utilizing a token economy program. *Journal of Psychiatric Nursing and Mental Health Services*, 1970, **8**, 31–35.

Herzog, T. Staff development in child management: Utilizing the principles of behavior shaping. *Journal of Psychiatric Nursing and Mental Health Services*, 1971, **9**, 12–14.

Kaufman, A., and Baron, A. Suppression of behavior by time-out punishment when suppression results in loss of positive reinforcement. *Journal of the Experimental Analysis of Behavior*, 1968, **11**, 595–607.

Kaufman, K. F., and O'Leary K. D. Reward, cost, and self-evaluation procedures for disruptive adolescents in a psychiatric hospital school. *Journal of Applied Behavior Analysis*, 1972, **5**, 293–309.

Kazdin, A. E., and Bootzin, R. R. The token economy: An evaluative review. *Journal of Applied Behavior Analysis*, 1972, **5**, 343–372.

Lee, D., and Znachko, G. Training psychiatric aides in behavior modification techniques. *Journal of Psychiatric Nursing and Mental Health Services*, 1968, **6**, 7–11.

Martin, G. L. Teaching operant technology to psychiatric nurses, aides, and attendants. In F. W. Clark, D. R. Evans, and L. A. Hamerlynck (Eds.), *Implementing Behavioral Programs for Schools and Clinics: Proceedings of the Third Banff International Conference on Behavior Modification*. Champaign, Ill.: Research Press, 1972.

Martin, G. L., and Pear, J. J. Short-term participation by 130 undergraduates as operant conditioners in an ongoing project with autistic children. *Psychological Record*, 1970, **20**, 327–336.

McNamara, J. R. Teacher and students as sources for behavior modification in the classroom. *Behavior Therapy*, 1971, **2**, 205–213.

McReynolds, W. T., and Coleman, J. Token economy: Patient and staff changes. *Behaviour Research and Therapy*, 1972, **10**, 29–34.

Meichenbaum, D. H., Bowers, K., and Ross, R. R. Modification of classroom behavior of institutionalized female adolescent offenders. *Behaviour Research and Therapy*, 1968, **6**, 343–353.

Nay, W. R. Written, lecture, modeling, and roleplaying as instructional techniques for parents. *Behavior Therapy*, 1974, in press.

Nay, W. R., and Legum, L. A color-coded discriminator in reprogramming a classroom for the mentally retarded. Paper presented at Southeastern Psychological Association, New Orleans, La., April 1973.

O'Leary, K. D., and Becker, W. C. Behavior modification of an adjustment class: A token reinforcement program. *Exceptional Children*, 1967, **9**, 637–642.

O'Leary, K. D., Becker, W. C., Evans, M. B., and Saudgras, R. A. A token reinforcement program in a public school: A replication systematic analysis. *Journal of Applied Behavior Analysis*, 1969, **2**, 3–13.

O'Leary, K. D., and Drabman, R. Token reinforcement programs in the classroom: A review. *Psychological Bulletin*, 1971, **75**, 379–398.

Panyon, N., Boozer, H., and Morris, N. Feedback to attendants as a reinforcer for applying operant techniques. *Journal of Applied Behavior Analysis*, 1970, **3**, 1–4.

Patterson, G. R., Cobb, J. A, and Ray, R. A social engineering technology for retraining aggressive boys. In H. E. Adams and I. P. Unikel (Eds.), *Issues and Trends in Behavior Therapy*. Springfield, Ill.: Thomas, 1973.

Patterson, G. R., Ray, R. S., and Shaw, D. A. Direct instruction in families of deviant children. *Oregon Research Institute Research Bulletin*, 1968, **8**, No. 9.

Phillips, E. L. Achievement place: Token reinforcement procedures in a home-style rehabilitation setting for "pre-delinquent" boys. *Journal of Applied Behavior Analysis*, 1968, **1**, 213–223.

Phillips, E. L., Phillips, E. A., Fixen, D., and Wolf, M. Achievement place: Modification of the behaviors of pre-delinquent boys within a token economy. *Journal of Applied Behavior Analysis*, 1971, **4**, 45–59.

Tharp, R. G., and Wetzel, R. J. *Behavior Modification in the Natural Environment*. New York: Academic Press, 1969.

Tyler, V. O., and Brown, G. D. Token reinforcement of academic performance with institutionalized delinquent boys. *Journal of Educational Psychology*, 1968, **59**, 164–168.

Walker, H., and Buckley, N. The use of positive reinforcement in conditioning attending behavior. *Journal of Applied Behavior Analysis*, 1968, **1**, 245–252.

Walker, H., and Buckley, N. K. Programming generalization and maintenance of treatment effects across time and across settings. *Journal of Applied Behavior Analysis*, 1972, **5**, 209–224.

CHAPTER 7

Learned Control of Cardiovascular Processes: Feedback mechanisms and therapeutic applications*

JASPER BRENER

It is well established that the precision and specificity of learned motor control may be substantially enhanced by the provision of exteroceptive feedback contingent upon effector action. Thus, for example, Basmajian (1963) demonstrated that when the activity of a single motor unit is amplified and presented to the subject as a sequence of auditory clicks, the subject rapidly acquires the ability to accurately control the rate of firing in that unit. Findings of this sort indicate that the specificity of voluntary motor control is limited only by the capacity of the feedback channel that transmits information from the effector mechanism to the control centers of the nervous system.

This general principle finds ready application in a variety of clinical settings. For example, Hardyck et al. (1966) utilized a similar feedback procedure to increase silent reading speed. These investigators, observing that subvocalization is a significant factor in reducing silent reading speed, provided their subjects with auditory feedback from the vocal musculature. When subjects were instructed to suppress the auditory feedback while reading, a complete cessation of subvocalization was obtained in one session. Furthermore, follow-up tests one month and three months after training indicated no recurrence of this symptom. A very similar technique was employed by Budzynski et al. (1970) in the treatment of tension headaches. Such headaches are caused by sustained tension of the scalp and neck muscles. Patients were provided with auditory feedback in the form of a tone which varied in pitch as a direct function of the *frontalis* EMG amplitude. Under these conditions all patients learned to reduce frontalis

*Research reported in this chapter was supported by NIMH Grant 17061.

EMG activity with an attendant reduction in the headaches. No recurrence of these symptoms was noted over a three-month follow-up.

The generality of the effects of exteroceptive feedback on the development of motor control was expanded when Razran (1961) reported an experiment by the Russian investigator Lisina on learned vasomotor control in humans. This investigator observed that when subjects were permitted to watch polygraphic records of their vasomotor activity they learned to avoid electric shock by vasodilation, although the unconditioned response to this stimulus was constriction. In the absence of such exteroceptive feedback, however, the vasodilatory avoidance response was not acquired. The significance of this report was its suggestion that voluntary control of visceral responses was not, as had previously been believed, precluded by inherent structural properties of the nervous system. In this case, provision of exteroceptive feedback led to the development of voluntary control over an autonomically mediated vascular activity. Since the time of Razran's report of this experiment, the literature on learned visceral and nervous system events has grown prolifically. The purpose of this chapter is to discuss the principles underlying such learning and to consider the theoretical and applied implications of these phenomena.

THE LIBERALIZATION OF VOLITION

Since its most archaic beginnings, Western science has explicitly denied the possibility that the internal workings of the body may be the object of willful manipulation. Although volition is traditionally seen as the cause of behavior, simple reflection tells us that we cannot specify how to execute any of the activities that we classify as voluntary. As Sherrington (1940) pointed out: "Our mind is unaware of how we do our standing, walking, running, and so on . . . it knows but the result" (p. 156). It furthermore appears that the illusion of voluntary control rests on the consequences of our actions rather than their antecedents. Thus Laszlo (1966) observed that when subjects are deprived of interoceptive feedback from their arm muscles, they were also robbed of the illusion of voluntary control. In this study Laszlo produced functional deafferentation of the limb by applying a pressure block. When sensations in the limb were lost, she instructed subjects to execute various responses of the hand. Although subjects complied with these instructions, they reported being unable to. Because the visceral afferent system is relatively underdeveloped and, as a consequence, visceral actions relatively indiscriminable, our long commitment to the concept of a nonvoluntary visceral system is scarcely surprising.

The new literature on operant and voluntary control of such processes therefore represents a substantial and revolutionary change in our view of the *modus operandi* of organisms. It strongly asserts that contrary to our traditional view, activities of the nervous system and viscera do not differ qualitatively from somatomotor activities in their reaction to response-contingent reinforcement and feedback.

The late and sudden emergence of such phenomena bears our close scrutiny. Although it may be argued with some force that the recent discovery of learned control of internal responses is due to the passing of a technological threshold in psychophysiology, a virtual dearth of published investigations of such phenomena prior to 1960 weakens this explanation. In fact when Skinner (1938) reported apparent success in conditioning vasomotor activity in the forearm of a human subject, the evidence was discounted. At the time, the view that visceral responses were members of an involuntary, reflexively controlled, and automatic system was too deeply entrenched to accomodate this datum. Similarly, the scientific community has been painfully slow in recognizing the fabled ability of yogis to exercise "voluntary control" over their viscera (Wenger et al., 1961). Such data could not readily be assimilated with our arduously derived dualistic view of the organism. Since its earliest beginnings, biology has been committed to a model of the organism that incorporates a mechanical entity and a more ephemeral volitional or rational entity. Current physiology textbooks continue to make copious reference to the "voluntary" and "involuntary" response systems. It would therefore seem more correct to attribute the late emergence of learned visceral control to the dissolution of such common prejudices relating to the *modus operandi* of organisms rather than to a technological lag.

It seems defensible to argue that what we are seeing in this literature is a significant reemergence of a mechanistic view of the organism. The significance of the movement is that it broaches the nature of volition in a more direct and empirical fashion than ever before. The traditional concept of volition as a final cause of behavior has led science away from an objective description of human behavior and has established a barrier around psychology that is virtually impenetrable by other biological sciences. As Blanchard (1958) suggested, "You are too much preoccupied with the ends to which the choice would be a means to give any attention to the causes of which your choice may be an effect" (p. 21). By establishing that visceral activities are amenable to learned control, this new literature not only identifies a potentially valuable therapeutic tool but, in addition, leads us to more critically examine the labels "voluntary" and "involuntary" that we so freely employ in the description of behavior. Perhaps the liberalizing of the concept of volition that is implied by this literature will lead us to more seriously examine the causes of voluntary activity.

VOLUNTARY AND INVOLUNTARY

Traditionally the concepts of "voluntary" and "involuntary" are viewed as opposite poles of a behavioral continuum. Circumscribed activities are seen as falling somewhere along this linear continuum. Although physiology has tended to assume that such voluntary-involuntary distinctions are based on stable structural differences in respective neural control circuits, psychology, particularly in its applied clinical aspects, has assumed that the boundaries separating these classes of behavior are not immutable. In fact, much of clinical practice may be described as an attempt to alter the status of a response from involuntary to voluntary. Although the literature on learned visceral control is more easily assimilated by the latter approach, it should be recognized that this is primarily because psychology has avoided making the definitions of voluntary and involuntary explicit. Although linguistically these terms are opposites, operationally they are not.

Whatever universal meaning accrues to the concept of voluntary behavior is derived from its operational usage. In this context, a voluntary response is one that is systematically influenced by instructions. To establish whether a particular activity is voluntary, an individual is instructed to produce or inhibit the response in question. Compliance with the instruction is the only objective criterion to be employed in the classification of the response as voluntary or not. If the instructions fail to influence the activity in the appropriate manner, the voluntary status of the response is not established. Repeated failure to demonstrate instructional control over a response establishes the *nonvoluntary* status of that response. Since such voluntary characteristics of a response are assumed to rely on the fulfillment of certain training procedures, it is also assumed that the nonvoluntary status of a response may be reversed by the application of the appropriate procedures.

Involuntary responses are operationally defined as those that are reliably elicited by a narrowly delineated class of stimuli in the absence of any other conditions. The major implication of the clause relating to the absence of any other conditions in the involuntary production of a response is that this form of control is intrinsically embedded in the structure of the organism. Needless to say, the ability of an eliciting stimulus to produce its associated involuntary response is to some extent determined by the prior treatment of the recipient organism. Thus, for example, food powder in the mouth will not elicit salivation in a satiated dog. In satiated dogs, therefore, it might be said that salivation to food powder is not an involuntary response. In this instance, salivation may be termed a ''noninvoluntary'' response; certainly it would not be called a voluntary response.

It is therefore proposed that voluntary and involuntary represent two independent dimensions in the classification of behavior rather than being opposite poles of a linear continuum. Numerous responses of the striate musculature such as eye-blinking, knee-jerking, respiration, and limb withdrawal display easily demonstrable voluntary and involuntary characteristics; that is, they may be systematically influenced by instructions and eliciting stimuli. To this array of responses that are amenable to both forms of control, we may now also add the visceral and nervous system activities reported in the recent literature. Hence it seems to be unwarranted to suggest that the structural attributes of an effector system preclude the demonstration of either voluntary or involuntary responses in that system. In other words, the inability to demonstrate either voluntary or involuntary activities in a given effector system reflects deficits in the demonstration operations rather than impenetrable anatomical barriers implicit in the response apparatus.

It is proposed, then, that all responses are amenable to *both* voluntary *and* involuntary control. The task of psychophysiology and related biological disciplines is to specify the conditions under which the voluntary and involuntary characteristics of different effector systems may be reliably demonstrated. The operations employed to demonstrate such behavioral characteristics will be predicated upon the model of functioning assumed to underlie the voluntary and involuntary response processes. In view of this, an examination of the relative merits of established approaches to the analysis of behavior appears to be in order. Since the demonstration of involuntary characteristics in a response is relatively unequivocal, discussion of these procedures is unnecessary. It should nevertheless be recognized that the eliciting stimuli for involuntary responses may vary greatly in their complexity and in their locus of application.

OPERANT AND VOLUNTARY CONTROL

Perusal of the literature on learned visceral control indicates that the techniques employed in the training of such control are referred to either as operant conditioning or as voluntary control procedures. Thus Brener (1966) employed a shock-avoidance contingency to train heartrate increases and decreases in human subjects, whereas Brener and Hothersall (1966) employed instructions and feedback stimuli to achieve the same end. Within the context of the approach adopted here, no substantial distinction is made between the processes of operant and voluntary control. An operant response is defined as one that is reliably influenced by a discriminative stimulus; a voluntary response, as one that is reliably influenced by an instructional stimulus. In other words, instruction and discriminative stimuli are considered to be members of a general class of environmental events that may be termed conditioned or learned initiating stimuli. Neither discriminative nor instructional stimuli display systematic unconditional influences on the response that they eventually come to control: the response-controlling properties of these events is conditional upon certain prior treatments. Examination of these prior treatments amplifies the operational similarity of the voluntary and operant responses.

Although it is well known that operant-controlling (discriminative) properties may be established in an otherwise neutral stimulus by presentation of that stimulus during the reinforcement of a response, the operations involved in establishing equivalent properties in instructional stimuli have not been made explicit. It was, however, noted earlier that the provision of exteroceptive feedback of effector action enhances learned control over the activities of the effector. Conversely, it is well established that disturbances of exteroceptive feedback consequent upon effector action lead to disruption of motor control (Chase et al., 1959; Smith et al., 1960). Since the reinforcing stimuli conventionally employed in operant conditioning may also legitimately be considered members of the general class of exteroceptive feedback stimuli, it is proposed that the availability of response-contingent stimulation is prerequisite to the demonstration of either the voluntary or operant characteristics of a response.

The principal distinction between feedback stimuli and reinforcing stimuli is that the incentive properties that are intrinsic to the latter must be established in the former by appropriate manipulations. However, even this difference is relative. It will be recognized that the reinforcing properties of very few stimuli are unconditional. Thus, for example, food will exhibit reinforcing properties only provided that the recipient organism is food-deprived. The difference between those events termed "secondary" or "conditional" reinforcers and those called feedback stimuli is marginal. It will also be noted that reinforcing and feedback stimuli are subject to similar manipulations (delay, magnitude, probability, and density) in relationship to the behavior upon which they are contingent, and that these manipulations result in similar influences on such behaviors. Given the functional similarity of instructional and discriminative stimuli on the one hand and feedback and reinforcing stimuli on the other, a strong case can be made for the operational equivalence of voluntary and operant behaviors. The basic operations involved in the demonstration of these two classes of behavior are as follows:

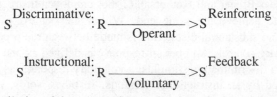

Despite the similarity of these paradigms, the analytical models associated with the operant and feedback approaches to learned motor control differ in a significant fashion.

Within the traditional conditioning framework, reinforcement is posited as a final cause of behavior; the motor skills literature has not accorded feedback this status. Whereas the reinforcement model postulates that reinforcement functions to "stamp in" connections between stimuli and responses, the feedback model provides a framework within which this "stamping in" function may be analyzed. Although no system provides explanatory concepts that are immune to further reduction, it is nevertheless true that certain systems permit finer-grain analyses than do others. The principle of reinforcement which is axiomatic in the reinforcement approach to behavior control is derivative from more basic axioms in the feedback approach. The primary benefit of the latter approach is that by specifying how response-contingent stimulation leads to the development of learned motor control, it generates a more flexible and comprehensive model in terms of which the development of such control may be better understood. This conceptual framework in turn suggests the procedural means whereby the development of voluntary motor control may be more precisely influenced.

THE FUNCTIONS OF FEEDBACK STIMULI

As has already been mentioned, feedback from an effector is a necessary condition for the development of voluntary control over the activities of that effector. Furthermore, it appears that the development and maintenance of voluntary control is dependent on at least two modes of feedback: interoceptive and exteroceptive. Thus we may observe that functional (Laszlo, 1966) or structural (Mott and Sherrington, 1895) interruption of the afferent neural pathways leads to an impairment of voluntary control. Loss of exteroceptive feedback is also observed to interfere with the acquisition of voluntary control, as in the case of speech acquisition in deaf individuals. What is assumed to be a minimal voluntary control circuit is illustrated in Figure 1. In addition to incorporating the feedback pathways just referred to, this circuit comprises components representing a central sensory integrator, a central motor controller, an efferent motor pathway, and an effector apparatus. A more complete description of this model has been provided elsewhere (Brener, 1974).

The interoceptive afferent stimuli contingent upon the execution of an act represent an extremely precise definition of the topographical dimensions and intensive characteristics of an effector action. The occurrence of such stimuli therefore provides an adequate basis upon which the nervous system can evaluate effector action and provide the necessary corrective signals. James (1890) proposed that ''A supply of ideas of the various movements that are possible left in the memory by experiences of their involuntary performance is thus the first prerequisite of voluntary life'' (p. 488). It is assumed here that the regulation of motor action is based on a comparison of the immediate sensory consequences of the act with the memory or image of past occurrences of the act (von Holst, 1954). In accordance with the *ideomotor* theory of voluntary action proposed by James (1890), the formation of the RI (response image) is assumed to rest upon the pairing of exteroceptive stimuli with the interoceptive consequences of the act. As a function of this procedure the exteroceptive stimuli come to elicit the pattern of central activation (the RI) that in the past had been produced by interoceptive feedback from the effectors. Elicitation of an RI is further assumed to lead to the selection and activation of a motor program ap-

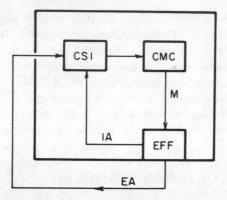

Figure 1. Minimal voluntary control circuit. *Abbreviations:* CSI = central sensory integrator; CMC = centrol motor controller; M = efferent motor pathways; Eff = effector apparatus; IA = interoceptive afferent pathway; EA = exteroceptive afferent pathway;

The development of voluntary control is assumed to rest upon the pairing of interoceptive afference transmitted via the IA pathway and exteroceptive afference transmitted via the EA pathway to the CSI. As a function of this pairing operation, the EA stimulus acquires the property of eliciting the pattern of excitation in the CSI that was previously contingent upon activation of the IA pathway by Eff activity. This pattern of central excitation is termed the response image (RI) and its activation leads in turn to the selection and activation of a pattern of activity in the CMC which is appropriate to the production of the response specified in the RI. CMC activation leads in turn to Eff action via the efferent pathways (M). The interoceptive afference consequent upon Eff activity is compared in the CSI with that specified by the RI. If the two are in accord, the act is completed; if not, additional motor signals are generated.

propriate to the production of effector activity which has as its consequence the pattern of interoceptive afferentation specified in the response image. It should be noted that these processes are assumed to operate only during the acquisition of learned motor control. Following acquisition and with further training, central feedback apparently assumes a more important and peripheral feedback a less important role in behavioral regulation (Kimble and Perlmuter, 1970).

Since the occurrence of striate muscle responses such as moving a limb leads to both interoceptive (feeling the movement) and exteroceptive (e.g., seeing the movement) feedback, the pairing operation necessary for the formation of an exteroceptively controlled RI occurs naturally. This natural process may conceivably provide the basis of imitative behavior. Thus seeing a particular limb movement leads to the elicitation of an RI, which was formed by the prior association of similar visual stimuli with the interoceptive consequences of the act in question. The development of instructional control over a response would depend on the prior pairing of the verbal labels employed in the instruction (exteroceptive feedback) with the interoceptive consequences of the act. By the process of higher-order conditioning, the verbal stimuli may also come to evoke the RI by being paired with the exteroceptive feedback stimuli consequent upon an act.

The process whereby the interoceptive and exteroceptive stimuli contingent on an act become associated is well described by the concept of "calibration." As this term implies, the consistent covariation of these stimuli leads to a graduation of the interoceptive variations in terms of the dimension represented by the exteroceptive stimulus variation. Thus the ability of an individual to identify and verbally describe the position of his arm without looking at it is assumed to rely on the prior calibration of the interoceptive consequences of arm positioning in terms of visually and verbally defined reference systems. It will be noted then that two demonstrable effects of calibration are proposed:

1. Calibration will lead to the development of RI-eliciting properties in the exteroceptive feedback stimulus.
2. Calibration will lead to an improvement in the ability of the subject to discriminate and describe effector activity in terms of the calibrating referent.

Before going on to discuss the application of this model to the development of cardiovascular control, the question of therapeutic feedback procedures will be considered briefly. As mentioned earlier, disturbances of either interoceptive or exteroceptive feedback disrupt voluntary control of the effector in question. Although such impairments of control may be remedied by the provision of additional exteroceptive feedback, the nature of the remedy effected by this procedure is substantially different for the cases of interoceptive and exteroceptive deafferentation, respectively.

An example of interoceptive deafferentation is contained in the control of postural and ambulatory responses in patients with *tabes dorsalis*. Among other effects, this disease results in deafferentation of the lower limbs. Patients suffering from *tabes dorsalis* are able to maintain an erect posture only when visual cues are available. When such exteroceptive feedback is withdrawn, the patient begins to sway and will eventually fall. Ambulation in such patients also relies heavily on both visual and auditory cues, and even in the presence of such exteroceptive feedback, motor adjustments involving the deafferented limbs are gross and inaccurate. Of particular importance to the topic currently under consideration is the observation that these individuals cannot control the deafferented effectors in the absence of exteroceptive feedback. Such feedback substitutes for the deficient interoceptive feedback and provides a crutch for performance (Bilodeau, 1969).

A very different picture is presented by cases in which the disturbance in voluntary control is due to exteroceptive deafferentation, as in the case of speech acquisition in deaf individuals. Here the pairing of tactile or visual exteroceptive feedback with variations in the activities of the vocal apparatus serves to calibrate the interoceptive feedback deriving from these activities. Following such a procedure, the patient is able to discriminate the sensations (based upon interoceptive feedback) associated with effector activities involved in the production of the various speech sounds and sensed via the visual or tactile exteroceptive feedback display. Following calibration of interoception from the vocal apparatus in terms of its auditory consequences, the deaf individual is able to maintain articulate speech in the absence of exteroceptive feedback. In such cases, then, exteroceptive feedback serves a learning rather than performance function.

CONTROL OF CARDIOVASCULAR RESPONSES

Given the importance of interoceptive and exteroceptive feedback to the development of voluntary motor control, it is not surprising that voluntary visceral control is inconspicuous. Not only are the viscera less prolifically innervated than the striate muscles, but their cortical projections are small and poorly defined. Furthermore, during their normal course of action, the viscera produce little discriminable exteroceptive feedback. Within the framework of the model of voluntary control described previously, the provision of exteroceptive feedback of visceral activity appears to be a necessary prerequisite to the development of control over the activities of this response system. Provision of such feedback may be accomplished by transducing visceral effector activity and transforming it into an exteroceptively discriminable stimulus.

A simple method of providing exteroceptive feedback of heart rate (HR) is illustrated in Figure 2. Each R wave of the subject's EKG is transformed into a square wave of constant amplitude and duration (Brener, 1966b). These pulses are then transmitted to an analysis circuit which compares the intervals between successive heartbeats (the IBI, or interbeat interval) to a standard interval based on the subject's modal preconditioning IBI (Figure 2a). If the IBI is greater than the criterion interval (a low HR), the subject is presented with a low-pitched tone; if the IBI is shorter than the criterion interval (a high HR), the subject is presented with a brief high-pitched tone. Under these conditions when subjects are instructed to produce high-pitched tones in the presence of one visual stimulus and low-pitched tones in the presence of another stimulus, they rapidly learn to control their HR's. The results of executing this procedure on a subject for three sessions each comprised of 24 alternating 1-minute increase (produce high-pitched tones) and decrease (produce low-pitched tones) trials are illustrated in Figure 2c. It is seen here that the increase and decrease instructions lead to discrete, nonoverlapping IBI distributions. Since this observation indicates that HR was systematically influenced by instructions, it may be concluded that under conditions of exteroceptive feedback, this response of the cardiovascular system is subject to voluntary control.

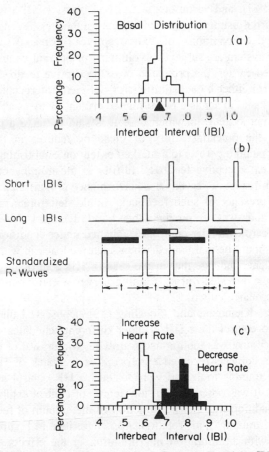

Figure 2.   Method of providing exteroceptive HR feedback. (a) Pretraining IBI distribution. The shaded triangle indicates criterion according to which high and low HR's are classified. (b) Method of classifying IBI's. Each IBI is measured against the criterion illustrated by the horizontal bars [equal to the value indicated by the traingle in (a)]. If an IBI is longer than the criterion (low HR), it is classified as a long IBI; if it is shorter than the criterion (high HR), it is classified as a short IBI. The terminal HR control performance of the subject whose pretraining IBI distribution is shown in (a) is illustrated by (c), which indicates discrete IBI distributions in response to the instructions to produce high-pitched tones associated with short IBI's (increase HR) and the low-pitched tones associated with long IBI's (decrease HR).

Variations of this procedure have been employed to establish voluntary control over a wide range of cardiovascular responses in humans. These include systolic blood pressure (Brener and Kleinman, 1970; Shapiro et al., 1969), diastolic blood pressure (Brener, 1974), HR (heartrate) increases and decreases (Shearn, 1962; Brener and Hothersall, 1966, 1967; Engel and Chism, 1967; Engel and Hansen, 1966), control of HR variability (Hnatiow and Lang, 1965;

Lang et al., 1967), and vasomotor activity (Lisina, 1961; Snyder and Noble, 1968). This partial listing of reported effects establishes beyond any reasonable doubt that under conditions of exteroceptive feedback, responses of the cardiovascular system are subject to voluntary or operant control.

As mentioned earlier, the provision of exteroceptive feedback may facilitate voluntary control either by substituting for deficient interoceptive feedback, in which case it is said to act as a performance crutch, or by establishing an exteroceptive referrent system, in which case it is said to serve a calibrating function. Clearly, the potential utility of these procedures in the treatment of cardiovascular pathology rests to a marked extent on establishing which of these two functions exteroceptive feedback fulfills in the training of cardiovascular control. If such feedback served as a performance crutch, then the control evidenced in the presence of such feedback should deteriorate rapidly when the feedback is withdrawn. If, on the other hand, feedback serves a calibrating function, then cardiovascular control established under conditions of exteroceptive feedback should be maintained when such feedback is withdrawn. Several sources of evidence indicate that in the case of HR control at least, the exteroceptive feedback provided during training serves a calibrating function rather than as a performance crutch.

Thus Brener, Kleinman, and Goesling (1969) observed that when subjects were trained to control their HR's under different schedules of exteroceptive feedback, the control was maintained following withdrawal of the feedback. In this experiment subjects received exteroceptive feedback of HR on 0, 50, or 100 percent of training trials and were tested for HR control in the absence of such feedback. It was observed that the degree of control exhibited by subjects in the latter condition was a direct function of the amount of feedback they had received during training. This relationship is described in Figure 3. These data, then, fit well with a calibration interpretation of the effects of exteroceptive feedback. The more exteroceptive feedback made available to subjects during training, the better able they were to control their HR's in the absence of feedback. In terms of the model proposed above, it is assumed that the exteroceptive feedback served to calibrate interoceptive feedback contingent upon HR variations, thereby enabling subjects to identify instances of high and low HR's. The more feedback provided during training, the more precisely these HR response images were defined and the greater was the magnitude of the HR response subsequently evoked by the instructions.

Of particular interest in these data is the observation that subjects in the 0 percent group not only displayed some evidence of HR control, but that this control improved as a function of training (from Session 1 to Session 2). These data again suggest that interoceptive feedback associated with HR performance is discriminable and can serve as the basis for the voluntary regulation of this activity. The source of such feedback is, however, not identified by these exper-

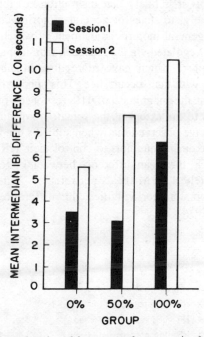

Figure 3. Heart rate control as a function of the amount of exteroceptive feedback provided during training. The mean intermedian IBI differences were computed by subtracting the median IBI displayed during increase trials from the median IBI displayed during decrease trials for each subject and then taking the mean of these differences for each group. A positive intermedian IBI difference therefore indicates that subjects were displaying higher heart rates on increase trials than on decrease trials. (From J. M. Brener, R. A. Kleinman, and W. J. Goesling, Heart rate control following different exposures to augmented sensory feedback *Psychophysiology*, **5:**510–516, 1969. Copyright (1969) by the Society for Psychophysiological Research. Reproduced by permission.)

iments. Since the HR response is embedded in a complex of other responses, including somatomotor and respiratory activities, it is likely that subjects employ the interoceptive feedback contingent on these related activities in order to identify instances of the appropriate HR response rather than the relatively indiscriminable feedback from the cardiovascular system itself.

In support of this possibility is the observation that subjects generally are better able to produce HR increases than HR decreases on command. Whereas HR increases frequently lead to discriminable pulsatile thoracic and auditory sensations, normal HR slowing is not associated with discriminable sensations. By virtue of their greater discriminability, HR increases are more readily identifiable and therefore may be associated more readily with the collateral sensations arising from the somatomotor and environmental contexts in which such responses occur. Thus it is likely that instructions to increase and decrease the HR lead, respectively, to states of general motoric activation and quiescence. Furthermore, this general motoric adjustment in which HR responses are embedded is probably regulated via the feedback from somatomotor components of the response complex, which have more discriminable interoceptive consequences associated with their occurrence. This speculation gleans support from the observation that the magnitude of HR responses produced by instructions is inversely related to the extent of the somatomotor constraint imposed on the subject. Thus we have observed that when subjects are instructed not to breathe irregularly or move during attempts to control their HR's in the absence of exteroceptive feedback, the mean difference between increase and decrease conditions is approximately 3 BPM (beats per minute). When no verbal constraints are placed upon somatomotor activities, this difference rises to approximately 7 BPM (Brener, 1974).

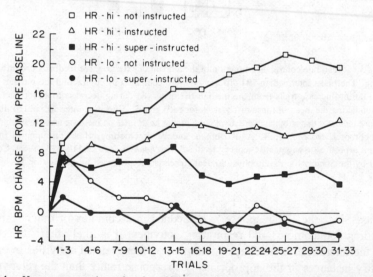

Figure 4.   Heart rate control as a function of instructional constraints on somatic activity. Subjects in the superinstructed group received instructions not to move and were required to breathe at a rate indicated by a pacing stimulus. Subjects in the instructed group received instructions not to move but did not have their respiration paced. Subjects in the not-instructed group did not receive any instructions relating to the control of somatic activities. (From P. A. Obrist, J. L. Howard, J. G. Lawler, R. A. Galosy, K. A. Meyers, and C. J. Gaebelein, The cardiac somatic interaction. In P. A. Obrist, A. H. Black, J. Brener, and L. V. DiCara (Eds.), *Current Trends in Cardiovascular Psychophsiology*, Chicago: Aldine-Atherton. Copyright (1974) Aldine-Atherton, Inc. Reproduced by permission.)

A similar effect has been reported by Obrist et al. (1974) during a procedure involving the avoidance conditioning of HR. These data are illustrated in Figure 4. It will be noted (1) that the HR increases are far more pronounced than the HR decreases and (2) that the level of control is inversely related to the extent of somatomotor constraint specified in the instructions to the various groups. Thus although these data support the contention that responses are discriminable, they also suggest that such discriminations are based on interoceptive feedback from the somatomotor correlates of IIR responses rather than upon cardiovascular afferentation per se. The importance of establishing that cardiovascular afferentation is discriminable relates again to the clinical applications of these procedures. If it were the case that voluntary cardiovascular control was immutably based on feedback from the somatomotor activities that accompany cardiovascular change, then in terms of the model of voluntary control proposed here, cardiovascular responses could only be controlled insofar as the entire somatocardiovascular Gestalt could be controlled. Since certain cardiovascular pathologics such as essential hypertension are marked by a dissociation between levels of somatomotor and cardiovascular activity, such a constraint would severely limit the potential utility of these procedures.

Although the study of interoceptive discrimination has received considerable attention in the Soviet Union (Razran, 1971), this area of research has been sorely neglected in the West. Nevertheless, the operant discrimination paradigm does lend itself well to the study of these processes and in view of the foregoing considerations, it was decided to examine the effects of cardiovascular interoceptive discrimination training upon subsequent control of heart rate. In this experiment (Kleinman, 1970), subjects were required to press a button whenever and as soon as they sensed a heart beat (HB). Calibration trials on which subjects heard a brief tone on each HB and were not required to press the button were interspersed between discrimination trials. Employing a measure of the latencies from HB's to button presses, evidence that subjects learned to discriminate the occurrence of HB's was obtained.

In terms of the model of voluntary control proposed here, such an enhancement in the ability of subjects to discriminate the interoceptive consequences of effector action should lead to a parallel enhancement in their ability to control the activities of the effector in question. This prediction was borne out by a comparison of HR control in subjects who had been submitted to the HB discrimination procedure with subjects who had been submitted to a control procedure not involving HB discrimination. Subjects trained to discriminate their HB's subsequently displayed better control of HR with and in the absence of exteroceptive HR feedback.

It may be concluded then that a variety of cardiovascular responses are subject to instructional control. Although the level of control evidenced is a function of the amount of exteroceptive feedback provided during training, such control may be maintained when the feedback is withdrawn. On the basis of this observation, it is assumed that such feedback serves to calibrate the interoceptive feedback cues consequent upon the cardiovascular activity in question or upon other activities that form the general response set in which the cardiovascular response is embedded. Further evidence suggests that cardiovascular afferentation per se may be discriminated, thereby providing the possibility of generating specific control over the cardiovascular component of the general response set.

THE SPECIFICITY OF LEARNED CARDIOVASCULAR CONTROL

The question of whether cardiovascular activities may be modified independently of the somatomotor responses they accompany during normal functioning has been the subject of considerable debate. Both behavioral (Obrist and Webb, 1967) and neurophysiological (Germana, 1969) evidence supports the idea that these motor activities are integrated at a central level and represent peripheral manifestations of a single central process. This idea is to be contrasted with the traditional notion that the cardiovascular system responds in a reflexive fashion to the peripheral demands of the striate musculature. The latter model of functioning carries with it the implication that cardiovascular learning is an artifact of somatomotor learning and has been the subject of an exchange of views between Smith (1954, 1964a, 1964b) and Black and Lang (1964). In this controversy, Black and Lang provided evidence to indicate that cardiovascular responses could be classically conditioned in curarized dogs. Since this drug produces complete flaccid paralysis of the striate musculature in appropriate doses, the possibility of somatic afferentation eliciting cardiovascular responses was prevented. Although this debate was not satisfactorily resolved, the procedure of curarization was employed again by Trowill (1967) and Miller and DiCara (1967) to demonstrate that operant HR conditioning was independent of somatomotor influences.

The range of operant cardiovascular effects demonstrated in curarized rats is very impressive (Miller, 1969; DiCara, 1970). Although the basic effects reported by these investigators have been independently replicated by Hothersall and Brener (1969) and Slaughter et al. (1970), recent replication difficulties (Miller and Dworkin, 1974; Brener et al., 1974; Hahn, 1974; Roberts, 1974) indicate that operant cardiovascular phenomena in curarized animals are not as robust as was previously suggested. Were it not for these difficulties, the reported phenomena would represent definitive evidence of response specificity within the cardiovascular system. These phenomena include operant control of differential vasomotor activity in the two ears of a rat (DiCara and Miller, 1968) and conditioning of the P-R interval of the rat EKG independently of the R-R interval (Fields, 1970). Oddly enough, although these procedures appear to be effective in developing operant control over specific elements of cardiovascular activity, they do not effectively establish a case for the independence of somatomotor and cardiovascular control.

For example, DiCara and Miller (1969) conditioned HR increases in one group of curarized rats and HR decreases in another group. When these subjects were subsequently tested for retention of the conditioned HR response in a noncurarized state, it was observed that subjects which had been reinforced for HR increases under curare displayed higher respiration rates and general activity levels than subjects that had been reinforced for HR decreases. Since under curare there was no chance of fortuitous reinforcement of respiratory and activity responses, it must be concluded that the reinforcement contingencies operated to modify the activity of some central process responsible for the control of HR and the biologically related phenomena of respiration and somatomotor activity. Curare simply prevented the experimenter from observing the latter manifestations of this process during conditioning.

Further support for this interpretation derives from a study by Goesling and Brener (1972). If it is assumed that cardiovascular and somatomotor responses represent two components of a single motor adjustment complex, then it should follow that the cardiovascular component of a learned variation of this somatocardiovascular Gestalt should be observable in the curarized preparation, since curare blocks only the peripheral manifestations of the somatic component. To investigate this possibility, one group of freely moving rats was trained to be active and a second group was trained to be immobile using a shock-avoidance procedure. When the activity and immobility responses had been acquired, all subjects were curarized and submitted to HR conditioning using a shock avoidance procedure similar to that employed in the precurare treatment. Half the subjects in each group were reinforced for HR increase and the other half for HR decreases. The results, which are presented in Figure 5, indicate that the general motoric adjustment established in the precurare treatments were more significant determinants of HR change under curare than the reinforcement contingencies implemented under curare. In particular, subjects that had been trained to be active all displayed HR increases under curare, whereas those that had been trained to be immobile all displayed HR decreases. Thus it may be concluded that even under curare, the effects of somatomotor learning continue to be manifested.

Because the curarized, artificially respirated rat is subject to a multitude of abnormal influences (Brener et al., 1974), it is difficult to develop general principles of cardiovascular control through the study of this preparation. However, recent studies involving intact preparations indicate that feedback procedures alone may be effective in developing very specific control of cardiovascular responses.

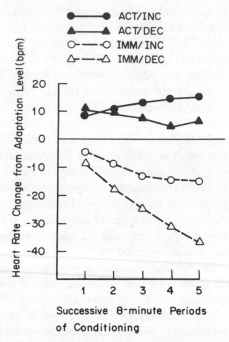

Figure 5.   Heart rate conditioning under curare as a function of precurare treatment and reinforcement contingencies imposed under curare. In the legend ACT/ and IMM/ refer to whether subjects were trained to be active or immobile prior to curarization, whereas /INC and /DEC refer to whether they were reinforced for HR increases or decreases under curare. (From J. Brener, E. Eissenberg, and S. Middaugh, Respiratory and somatomotor factors associated with operant conditioning of responses in curarized rats. In P. A. Obrist, A. H. Black, J. Brener, and L. V. DiCara (Eds.), *Current Trends in Cardiovascular Psychophysiology.* Chicago: Aldine-Atherton. Copyright (1074) by Aldine-Atherton, Inc. Reproduced by permission.)

It was mentioned earlier that the pattern of interoceptive feedback contingent upon a response provides a precise description of the topographical dimensions and intensive characteristics of that response. When an exteroceptive feedback stimulus is consistently paired with a response, it acquires the property of eliciting the pattern of central excitation previously elicited by the interoceptive feedback contingent on that response (the RI). However, because the activities of organisms tend to occur in functionally related constellations rather than as discrete and autonomous events, when an exteroceptive feedback stimulus is made contingent on a given response, it will also necessarily be contingent on the other responses forming the functional unit of which the given response is a member. Following such a calibration procedure, when an individual is instructed to produce the exteroceptive feedback stimulus, the behavioral adjustment that ensues will identify the other components of such a functional behavioral unit. Thus by measuring a broad spectrum of activities during voluntary control experiments, it is possible to examine the intrinsic organization of motor activities.

It has been observed, for example, that when individuals are trained to control their systolic blood pressures (BP) under conditions of exteroceptive feedback of BP, systematic changes in BP occur in the absence of correlated changes in HR (Shapiro et al., 1969; Shapiro et al., 1970; Brener and Kleinman, 1970). The relationship observed between these two cardiovascular variables in the Brener and Kleinman experiment is illustrated in Figure 6. It is seen here that although the BP's of experimental and control subjects diverge significantly, the HR's of these two groups display considerable overlap. Thus it may be concluded that exteroceptive feedback of systolic BP identifies a behavioral unit of which HR responses are not a component.

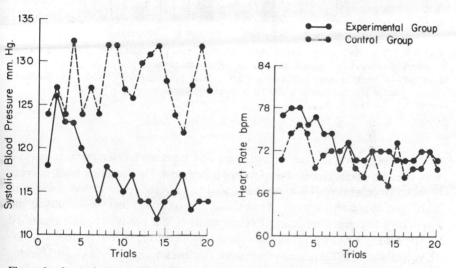

Figure 6. Learned control of systolic blood pressure in humans and associated HR changes. Subjects in the experimental group were instructed to decrease the rate of an exteroceptive feedback stimulus which was related to their systolic blood pressures, whereas subjects in the control group were instructed simply to attend to the feedback display. (From J. Brener, and R. A. Kleinman, Learned control of decreases in systolic blood pressure. *Nature*, **226**(5250):1063–1064, 1970. Copyright (1970) by Macmillan Journals Ltd. Reproduced by permission.)

To explore more fully the nature of the behavioral adjustments induced by the provision of HR and BP feedback, an experiment was recently undertaken (Brener and Shanks, 1974) in which different combinations of instructions and feedback were investigated. Data drawn from this experiment are presented in Figure 7. These data illustrate the influence of HR and BP feedback on four

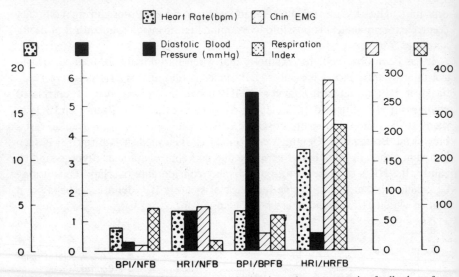

Figure 7. The effects of instructions alone and instructions plus exteroceptive feedback on four measures of activity. The symbols employed to identify the different groups are interpreted as follows: BPI/ = blood pressure instructions; HRI/ = heart rate instructions; /NFB = no feedback; /BPFB = blood pressure feedback; /HRFB = heart rate feedback.

measures of activity. It can be observed that whereas BP feedback leads to a very specific enhancement of the level of BP control, HR feedback leads not only to an enhancement of HR control but also to substantial correlated changes in EMG and respiratory activity. Thus it may be concluded that striate muscle and respiratory responses are integral components of the behavioral unit identified by HR feedback but not of the behavioral unit identified by BP feedback.

As Schwartz (1972) recently indicated, feedback techniques may also be employed effectively in exploring the extent to which demonstrably independent cardiovascular activities are amenable to learned integration and differentiation. This investigator provided different groups of subjects with exteroceptive feedback stimuli that were contingent upon combinations of responses rather than single responses. In particular, one group of subjects received feedback when both HR and BP were increasing ($BP_{up}HR_{up}$), another group when both measures were decreasing ($BP_{down}HR_{down}$), a third group when BP was increasing and HR decreasing ($BP_{up}HR_{down}$), and a final group when BP was decreasing and HR increasing ($BP_{down}HR_{up}$). The results of instructing subjects to produce the exteroceptive feedback stimulus are presented in Figure 8. As can be seen, voluntary control of integrated or differentiated patterns of cardiovascular responding were predictably produced by this simple procedure. Schwartz mentions that the training of integrated BP-HR decreases (BP$_{down}$HR$_{down}$) may have application in the alleviation of pain associated with *angina pectoris*.

One clearly defined factor limits the specificity of the behavioral adjustments that may be produced by this method. This is specified by the biological constraints implicit in the structural and functional characteristics of the organism. In fact, as Black (1974) recently noted, the techniques of operant or voluntary visceral control may well be useful tools in the empirical definition of these boundaries. This investigator recently reported the application of a dissociative conditioning contingency in which rats were reinforced for increasing their HR's while standing still (as measured by ambulation in a wheel). It was observed that in most of the subjects this contingency led to increases in somatic activity which were not involved in ambulation together with a correlated increase in HR. Although some evidence of increases in HR above the level of that normally observed in still subjects was forthcoming, in no case did the HR level achieve that of subjects in a moving state. This observation accords with others reported in this chapter: the intrinsic integration of somatomotor and cardiovascular activities is not readily amenable to modification by conditioning and feedback procedures.

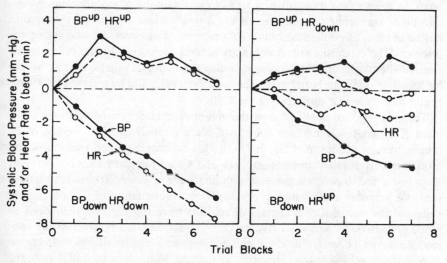

Figure 8. Learning of blood pressure/heart rate integration and differentiation under conditions of exteroceptive feedback. (From G. Schwartz, Voluntary control of human cardiovascular integration and differentiation through feedback and reward. *Science*, **175**:90–93, 1972. Copyright (1972) by the American Association for the Advancement of Science. Reproduced by permission.

CLINICAL APPLICATIONS OF VOLUNTARY CARDIOVASCULAR CONTROL

The application of the techniques described to the treatment of functional cardiovascular pathologies is presently in its infancy. Nevertheless, the results of recent reports suggest that these techniques may well provide an extremely powerful therapeutic tool. The potential efficacy of these methods has been tested in the training of voluntary control of cardiac arrhythmias and of blood pressure in populations of cardiac patients.

Whereas the physiological mechanisms involved in arrhythmic activities of the heart are fairly well known, the mechanisms involved in chronic elevations of blood pressure are for the most part unspecified. Although it is possible in some cases to trace the causes of high blood pressure to some structural or functional defect in one or more of the many systems involved in the regulation of this variable, in the vast majority of cases elevations of blood pressure are unaccompanied by any other discernible malfunction. Where the etiology of sustained high blood pressure (greater than 140/80 mm Hg) is not discernible, this condition is termed "essential hypertension." Elevations of blood pressure tend to be progressive and the higher the pressure, the greater are the attendant dangers of coronary artery disease and cerebrovascular accidents. In view of this, essential hypertension is generally treated pharmacologically (diuretics, sympathetic blocking agents, and tranquilizers) so as to maintain the blood pressure in normal limits and arrest the progress of the disease. Since essential hypertension has no obvious physiological cause, its treatment must necessarily be symptom-oriented. The establishment of voluntary control over this variable offers an attractive alternative to chemotherapy. It also seems logical that a disease which by default is often attributed to psychogenic factors should be treated by a therapeutic procedure that operates via the CNS.

The only reported application of the voluntary control procedure to the treatment of hypertension involves a study of seven patients over an average of 22 training sessions (Benson et al., 1971). In this experiment, decreases in systolic blood pressure resulted in brief auditory and visual feedback stimuli. Subjects were instructed to produce these stimuli and were rewarded for each twentieth feedback stimulus combination produced by the presentation of a photographic slide and the payment of 5 cents. All subjects were run until no reductions in blood pressure were noted on five successive sessions. All but one of the subjects displayed a decrease in blood pressure over training, resulting in a decrease from a mean of 164.9 mm Hg prior to training to a mean of 148.4 mm Hg over the last five training sessions. Although these results provide a good basis for the development of this therapeutic method in the treatment of hypertension, they do not in themselves establish its therapeutic utility. For the treatment to be effective, it must be established (a) that the control developed in the laboratory may be maintained in the outside world and (b) that the control may be maintained in the absence of exteroceptive feedback. The second requirement is imperative in the case of blood pressure control since a portable means of monitoring and providing exteroceptive feedback of this variable has not yet been established.

Both of these requirements are admirably met in the studies by Engel and his associates (Weiss and Engel, 1971; Engel and Bleecker, 1974) on the control of abnormal heart rhythms in a population of cardiac patients. Cardiac arrhythmias may be defined as any abnormality in the rate or rhythm of the heart. Such arrhythmias may derive from an abnormally high or low rate of impulse formation in the sinoatrial node, which is the normal pacemaker of the heart (sinus tachycardia and sinus bradycardia). Alternatively, arrhythmias may arise from the initiation of heart beats in foci other than the sinoatrial node (ectopic rhythms) or from lesions in the conduction pathways that transmit the wave of depolarization from the sinoatrial node through the myocardium.

Patients in each of these groupings have been studied by Engel and his group and their evidence to date is largely positive. Not only have patients who were unresponsive to more traditional therapeutic procedures such as chemotherapy learned to control their abnormal rhythms in the laboratory, but in addition this control has been maintained following treatment.

The basic procedure employed by these investigators is very similar to that previously described. Treatment involves first establishing control over heart rate under conditions of exteroceptive feedback. When evidence of heart-rate control develops, the exteroceptive feedback is gradually withdrawn. Under these conditions most patients demonstrate an ability to regulate their arrhythmias on the basis of internal cues.

Several findings have emerged from this research which have implications not only for the clinical application of feedback methods but also for the understanding of voluntary control processes in general. First, the degree of control exhibited by patients in these studies greatly exceeds that reported for normal humans. For example, a patient who displayed between 12 and 18 premature ventricular contractions (PVC's) per minute at the inception of training reduced the rate of these abnormal heart beats to less than 0.5 per minute during training. Another patient displaying sinus tachycardia reduced her rate from a four-year average of 106 to 75 BPM per minute. Although numerous nonprocedural physiological factors may contribute to the magnitude of these effects, it should be noted that the subjects were run over many sessions of training and were highly motivated to learn the appropriate responses. This is to be contrasted with the undergraduate "volunteer" subjects employed in experimental studies who are usually run for one session and whose successful performance in the experiment is not of vital importance to them.

Second, it should be noted that the voluntary cardiovascular control established in the laboratory has been observed to persist in the extralaboratory situation for periods of up to five years. In other words, these procedures did not lead to a temporary suppression of the pathological symptom, as chemotherapy by antiarrhythmic drugs would, but rather they resulted in the successful rehabilitation of seemingly disabled individuals without the need for continued medication. Not only is continued reliance on medication a nuisance, but in certain cases the side effects of the medication may be almost as disabling as the disease itself. It will be recognized that the ability of individuals to maintain control in the absence of exteroceptive feedback suggests that such feedback provided early during training served the calibration functions described earlier in this chapter. Further evidence in support of this contention is that a number of patients in these studies reported that following training they were able to discriminate and control instances of the arrhythmia for which they had been treated. This ability was undoubtedly facilitated by the procedure of "weaning" subjects from the exteroceptive feedback during training.

Finally, it should be noted that the effects produced were not specific to the symptoms that patients were taught to control. For example, a patient who was taught to control sinus tachycardia not only displayed a reduction in heart rate, but her blood pressure fell from 140/80 to 115/75 mm Hg. Treatment for a supraventricular tachycardia in another patient led not only to bringing this disorder under control but also to a decrease in the size of his enlarged liver and heart. These observations lend further support to the assertion that training of voluntary cardiovascular control represents a potentially effective means of treating a variety of pathologies in this effector system.

CONCLUSIONS

Judging from the literature on voluntary and operant control of visceral and nervous system events, we are forced to concede that voluntary control is a far more ubiquitous phenomenon than we had previously envisaged. Despite the pervasiveness of this form of motor control, however, it will be recognized that its development does rest on the availability of certain structurally based processes. These have been defined in this chapter as the minimal voluntary control model. Whereas prosthetic devices may be employed to augment or substitute for deficient feedback pathways, damage to the central sensory or motor circuits, efferent, or effector processes may well preclude the development of voluntary control. However, given an organism that displays centrally controlled variations in the activities of an effector system, there is no evidence to suggest that given variants of this activity may not be brought under voluntary control by employing feedback procedures of the sort described in this chapter.

REFERENCES

Basmajian, J. V. Conscious control of single nerve cells. *New Scientist*, 1963, **369**, 661–664.

Benson, H., Shapiro, D., Tursky, B., and Schwartz, G. E. Decreased systolic blood pressure through operant conditioning techniques in patients with essential hypertension. *Science*, 1971, **173**, 740–742.

Bilodeau, I. McD. Information feedback. In E. A. Bilodeau and I. McD. Bilodeau (Eds.), *Principles of Skill Acquisition*. New York: Academic Press, 1969.

Black, A. H. Operant autonomic conditioning: The analysis of response mechanisms. In P. A. Obrist, A. H. Black, J. Brener, and L. V. DiCara (Eds.), *Current Trends in Cardiovascular Psychophysiology*. Chicago: Aldine-Atherton, 1974.

Black, A. H., and Lang, H. M. Cardiac conditioning and skeletal responding in curarized dogs. *Psychological Review*, 1964, **71**, 80–85.

Blanchard, B. The case for determinism. In S. Hook (Ed.), *Determinism and Freedom*. New York: New York University Press, 1958.

Brener, J. Heart Rate. In P. Venables and I. Martin (Eds.), *A Manual of Psychophysiological Methods*. Amsterdam: North Holland Publishing Company, 1966. (a)

Brener, J. Heart rate as an avoidance response. *Psychological Record*, 1966, **16**, 329–336. (b)

Brener, J. A general model of voluntary control applied to the phenomena of learned cardiovascular change. In P. A. Obrist, A. H. Black, J. Brener, and L. V. DiCara (Eds.), *Current Trends in Cardiovascular Psychophysiology*. Chicago: Aldine-Atherton, 1974.

Brener, J., Eissenberg, E., and Middaugh, S. Respiratory and somatomotor factors associated with operant conditioning of cardiovascular responses in curarized rats. In P. A. Obrist, A. H. Black, J. Brener, and L. V. DiCara (Eds.), *Current Trends in Cardiovascular Psychophysiology*. Chicago: Aldine-Atherton (in press).

Brener, J., and Hothersall, D. Heart rate control under conditions of augmented sensory feedback. *Psychophysiology*, 1966, **3**, 23–28.

Brener, J., and Hothersall, D. Paced respiration and heart rate control. *Psychophysiology*, 1967, **4**, 1–6.

Brener, J., and Kleinman, R. A. Learned control of decreases in systolic blood pressure. *Nature*, 1970, **226**, 1063–1064.

Brener, J., Kleinman, R. A., and Goesling, W. J. Heart rate control following different exposures to augmented sensory feedback. *Psychophysiology*, 1969, **5**, 510–516.

Brener, J., and Shanks, E. The interaction of instructions and feedback in the training of cardiovascular control. Unpublished manuscript, 1973.

Budzynski, T., Stoyva, J., and Adler, C. Feedback-induced muscle relaxation: Application to tension headache. *Journal of Behavior Therapy and Experimental Psychiatry*, 1970, **1**, 205–211.

Chase, R. A., Harvey, S., Standfast, S., Rapin, I., and Sutton, S. Comparison of the effects of delayed auditory feedback on speech and key tapping. *Science*, 1959, **129**, 903–904.

DiCara, L. V. Learning in the atonomic nervous system. *Scientific American*, 1970, **222**, 30–39.

DiCara, L. V., and Miller, N. E. Instrumental learning of vasomotor responses by rats: Learning to respond differentially in the two ears. *Science*, 1968, **159**, 1485–1486.

DiCara, L. V., and Miller, N. E. Transfer of instrumentally learned heart-rate changes from curarized to non-curarized state: Implication for a mediation hypothesis. *Journal of Comparative and Physiological Psychology*, 1969, **68**, 159–162.

Engel, B. T., and Bleecker, E. R. Application of operant conditioning techniques to the control of the cardiac arrhythmias. In P.A. Obrist, A.H. Black, J. Brener, and L.V. DiCara (Eds.), *Current Trends in Cardiovascular Psychophysiology*. Chicago: Adline-Atherton, 1974.

Engel, B. T. and Chism, R. A. Operant conditioning of heart rate speeding. *Psychophysiology*, 1967, **3**, 418–426.

Engel, B. T., and Hansen, S. P. Operant conditioning of heart rate slowing. *Psychophysiology*, 1966, **3**, 176–187.

Fields, C. Instrumental conditioning of the rat cardiac control systems. *Proceedings of the National Academy of Sciences, USA*, 1970, **65**, 293–299.

Germana, J. Central efferent processes and autonomic-behavioral integration. *Psychophysiology*, 1969, **6**, 78–90.

Goesling, W. J., and Brener, J. Effects of activity and immobility conditioning upon subsequent heart-rate conditioning in curarized rats. *Journal of Comparative and Physiological Psychology*, 1972, **81**, 311–317.

Hahn, W. H. The learning of autonomic responses by curarized animals. In P. A. Obrist, A. H. Black, J. Brener, and L. V. DiCara (eds.), *Current Trends in Cardiovascular Psychophysiology*. Chicago: Aldine-Atherton, 1974.

Hardyck, C. D., Petrinovich, L. F., and Ellsworth, D. W. Feedback of speech muscle activity during silent reading: Rapid extinction. *Science*, 1966, **154**, 1467–1468.

Hnatiow, M. and Lang, P. J. Learned stabilization of cardiac rate. *Psychophysiology*, 1965, **1**, 330–336.

Hothersall, D., and Brener, J. Operant conditioning of changes in heart rate in curarized rats. *Journal of Comparative and Physiological Psychology*, 1969, **68**, 338–342.

James, W. *Principles of Psychology*. New York: Holt, 1890.

Kimble, G. A. and Perlmuter, L. C. The problem of volition. *Psychological Review*, 1970, **77**, 5, 361–384.

Kleinman, R. *Development of voluntary cardiovascular control*. Unpublished doctoral dissertation, University of Tennessee, 1970.

Lang, P. J., Sroufe, L. A., and Hastings, J. E. Effects of feedback and instructional set on the control of cardiac rate variability. *Journal of Experimental Psychology*, 1967, **75**, 425–431.

Laszlo, J. I. The performance of a simple motor task with kinaesthetic sense loss. *The Quarterly Journal of Experimental Psychology*, 1966, **18**, 1–8.

Miller, N. E. Learning of visceral and glandular responses. *Science*, 1969, **163**, 434–445.

Miller, N. E., and DiCara, L. V. Instrumental learning of heart rate changes in curarized rats: Shaping and specificity to discriminative stimulus. *Journal of Comparative and Physiological Psychology.* 1967, **63,** 12–19.

Miller, N. E., and Dworkin, B. R. Visceral learning: Recent difficulties with curarized rats and significant problems for human research. In P. A. Obrist, A. H. Black, J. Brener, and L. V. DiCara (Eds.), *Current Trends in Cardiovascular Psychophysiology.* Chicago: Aldine-Atherton, 1974.

Mott, F. W., and Sherrington, C. S. Experiments upon the influences of sensory nerves upon movement and nutrition of the limbs. *Proceedings of the Royal Society, London,* 1895, **57,** 481–488.

Obrist, P. A., Howard, J. L., Lawler, J. G., Galosy, R. A., Meyers, K. A., and Gaebelein, C. J. In P. A. Obrist, A. H. Black, J. Brener, and L. V. DiCara (Eds.), *Current Trends in Cardiovascular Psychophysiology.* Chicago: Aldine-Atherton, 1974.

Obrist, P. A., and Webb, R. A. Heart rate conditioning in dogs: Relationship to somatic-motor activity. *Psychophysiology,* 1967, **4,** 7–34.

Razran, G. The observable unconscious and the inferable conscious in current Soviet psychophysiology: Interoceptive conditioning, semantic conditioning, and the orienting reflex. *Psychological Review,* 1961, **68,** 81–147.

Razran, G. *Mind in Evolution: An East-West Synthesis of Learned Behavior and Cognition.* Boston: Houghton Mifflin, 1971.

Roberts, L. Comparative studies of operant electrodermal and heart rate conditioning in curarized rats. In P. A. Obrist, A. H. Black, J. Brener, and L. V. DiCara (Eds.), *Current Trends in Cardiovascular Psychophysiology.* Chicago: Aldine-Atherton, 1974.

Schwartz, G. Voluntary control of human cardiovascular integration and differentiation through feedback and reward. *Science,* 1972, **175,** 90–93.

Shapiro, D., Tursky, B., Gershon, E., and Stern, M. Effects of feedback and reinforcement on the control of human systolic blood pressure. *Science,* 1969, **163,** 588–590.

Shapiro, D., Tursky, B., and Schwartz, G. E. Control of blood pressure in man by operant conditioning. Circulation. *RES,* 1970, **271,** 27–32.

Shearn, D.W. Operant conditioning of heart rate. *Science,* 1962, **137,** 530–531.

Sherrington, C. *Man on his Nature.* London: Penguin Books, 1940.

Skinner, B. F. *The Behavior of Organisms.* New York: Appleton-Century-Crofts, 1938.

Slaughter, J., Hahn, W., and Rinaldi, P. Instrumental conditioning of heart rate in the curarized rat with varied amounts of pre-training. *Journal of Comparative and Physiological Psychology,* 1970, **72,** 356–359.

Smith, K. Conditioning as an artifact. *Psychological Review,* 1954, **61,** 217–225.

Smith, K. Curare drugs and total paralysis. *Psychological Review,* 1964, **71,** 77–79. (a)

Smith, K. Comment on the paper by Black and Lang. *Psychological Review,* 1964, **71,** 86. (b)

Smith, W. M., McCrary, J. W., and Smith, K. U. Delayed visual feedback and behavior. *Science*, 1960, **132**, 1013–1014.

Snyder, C., and Nobel, M. Operant conditioning of vasoconstriction. *Journal of Experimental Psychology*, 1968, **77**, 263–268.

Trowill, J. A. Instrumental conditioning of the heart rate in the curarized rat. *Journal of Comparative and Physiological Psychology*, 1967, **63**, 7–11.

von Holst, E. Relations between the central nervous system and the peripheral organs. *British Journal of Animal Behavior*, 1954, **2**, 89–94.

Weiss, T., and Engel, B. T. Operant conditioning of heart rate in patients with premature ventricular contractions. *Psychosomatic Medicine*, 1971, **33**, 301–321.

Wenger, M. A., Bagchi, B. K., and Anand, B. K. Experiments in India on "voluntary" control of heart and pulse. *Circulation*, 1961, **24**, 1319–1326.

CHAPTER 8

Behavioral Tactics for Clinical Cardiac Control

EDWARD B. BLANCHARD and ROBERT W. SCOTT

This chapter consists of three parts: first, a review of the literature on operant conditioning of heart rate (HR) in humans through the spring of 1971 when the series of experiments reported here was begun; second, a description of the first four phases of our own research program which spanned the period 1971-1972; and finally, an integration of our results with newer reports from other centers and a brief description of directions for future research.

PREVIOUS RESEARCH ON THE OPERANT CONDITIONING OF HEART RATE, 1962–1971

With the pioneering work of Miller and his colleagues (summarized in Miller, 1969) showing conclusively that autonomic responses can be controlled through operant conditioning without peripheral mediation, the whole repertoire of autonomic responses became potentially open to central, and possibly voluntary, control. Paralleling, and even in some cases preceding, Miller's work with rats has been a growing literature on the topic of the operant conditioning and/or establishment of self-control of cardiovascular processes in humans.

For purposes of this review a clarification of terms is needed. The two operations or procedures, operant conditioning and self-control through the use of external sensory feedback, are used interchangeably. In the studies with human subjects which have labeled the process involved as operant conditioning (Engel and Hansen, 1966; Engel and Chism, 1967a, 1967b; Levene, Engel, and Pearson, 1968; Headrick, Feather, and Wells, 1971), subjects usually received a combination of feedback or information assessing the adequacy of their performance and small amounts of money which were contingent upon performance. In the studies which have labeled the process self-control through the use of

273

exteroceptive feedback, subjects received only feedback about the adequacy of their performance. No one has yet shown that the rewards are necessary, sufficient, or even facilitative to the subjects' acquiring the desired response.

The rewards in most of these studies may serve more to provide the subject with information about the adequacy of his response than as an incentive for the production of the response. Certainly it has been shown that feedback functions as a reinforcer, since providing it to the subject leads to an increased likelihood of his producing the desired response, and removing it leads to a decrement in this likelihood. Thus the two operations are inextricably confounded since one must give the subject feedback as to adequacy of performance when giving him contingent rewards and since feedback or information has been shown to function as a reinforcer. It may be possible to separate the incentive and informational functions of rewards but this has not yet been done.

In Figure 1 the studies involving change in HR as the dependent variable are summarized in terms of mean experimental change in HR. Omitted from this figure and from intensive consideration by this review are studies by Shearn (1962), Frazier (1966), and Brener (1966), all of which used a shock avoidance procedure. Basic to these studies was a situation whereby a subject could avoid mild but painful electrical shocks by emitting an HR of the appropriate magnitude. These studies, which did show that subjects could learn some degree of HR control, are omitted because such a paradigm was not thought to be relevant for clinical practice. The studies which are included are based on positive incentives or sensory feedback, both of which are considered practical clinical procedures. As the following review of these studies shows, each of the principal investigators uses a somewhat different experimental paradigm.

Engel and his associates (Engel and Hansen, 1966; Engel and Chism, 1967a; Levene, Engel, and Pearson, 1968) demonstrated slowing (1966), speeding (1967b), and alternate speeding and slowing of HR within a single session (1968) using an "operant conditioning" procedure. Subjects, always normal college students, males in 1966 ($n = 10$) and 1967a ($n = 5$) and females in 1968 ($n = 5$), received binary visual feedback in the form of a light onset for each interbeat interval (IBI) that differed from the set point in the appropriate direction. The set point was the median of each individual subject's distribution of IBI's collected during a baseline period. In all of these studies subjects could earn 1/4 or 1/2 cent per second that they kept the light on.

Subjects were run for six 1-hour sessions in the first two studies and for two 1-hour sessions for the third. In each session there was an adaptation period, a 5- to 8-minute baseline recording period, and then a continuous period of 25 minutes during which the subject was told to control the light. In all cases subjects were told they were participating in a conditioning experiment but not that the correct response was an appropriate change in HR. In each of the first two studies, five yoked controls who received false HR feedback were run. No controls were used in the third (1968) study.

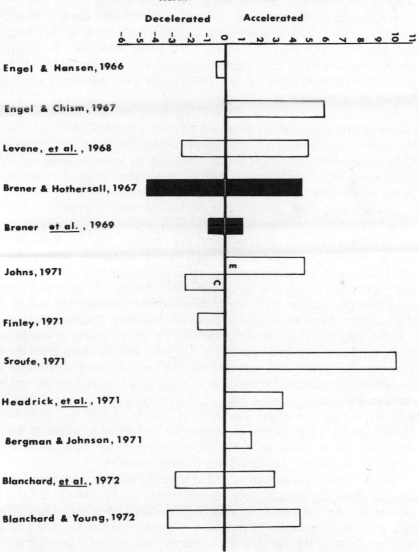

Figure 1.   Summary of human heart rate control research through 1971.

Of the ten subjects used in the HR slowing study, five showed evidence of gaining control of HR with decreases in HR ranging from -1.2 to -2.6 beats per minute (BPM) ($\overline{X} = -1.96$). The other five were not able to gain control despite the fact that three of five knew the correct response. None of the five successful subjects guessed the correct response. Mechanisms used by successful subjects were identified as "relaxation" or "concentrating on the task."

A reanalysis of the data from this study for *all* experimental subjects, no just those whom the authors labeled as successful in learning to slow HR, reveals that the mean change in HR was -0.5 BPM. Moreover, the significant decrease reported by the experimenters appeared on closer examination to be the result of an HR increase on the part of the control group rather than a decreased HR for experimental subjects.

All five subjects used in the HR speeding study showed evidence of gaining control of HR with increases from $+4.2$ to $+9.8$ BPM ($\overline{X} = +5.9$). Two of the controls also showed noticeable increases in HR, $+6.6$ and $+7.0$ BPM. Only one experimental subject became aware of the response being measured. Mechanisms used were identified both as "concentration" and "relaxation," which were similar to those used by the control subjects.

Although the authors conclude that cardiac acceleration appeared to be more easily learned than deceleration, reexamination of their data seriously attenuates the strength with which this conclusion can be made. The 5.6 BPM increase for the control group in the HR slowing study is essentially equal to the 5.9 BPM increase for the experimental group in the investigation that purported to demonstrate HR acceleration using identical techniques. It seems unwarranted to attribute one increase to chance or noncontingent reinforcement (yoked controls) and an equivalent increase to experimental effects (feedback group).

In the study by Levene et al. (1968) trials on which the subject was to alternately accelerate and decelerate HR at 1-minute intervals were given for two 1-hour sessions. The results indicated that HR increases were significantly different from HR decreases. Differences in group means between resting and self-control trials were -2.5 and $+4.8$ BPM for lowering and raising attempts, respectively. Large intersubject variability in control of HR was again noted. There was also a high degree of intersubject variability in length of training time (two to four 1-hour sessions). Moreover, only two of the five subjects learned to consistently vary their HR's in both directions.

Since no control groups were used and since the subjects were given varying amounts of training time, the only conclusion that can be drawn is that individuals can be taught HR self-control in both directions using exteroceptive feedback to provide knowledge of results. It is unfortunate that the only available measure of resting HR was obtained before the introduction of the experimental procedure and also that acceleration and deceleration attempts were alternated without allowing HR to return to an approximation of its baseline level before attempting to produce change in the opposing direction. This immediate alternation introduces the possibility of a rebound effect that could positively bias the results. Merely adjusting the criterion HR so that it falls at the median of the HR distribution from the beginning of a 1-hour session does not seem to deal adequately with the possibility of intratrial fluctuations. This criticism is based on the reports by Brener and Hothersall (1966, 1967) that HR showed a constant decline within a single session.

In all of Engel's studies a shaping procedure was used during training sessions: after determination of the median HR, the set point was initially a value which made subjects successful on 80 percent of the trials. This was subsequently changed to a median for data collection trials.

Brener and his associates (Brener and Hothersall, 1966, 1967; Brener, Kleinman, and Goesling, 1969) demonstrated both speeding and slowing of HR in the same subject within a single session using differential binary auditory feedback. In all of the studies subjects received the feedback of a high-pitched tone of 100-millisecond duration for IBI's shorter than the mode of the distribution of IBI's collected during a baseline period, indicating a faster HR, and a low-pitched tone for IBI's longer (slower HR) than the modal value. Subjects were asked to try to elicit either one tone or the other at various stages of the experiment. In the two studies by Brener and Hothersall, subjects were not told that the tones were related to HR. In the third study they were so informed. In all studies self-control trials of approximately 1 minute (50 IBI's) were alternated with 30-second periods of no feedback. Also, in all three studies the subjects were instructed to try to control the tone, or their HR, by "mental processes only" rather than using breathing or muscle tensing. In all of the studies normal college students were used.

In the first study, involving five subjects, four trials of raising HR were alternated with four trials of lowering HR. Subjects gave significantly fewer short IBI's in the final lowering trial than in the final raising trial, indicating successful control of HR. This study is not summarized in Figure 1 because the data are not reported in a form from which mean change in HR, upward or downward, can be calculated. In the other two studies by Brener, it was possible to calculate a mean raise-lower difference, however, it was still not possible to determine the mean acceleration or mean deceleration of HR from some baseline level.

Postexperimental interviews revealed that no subjects knew that the feedback was related to HR and the mechanisms reported by subjects were said to be "extremely variable." The recordings of respiration rate during the sessions indicated a possible relationship between HR and respiration.

To control for the respiration effect of faster, erratic breathing associated with increased HR, Brener and Hothersall (1967) taught subjects to breathe in a paced manner while utilizing their feedback paradigm. Then, after an appropriate adaptation period, each of the five subjects was given six trials on which the subjects were to raise their HR and six for lowering. Even with respiration rate controlled, the subjects were able to produce significant changes in HR as desired. The differences between lowered and increased HR's varied from 1 to 7 BPM. Self-control tended to improve between trials.

Brener's third study (1969) differs from the preceding two in that subjects were informed that the purpose was to change their HR and what the feedback contingencies were. In the first part ten subjects were given 12 trials of approximately 60 seconds on which they were to raise their HR alternated with 12 trials on which HR was to be lowered. A 30-second rest period was interposed between self-control trials. No feedback was given during this study, yet subjects had HR's significantly ($p < .01$) higher on "increase HR" trials than on "decrease HR" trials. The difference was relatively small, however, ranging from 1 to 3.5 BPM.

In the second part of the study, five subjects were given differential binary auditory feedback on either 100, 50, or 0 percent of the 12 trials, 6 to raise HR and 6 to lower. Interposed among these were three pairs of trials on which no feedback was given and on which the data for the study were gathered. Two sessions were run on different days. There was also significantly better control evidenced during the second session than during the first. No results were reported on either the mechanisms used or on the subject variability in degree of control.

Related to the no feedback portion of the study by Brener et al. (1969) is a recent study by Bergman and Johnson (1971). They also demonstrated that normal college students can show brief significant changes in HR with no feedback whatsoever. They measured HR on the first six beats after a stimulus onset which signaled subjects to try to change their HR in a particular direction. For these six beats those subjects in the increase HR group had a significantly higher HR ($\bar{X} = 1.5$ BPM) than a no-change control group, and the decrease HR group was significantly lower ($\bar{X} = -1.0$ BPM) than the controls. HR's were measured relative to prestimulus HR. In a replication, subjects were again able to raise HR more than controls, but the subjects in the decrease group could not lower their HR significantly. During a reversal neither self-control group differed significantly from the controls.

Johns (1971), using a differential binary auditory feedback procedure very similar to that of Brener et al. (1969), investigated the effects of feedback and instruction on self-control of HR when both respiration rate and gross body movement were controlled. His study used normal college females ($n = 5$ per cell) for a single session in which 70-second trials of both acceleration and deceleration of HR were given. Johns found a significant effect of instructions but none of feedback: his subjects who were informed of the HR-feedback signal relation, who received feedback, and who were instructed to change their HR were able to raise their HR ($\bar{X} = +4.6$) but not lower it; subjects who were instructed to change HR but not given feedback could lower it ($\bar{X} = -2.3$ BPM) but could not raise it. Both of these groups showed differences in HR between acceleration and deceleration trials, whereas there were no such differences for the two groups who were not instructed to change their HR. It was not clear what the noninstructed subjects who received feedback were told about the auditory signal nor was it clear how the feedback signal was linked to the response. Various cognitive mechanisms were reported by subjects as the means they used to "mentally" make their hearts beat faster or slower.

Finley (1971) used a continuous proportional visual feedback paradigm to teach self-control of cardiac deceleration. Twenty college students, ten per condition, were given either correct or incorrect feedback of their HR and were told to keep the meter pointer in what was the lower HR range. They were not informed that HR was the appropriate response. Subjects each received five 5-minute feedback trials separated by 5-minute rest, or no-feedback, periods. Subjects receiving true feedback were able to lower their HR during feedback trials significantly more than on trials when no feedback was available ($\Delta \overline{X} = -1.7$ BPM) and more than subjects receiving incorrect feedback ($\Delta \overline{X} = -1.5$ BPM). The latter group showed an increase in HR when receiving the false feedback and a decrease when there was no display, pointing out the disruptive effects of false feedback.

Headrick, Feather, and Wells (1971) used continuous proportional auditory feedback in a study of HR raising and lowering by separate groups of college students. Their subjects were not informed of the relation of the feedback signal to HR. In the one session of their study, subjects could raise ($\overline{X} = +2.5$ to 4.0 BPM) but could not lower their HR during the ten 60-second trials. An important aspect of their study was the treatment of the data: HR on experimental trials was compared to that of an immediately preceding baseline to control for overall changes during the session.

Self-Control of Heart Rate Variability

Lang and his associates (Hnatiow and Lang, 1965; Lang, Sroufe, and Hastings, 1967; Sroufe, 1969) demonstrated a reduction of HR variability using continuous proportional visual feedback. In these studies the self-control task, the instructions, and the feedback procedures were the same. The 1967 study served to replicate the findings of the first and to provide additional controls for competing explanations of the findings. In all studies the experimental subjects, normal college males, were told that their task was to keep their HR's as steady or constant as possible by keeping a pointer within a specified range on a visual display. The range was actually ± 3 BPM of the mean of a distribution recorded and calculated during the last 5 minutes of the adaptation period. Three 5-minute self-control trials were separated by 7-minute periods during which no feedback was available. In the first study (1965) the control subjects were instructed in the same manner as the experimental subjects but were given false feedback. In the second study (1967) one control group was given the same instructions, but the feedback they received was that given to their yoked experimental subjects. Two other groups were included, in one of which subjects were given accurate feedback but not informed as to what it represented. Their task was merely to track the pointer in its variations rather than control it. The third group received the same instructions as the second but feedback from the HR of their yoked control partner.

In both studies the experimental subjects showed a significantly greater percentage of time within the specified range (approximately 2.5 out of 5 minutes possible, as opposed to control subjects who averaged under 2 minutes), and a lower standard deviation for their HR distribution (lower by about 10 BPM) than any of the controls. These studies also found significantly greater control of variability when experimental subjects were given feedback than when the feedback was not available to them. No results on intersubject variability in gaining control or the cognitive mechanisms by which it was obtained were reported. Respiration was monitored in all cases and variations in it were statistically ruled out as the principal control method.

Sroufe (1969) modified this basic paradigm to include stricter control procedures to eliminate a possible respiratory explanation of reduced cardiac variability. Thirty subjects were taught to breathe at fixed rates (14, 16, 18 per minute) and at constant amplitudes. Ten subjects were given no respiratory restrictions. The third and fourth sessions were identical to the basic procedure of Lang et al. (1967) with half the subjects in each group providing the feedback for themselves and their yoked control partners. The data presented were collected during the fifth session in which 1-minute presentations of feedback and no feedback were alternated for four presentations of each. There were three such blocks of eight trials with a 3-minute rest period between blocks.

Results added support to previous findings that experimental subjects showed greater reduction of HR variability when feedback was present than when it was absent. They also decreased the standard deviation of their HR distribution, whereas subjects with inaccurate feedback tended to become slightly more variable as the session progressed. While manipulating respiration rate appeared to produce minimal results, there was one unique finding demonstrated in this report. Comparison of subjects with controlled respiration to those without restrictions indicated that both were able to reduce significantly HR variability, but the former were less successful at the end than at the beginning of the session. Sroufe attributed this to the fatiguing effects of attempting to control both HR and respiration concurrently.

Clinical Application of Self-Control of Heart Rate

In turning from the literature on self-control of HR with normal subjects to the area of demonstrated clinical applications, the scarcity of studies becomes readily apparent. Engel and Melmon (1968) presented a brief report on the application of operant conditioning procedure to patients with cardiac disorders. They treated four patients with different cardiac arrhythmias, including atrial fibrillation, atrial and ventricular tachycardia, and premature ventricular contractions (PVC), by teaching them to regulate their HR and heart rhythm using Engel's operant conditioning paradigm. Three of the four achieved sustained effects which continued several months. Details of the treatment procedure were not presented.

None of the other investigators in this area reported clinical application of the research on the self-control of HR.

Summary of Previous Research

As of early 1971 several points seemed clear: the fact of self-control of HR through the use of feedback and/or reinforcement was well established. However, with rare exception, control had been demonstrated in normal college students rather than patients with cardiac disorders. Moreover, the changes reported were small, in the range of 1 to 6 BPM. Although this magnitude of change was sufficient to be significant *statistically*, it was far from being *clinically* significant. Furthermore, the changes have tended to be demonstrated for relatively short trials (modal trial length is about 1 minute). Finally, most studies have used only one or two experimental sessions.

Goals of Our Research

Our research program sought to rectify most of the faults found in the previous research in this area by having as its goals: (a) the obtaining of large-magnitude, clinically significant changes in HR over relatively long experimental trials, and (b) maintaining the changes over successive days. A final aspect of our research program was the utilization of patients suffering from tachycardia as subjects in addition to normal individuals.

BEHAVIORAL TACTICS FOR CLINICAL CARDIAC CONTROL

This section describes a series of experiments conducted from early 1971 through late 1972. This research was conducted in four phases and will be described in terms of these phases. In all of the experiments reported there are certain methodological similarities. These are described first.

Commonalities of Methodology

Each subject was initially informed that he was participating in a research program which involved the monitoring of various aspects of his internal behavior. He was also told that the response being monitored was not related to respiration or to muscle tension and that he was therefore to relax and breathe normally during all experimental trials. As will be indicated later, some subjects were informed of the nature of the response as part of the particular experiment in which they participated.

During each experimental session, subject was comfortably seated in a reclining chair in a sound-attenuated chamber. On his arms and legs were placed electrodes through which to monitor the electrocardiogram (EKG). The subject's HR was recorded on a Model 7 Grass Polygraph using a 7P4 Tachograph preamplifier and various other counters and recorders. This equipment was electronically coupled via a Schmitt trigger with a television set or a pair of running time meters which faced the subject in the chamber so that during certain experimental trials subject's HR could control the operation of the television picture or the meters. The running time meters were a pair of clocks which accumulated seconds of correct and incorrect response, that is, subject's HR above or below a specified rate, depending on whether HR was being accelerated or decelerated.

All sessions lasted 40 minutes. The first 20 minutes constituted an adaptation period during which the subject's HR was recorded while he sat quietly in the experimental room. The last 20 minutes comprised the experimental trial during which the experimental procedures were employed. Sessions were usually held daily.

Experimental Design

All of the experiments reported here are of the single subject reversal, or ABA, design. Basic to this design is the establishment of a stable baseline level of the target behavior (A), introduction of an experimental manipulation (B), and removal of the experimental manipulation and a return to baseline conditions (A). In some experiments several experimental manipulations might be introduced sequentially or in an additive fashion, but the final phase was always a return to baseline conditions.

The number of trials needed to complete any condition was dependent on subject's performance in relation to the criterion determined by the experimenter. However, no condition was terminated until subject's mean HR showed stability over days. Stability was defined as three consecutive trials in which HR evidenced less than 10 percent variability; that is, the HR value for any trial was within ±5 percent of the mean HR for three consecutive trials.

Because of the nature of the design, statistical analyses of the results were not necessary. Rather, results are shown in the form of graphic representation of the data with changes in level and slope indicating the relative effectiveness of experimental manipulations.

Two basic kinds of experiment are presented: (a) analog experiments in which the HR of normal volunteers is accelerated and (b) clinical experiments in which the HR of patients with tachycardia is decelerated. The subjects for all of the analog experiments were college students who participated as paid volunteers. All were reported to be in good health and on no medication. The subjects for the clinical experiments were a heterogeneous group.

The strategy was to try a procedure first in an analog experiment. If it was successful then the next step was to demonstrate the usefulness of the procedure with a clinical case. The importance of the last step is stressed because analog experiments have a value only if factors discovered in them can be shown to have relevance for a clinical population.

PHASE 1: CONSTANT CRITERION

EXPERIMENT 1

Subject. The subject was a 20-year-old normal male.

Experimental Conditions. In this experiment the reinforcer was access to the video portion of commercial television programs. At all times when the television was used, the audio portion of the program was available to the subject on a noncontingent basis, but the video could be turned on or off depending on the experimental procedure.

The first condition employed (baseline) involved the determination of resting HR. During this time HR was monitored for 40 minutes while the subject sat in the experimental room. This baseline condition was terminated when HR stabilized.

The second condition consisted of the noncontingent presentation of television (NCTV) during the experimental trials. This condition was included to determine whether the presentation of television per se affected HR and was terminated when the subject's HR stabilized.

During the third condition television was made contingent (CTV) on an increase in HR. At the beginning of this condition the subject was informed that the television picture would operate only when he was making the "correct" response with respect to his internal behavior. He was instructed to keep the television picture on as much as possible. The *criterion* HR required of the subject in order to receive reinforcement was 5 BPM above his baseline level throughout the 20-minute experimental trial. When subject's mean HR remained at or above this criterion for three consecutive experimental trials the criterion was raised five beats. This procedure was continued until the subject's HR was 20 percent higher than his baseline HR for three consecutive trials. The fourth condition for this subject was the same as condition two—the television picture was presented noncontingently. This condition was included to determine the extent of reversal of HR when the contingency was removed.

Results. The data for this subject are presented in Figure 2. From a resting rate of 65 BPM in the baseline condition there was no significant acceleration of HR in the noncontingent reinforcement condition. During the third condition, through the use of shaping and contingent television, the subject's HR was accelerated to a rate of 82 BPM. In the fourth condition, noncontingent reinforcement, the subject's HR dropped to an average of 70 BPM, which approximated operant level.

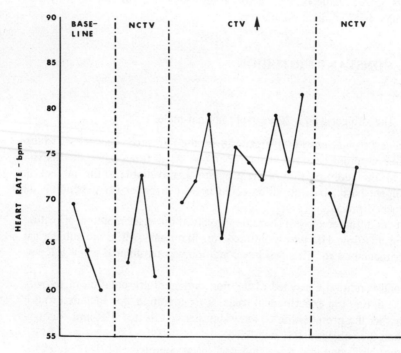

TRIALS

Figure 2.   Heart rate in beats per minute for Subject 1 for all conditions of the experiment. (From R. W. Scott, R. D. Peters, W. J. Gillespie, E. B. Blanchard, E. D. Edmunson, and L. D. Young. The use of shaping and reinforcement in the operant acceleration and deceleration of heart rate. *Behaviour Research and Therapy,* **11:**179-186, 1973. Copyright (1973) by Pergamon Press. Reproduced by permission.)

EXPERIMENT 2

The first experiment was an analog involving the acceleration of HR in a normal individual. The second experiment involved a clinical patient to illustrate the feasibility of this procedure for deceleration of HR.

Subject. The subject was a 61-year-old male psychiatric patient diagnosed as suffering from chronic anxiety and manifesting a moderately elevated HR. He suffered from no coronary disease and was on no medication throughout the duration of the experiment.

Experimental Conditions. This subject received the same conditions as the first except that an attempt was made to decelerate HR. A fifth condition was employed because of the failure to obtain a significant reversal of HR in the fourth condition. This final condition was similar to the third except that television was introduced contingent on HR acceleration in an attempt to return the subject's HR to its operant level.

Results. The data are presented in Figure 3. The resting baseline for this subject was 87 BPM. During the presentation of noncontingent television (NCTV) there was a decrease in HR to 80 BPM. In the third condition, contingent television (CTV), the subject's HR was lowered in 13 trials to the normal range, averaging 71 BPM for the final two trials. In the fourth condition there was no significant reversal of the decelerated HR after 13 trials of noncontingent reinforcement. In the final condition subject's HR was accelerated to its initial resting rate by the reinstatement of contingent television for 23 trials in which the subject had to increase his HR for reinforcement.

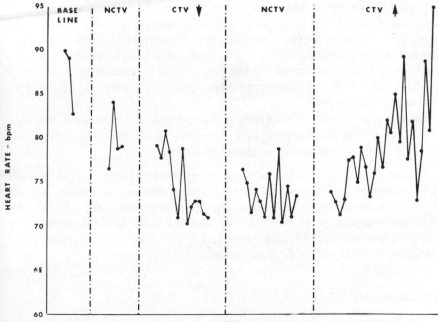

TRIALS

Figure 3. Heart rate in beats per minute for Subject 2 for all conditions of the experiment. (From R. W. Scott, R. D. Peters, W. J. Gillespie, E. B. Blanchard, E. D. Edmunson, and L. D. Young. The use of shaping and reinforcement in the operant acceleration and deceleration of heart rate. *Behaviour Research and Therapy*, **11;**179-186, 1973. Copyright (1973) by Pergamon Press. Reproduced by permission.)

EXPERIMENT 3

The results of Experiments 1 and 2 were highly encouraging in that large-magnitude changes in HR were generated and maintained over successive sessions. It was felt, however, that changing to a more potent reinforcer might improve the efficiency of the paradigm employed in the first two experiments. Experiment 3, therefore, was an analog experiment designed to replicate the first experiment with some important methodological changes included.

Subject. The subject was a 20-year-old male whose basal HR was below the normal range.

Experimental Conditions. Among the changes in this experiment was the use of a different reinforcer, money. This change was introduced because of some mild dissatisfaction expressed by this subject with the ongoing commercial television fare. The subject was given 1 cent for every 10 seconds of correct responding (i.e., emitting HR above the criterion level for each trial), as recorded on the running time meters.

A second change was that television was presented noncontingently to the subject during the baseline condition (Condition 1). This was done for several reasons: (a) it increased the comparability of this experiment to the first experiment; (b) it was felt that an adequate control in baseline would require a visual stimulus to which the subject attended, since focusing of attention might have some effect on HR (Lang et al., 1967). Commercial television programs were used since, a priori, it seemed that the subject would attend to this meaningful material more readily than to some other stimulus complex such as random movement of the meters.

Except for the change in reinforcer just mentioned, the acquisition condition of this experiment was the same as in the earlier experiment. The final condition (Condition 3) was, again, a return to baseline.

Results. The data for this experiment are graphed in Figure 4. The average HR during the baseline administration of noncontingent television was 47 BPM. Over 26 trials of shaping and contingent reinforcement, the subject's HR increased to an average 63 BPM over the final six trials. In the third condition (return to baseline) the subject's HR returned essentially to its operant level, averaging 50 BPM for the final three trials.

Discussion

At this point the employment of positive reinforcement in an operant paradigm appeared to provide an effective means for producing large changes in HR and for maintaining these changes over successive sessions. Functional relationships between the manipulation of the reinforcement and changes from operant levels were established and maintained effectively.

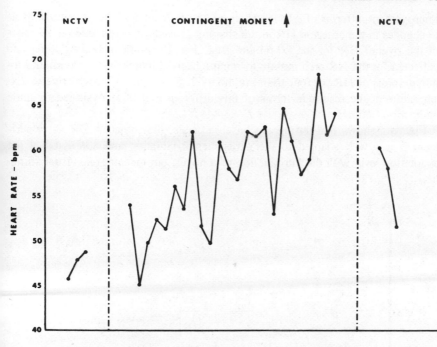

Figure 4. Heart rate in beats per minute for Subject 3 for all conditions of the experiment. (From R. W. Scott, R. D. Peters, W. J. Gillespie, E. B. Blanchard, E. D. Edmunson, and L. D. Young. The use of shaping and reinforcement in the operant acceleration and deceleration of heart rate. *Behaviour Research and Therapy*, **11**:179-186, 1973. Copyright (1973) by Pergamon Press. Reproduced by permission.)

The demonstration that HR could be controlled with conditioning procedures was not new. However, the fact that changes in HR of relatively large magnitude were demonstrated and maintained for longer periods of time greatly enhances the assumption that operant conditioning procedures offer potential for viable treatment of certain cardiac disorders.

In the second experiment, where the subject's HR, once decelerated, did not return to its operant level when the contingency was removed, was a somewhat puzzling finding that will be discussed later. In any event, it was possible to show that his HR could be brought under operant control by the final experimental condition in which it was accelerated to its original level.

Changing the Unit of Analysis

These experiments were highly gratifying; however, they were still of a somewhat preliminary nature and the procedure involved seemed to be in need of improvement in terms of efficiency. It will be remembered that all decisions as to changes in the criterion HR in the shaping procedure were made on the basis of the overall HR for the 20-minute trial. For Experiment 3, data were also collected for the HR on a minute-to-minute basis. Figures 5 to 8 are minute-to-minute plots of HR for four trials, numbers 2, 5, 10, and 12, respectively. Examination of the results in terms of this different unit of analysis led to some interesting findings.

Figure 5 shows that during the baseline trials, the subject's HR in Experiment 3 was well adapted to the experimental situation and continued at the adaptation level with the introduction of a novel, but meaningful, visual stimulus.

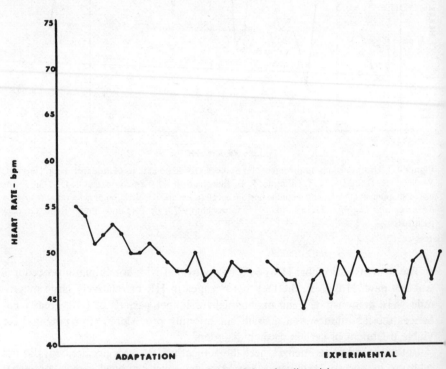

Figure 5.   Minute-to-minute heart rate for Subject 3 for a baseline trial.

In Figure 6 the results are presented for a trial in which success was achieved; that is, the subject's HR during the experimental trial met the criterion level indicated on the figure. It is clear that this subject's HR accelerated from the adaptation level to meet the criterion, but that no further acceleration was present during the trial.

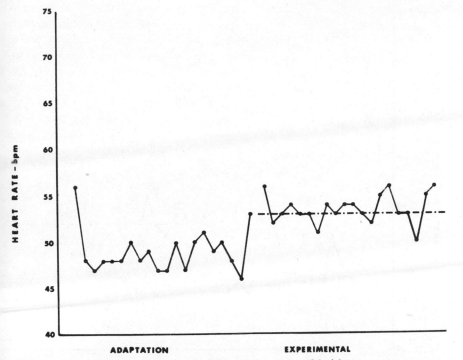

Figure 6. Minute-to-minute heart rate for Subject 3 for a successful trial.

Figure 7 shows a trial on which the subject's HR initially accelerated to meet the criterion but then gradually decreased during the trial. Since the criterion for reinforcement was held constant for the entire trial, there was no way to intervene in this process.

Finally, in Figure 8 the results for an unsuccessful trial are presented. In this trial there was still the initial surge in HR found in nearly all of the experimental trials. However, in this instance, because of the level of the criterion, the subject never reached the criterion and thus never received any reinforcement. This failure of the subject to receive any reinforcement for the entire trial is analogous to being placed on extinction.

These findings, which resulted from using a different unit of analysis for the data, led to a search for a better, more flexible shaping procedure. Several features seemed desirable: (a) the procedure should capitalize on the initial surge toward the criterion, which subjects typically showed; (b) it should allow for decreases as shown in Figure 7 and be able to intervene in them; and (c) it should constantly challenge the subject.

After several attempts at developing such a strategy, the shaping procedure described in the next section was developed. Its essence was the use of a *varia-*

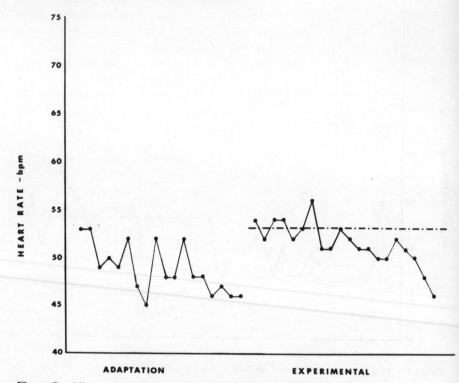

Figure 7.   Minute-to-minute heart rate for Subject 3 for an initially successful trial.

ble criterion (VC), changed on a minute-to-minute basis to maximize the contact with the reinforcement contingency which the subject experienced.

An interesting aside revealed by these data is that subjects showed evidence early in the acquisition trials of learning the response. This evidence was in terms of the initial ''surge'' toward the criterion they showed during the first few minutes after the experimental trial began. This surge was present both in subjects whose HR was being accelerated and in those whose HR was being decelerated. In the latter subjects the surge was of a lower magnitude but was fairly consistently in the appropriate (downward) direction.

PHASE 2: CONSTANT CRITERION TO VARIABLE CRITERION

This section describes three experiments in which subjects were initially run on the constant criterion procedure and then switched to the new variable criterion procedure. Two of the experiments are analog studies and one is a clinical case.

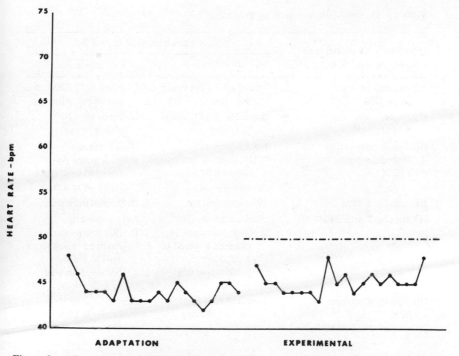

Figure 8.   Minute-to-minute heart rate for Subject 3 for an unsuccessful trial.

Variable Criterion Shaping Procedure

The new variable criterion shaping procedure involved changing the criterion which the subject had to achieve in order to receive reinforcement on a minute-to-minute basis according to an empirically derived set of rules. The exact decision rules are presented in Table 1.

EXPERIMENT 4

Subject. The subject for Experiment 4 was an 18-year-old female.

Experimental Conditions. The first three conditions of this experiment were the same as those for Experiment 1: baseline, during which the subject sat quietly; next the reinforcer, the video portion of ongoing commercial television programs (the audio portion was available noncontingently throughout the experiment), was delivered to the subject noncontingently (NCTV). In the third condition the video portion of the television program was made contingent (CTV) and an attempt was made to accelerate subject's HR using the constant criterion (CC) shaping procedure.

Table 1.   Variable Criterion Shaping Procedure

If Subject's HR Relative to Criterion on Trial N is:	Criterion on Trial $N + 1$ Is:	
	Acceleration	Deceleration
HR exceeds by 4 or more BPM	Raised to 2 BPM below behavior	Lowered to 2 BPM above behavior
HR exceeds by 2 or 3 BPM	Raised to 1 BPM below behavior	Lowered to 1 BPM above behavior
HR equals criterion or exceeds criterion by 1 BPM	Held 1 minute If HR remains unchanged raised 1 BPM on trial $N + 2$	Held 1 minute If HR remains unchanged lowered 1 BPM on trial $N + 2$
HR fails by 1 BPM	Held indefinitely	Held indefinitely
HR fails by 2 or 3 BPM	Held 1 minute If HR remains unchanged lowered to 1 BPM above behavior on trial $N + 2$	Held 1 minute If HR remains unchanged raised to 1 BPM below behavior on trial $N + 2$
HR fails by 4 or more BPM	Lowered to 2 BPM above behavior	Raised to 2 BPM below behavior

In the first three experiments the subjects were not informed of the nature of the response they were to control. In the fourth condition of Experiment 4, the subject, who was likewise ignorant of the response, was informed (I) of its nature. Otherwise the procedure was the same as in the preceding condition. This condition was included as a test of the allegedly detrimental effect knowledge of the response has on the self-control of HR (Engel and Chism, 1967a; Engel and Hansen, 1966).

In the next condition the variable criterion (VC) shaping procedure, using contingent television as the reinforcer, was introduced. In the final condition the experimental analysis was completed by again giving the subject access to the reinforcer on a noncontingent basis (NCTV).

The number of trials in any condition was dependent on the subject's performance. However, no condition was terminated until stability was achieved.

Results. The average HR for the 20-minute experimental trials is presented in two-day blocks for this experiment and all subsequent ones. In conditions for which there were only three trials, the two points plotted represent the average of Trials 1 and 2 and of Trials 2 and 3.

The baseline HR was 75 BPM. The presentation in Condition 2 of noncontingent reinforcement had no effect. The implementation in Condition 3 of the contingency and constant criterion shaping procedure led to an initial increase of about 5 BPM. However, 16 trials in this condition resulted in little overall increase. Informing the subject of the nature of the response in Condition 4 had no effect: it neither facilitated an increase in HR nor was it deleterious, leading to less self-control.

The introduction of the variable criterion procedure resulted in an increase in HR of 15 BPM for the final three trials as may be seen in Figure 9. HR for the final trial was 91 BPM. In the final condition the subject's HR returned to its baseline level.

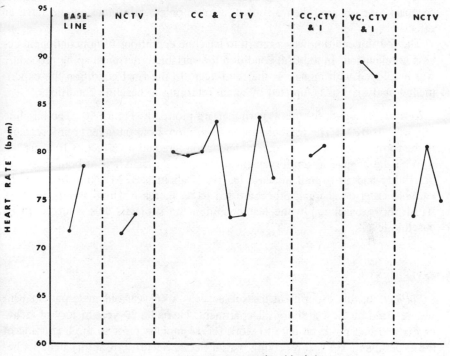

TRIALS (in two day blocks)

Figure 9. Heart rate in beats per minute for Subject 4 for all conditions of the experiment.

EXPERIMENT 5

Experiment 5, a second analog experiment, served as a replication of Experiment 4, with some important methodological differences.

Subject. The subject for this experiment was a 20-year-old female.

Experimental Conditions. The fifth subject was informed of the nature of the response from the very beginning. The first condition of the experiment was baseline, during which the initial reinforcer, access to the video portion of ongoing commercial television programs, was delivered to the subject noncontingently until her HR met the criterion for stability. In the second condition reinforcement was made contingent (CTV) on an accelerated HR using the constant criterion (CC) shaping procedure.

The next condition provided a test of an important theoretical question as to whether this procedure is, in fact, operant conditioning. Everything was held constant except that the reinforcement was changed to money. If reinforcement really does play a part in the procedure as an incentive over the knowledge of feedback one obtains, then a shift to a more potent reinforcer should have an effect.

The fourth condition was a return to baseline conditions of noncontingent access to television. In the fifth condition the variable criterion shaping procedure was employed with money as the reinforcer. In the final condition the experimental analysis was completed by again returning to baseline conditions.

Results. The data for this experiment are plotted in Figure 10. The baseline HR was 70 BPM. The presentation in Condition 2 of contingent reinforcement in the form of access to commercial television fare had no effect in 10 trials.

With the change in reinforcement to money, 24 trials led to both increased variability and an overall increase in HR of about 5 BPM. Nine trials on the variable criterion shaping procedure led to an increase which stabilized at 15 BPM above baseline. In the last condition the subject's HR returned to its baseline level.

EXPERIMENT 6

Subject. In this experiment the subject was a 46-year-old male patient who was referred by the Cardiology Department. He had a 20-year history of tachycardia and had not been able to work for 14 months prior to the beginning of the experiment. He was receiving partial Social Security disability benefits because of his condition. He had been taking approximately 40 milligrams of Librium per day for 14 months before the experiment. During the course of the experiment he decreased his medication on his own to less than 10 milligrams per day.

Experimental Procedures. Since this individual was a clinical case and was taking part in the experiment as a form of treatment, he was informed of the response being conditioned. Also, money rather than access to television was used as the reinforcer throughout the experiment.

Condition 1 consisted of baseline trials during which noncontingent television was presented. In Condition 2 the attempt was made to decelerate HR using the constant criterion (CC) shaping procedure with money as a reinforcer. In

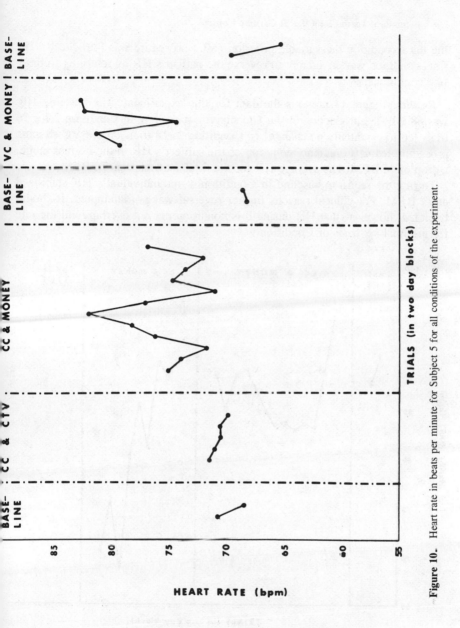

Figure 10. Heart rate in beats per minute for Subject 5 for all conditions of the experiment.

the third condition the variable criterion (VC) procedure was introduced. The final condition was an attempt to reverse the patient's HR by returning to baseline conditions.

Results. Figure 11 presents the data for this experiment. The baseline HR was 88 BPM. Introduction of the CC shaping procedure in Condition 2 for 26 trials led to essentially no change. In Condition 3, 18 trials on the VC shaping procedure led to a dramatic reduction of the subject's HR to the normal range, a drop of 16 BPM. His average HR for the final six trials was 72 BPM.

During the return to baseline in Condition 4 this individual's HR stabilized at 77 BPM. For clinical reasons further reversal was not attempted. It should be noted, however, that HR during this condition did not overlap with the rate for the final six trials of Condition 3.

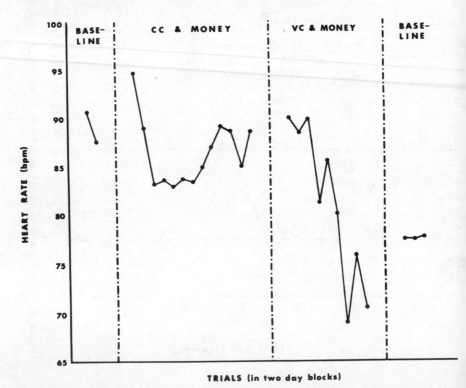

TRIALS (in two day blocks)

Figure 11.   Heart rate in beats per minute for Subject 6 for all conditions of the experiment.

Discussion

Experiments 4, 5, and 6 seem to point out the advantage of the VC procedure over the CC procedure in terms of both efficacy and efficiency: The VC procedure was effective in instances where the CC procedure was not and also tended to produce changes more rapidly. The changes in HR obtained by the VC procedure, at the time the work was done, surpassed any published results in terms of magnitude of change, length of experimental trial for which the change was demonstrated, and stability of the altered HR.

Another observation is worth noting. In subjects whose HR was decelerated in both Experiment 6 and in a previous experiment there were preexperimental complaints of being anxious, tense, or nervous. There was a decrease in these verbalizations concurrent with the deceleration of HR. Furthermore, there were other anecdotal data relating to clinical improvement. The sixth subject, whose verbal report of feeling less anxious coincided with the middle of the VC shaping procedure (Condition 3), actively sought and obtained employment toward the end of treatment. This was his first gainful employment in over 16 months and came in spite of his receiving Social Security disability benefits because of his chronic tachycardia. For the clinical subject in the earlier study, there were reports from the ward of improved behavior and a decrease in tricophilic behavior which had previously been observed at a high rate.

Results from experiments in this phase also shed some light on two important theoretical controversies in the biofeedback research area. The first of these concerns whether subjects should be informed of the nature of the response being conditioned. Reviewing the literature, one finds considerable difference of opinion on this point. For instance, Engel and his associates (Engel and Hansen, 1966; Engel and Chism, 1967a; Levene et al., 1968) did not inform their subjects, nor did Finley (1971). Brener and his colleagues initially did not inform their subjects of the nature of the response (Brener and Hothersall, 1966, 1967); however, in a later study (Brener et al., 1969) they changed their procedure and did inform them. Further, Headrick et al. (1971) did not inform the subjects in the group experiment of their study. Among those who have consistently informed their subjects of the nature of the response from the outset have been Sroufe (1971), Bergman and Johnson (1971), and Blanchard and his associates (Blanchard, Young and McLeod, 1972; Blanchard and Young, 1972). We ourselves have been inconsistent on this issue within the present studies.

This apparent difference of opinion as to whether or not to inform subjects seems to have developed because of a post hoc finding by Engel and Hansen (1966). They reported that subjects who do not correctly infer the nature of the response being conditioned show greater changes than those who do. At the conclusion of the experiment, subjects were asked what response they were controlling. The five subjects who showed evidence of learning the HR deceleration response did not know the nature of the response; however, four of the five nonlearners in the experimental condition did guess the correct response. The performance of the second group was no better than that of the control subjects who were given false feedback.

These results seem to have been the beginning of a myth that knowledge of the response *caused* poorer performance in control of HR. For instance, Headrick et al. (1971) state, "Subjects were misled concerning the response being conditioned on the basis of observations by other investigators (Engel and Hansen, 1966) that *awareness* of the contingency between HR and feedback *tended to result in poorer performance*" (italics added).

The way to settle this controversy is to treat knowledge of the response as an independent variable to be manipulated. This was done in Experiment 4 (see Figure 9) by informing the subject of the nature of the response while continuing her in the CC treatment. The results showed neither an increase nor decrease in HR. Thus, rather than knowledge of the response being detrimental to self-control, it seemed to be inconsequential. A recent study by Bergman and Johnson (1972) also addressed this question directly in a short-term group study and found that correct knowledge of the response conferred a significant advantage to subjects over those who were not informed of it.

The second controversy surrounds the role of reinforcement in biofeedback studies. Engel and his associates refer to their operations as operant conditioning. In addition to binary visual feedback, their subjects were given small sums of money for accumulated experimental time during which their HR was either above or below a criterion HR. All of the other studies of HR change are described in terms of self-control established through external sensory feedback. It is possible, of course, to construe all of these studies as examples of operant conditioning in which the reinforcement is knowledge of results. On the other hand, it is equally possible to construe the reinforcement in informational terms as binary feedback, since subjects receive reinforcement if they are correct and do not receive it if they are not making the correct response.

If one considers knowledge of results to be a reinforcer, feedback and reinforcement are inextricably confounded in the feedback studies. Therefore it is not possible to settle the question merely by giving one group of subjects feedback and a second group reinforcement and then comparing their performance. However, it is possible to tell if reinforcement is providing something beyond information by switching from a less desired to a more desired reward while holding information content constant and then noticing if the response reflects this change. In Experiment 5 (see Figure 10) the reinforcer was switched within the CC procedure resulting in an overall increase in HR of about 5 BPM, which does seem to provide partial confirmation of the efficacious role of reinforcement as an incentive.

PHASE 3: VARIABLE CRITERION

Following the successful application of the VC procedure to subjects previously run on the CC procedure, the next logical step was to run subjects on the VC procedure from the very beginning. This section of the chapter describes three experiments (two analog, one clinical) in which this was done.

EXPERIMENT 7

Subject. The subject for this analog experiment was a 19-year-old normal female.

Experimental Conditions. During this experiment the VC procedure was employed exclusively. Condition 1 was the same as in previous studies, noncontingent television was presented during the experimental trial. In Condition 2 money was used as the reinforcer in the variable criterion shaping procedure. Phase 3 represented a return to baseline conditions. The subject was not told the nature of the response being conditioned.

Results. Figure 12 presents the data for this experiment. This subject's baseline HR was 56.5 BPM. In six trials during Condition 2, the VC procedure resulted in a rise of 30 BPM to an average rate of 87 BPM for the final three trials. In the reversal (Condition 3) nine trials were necessary for the subject to return to her resting HR and show stability.

EXPERIMENT 8

Subject. The subject for this analog experiment was a 22-year-old normal male.

Experiment Conditions. This experiment was an exact replication of Experiment 7.

Results. The subject's baseline HR was 68 BPM. As may be seen in Figure 13, eight trials with the variable criterion shaping procedure led to an increase of over 35 BPM with an average HR for the final three trials of 106 BPM. Nine trials were necessary for the subject's HR to return to a stable level of 69.5 BPM.

EXPERIMENT 9

In keeping with the aim of systematically attempting to replicate results from analog experiments with clinical cases, a clinical experiment was conducted.

Subject. The subject for the ninth experiment was a 50-year-old male patient on the Psychiatry Department Inpatient Unit. He had a diagnosis of anxiety neurosis. This patient had a 26-year history of various complaints, including tachycardia, and had not been gainfully employed for 27 months before the experiment because of tachycardia and feelings of "anxiety and weakness." He was on no medication during the experiment. He was paid at the rate of $1.50 per

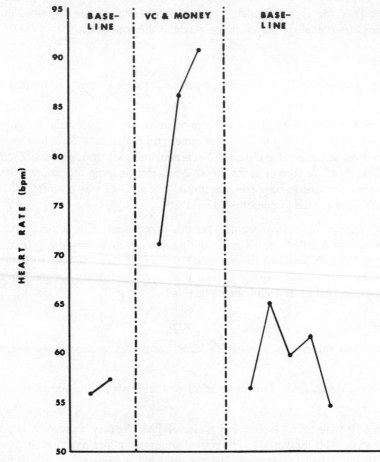

Figure 12.   Heart rate in beats per minute for Subject 7 for all conditions of the experiment.

session and was informed of the response being conditioned.

Experimental Conditions. The conditions in this experiment were the same as those in Experiments 7 and 8 with one exception: During the second condition the subject's HR was decelerated using the VC procedure.

Results. The client's baseline HR was 96 BPM. Nineteen trials with the shaping procedure led to a decrease of 14 BPM, as may be seen in Figure 14. In the return to baseline conditions his HR did not return to its high level. Instead, over eight trials it remained decelerated, stabilizing at approximately 78 BPM.

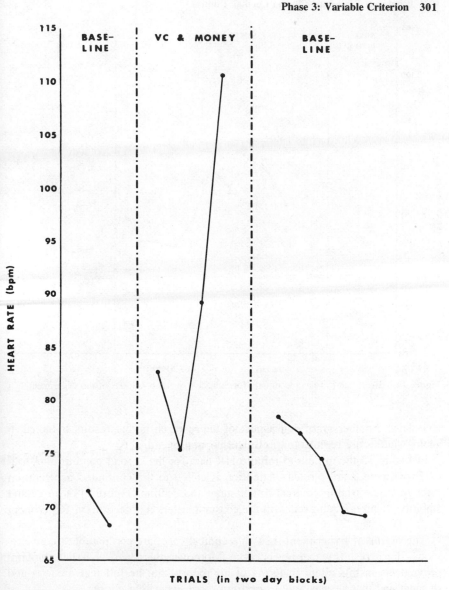

BASE-
LINE

VC & MONEY

BASE-
LINE

Figure 13.   Heart rate in beats per minute for Subject 8 for all conditions of the experiment.

Discussion

These three experiments highlight even more the advantage of the VC procedure over the CC procedure. In Experiments 7 and 8 changes of magnitudes
superior to any reported elsewhere were obtained and maintained over succes-

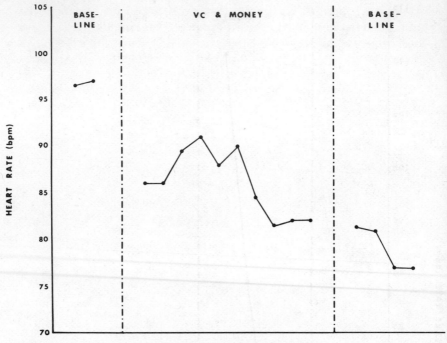

Figure 14.   Heart rate in beats per minute for Subject 9 for all conditions of the experiment.

sive days. Another gratifying aspect of the research is that results obtained in analog studies are replicable in clinical population subjects.

In Figure 15 the minute-to-minute HR data for the second conditioning trial of Experiment 7 are plotted. Attention is called to the continued acceleration throughout the trial in contrast to the surge and decline (Figure 7) or surge and stability (Figure 6) achieved with the constant criterion procedure in Experiment 3.

The results of Experiment 9, with a clinical case, are comparable to our previous clinical results with this procedure. Moreover, there were concomitant improvements in this client in terms of his reports that he felt less anxious and stronger and that he was able to perform more household chores.

In this experiment, the failure of the HR, once decelerated, to return to its prior high pathological level is a phenomenon that had been observed in our laboratory previously. This repeated finding of resistance to extinction of an HR decelerated to the normal range has the clinical implication that a high degree of generalization may be available from this procedure.

The resistance of a decelerated HR to extinction is in sharp contrast to our experiments in which HR has been accelerated. In these latter cases, HR readily returns to baseline level once the extinction procedure is instituted. A possible explanation for this phenomenon may be found in terms of homeostasis. An accelerated HR is outside the normal range for a particular individual; removal of the contingency results in a return to his normal range. For subjects whose HR is decelerated, however, the terminal behavior is now within the generally accepted normal range. For extinction to occur in these cases, a change antagonistic to homeostasis would be required and should occur only with some difficulty.

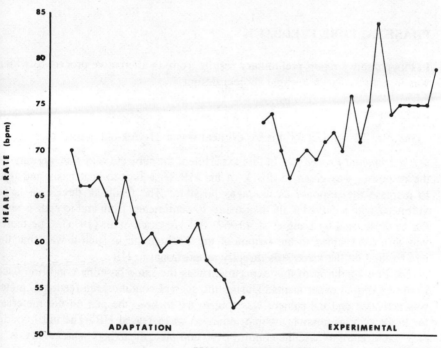

TRIAL 6 – EXPERIMENTAL

Figure 15. Minute-to-minute heart rate for Subject 7 using the variable criterion procedure.

In contrast to the verbal reports of our patients of feeling less tense and anxious when HR is decelerated, the subject in Experiment 7 reported during the final experimental trials when her HR was 94 BPM that she felt tense and anxious. Headrick, Feather, and Wells (1971) reported that their subjects who achieved large-magnitude HR increases also complained of feeling anxious toward the end of the experiment.

It may well be the case that verbal reports of "feeling anxious" and other "cognitive" responses are correlated with autonomic responses such as elevated HR, but that the causal relation may hold either way. Typically, the method of attacking the problem of anxiety has been to aim at the cognitive realm through either psychotherapy or one of the behavioral approaches such as systematic desensitization (Wolpe, 1958) with the autonomic response treated as a dependent variable (e.g., Lang, 1969; Leitenburg, Agras, Butz, and Wincze, 1971). This research suggests the possibility of a different approach: treating HR as the independent variable and exploring the possibility that manipulation of HR will cause changes in self-report and other behavior.

PHASE 3A: PURE FEEDBACK

In this phase we report preliminary results from an alternative procedure which was investigated with a single subject design.

EXPERIMENT 10

Subject. The subject for this experiment was a 21-year-old normal male.

Experimental Procedure. In this experiment the subject, who was ignorant of the response, was given feedback of his HR on a beat-to-beat basis and told to increase the response as much as possible. The feedback device, a large voltmeter with a curved scale measuring 20 centimeters from end to end, is similar to those used by Lang et al. (1967) and Headrick et al. (1971). The meter was directly coupled to the output of the Tachograph in such a way that the pen reading on the meter was directly proportional to HR.

The first condition of this experiment was the same baseline condition used in the preceding experiments. During the second condition the feedback meter was activated and the subject was told to try to keep the pen on the meter as far to the right as possible, which indicated an increased HR. The third condition was a return to baseline conditions to complete the experimental analysis.

Results. This subject's baseline HR was 63 BPM. As seen in Figure 16, six trials with proportional visual feedback alone led to an increase in HR of 21 BPM with an average HR on the final four trials of 84 BPM. Ten trials in the return to baseline led to a decrease in HR to 71 BPM. Although this did not represent a complete reversal, it should be noted that there is no overlap between HR in the feedback and baseline condition.

The results of Experiment 10 expand the range of procedures available for achieving large-magnitude changes in HR which can be maintained over successive days. Although the results are preliminary and in need of replication both in normal and clinical populations, they are encouraging. These results also fur-

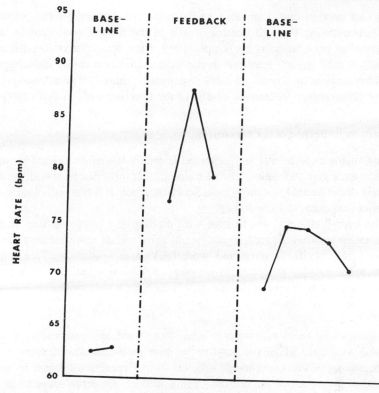

Figure 16.   Heart rate in beats per minute for Subject 10 for all conditions of the experiment.

ther confuse the picture of the role reinforcement plays in self-control experiments since, in this case, the only reinforcement is knowledge of results.

PHASE 4: STIMULUS CONTROL

As impressive as these results are in terms of magnitude of change and duration for which it was maintained, and in spite of a number of replications, they are only the first step in the development of behavioral procedures for achieving clinical cardiac control. The ultimate goal of such procedures would be to teach the patient to control his HR in his natural environment.

One strategy for achieving this generalization of laboratory effects to the natural environment involves a three-step training program: (a) bringing the change in HR under stimulus control in the laboratory; (b) transferring, in the laboratory, the controlling stimulus from an external one controlled by the experimenter to an internal one, such as a verbalization, controlled by the patient; and (c) demonstrating this self-control of HR in the natural environment. Such a strategy has been reported by Wolpe (1969) for teaching anxious patients how to control their anxiety reactions in the natural environment by inducing a feeling of relaxation as a result of a self-command "relax." The studies presented in this phase report preliminary results of the first two steps in this strategy.

Common Experimental Procedures

Three analog experiments are presented in which the subjects used in previous studies were given stimulus control training. All three subjects had, of course, already demonstrated that they could accelerate their HR markedly under the appropriate experimental conditions.

The overall strategy was to start with the terminal phase of Step 1, that is, to ascertain to what degree subjects could demonstrate stimulus control of HR without any specific training and work backward, systematically adding elements to the training procedure as necessary to obtain stimulus control and then removing them to see what degree of stimulus control remained.

Subjects

The subjects in these experiments were those used in Experiments 5, 8, and 10. All were paid $1.50 per session for their participation. Moreover, before the beginning of this experiment, subjects from Experiments 8 and 10 were informed of the nature of the response being studied; the other subject had previously been informed of the response.

Of necessity, all subjects were terminated at the end of the school term. Since, as the results show, subjects made progress at different rates, this termination left subjects in varying stages of acquisition of self-control of HR.

Apparatus

In addition to the same recording and feedback apparatus used in previous studies, a panel containing two lights was mounted in the experimental chamber in plain view of the subjects. The onset of these lights, which served as the S^D and S^Δ for the stimulus control trials, was controlled remotely from the equipment room. Timing of the duration of the S^D and S^Δ periods was done by the timer operating the printout counter.

Procedure

In this study, as in the first one, several aspects of the procedure were common to all experiments. Experimental sessions lasted 40 minutes and consisted of a 20-minute adaptation period followed by a 20-minute experimental trial.

The baseline procedure used with all subjects was that described for previous studies with the exception that more rigorous criteria for stability were imposed: four consecutive trials instead of three on which HR evidenced variability of less than 10 percent of baseline HR.

All subjects were started on the same procedure to see whether, as a result of prior training procedures, they could show stimulus control of HR initially. After the completion of the 20-minute adaptation period, 5-minute periods signaled by a light (S^D) during which the subject was to raise his HR were alternated with 5-minute periods signaled by a second light ($S^\triangle$) during which the subject was told to rest and not try to change his HR. Thus two 5-minute S^D periods were given along with two 5-minute $S^\triangle$ periods. This procedure is referred to as stimulus control.

EXPERIMENT 11

Procedure. The subject from Experiment 5 was used in this experiment. The first two conditions for this experiment were the baseline procedure and stimulus control procedure described above. After 11 trials of the stimulus control procedure the subject showed no sign of extinguishing. This finding demonstrated the advantage of determining the degree of terminal behavior present in the subject's repertoire at the beginning of the experiment. At this point, Step 2 of the generalization training program was initiated: Control of S^D onset and offset was transferred from an external stimulus controlled by the experimenter to self-command controlled by the subject. The subject was asked to change her HR when she was ready after the adaptation period and to signal the experimenter by saying "raise" (S^D) or "rest" ($S^\triangle$) when she was raising her HR or resting.

Results. In Figure 17 the data for Experiment 11 are presented in terms of HR. The average values for each S^D and $S^\triangle$ period of each trial are plotted as are the values for the baseline trials.

To make the results easier to follow, in Figure 18 the degree of control of HR is expressed as an index-of-change in BPM. This change score was calculated by first finding the average HR for each 5-minute S^D or $S^\triangle$ period, then subtracting the HR for the $S^\triangle$ period from that for the following S^D period, and finally averaging the changes for the two S^D periods. The final 5 minutes of the adaptation period were used for the first $S^\triangle$ interval. (This change score is also used to present the results of the remaining two experiments.)

The subject's baseline HR was 67 BPM and the range of HR was 5 BPM for the final four baseline trials. On each of the graphs of the change score, the baseline degree of variability in HR is plotted, expressed as the difference in HR from highest to lowest baseline trial. As can be seen in Figure 18, 11 trials of the stimulus control procedure of Condition 2 resulted in an average degree of control of 14 BPM, ranging from 9 to 18.7 BPM.

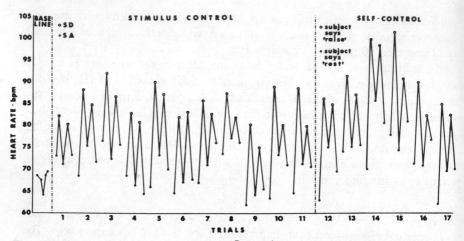

Figure 17. Heart rate in beats per minute for each S^D and $S^\triangle$ period in all conditions of Experiment 11.

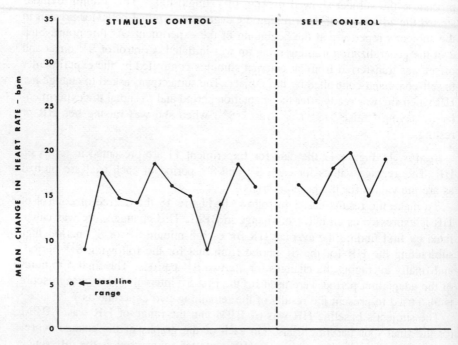

Figure 18. Mean change in heart rate in beats per minute from $S^\triangle$ to S^D periods for all conditions of Experiment 11.

At this point Step 2 of the generalization training, "self-control" of HR, was initiated. Six trials on this procedure where the subject controlled the signal for raising HR and resting resulted in an average degree of control of 17.2 BPM.

For the trials in Condition 3, HR was calculated by counting actual number of heart beats during each interval and dividing by the length of interval. The subject's timing was fairly consistent with the earlier procedure, averaging 5.6 for the S^D periods and 4.4 minutes for the $S^\triangle$ periods (see Figure 19).

EXPERIMENT 12

Experimental Conditions. The subject from Experiment 8 was used for this experiment. The first two conditions, baseline and stimulus control, were the same as in Experiment 11. In the third condition the subject was also given visual feedback proportional to his HR on a continuous basis during both S^D and S periods. The feedback apparatus was that used in Experiment 10. This subject had no prior experience with this apparatus. The fourth condition saw the addition of the variable criterion shaping procedure, utilizing the running time meters, to the feedback and stimulus control conditions. In the fifth condition the variable criterion shaping procedure was removed, leaving only the feedback and stimulus control procedures in effect. In the sixth condition the feedback was removed and the variable criterion shaping procedure was added to the stimulus control procedure. The shaping procedure was removed in condition 7, a baseline condition, and reinstated in the final condition.

Results. As can be seen in Figure 20, the subject's baseline HR was 70 BPM and the range of HR was 2.5 BPM. During the first five stimulus control trials of Condition 2, his degree of HR control dropped from 4.2 BPM to a negative value of −0.5 BPM, indicating average change in the incorrect direction. During the five trials of Condition 3, control improved slightly. The addition of the variable criterion shaping procedure for five trials in Condition 4 led to a dramatic increase in control, averaging 19.1 BPM. A return in Condition 5 to the procedures of Condition 3 showed a steady decline in degree of control. Reinstatement of the variable criterion shaping procedure without the feedback in Condition 6 for two trials resulted in an average degree of control of 27.5 BPM. A return to the stimulus control procedure of Condition 2 for five trials showed that some degree of control remained, ranging from 5.5 to 10.1 BPM. Finally, in Condition 8, a return to the procedures of Condition 6 for three trials showed a reinstatement of control with the index ranging from 10.7 to 29.2 BPM.

EXPERIMENT 13

Experimental Conditions. The subject from Experiment 10 was used in this experiment. The first three conditions for this experiment were the same as in

Experiment 12: baseline, stimulus control, and the addition of feedback to stimulus control procedure. The experimental analysis of this subject was completed by returning to the stimulus control procedure for the fourth and final condition.

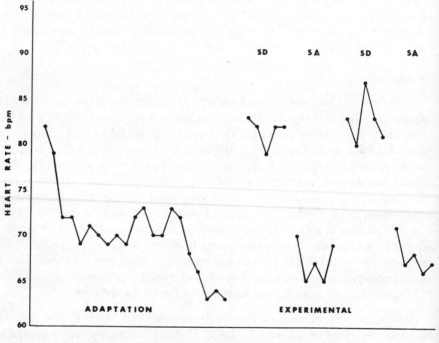

Figure 19.   Heart rate in beats per minute on a minute-to-minute basis for an entire session in the stimulus control condition.

Results. In Figure 21 it can be seen that the subject's baseline HR was 66 BPM and the range of HR was 5.5 BPM. During the initial trials on the stimulus control procedure, the degree of control ranged from 6.5 to 11.3 BPM and averaged 9.2 BPM. The addition of feedback to the stimulus control procedure resulted in an increase in degree of control, averaging 15.8 BPM for the four trials. In Condition 4 a return to the procedure of Condition 2 for five trials resulted in an average degree of control of 21.5 BPM.

Respiration Effects

An issue in the field of self-control of cardiac function surrounded by much controversy is the relative importance of mediational variables. Although media-

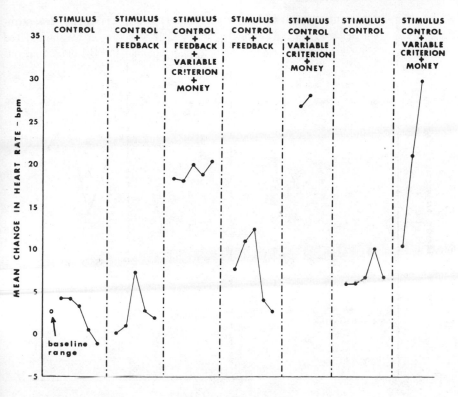

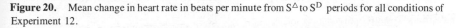

TRIALS

Figure 20.   Mean change in heart rate in beats per minute from S^Δ to S^D periods for all conditions of Experiment 12.

tion by means of cognitive or unspecified skeletal muscular mechanisms has been suggested, the primary focus of the mediation controversy has been on the effects of respiratory variables. Experimental procedures designed to determine whether the obtained HR change resulted from respiratory changes fall into four general categories. Although no investigator failed to monitor respiration, some did little else. Brener and Hothersall (1966) and Brener et al. (1969) report monitoring respiration but do not mention any instructions concerning breathing, nor do they report any analyses of the observed differences.

Engel and his associates (Engel and Chism, 1967a; Engel and Hansen, 1966; Levene et al., 1969) gave all subjects in their investigations the explicit instructions not to change their breathing pattern from normal. Again, however, only monitoring and visual inspection of the data were used to reach the conclusions that respiration did not change significantly and that the observed HR differences did not result from respiratory changes. Levene et. al. (1969) did carry

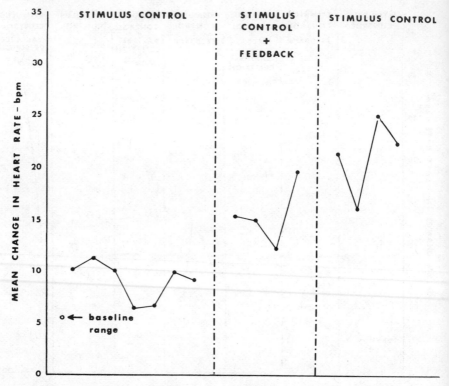

Figure 21. Mean change in heart rate in beats per minute from $S^\triangle$ to S^D periods for all conditions of Experiment 13.

the investigation a step further by teaching two subjects whose respiration rates (RR) were variable to duplicate their earlier RR through a pacing technique. This resulted in changes in HR variability but not in overall HR. When subjects were then asked to imagine the "cue" stimuli, changes were evidenced in both HR and RR but no awareness of these changes was reported.

The third approach to the problem, manipulation of RR to insure its constancy during HR conditioning sessions, was employed by Brener and Hothersall (1967), Johns (1971), and Sroufe (1969) and basically consists of having subjects pace their respiration to a metronome or rhythmic puff of air set at their adaptation RR. Even with RR held constant experimentally, subjects were still able to alter their HR significantly in the appropriate direction. However, as Sroufe pointed out, ability to control HR appears to deteriorate within a session when subject is attempting to control two systems simultaneously.

The final method used (Finley, 1971; Headrick et al., 1971; Hnatiow and

Lang, 1965; Lang et al., 1967) to insure that changes in HR are not the result of respiratory differences is to monitor, analyze, and control statistically through covariance analyses any systematic variations in respiration that are found. There have been no significant relationships between HR change and respiratory changes with two minor exceptions: Headrick et al. (1971) found a significant correlation between breathing amplitude and HR for one subject; and Hnatiow and Lang's (1965) single significant correlation was between average HR deviation during the final no-feedback period and the average inspiration to total cycle ratio for the final feedback period.

A summary of cardiorespiratory relations is not complete without the inclusion of two studies that focus specifically on them. In the earlier investigation (Engel and Chism, 1967b) 20 percent changes in RR sustained for a 10-minute period did not cause changes in average HR. However, an inverse relation was noted between RR and HR variability. Sroufe's (1971) series of three experiments was broader in scope since he manipulated respiratory volume in addition to RR. Changes in respiratory volume affected both the level and variability of HR, with deeper breathing producing a higher but more variable HR.

In light of the evidence, monitoring of respiratory variables seems mandatory for those investigations attempting to show HR control. However, monitoring alone is not sufficient; the effects of respiratory changes must be controlled either experimentally or statistically to eliminate this possible source of confounding. As Sroufe (1971) has so aptly observed, "The fact that cardiac control is possible with respiration experimentally controlled merely suggests that Ss *can* control rate independent of respiration, not that respiration is of minor importance" (p. 654). Sroufe's series of experiments elucidates a point of considerable relevance to those investigations concerned with self-control or operant conditioning of HR; that is, both respiratory rate and volume are important variables and a decision not to consider them should not be made arbitrarily. In fact, when level of HR is the dependent variable, as with a clinical population, respiratory volume seems to be a much more significant variable than RR.

Being aware of the research on the relationship between HR and RR and of the need to take respiration into account, the authors' initial approach was to instruct subjects not to alter their breathing pattern. Later, in Experiments 7 to 13, the authors began to monitor respiration and analyze the results on it separately.

Respiration rate was monitored by attaching a Hewlett-Packard microswitch respiration transducer to an elastic band around a subject's chest in such a way that very small chest expansions or contractions (0.4 millimeter) were detected. The output of the microswitch, an all-or-nothing signal, was fed directly to the input of a 7 DA driver amplifier. A Schmitt trigger was used to detect the output of this channel and send a pulse to a separate channel of the Grason-Stadler printout counter of RR in respirations per minute.

Results on RR

Inspection of the RR data revealed no systematic relation over subjects between RR and HR in Experiments 7 to 10. This was confirmed by calculating a t test for correlated means between mean adaptation and experimental RR for all trials for the subjects ($t = 1.75$, $df = 3$, $p > .05$). Subjects apparently were following the instructions by not trying to alter their breathing pattern. The respiration data from Experiments 11 to 13 were subjected to a one-way analysis of variance with repeated measures on the five data collection periods (three $S^{\triangle}$'s and two S^D's). This analysis revealed no systematic variation across subjects and experimental periods of RR ($F < 1.0$).

Discussion of Experiments 11 to 13

Although the results of the three experiments must be regarded as preliminary, they are certainly encouraging in that they demonstrate that a high degree of stimulus control of change in HR can be obtained, averaging 19.3 BPM for the terminal phase of the three experiments. More heartening still are the results obtained in Experiment 11 in which true self-control of HR was demonstrated for reasonably long periods and with clinically significant degrees of change. These results are novel in the HR literature since increases and decreases were initiated by the subject rather than the experimenter and were obtained with no feedback being given the subjects.

The demonstration in Experiments 11 to 13 of the feasibility of using a stimulus control paradigm to teach the generalization of self-control of HR, when combined with the results of earlier experiments which reported procedures for obtaining large-magnitude changes in HR in the laboratory, seem to show that a behavioral strategy for clinical cardiac control is possible and practical. This enthusiastic claim must be tempered, of course, by several qualifications. First, the authors' best results were obtained in the experimental chamber. There is a great need to extend the results from the laboratory to the natural environment; that is, to follow Step 3 of the generalization technique.

Second, these are mainly the results of analog experiments—experiments on the acceleration of HR in normal subjects. What is needed is replication of the stimulus control results with clinical subjects suffering from tachycardia. The authors' results to date, however, do suggest that such a replication is quite possible since all their previous analog results have been replicated with clinical cases whose HR was being decelerated.

It seems that the degree of stimulus control and self-control of HR achieved is a function of either the individual subject or his training history. Although run on different training procedures, the subjects in Experiments 12 and 13 achieved similar magnitude changes in HR with a similar number of training trials. Moreover, when the specific training procedure under which a subject initially learned HR acceleration was reinstated in the stimulus control training, both subjects performed well. However, when returned to the stimulus control condition, the subject in Experiment 13 continued to show a high degree of control whereas the other subject did not. Moreover, this subject did poorly on the procedure that worked with the first subject. Thus prior training does seem to make a difference, but the nature of the difference is unclear at this point.

The picture is further clouded by the success of the subject in Experiments 5 and 11. Although she was trained on the sae procedure as the subject in Experiments 8 and 12, she was successful at demonstrating both stimulus control and self-control. One difference between these subjects is that the former received many unsuccessful training trials with the CC procedure before being run successfully on the VC procedure.

A study by Weiss and Engel (1971) sheds some light on this apparent inconsistency. In their study of conditioning PVC rate in patients with cardiac arrhythmias, success in the hospital and generalization outside of it were related to absolute number of training trials; the more trials, the more likely was success. Thus a history of more training trials may be the cause of this subject's success.

Further research is needed to answer a second question of whether subjects already have the ability to demonstrate self-control of HR when they begin the experiment. To test this, one needs to select naive subjects through the procedure of testing for terminal behavior initially and then work "backward" through the training procedure to see how much training is necessary for the subject to obtain self-control.

This study, like many others, raises more questions than it answers. However, it does seem to show that behavioral tactics can be developed to achieve clinically significant control of HR.

DISCUSSION

The state of research in the area of the self-control of HR at the time the present research was initiated was characterized by the following:

1. The fact of the control of human HR through operant conditioning and/ or biofeedback procedures was well-established.

2. The magnitude of change reported was relatively small, in the range of 1 to 6 BPM.

3. The length of experimental trial used was relatively short, in the range of 1 to 5 minutes.

4. Relatively few experimental sessions were run, in the range of 1 to 5.

5. Results were reported for the most part in terms of changes within a session rather than changes maintained over successive sessions.

While the present research was in progress, two studies were published which correct some of the faults just listed. Headrick et al. (1971) achieved consistent increases in HR of 30 BPM in a single subject run for many trials. They used a form of visual feedback and no reinforcement other than verbal encouragement and knowledge of results. Despite the magnitude of change obtained, there were several problems with the Headrick et al. study: (a) trials were only 1 minute long; (b) changes were reported within a single session from a baseline level rather than being maintained over successive sessions; and (c) despite more than 60 trials, the subject was unable to lower his HR by more than 4 or 5 BPM.

More recently, Stephens, Harris, and Brady (1972) reported on 4 subjects, selected from a sample of 25, all of whom showed large-magnitude changes in HR in one or both directions. Stephens et al. used both auditory and visual feedback and a reinforcement procedure based on money. The trial length varied from 5 to 30 to 60 minutes, and 18 to 19 sessions were run. Changes ranged from about 25 BPM increases to 6 to 10 BPM decreases in two subjects. Part of the trials were similar to the present authors' stimulus control procedure with results comparable in terms of magnitude of change.

The latter study suffers from two minor faults. First, the changes were reported for within-session alterations in HR and were not maintained over days. Second, no attention seems to have been paid to establishing a stable baseline HR against which to compare the results.

Thus, in spite of these two recent reports, the results the present authors have reported here are unique in the literature on several counts:

1. Actual clinical application of biofeedback procedures to HR per se.

2. The magnitude of decrease in HR is superior to any reported elsewhere and the increases obtained with the VC procedure are comparable.

3. The changes have been maintained over successive sessions (days) and came off a stable baseline.

4. True self-control in the absence of any feedback or reinforcement was demonstrated in Experiment 11 and to a lesser degree in Experiment 13.

Clinical Applications

Although there has been much speculation about the possible applications of biofeedback procedures to clinical problems, the actual research into this area is very sparse. There has been one good uncontrolled study of the application of biofeedback procedures to cardiac arrhythmias, that of Weiss and Engel (1971).

Although there have been several brief reports (Engel and Melmon, 1968; Weiss and Engel, 1970) on the operant conditioning of cardiac arrhythmias, all of the data seem to be summarized in one article by Engel and his associates

(Weiss and Engel, 1971). Their study contains detailed reports on eight patients suffering from premature ventricular contractions (PVC's) who were all treated in approximately the same experimental paradigm.

The paradigm was, for the most part, a replication of the procedures used in Engel's three previous studies. Patients were given binary visual feedback as to whether their HR was at or beyond the desired HR in the appropriate direction. Evidently the shaping procedure that had been used in earlier studies by Engel (Engel and Chism, 1967a; Engel and Hansen, 1966) was not employed. Also, in this study, contrary to the previous work with normals, patients were fully informed of all the details of the experiment, especially the response being monitored.

Unlike Engel's earlier studies, subjects were not given monetary rewards for time accumulated in the correct direction. Despite the ommission of this tangible reinforcer, the authors still describe their study in terms of "operant conditioning" rather than self-control through feedback.

Patients were given one to three training sessions per day which consisted of one 34-minute or two 17-minute self-control trials following a 20-minute baseline. The HR criterion was determined from the last 10 minutes of this baseline.

Most patients were run under four conditions and some under a fifth. There were, in the usual order, HR speeding, HR slowing, alternately speeding and slowing HR for 1- to 4-minute trials, and then a control of HR variability condition. In this final condition subjects received binary feedback (light onset) when their HR stayed within a 10 BPM range. The nature of this feedback arrangement provided subjects with feedback of the occurrence of each PVC. The fifth condition, in which four of the patients were run, consisted of a gradual removal of feedback. Feedback was alternately presented and removed; the initial ratio of 1 minute of feedback to 1 minute without was extended to 1 minute on and 7 off. In this final phase subjects did as well without feedback as with it, indicating that true self-control had been learned.

Total number of training sessions ranged from 22 to 77 with a mean of 57.5. The five cases that can be considered successes all had 47 or more training sessions.

The results can be evaluated in two ways: first, in terms of practical outcome or the number of patients who showed evidence of learning to control their PVC's in hospital and on follow-up. The second way to evaluate the results is in terms of the relative degree of success subjects had in each condition in actually controlling HR.

Four of the eight patients had a significantly reduced frequency of PVC's after the training procedure as measured in the ward and at a follow-up 3 to 21 months afterward. A fifth patient did not have a significant reduction in PVC rate but did learn to recognize their occurrence and was able to control them at home through resting. The other three patients showed no evidence of learning to control PVC's.

In terms of the degree of success subjects had in each condition, summarized as the ratio of patients who demonstrate self-control with a procedure compared to the total number of patients given that kind of training, the following results were obtained: HR speeding, 2/7; HR slowing, 6/8; alternative speeding and slowing, 5/5; control of HR variability, 7/8; fading of feedback, 4/4.

There are two obvious criticisms that can be leveled at this otherwise excellent example of an uncontrolled clinical study. The first is the lack of a control group of patients who were either untreated or given some equally time-consuming and involving placebo task. This criticism is obviated to some degree because of the prolonged baseline period prior to the experimental phase during which PVC's were noted. The documented history of PVC's ranged from 3 months to 8 years, with a mean of 3 years. Despite this, one would hope that a next step would be a controlled outcome study of the procedure.

The second criticism is the obvious confounding of several aspects of the training procedure. One does not know whether the entire sequence of training procedures is necessary or only part of them. An obvious next step is to isolate which parts of the training procedure are necessary, facilitative, or superfluous, in order to improve efficiency. One point that does emerge from reanalysis of the results is that improvement is significantly ($p = .05$, Fisher's exact probability test) related to receiving 47 or more training sessions. The requirement of a large number of trials to achieve significant clinical changes agrees with the findings of the present authors (Experiments 6 and 9).

Future Directions

At the end of any presentation of a systematic set of research studies two questions occur: So what? and What next? To the "So what?" the answer would be that a fairly efficient and reliable procedure for obtaining stable large-magnitude changes in HR has been developed. Furthermore, clinical efficacy of the procedure has been demonstrated in a limited set of cases.

The answer to the second question is a bit more involved. Future research will probably take three directions. First, additional analog studies using the pure feedback procedure of Experiment 10 seem warranted to confirm its efficacy. A second set of analog studies is necessary to extend the work on stimulus control, Experiments 11 to 13, and to develop a procedure in which there is true generalization or transfer of self-control of HR from the laboratory setting to the subject's natural environment. A technical problem will have to be solved to make such work feasible—adequate remote monitoring of HR.

The second set of studies the present authors want to complete are additional clinical experiments. These include use of the pure feedback procedure and the establishment of stimulus control with subjects whose HR was being decelerated. Finally, we hope to run a clinical trial of several patients using the VC procedure.

One final aspect of the new clinical studies would be to include an additional control condition in the single-subject experiments during which subjects would attempt to control HR without any feedback or reinforcement. Such a condition would control for some of the instructional effects identified by Bergman and Johnson (1971, 1972).

As interesting and important as IIR is, the most important clinical application of these techniques would be not to tachycardia but to patients suffering from essential hypertension. This constitutes a major health problem in the United States, affecting up to 10 percent of the population. The standard way of dealing with this disorder is through antihypertensive drugs. Unfortunately, there are serious side effects from some of these so that a nonpharmocological approach would be very valuable. Thus the final phase of the work of the present authors is to determine the extent to which the technology developed for dealing with HR can be applied to elevated blood pressure.

ACKNOWLEDGMENTS

The authors would like to acknowledge the financial support of the National Heart and Lung Institute whose grant, 1RO1HL14906-01, in part supported this research and preparation of this manuscript.

The authors also acknowledge the able assistance of several of their colleagues who collaborated on one or more of the experiments presented in this chapter: Eileen D. Edmundson, William R. Gillespie, Douglas R. Peters, and Larry D. Young. The authors further acknowledge the advice, support, and encouragement provided them by Dr. W. Stewart Agras throughout this project.

REFERENCES

Bergman, J. S., and Johnson, H. J. The effects of instructional set and autonomic perception on cardiac control. *Psychophysiology*, 1971, **8**, 180–190.

Bergman, J. S., and Johnson, H. J. Sources of information which effect training and raising of heart rate. *Psychophysiology*, 1972, **9**, 30–39.

Blanchard, E. B., and Young, L. D. Relative efficacy of visual and auditory feedback and self-control of heart rate. *Journal of General Psychology*, 1972, **87**, 195–202.

Blanchard, E. B., Young, L. D., and McLeod, P. G. Awareness of heart activity and self-control of heart rate. *Psychophysiology*, 1972, **9**, 63–68.

Brener, J. Heart rate as an avoidance response. *Psychological Record*, 1966, **16**, 329–336.

Brener, J., and Hothersall, D. Heart rate control under conditions of augmented sensory feedback. *Psychophysiology*, 1966, **3**, 23–28.

Brener, J., and Hothersall, D. Paced respiration and heart rate control. *Psychophysiology*, 1967, **4**, 1–6.

Brener, J., Kleinman, R. A., and Goesling, W. J. The effects of different exposures to augmented sensory feedback on the control of heart rate. *Psychophysiology*, 1969, **5**, 510–516.

Engel, B. T., and Chism, R. A. Operant conditioning of heart rate speeding. *Psychophysiology*, 1967, **3**, 418–426. (a)

Engel, B. T., and Chism, R. A. Effect of increases and decreases in breathing rate on heart rate and finger pulse volume. *Psychophysiology*, 1967, **4**, 83–89. (b)

Engel, B. T., and Hansen, S. P. Operant conditioning of heart rate slowing. *Psychophysiology*, 1966, **3**, 176–187.

Engel, B. T., and Melmon, L. Operant conditioning of heart rate in patients with cardiac arrhythmias. *Conditional Reflex*, 1968, **3**, 130.

Finley, W. W. The effect of feedback on the control of cardiac rate. *The Journal of Psychology*, 1971, **77**, 43–54.

Frazier, T. W. Avoidance conditioning of heart rate in humans. *Psychophysiology*, 1966, **3**, 188–197.

Headrick, M. W., Feather, B. W., and Wells, D. T. Undirectional and large magnitude heart rate changes with augmented sensory feedback. *Psychophysiology*, 1971, **8**, 132–142.

Hnatiow, M., and Lang, P. J. Learned stabilization of cardiac rate. *Psychophysiology*, 1965, **1**, 330–336.

Johns, T. R. Heart rate control in humans under paced respiration and restricted movement: The effect of instructions and exteroceptive feedback. Paper presented to the 79th Annual Convention of American Psychological Association, 1971.

Lang, P. J. The mechanics of desensitization and the laboratory study of human fear. In C. M. Franks (Ed.), *Behavior Therapy: Appraisal and Status*. New York: McGraw-Hill, 1969.

Lang, P. J., Sroufe, L. A., and Hastings, J. E. Effects of feedback and instructional set on the control of cardiac rate variability. *Journal of Experimental Psychology*, 1967, **75**, 425–431.

Leitenberg, H., Agras, W. S., Butz, R., and Wincze, J. Relationship between heart rate and behavior change during the treatment of phobias. *Journal of Abnormal Psychology*, 1971, **78**, 59–68.

Levene, H. E., Engel, B. T., and Pearson, J. A. Differential operant conditioning of heart rate. *Psychosomatic Medicine*, 1968, **30**, 837–845.

Miller, N. E. Learning of visceral and glandular responses. *Science*, 1969, **163**, 434–445.

Shearn, D. W. Operant conditioning of heart rate. *Science*, 1962, **137**, 530–531.

Sroufe, L. A. Learned stabilization of cardiac rate with respiration experimentally controlled. *Journal of Experimental Psychology*, 1969, **81**, 391–393.

Sroufe, L. A. Effects of depth and rate of breathing on heart rate and heart rate variability. *Psychophysiology*, 1971, **8**, 648–655.

Stephens, J. H., Harris, A. H., and Brady, J. V. Large magnitude heart rate changes in subjects instructed to change their heart rates and given exteroceptive feedback. *Psychophysiology*, 1972, **9**, 283–285.

Weiss, T., and Engel, B. T. Operant conditioning of heart rate in patients with premature ventricular contractions. Paper presented to 1970 meeting of Society for Psychophysiological Research, New Orleans, La.

Weiss, T., and Engel, B. T. Operant conditioning of heart rate in patients with premature ventricular contractions. *Psychosomatic Medicine*, 1971, **33**, 301–321.

Wolpe, J. *Psychotherapy by reciprocal inhibition*. Stanford: Stanford University Press, 1958.

Wolpe, J. *The Practice of Behavior Therapy*. New York: Pergamon Press, 1969.

CHAPTER 9

Interventions with
Psychotic Behaviors

ROBERT PAUL LIBERMAN, CHARLES WALLACE, JAMES TEIGEN, AND
JOHN DAVIS*

Although evidence is increasing for a genetic-biological component associated with the schizophrenias (Wender, 1969; Kety, 1972; Rosenthal, Wender, Kety, Schulsinger, Welner, and Ostergaard, 1968), there have been no recent break-throughs in somatic treatments for these disorders. Chlorpromazine and its pharmacologic congeners are still the mainstays of treatment that they were in 1960. Since that time, enthusiasm for traditional psychotherapeutic approaches to schizophrenia has waned because there is excellent empirical evidence that psychotherapy adds little or nothing to the effect of phenothiazines in the treatment of acute or chronic schizophrenics (May, 1968; Grinspoon, Ewalt, and Shader, 1967).

The revolutionary changes in the delivery of mental health services through community mental health centers have largely bypassed the hundreds of thousands of chronic psychotic patients who currently constitute about two-thirds of the resident populations in public mental hospitals. Of patients released from hospitals each year, 90 percent have been hospitalized for one year or less (Padula, Glasscote, and Cumming, 1968). Only 3 percent of patients released have spent five or more years in the hospital. This large reservoir of chronic patients is likely to increase since the proportion of first-admission psychotics who never leave the hospital, combined with the readmissions who subsequently become long-term residents, range between 20 and 75 percent of all admissions in various states (Paul, 1969). In their brief-stay, inpatient facilities, community open-door mental health centers offer crisis intervention treatment to acutely psychotic individuals. Persons needing longer duration of treatment or who are

*The opinions or conclusions stated in this chapter are those of the authors and are not to be construed as official or as necessarily reflecting the policy of the California Department of Mental Hygiene or the University of California.

323

repeatedly troublesome to the community with acting out behavior are referred to the state or VA hospitals for custodial care. Admission to a long-stay hospital is frequently an environmental trap for patients. A person continuously hospitalized for two years has only a 6 percent chance for eventual discharge, a rate which has not changed in this century.

Two general categories of psychotic individuals present a major challenge to American mental health practitioners. In one group the patients are relatively young, have periodic psychotic episodes or are consistently provocative with high rates of verbal and/or physical abusiveness. They are early labeled as deviant and are experienced as intolerable by their families and community agencies. When the community resources lose patience, these individuals are sent to a custodial institution.

The second class of psychotic patients consists of those whose long stay in custodial environments has produced a social breakdown syndrome (Zusman, 1967). As a result of contingencies operating in public mental hospitals, long-term patients are conditioned to be compliant, passive, and socially and vocationally incompetent.

Social and occupational skills that patients possess upon entering a hospital, board-and-care, or nursing home are frequently extinguished by the lack of any positive consequences to maintain them. Patients are not "paid off" for grooming themselves nicely, cooking their meals, using the telephone, asserting their desires for changes in the ward atmosphere, or for working in a hospital job. Instead, the bulk of reinforcement from the staff—whether it be in the form of attention and interest or in the passing out of cigarettes—is focused on patients being compliant, quiet, and docile. In many institutions the staff can hardly be blamed, since they are frequently overworked and overwhelmed by the numbers of patients. What happens is a mutually reinforcing state of affairs: The patients are rewarded for their compliance and the staff are, in turn, rewarded by the ease of routines and low levels of emotional outbursts by the patients.

Ironically, the more effective the patient is in adapting to the hospital the more he is viewed as someone requiring continued hospitalization and the greater the problem for him of adjusting to the community if he is released. "Institutionalitis" is a maladaptive behavior pattern produced by the contingencies of reinforcement that impinge on both patients and staff in large public mental hospitals. It is no accident that many studies of the release patterns of chronic mental patients have shown very high correlations between length of stay in the hospital, low discharge rate, and likelihood of readmission if discharged.

This challenge to the therapeutic effectiveness of clinicians and mental health administrators will not be met by training more professionals to engage in subjectively satisfying and enthralling relationship, insight-oriented, encounter group, Gestalt, and other "new" therapies. The verbal interaction, bioenergetic, and other supposedly "humanistic" approaches to treatment will satisfy and perhaps help many well-functioning or neurotic individuals suffering from boredom, emotional inhibitions, transient anxieties, and depressions. Whereas one-third of these neurotic individuals would achieve amelioration of their dysphoria "spontaneously" without any treatment, the placebo effect does not so easily produce remissions in psychotics. Neither will fresh bricks and mortar or shiny furniture of new mental health centers by themselves produce therapeutic answers to behavioral riddles posed by hard-core, process schizophrenics. Grafting on the methods of the past will not be sufficient to reach the goals set by our ideological architects of community mental health to reduce the morbidity and duration of hospitalization of those with major mental illness.

BEHAVIOR MODIFICATION

Significant new advances have been made in the application of operant conditioning to the treatment of the schizophrenias. Applied operant conditioning has produced a variety of effective treatment approaches, data on the interaction between environment and drugs in behavior change, and a new emphasis on empirical and experimental methods in the treatment of psychotics.

Operant conditioning had its roots in the psychological formulation of the *law of effect* by Thorndike around the turn of the century, but it did not gain wide experimental support until Skinner's *The Behavior of Organisms* and *The Science of Human Behavior* (Skinner, 1938, 1953). Most of the basic principles of behavior were elucidated in animal, laboratory studies and were rarely applied to human patients until the 1950's when Lindsley, Ferster, and other students of Skinner began to modify the behavior of schizophrenic adults and autistic children. The first studies used single subjects, showing that presentation of reinforcement produced increases in desired behavior and withdrawal of reinforcement produced decreases in undesirable behavior. By 1963 Ay lon and Azrin (1968) had established the first *token economy*, the application of reinforcement principles to an entire ward of patients.

A book reviewing the first ten years of behavior modification included work conducted with mute and withdrawn psychotics, autistic children, phobics, ticquers, stutterers, retardates, and apathetic students (Ullmann and Krasner, 1965). The original studies were carried out with "hopeless" patients on back wards because the pioneers in behavior modification met less resistance from jealous, vested interests of traditional clinicians. For a more current view of the status of behavior modification, the reader is encouraged to peruse recent publications in the field (Yates, 1969; Bandura, 1969; Liberman, 1972). The revolution that behavior modification caused in psychology has now spread to education, rehabilitation, criminal corrections, and even psychiatry.

This chapter is divided into two parts. In the first section, the use of behavior modification with schizophrenics is reviewed and placed in the context of such issues as staff training, generalization of treatment effects, cost-benefit analysis, and placebo effects. Much of this section has been previously published in the NIMH *Schizophrenia Bulletin* (Liberman, 1972 c). The second part of the chapter consists of a descriptive catalog of individualized behavior modification programs developed and applied to 25 consecutive psychotic patients admitted to the Clinical Research Unit of Camarillo State Hospital from 1970 to 1972.

ISSUES IN THE BEHAVIORAL TREATMENT OF CHRONIC PSYCHOTIC INDIVIDUALS

Interventions with Chronic Psychotics: The Token Economy

The initial studies of behavior modification in psychiatric settings were carried out on back wards of public mental hospitals. The systematic approach with chronic patients that has been formulated since 1960 uses clear specification of treatment goals and contingencies of reinforcement. Similar to the monetary system which motivates much of our behavior, the system of behavioral interventions with chronic psychotics is called the *token economy*. Instead of receiving food, bed, privileges, and small luxuries like cigarettes free of charge as in a custodial setting, patients must work and perform at a higher level of functioning to earn tokens, which then can be exchanged for the good things of life. Each patient's goals are calibrated periodically to his or her own previous level of behavior.

The aim of a token economy is to induce more socially appropriate behavior in patients, on a ward-wide basis, through the use of tokens. The tokens serve as common currency for a wide variety of back-up reinforcers which then can be chosen on an individual basis by the patients. The token economy also enables the staff to reinforce immediately adaptive behavior by rewarding the patient with a token rather than having him wait to receive some desired item or privilege at a later time. It is well known in both laboratory and clinical studies that immediate reinforcement is much more effective in the teaching of new behaviors than is delayed reinforcement. The dispensing of tokens is accompanied by the staff member's giving praise and recognition to the patient. Ultimately, this *social reinforcement* will supplant the tokens as the motivational support for the patient's behaviors.

The emphasis in the token economies, then, is to make the patients' responses have clear-cut, consistent consequences. Presenting a shaved face in the morning, grooming oneself carefully, participating in the ward clean-up, and working on a hospital job all have the consequence of being reinforced with tokens. On the other hand, failure to engage in socially appropriate behavior leads to absence of reinforcement (extinction of maladaptive behavior) or occasionally to punishment (i.e., fines) where tokens are taken away from the patient.

In the token economy the patient's behavior does mean something—and patients are required to take responsibility for their behavior just as we do in the real world. No patient in the token economy starves or goes without a bed, however. If too few tokens are earned during the day, the patient must subsist in a "welfare state." He must eat his meals on a steel tray rather than use more pleasant dinnerware; he must do without cigarettes and TV; and he must sleep on a hard cot rather than a comfortable bed. Thus tokens are immediate rewards that can be used to improve behavior much as money does in our natural economy. Ayllon and Azrin (1968) present an excellent description of the token economy, describing their pioneering efforts with this system.

Figure 1 shows some of the reinforcers used to back up the tokens in a behavior modification project at Patton State Hospital in California (Gericke, 1965). Patients who have the price in tokens can sleep in pleasant sleeping quarters with bedspreads, curtains, and side tables; those without the tokens must sleep in more barren settings. The same differentiation of consequences is attached to eating behavior.

What have been the results of these behavior modification experiments in the token economy? Figure 2 graphs the effect that tokens have on work performance on ward and hospital jobs at Anna State Hospital in Illinois (Ayllon and Azrin, 1968). When tokens are provided to patients contingent upon their work efforts, the patients show high levels of activity. When tokens are withdrawn or given "free" without any need to work, the patients' participation rapidly declines. It is clear from the data, derived from an ABAB design, that the tokens are crucial in maintaining high levels of performance. Findings from studies such as these, using patients as their own controls, have been replicated many times in different hospitals.[1]

Multiple baseline designs have also demonstrated the efficacy of behavioral interventions with chronic schizophrenics. In two schizophrenics with different types of hallucination, reinforcers contingent on a decrease and then cessation of each type of hallucination resulted in a sequential, time-correlated diminution and termination of each hallucination (Richardson, Karkalas, and Lal, 1973).

Liberman, Teigen, Patterson, and Baker, (1973) carried out a multiple baseline study of delusional speech in four chronic paranoid schizophrenics. Each patient had a characteristic set of delusional topics which occurred at a baseline rate during four 10-minute structured interviews spaced throughout the day. During the baseline period, each patient had a 40-minute, unstructured, informal "chat" with a favorite staff member in the evening over snacks. Except for the informal evening chat and the four structured daily interviews, patients were deprived of conversation with staff. The evening chat was thus established as a

---

[1]Additional information and research can be found in T. Ayllon and N. H. Azrin, *The Token Economy: a Motivational System for Therapy and Rehabilitation.* New York: Appleton-Century-Crofts, 1968.

Cots like this one were provided for patients who did not have a token to pay for a standard hospital bed with innerspring mattress.

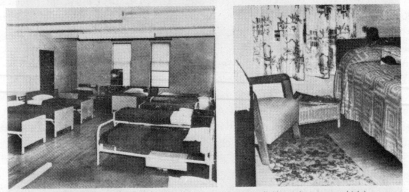

Sleeping facilities for patients in the orientation group (left) and therapy group (right).

Dining facilities in the same room for patients in the orientation group (left) and therapy group (right).

Figure 1. "Back-up" reinforcers for patients in a token economy at a state hospital. (From O. Gericke. Practical use of operant conditioning procedures in a mental hospital. *Psychiatric Studies and Projects*, **3:**1-10, 1965. Copyright (1965) by the American Psychiatric Association. Reproduced by permission.)

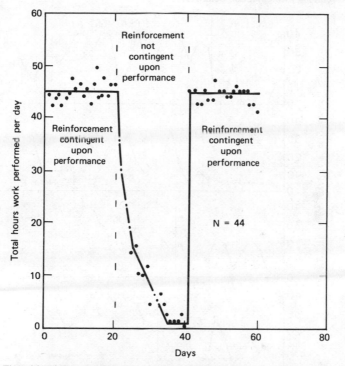

Figure 2. The critical influence of contingent token reinforcement for maintaining work behavior in chronic psychotics. (From T. Ayllon, and N. H. Azrin. The measurement and reinforcement of behavior of psychotics. *Journal of the Experimental Analysis of Behavior*, **8**:357-383, 1965. Copyright (1965) by the Society for the Experimental Analysis of Behavior, Inc. Reproduced by permission.)

reinforcer for the patients, particularly since they could talk about anything they wanted, including their delusions. Sequentially, over time, each patient was placed on a contingent schedule of reinforcement whereby the amount of time for the evening chat depended on the duration of rational speech during the 10-minute interviews during the day. There was a direct 1–1 relation between the duration of rational talk, timed from the start of the interview to the onset of delusional speech, and the length of the evening chat earned (see Figure 3). In some cases rational speech increased to a level 600 percent over baseline. Thus delusions, a high-frequency verbal behavior, were used to build up rational verbalizations which had previously occurred at low frequency. Generalization of the patients' greater rationality also was shown in the noncontingent evening chats where delusional speech decreased and realistic talk increased. The delusional speech of paranoid schizophrenics represents a response class that has

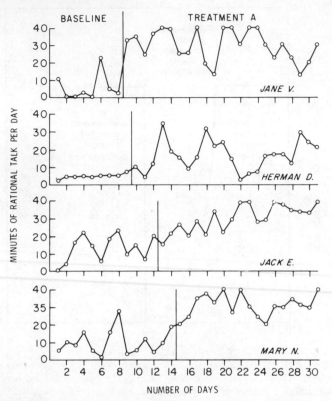

Figure 3. Duration of rational speech before onset of delusions in four 10-minute interviews under baseline and contingent social reinforcement (Treatment A) conditions. (From R. P. Liberman, J. Teigen, R. Patterson, and V. Baker. Reducing delusional speech in chronic, paranoid schizophrenics. *Journal of Applied Behavior Analysis,* **6:**57-64, 1973. Copyright (1973) by the Society for the Experimental Analysis of Behavior, Inc. Reproduced by permission.)

great clinical significance since epidemiological studies indicate that the most frequent type of abnormal behavior leading to readmission of previously hospitalized schizophrenics is verbalization of delusional and bizarre ideas. (Wing et al. 1964).

In a now classic study, Ayllon and Haughton (1964) reported the effectiveness of contingent attention, approval, and tangible reinforcers on increasing and then decreasing grandiose delusions in a single patient. This was paralleled by a decrease followed by an increase in neutral talk when the respective contingencies were focused on the rational speech.

Some of the most disastrous effects of long-term institutionalization of mental patients are an exaggerated constriction of interpersonal responses and withdrawal from social interaction. The "good" patient in a custodial setting is a

UNSTRUCTURED SETTING GROUP

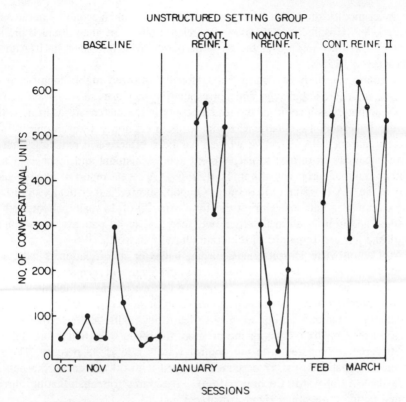

Figure 4.   Conversation among group members under baseline, contingent, and noncontingent reinforcement conditions. (From R. P. Liberman. Reinforcement of social interaction in a group of chronic mental patients. In R. Rubin, H. Fensterheim, J. Henderson, and M. Kushner, (Eds.), *Advances in Behavior Therapy*, New York: Academic Press, 1972, p. 156.)

quiet, unobtrusive one. Enhancing the social repertoires of such patients is critical for their being capable of leaving the hospital and for adjusting to and remaining in the community. Competence in carrying on conversations is instrumental in developing relationships, asking for directions, obtaining necessities, and, in general, navigating the social pathways required for a successful adaptation to community life.

One study (Liberman, 1972a) involved four chronic schizophrenic women, hospitalized over 15 years each, whose social conversation was reliably and quantitatively recorded during 50-minute group sessions. Contingent token reinforcement increased conversational participation by four to five times over the baseline and noncontingent reinforcement phases (see Figure 4).

More conventional indices of improvement have also been documented using behavior modification with chronic psychotics. At a token economy in the Menlo Park VA Hospital in California, the release rate more than doubled the first year of token economy over the baseline period with the same staff (Atthowe and Krasner, 1968).

A controlled study at Patton State Hospital showed highly significant decreases in apathetic behavior and corresponding increases in social and recreational activities as a result of the token economy (Schaefer and Martin, 1966). At the Lakeshore Psychiatric Hospital a token economy with chronic schizophrenic and mentally defective women has been effective in reducing such bizarre behaviors as refusal to eat, violent acts, delusional and incoherent talk, mutism, and inappropriate affect (Paul, 1969). A recent report of a token economy at the VA Hospital in Roseburg, Oregon, showed a statistically significant improvement in patients. During the first year, 20 of 28 male patients left the hospital and only 2 returned. After two years, 32 of 44 patients treated on the ward had left and remained in the community (Ellsworth, 1969).

At Central State Hospital in Georgia, behavior modification is used with about 900 patients. The patients must work, participate in recreational activities, and display acceptable behavior if they are to earn tokens, which then can be used to purchase food, bed, clean clothes, privileges, and luxuries. The token system gives patients an opportunity to learn new skills and relearn forgotten ones. In the first six months of the program the token ward had a furlough rate of 80 percent compared with the control ward's rate of 38 percent. The rate of return of patients was 17 percent compared with 50 percent of the patients from the control ward (Cochran, 1969). Procedures for rehabilitating chronic mental patients are summarized in Table 1.

Table 1. Behavioral Procedures for Rehabilitating Chronic Schizophrenics

1. Precisely define the behavioral goals for each patient (therapeutic goals)
2. Measure the frequency of the desired behavior as it is exhibited by the patient (therapeutic progress)
3. Attach clear positive and negative consequences to adaptive and maladaptive behavior, respectively (contingencies of reinforcement)
4. Use instructions and prompts to evoke the desired behaviors
5. Reinforce patients for making small, discrete steps in the desired directions (shaping behavior)
6. Structure the hospital setting to approximate the real world outside (stimulus generalization)
7. Provide opportunities for patients to learn and practice vocational and housekeeping skills which have marketable value in the community or instrumental role value within the family
8. Prepare patients and significant others to live in mutually supportive ways in the community (prerelease training, aftercare). Teach significant others to use behavioral principles to maintain goals
9. Coordinate community resources to reinforce and back up the patient's coping efforts in adjusting to the community

Cost-Benefit Analysis

An important question to ask of any therapeutic approach is how much it costs in relation to the benefits it provides. The only cost-benefit analysis of programs designed for chronic mental patients is one reported from Kalamazoo State Hospital in Michigan (Foster, 1969). The overall purpose of the program was to determine the effectiveness of behavior modification techniques on a wide range of behaviors which had in common the effect of preventing the patients' adjustment in the community. The patients in this study were 32 male chronic psychotics ranging in age from 20 to 40. They were continuously hospitalized for a minimum of 2 years and an average of 10.7 years. A control group consisted of 32 similar patients with an average length of hospitalization of 8.2 years.

The behaviors the program sought to modify were self-care, abnormal verbal behavior, vocational deficits, lack of social skills, and aggressive and destructive behavior towards self, others, and the physical environment. Tokens were given to patients for approximating appropriate behavior and these tokens were then used to purchase a variety of items which were freely available to the control group—personal care items, candy, cigarettes, and television. Results of the study revealed that 9 patients were discharged from the experimental group and none from the control group. A complete cost record was kept of salaries, special supplies and equipment, and food and clothing. The token program cost $424 more than the custodial approach during the first year. However, if the 28 percent exit rate for the patients from the token economy were extrapolated to all patients in Michigan state hospitals who fit the selection criteria, there would be 255 discharges. If these 255 hypothetical patients remained out of the hospital for two years, the state would save $384,285.

This cost-benefit study raises a question: Who benefits from discharges of chronic mental patients? How are these benefits distributed across various sectors of society? It is one thing to demonstrate the savings of a token economy to the state Department of Mental Health and another to assess the effects on the foster families who accept these patients from the hospital. In this day of community mental health we all too often take for granted that the greater benefit is for the patient to be outside of the hospital. Before we can fully satisfy ourselves with this assumption, however, we should make some effort to evaluate the impact of the chronic mental patient upon his family and upon the community—in terms of both financial and emotional cost. There is also the need to establish the effects on the patients whose standard of living and behavioral repertoires may actually show no change or even a diminution upon leaving the hospital for the community. There is nothing magical about being in the community, and a chronic patient who has learned to be docile and unproductive in a hospital is as likely to settle into the back wards in the community as easily as he settled into the back wards in the hospital.

Another group which may or may not benefit from the release of chronic patients is the staff of the mental hospital. We may assume that the staff would be freed from the chore of caring for many chronic patients enabling them to deal more creatively with the acute patients or the residual patients still in the hospital. This assumption, however, must be tested against reality. There is no short-cut in doing the necessary research.

A definitive study of the token economy in comparison with a maximum push milieu therapy is under way in Illinois, supported by National Institute of Mental Health funds. This project will compare specific target behaviors of the patients in social, personal, grooming, and instrumental work areas using a constant staff that rotates between the two experimental wards (Paul, 1971). Cost-benefit analyses will also be performed including long-term follow-ups on patients who are released from the units into the community.

At the Oxnard (California) Mental Health Center, a comprehensive research project is applying behavioral assessment and modification to the full range of clinical problems presented in this open, short-term treatment setting (Liberman, 1971). We have successfully adapted the token economy to the Day Treatment Center where a wide variety of patients, including many acute schizophrenics, are treated and returned to function in the community. The average length of stay in the Day Treatment Center is six weeks.

The token economy is called the Coupon-Incentive Program. The goals of the Coupon-Incentive Program are to increase the rate and quality of participation of the day care patients and to decrease the nagging and hassling of apathetic patients by the staff. Positive consequences are now attached to patients' participation in the Center's program. The patients receive coupons for engaging in a wide variety of constructive behaviors, including O.T. projects, menu planning and meal preparations, participating in a weekly planning conference, and clean-up efforts. The coupons reinforce or reward these behaviors because they can be exchanged for a variety of desirable things—coffee and meals, special outings, bowling, group therapy, and private therapy time with individual staff members.

The incentive or reinforcement program functions on the honor system. The patients manage the program themselves, choosing a monitor every two weeks who dispenses and collects coupons, checks to be sure that jobs have been done, and consults with the staff on problems that develop. The incentive system is reviewed each week at a patient-staff planning conference and changes are made to keep it functioning smoothly. For example, the wages and prices in the economy are open to renegotiation and change depending upon supply and demand factors.

The Coupon-Incentive Program has markedly decreased the nagging by the staff and has freed patients and staff for more positive and productive involvements. For example, each patient, in addition to being involved in the Coupon-Incentive Program, has an individually structured behavior modification program which builds on his assets and remediates his deficits. The patients learn autonomy and self-management as well as showing much higher levels of participation in all facets of the treatment program. Experimental data from the program reveal the Coupon-Incentive system doubles the participation rate of the patients over baseline and noncontingent reinforcement periods. A film graphically demonstrating the incentive system in action is available from the senior author of this chapter.

Demand Characteristics of Behavior Modification Studies

Although objective and reliable measurement is the foundation of behavior modification research, such measurement is open to experimenter bias, expectancy effects, and experimental reactivity. Experimental reactivity refers to the tendency for experimental procedures and measurement operations to function as an unintended, independent source of influence on the behaviors being measured. There is ample evidence in the behavior modification literature, for instance, that experimenter or self-monitoring of behavior influences the frequency or probability of the target behavior (Johnson and Martin, 1973; Kanfer, 1970). Simply keeping track of one's behavior can increase that behavior over baseline.

Some of this source of distortion is controlled by the use of reversal designs where the presumably effective variables are removed or changed while the behavioral measurement continues. Another way to deal with the problem is to establish the ecological validity of treatment effects by demonstrating that significant changes occur not only in the experimental setting but also in the nonexperimental, "real-life" behavioral settings of the individual. It is possible, for instance, that a schizophrenic will decrease his delusional speech when observed in a treatment context but will not show any corresponding decrease where it really counts—in the community after discharge. Thus in behavior modification research, generalization of treatment effects to natural environments is crucial. This matter has been discussed at greater length by others (McFall and Lillesand, 1971; Liberman, 1968, 1971a; Kazdin and Bootzin, 1972).

Generalization

Although behaviors have been demonstrated to change as a function of the application or withdrawal of behavior modification procedures, little is known about the generalization of these changes. This includes both *stimulus* and *response* generalizations; the former occurs when the behavioral gains transfer to other settings, and the latter refers to the spread of treatment effects to behaviors which were not originally targeted as foci for intervention. Another important dimension of generalization is duration of behavior change over *time*. Very often in token economy programs, behavioral change continues only while contingent reinforcement is operative. Kazdin and Bootzin (1972) discuss this problem as follows:

> Generally, removal of token reinforcement results in decrements in desirable responses and a return to baseline or near baseline levels of performance. Because most researchers have used the ABA design, experimental studies have focused on the functional relationship of the reinforcement procedures to the dependent variables, rather than on the maintenance of the altered behavior. Generalization of treatment effects to extratreatment settings (community, home, place of employment) is usually not assessed directly but instead inferred from increased discharge or decreased readmission rates. Since discharge and readmission rates depend upon administrative decisions, increases and decreases can be accomplished without concomitant changes in the behavioral status of the patients. In summary, although token economies have been dramatically effective at changing behavior within the psychiatric hospital, there is little evidence that improvement is maintained outside of the institution. . . . Generalization should be planned rather than depended upon as an inadvertent consequence of the token program. (p. 359)

A wide variety of conditioning techniques can be used to facilitate generalization of treatment effects, including the following:

1. Select as target behaviors in the treatment setting those which will continue to be reinforced in the natural milieu.
2. Pair praise, acknowledgment, approval, and other social reinforcers with tangible reinforcers (tokens and other material rewards). In this manner, naturally occurring social reinforcers will maintain the behavioral gains after discharge.
3. Gradually fade out the tangible reinforcers, relying solely on social reinforcers.
4. Gradually draw in the natural environment; for instance, schedule increasing amounts of time in the community for patients as they approach discharge.
5. Simulate the natural environment with its stimulus characteristics in the treatment milieu, and reinforce behavior under these simulated conditions.
6. Train relatives and other caretakers in the community to carry out the reinforcement programs begun in the hospital. This approach, the corollary of technique 4 above, brings elements of the treatment milieu into the natural milieu.
7. Train patients to provide self-reinforcement for the behaviors under treatment.
8. Use intermittent and delayed schedules of reinforcement as the treatment proceeds.

The initial aim of token programs was to improve the functioning of chronic, institutionalized patients to a point where they would become more self-sufficient *within* the hospital. Generalization presents a further challenge; to shape patients' behaviors to a point where they can make successful adjustments to the community *outside* the hospital. Radical changes in treatment settings are required to meet the challenge of generalization.

Within an institutional setting there is little opportunity to restructure the patients' environment so that it dovetails more closely with the outside world. For example, cooking is done in centralized kitchens by hired personnel although patients would benefit from doing their own cooking in small, homelike kitchens where they could be systematically prompted and reinforced. The same is true for buying things in stores, talking on the telephone, and running a household. Budget management has been successfully built into the token programs by giving the patients their tokens only once a week. In-hospital work situations are not sufficiently like jobs in the community—money is not used as a medium of reinforcement, public transportation is not used to and from the job, and industrial therapy supervisors are not as demanding or production-oriented as foremen in the outside community.

To better meet this new challenge, some token programs are being restructured to provide living opportunities for patients that are more congruent with life outside the hospital. At Pacific State Hospital a small number of patients spend three nights a week living in a residence on the hospital grounds to better accustom themselves to the stimulus characteristics of community home living. Some also go into the nearby town to work at domestic and laundry jobs for which they are paid. Patients can take buses into the city to reacquaint themselves with the swirl of community life, stores, traffic, and crowds.

After numerous patients relapsed in board-and-care and family care homes, the staff at the Camarillo-Neuropsychiatric Institute Research Program realized that the contingencies of reinforcement in the homes were running counter to the contingencies at the Clinical Research Unit at Camarillo State Hospital (Liberman, King, and DeRisi, 1972). For example, some care operators did not give approval and praise for good personal appearance or high activity levels as long as the patient was "quiet." The Camarillo-Neuropsychiatric Institute Research team is now considering ways of bringing prospective family care operators into the program and introducing them to the goals and methods of reinforcement used on the unit. In this way continuity of contingencies will be maintained after discharge. One method, just begun, is to offer a weekly workshop in behavioral principles to family care operators. This is connected to the referrral network for placing former patients; thus operators who complete the workshop gain preference in receiving new residents for their homes.

Cognizant of the importance of tailoring the training situation closely to the criterion situation, the Palo Alto VA Hospital and the Oxnard (California) Day Treatment Center have developed an educational approach to community rehabilitation. Day care patients attend classes and workshops that offer training in vocational preparedness, consumerism, personal finances, recreation, transportation, humor, and dating. Generalization is facilitated by giving patients assignments to carry out the behaviors practiced in class in the community (Liberman, DeRisi, King, Eckman, and Wood, 1974).

The pioneering research conducted by Fairweather, Sanders, Cressler, and Maynard (1969) can serve as a prototype for programs moving toward greater congruence between therapeutic and community settings. In this research small groups of chronic patients were formed in the hospital and were reinforced with money and privileges for increasing their cohesiveness and cooperative task behavior as they lived and worked together as a unit in the hospital. When they were functioning well together in the hospital, they were placed as a self-contained group in a living situation outside the hospital where they continued to reside and work together (as a janitorial service). Supervision was provided initially but was gradually faded out as the patients proved to themselves and the staff that they could successfully adjust to the demands of community life as a mutually supportive unit. This ingenious shaping of the patient group (under conditions of structured activities) and the gradual movement, in time, to settings of greater congruence to independent community functioning represents a proper model for reinforcement programs that aim to help patients establish long-term and successful community adjustments. This type of approach is necessary if the "revolving door" cycle of discharge-readmission to public mental hospitals is to be remedied.

A frequently cited criticism of behavior modification is that it focuses on symptoms and not on the "whole person." The pejorative implication is that behavioral approaches produce isolated and sometimes artificial changes, turning individuals into robots. Data are accumulating that, on the contrary, improvement in behaviors pinpointed for behavioral interventions does spread to other behaviors as well (Paul and Shannon, 1966; Liberman, 1971c; Bootzin, 1971; Franks, 1969; Kale, Kaye, Wheland, and Hopkins, 1969).

Behavior modifiers are now beginning to seriously study multiple levels of behavior concurrently (Liberman, 1971c; Patterson, 1971). Changes in subjectively reported behaviors such as mood and satisfaction should parallel changes in overtly exhibited behaviors.

Response generalization can occur in behavior modification. It is to be hoped that the behaviors learned during treatment will be stepping stones or basic building blocks for more complex behaviors which generate social reinforcers in the milieu.

Expectancy and the Placebo Effect

Most studies evaluating the impact of behavior therapy on schizophrenics have utilized patients as their own controls in ABAB or multiple-baseline designs.

These experimental designs are powerful in elucidating the functional relationship between behavior and environmental conditions. However, factors other than the reinforcement contingencies per se could conceivably account for systematic changes in behavior. For instance, social contact and involvement between staff and patients might be greater during contingent reinforcement periods than during baseline or noncontingent reinforcement conditions. Staff expectancy may be a confounding factor, since all behavior modification programs include training of ward personnel which tends to convince nurses and technicians that reinforcement methods will be effective. Since the staff cannot be blind to the presence or withdrawal of contingencies, their expectancy for success is a contaminant mixed in with the intervention.

Expectancy has been shown to be a factor in the treatment effects obtained in certain behavioral methods, particularly systematic desensitization, which is used primarily for neurotics who are avoiding situations because of anxiety. A recent review of this problem concludes that a patient's expectancy becomes increasingly less important when he is exposed to effective behavioral change procedures (Bootzin, 1971). Most of the procedures described in this chapter have been demonstrated to be highly effective; thus expectancy probably plays a small role in behavior modification with schizophrenics.

Group designs with patients randomly assigned or matched to a variety of treatments provide the best controls for confounding factors in outcome studies. A definitive study of the token economy in comparison with a "maximum push" milieu therapy program is now under way in Illinois. Using a constant staff that rotates between the two experimental wards, this project will compare specific target behaviors in social, personal grooming, and instrumental work areas (Paul, 1971). When completed, this elegantly controlled, factorial study will shed more light on the role of confounding variables.

Most of the studies of the effects of the token economies have been carried out with the patients kept on constant maintenance doses of phenothiazines. However, a recent experiment indicates that behavior modification procedures alone can control the deviant behavior of schizophrenics without drugs. Paul and his colleagues (Paul, Tobias, and Holly, 1972) have reported a triple-blind study of phenothiazines versus placebos given to chronic, regressed patients after transfer to a token economy. After baseline measures were taken, half the patients were put on placebos for 16 weeks. The patients on placebos improved to the same degree as the drug group but much faster. They conclude that there is a dynamic interaction between the type of environment and drug response. In custodial or low-impact milieu programs, drugs produce an appreciable, significant effect over and above placebos; however, in a setting with carefully constructed and consistently applied reinforcement contingencies, the drugs may interfere slightly with the acquisition of adaptive behavior. Three other studies analyzing the effects of drugs and contingencies of reinforcement on behavior are reported in the second part of this chapter.

Staff Training

The *sine qua non* of any behavior modification program is an alliance between the research or professional staff and the clinical or paraprofessional personnel. Since the actual work with patients—the reinforcement of target behaviors—is done primarily by the nursing staff, the staff's training and cooperation are of first-order importance. A challenge to behavior modifiers concerned with innovation and diffusion of new methods is the training of administrative and staff personnel at all levels in the rationale, utility, and method of a learning approach to mental patients. It is fallacious to assume that mental health workers will change their habitual ways of managing patients quickly or easily. Just as the social breakdown syndrome is resistant to change in patients, the methods used by staff members to induce this syndrome are also resistant to change.

The innovator must bring to bear principles of reinforcement for modifying staff behavior as well as patients' behavior. They must receive careful training and there must be incentives built into the system to reward or "reinforce" their changing their methods. Time off for attending training sessions, bonuses for fulfilling the training course, and the constant attention and encouragement by a dedicated project director are all examples of needed incentives. Thus the principles of behavior that are applied to patients must also be taken into consideration when retraining of staff is undertaken. Similar attention must be given to the administrative hierarchies in the hospital. Vertical staffing patterns and authoritarian superintendents who receive status for managing large hospitals are inimical to a behavior modification approach. Administrators must be persuaded that the behavioral change of patients is more important than a high patient census or neat rows of beds that are well made. Vested interest, institutionalized staff members, and the persistence of past behavior (traditions) must all be contended with if the basic behavioral principles are to have a chance to succeed.

Experiences, both positive and negative, at various programs highlight the critical importance of staff training and motivation in the outcome of behavior modification projects. At Sonoma State Hospital a token program was instituted in a 70-bed unit of moderately retarded males who exhibited various behavior disorders including aggressiveness. Minimal prior training was given to the staff of psychiatric technicians, most of whom had been using custodial methods of control for many years. The project director was not able to give full-time attention to the unit. Understandably the program has not succeeded. Technicians did not learn to distribute tokens contingent on the desirable behavior of the patients. They gave tokens to patients who appeared to have been "good boys" regardless of whether the patients earned them according to the schedule. Consistent reinforcement for target behaviors thus was not possible. The project director rued the lack of initial training and the poor alliance between himself and the nursing staff, but because of it the program was scrapped.

On the other hand, programs at Patton and Pacific State Hospitals and the Menlo Park VA Hospital have succeeded primarily because time was taken to train the staff in the rationale and use of reinforcement techniques, and a member of the psychology department has remained in daily, close contact with the ward milieu and staff. At each place a psychologist is in attendance on the ward, monitoring the performance of the nurses and technicians and the responses of the patients. They are available for consultations with the nursing staff and are able to iron out problems on the spot. They provide morale boosts to the staff simply by their accessibility and willingness to collaborate on a clinical level. They lead frequent staff conferences and work with the nurses and technicians in revising, updating, and evaluating the individual programs for the patients. At Patton an intensive training program for technicians lasting several months produced personnel who were alert and effective reinforcers. An excellent training manual for ward personnel was written recently by Schaefer and Martin (1969).

Considerable suspiciousness and hostility on the part of the hospital administration toward the innovative reinforcement methods has been encountered by almost every project. There is no simple way to obviate such resistance to change, but Dr. T. Ball at Pacific undercut potential hostility by circulating throughout the hospital a memo explaining some of the controversial and frequently misunderstood features of a token economy before the program was begun. When the innovation is done with groundwork and attention to the needs of the clinical personnel, success will occur.

SPECIFIC BEHAVIORAL INTERVENTIONS WITH PSYCHOTIC INDIVIDUALS

The Clinical Research Unit (CRU) is a 12-bed coed unit located at Camarillo State Hospital, 50 miles north of Los Angeles. It is part of the Camarillo-Neuropsychiatric Institute (UCLA) Research Program. Since the CRU's inception in November 1970, 54 patients have been treated for an average patient stay of 122 days.

The treatment staff consists of 14 nursing personnel for 24-hour coverage, a research psychiatrist, a clinical psychologist, a psychiatric social worker, and a research technician. The nursing personnel include both licensed psychiatric technicians and registered nurses. Students in psychiatry, nursing, psychology, and social work at various levels of experience are involved in practical or research training on the CRU. The staff and unit costs are provided at hospital expense with some research support emanating from California Department of Health and NIMH sources.

The flow chart in Figure 5 describes the administrative operations of the

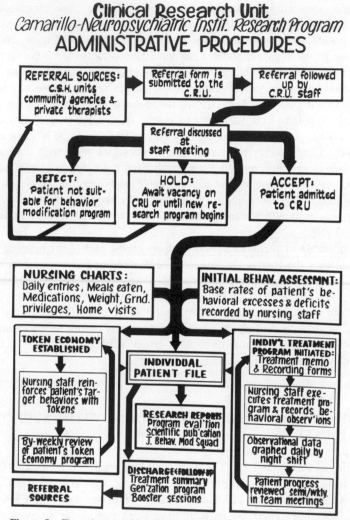

Figure 5. Flow chart detailing CRU administrative procedures.

CRU. Patients are referred to the CRU both from other units within the hospital and directly from agencies in the community. Certain patients who emit behaviors that are to be researched are also solicited from other units in the hospital. Each referral is screened by a nursing staff member who interviews the patient and discusses with the referring personnel such topics as the patient's behavioral excesses and deficits and their frequency, possible reinforcers, and ineffectiveness of past treatment modalities. The referral is discussed at a twice-weekly staff meeting, and the decision to accept or reject a referral is a cooperative decision made by all members of the treatment team.

The basic element in the CRU's treatment milieu is an individualized token economy which is used both for the completion of essential unit tasks and for the attainment of specific therapeutic goals for each patient. In addition to receiving tokens for getting up in the morning at the appropriate time, for grooming, and for room cleaning, patients are assigned various tasks according to their current level of functioning. These tasks are written on a standard data sheet which provides spaces for the indication of completion or noncompletion of tasks (see Table 2). All token economy programs are changed every two weeks in conjunction with the patient, who is given a copy of his or her program.

Apart from the token economy, individualized programs are developed which specify interventions for from one to three target behaviors for which the patient was referred to the CRU. To evaluate the effectiveness of these programs, a data collection and collation system has been developed which includes several steps (see Figure 5):

1. The frequency of the target behavior is determined by a variety of recording techniques ranging from continuous recordings, event recording during sessions, interval recording, and time sampling.

2. Data collection sheets are devised for each specific program.

3. Memos detailing each program are duplicated and distributed to all staff members' mailboxes, which are located in the nursing office.

4. A clipboard kept in the nurses' office for each patient contains that day's data collection sheet and all program memos pertaining to that particular patient.

5. Each day's data sheets are removed from the clipboards by the night shift (12 midnight to 8 AM shift), and results are graphed separately for each patient. New data sheets are then placed on the clipboards.

6. The data thus graphed provide day-by-day information to revise the individualized programs when necessary.

Since consistency in the application of contingencies is a *sine qua non* of behavior modification approaches, communication among all members of the treatment team and inhouse training are vital activities. Twice-weekly meetings are held in which patients' progress, program changes, referrals, and unit problems are discussed. These meetings are scheduled so that all three shifts attend at least one meeting per week. The program memos just discussed serve a vital communication function. A newsletter, *The Journal of the Behavior Mod Squad*, is distributed once a month to all staff members and interested hospital and community personnel. This mimeographed journal contains capsule summaries of each patient's progress and a humor section devoted to staff members (Patterson, Cooke, and Liberman, 1972). Training sessions in the techniques necessary to conduct the individualized programs are scheduled whenever a new

344

Table 2. Token Economy Target Behavior Review Form

Patient: _____ Therapist: _____ Date: _____

Target Behaviors for Coming Weeks: Based on Previous Assessment

Item		Token Amount and Schedule

UP, GROOM, ROOM

1. Up _____
2. Groom _____
3. Room _____

CHORES

1. _____
2. _____
3. _____

INDIVIDUAL

1. _____

ASSESSMENT: Check items completed. Use zero (0) if not completed

	Tu	W	Th	F	S	S	M	Tu	W	Th	F	S	S	M	% Success

1. Up
2. Groom
3. Room
1.
2.
3.
1.

SUGGESTED NEW GOALS

_____
_____
_____

program is to be implemented. Ten-week seminars on research and methodological topics are also scheduled regularly.

When it has been decided that a patient's program has reached its conclusion, the patient is transferred either to his home unit at Camarillo State Hospital or to a community facility. Whenever possible, the CRU staff works closely with the unit or agency personnel to continue the program and thus aid in generalization of behavior change from the CRU to the transfer facility.

Following are summaries of the programs of various patients who have been admitted to the CRU with a diagnosis of psychosis. These are grouped according to the major problem areas treated, and an introduction to the various groups precedes the summaries. The groupings are arbitrary and, to aid the reader, Table 3 indicates the patients treated for each major problem area.

It is important to note that consecutive cases referred to the CRU are reported here with treatment failures as well as successes. This is not a selection of cases designed to illustrate the potency of behavioral engineering; on the contrary, the authors feel that the "whoopee" style of behavior modification is past and that it is time to review soberly progress in the application of behavioral principles across a wide range of clinical problems.

It is also important to note that most of the case reports are of the AB design and, therefore, do not clearly demonstrate experimental control. The exigencies of clinical practice often do not allow the time to use a reversal design. Nevertheless, the use of an AB design does provide at least suggestive evidence concerning the effectiveness of the various procedures.

Delusional Speech

Individuals exhibiting a high frequency of verbalization of delusional or bizarre ideas are labeled "mentally ill." Bizarre speech, often grandiose or persecutory in nature, attracts a great deal of attention whether it takes place in the supermarket, on the assembly line, or in the confines of an institution. The surprise, fear, amazement, or amusement expressed by an audience powerfully reinforces the behavior. Long periods of hospitalization and repetitive brief tenures in community settings are consequences of delusional speech.

Extinction would be the treatment of choice if not for the intermittent reinforcement provided by other patients and visitors who do not ignore the bizarre verbal behavior. The positive correlation noted between hostility and rate of delusional speech expressed by some of the patients discussed below precludes the use of punishment techniques, which are difficult to administer to adults, engender anger in patients, and bear little resemblance to social interventions that can be practically employed in natural settings.

Immediate reinforcement of behaviors incompatible with delusional speech (e.g., rational speech, film editing, gardening chores) coupled with delayed incentives for increasing periods of delusion-free behavior were relatively effective

Table 3. Summary of Target Behaviors for Each Patient

| | | | | | | Problem Behavior | | | | | | | | | |
| | Verbal | | | | | Assault | | | | | | | | | |
Name	Delu-sion	Scream	Inau-dible	Ob-scene	Abuse	Self	Others	Prop-erty	Groom	Work	Hallu-cinate	Iso-late	Bizarre Motor	Sexual	Manip-ulate
J.E.	X														
J.V.	X				X				X						
M.N.	X														
H.D.	X														
B.G.									X		X				
B.R.										X	X		X		
M.B.										X		X			
J.O.						X								X	
R.V.							X		X	X					
V.Q.				X					X	X			X		
J.B.				X					X					X	
B.I.			X				X		X	X					
F.C.			X							X					
E.N.									X	X					
I.I.									X				X		
A.N.															X
W.N.					X		X								
I.P.	X											X			
M.V.	X									X					X
S.G.		X				X									
R.N.		X			X		X	X	X	X					
K.B.	X				X			X	X						
S.K.		X						X					X		
T.H.					X		X			X					
V.X.							X								
M.L.		X						X	X	X					
G.X.									X	X					
J.D.			X			X		X				X			
S.T.	X				X				X	X		X			
R.T.									X	X		X			
M.M.									X	X					X

in increasing rational and decreasing delusional speech. Individualization of reinforcement procedures is necessary for effective outcomes. The duration of the pretreatment history of delusional speech and the "tightness," consistency, and duration of the contingencies of reinforcement applied during treatment are relevant variables affecting outcome. Simply increasing rational speech without specifically suppressing delusional speech through targeting and probing procedures will not have any long-term impact on the verbal repertoires of delusional schizophrenics.

The following four case reports include various procedures designed to reduce or eliminate delusional speech and to substitute rational social interaction as an alternative to delusional or "crazy" talk.

CASE REPORT 1

Patient. J. E., a 64-year-old, white male, had been hospitalized at Camarillo State Hospital for more than 16 years. He was divorced, had one child, was wealthy, college educated, and had received a prefrontal lobotomy 15 years previously. He was not receiving medication. His psychiatric diagnosis was schizophrenia, paranoid type.

Problem Behaviors

1. High frequency of delusional speech.
2. Habitual carrying of a large briefcase filled with tools, newspaper clippings, and personal articles. The newspaper clippings were used to support his delusions.
3. Deficits in social and task-oriented skills.

Procedures

1. Delusional statements made by J. E. were separated into four topical categories. A high-frequency, regularly occurring behavior (staying up late with an elaborate "midnight snack") was made contingent upon avoiding delusional topics sequentially in each of the four categories of a multiple-baseline design. The number of interviews which contained a delusional statement out of four total interviews per day determined the hour at which he had to go to bed. All contingencies were then removed to determine the effect on the frequency of delusional talk (reversal period). Subsequently, the early bedtime contingency was reinstated if any delusional category was mentioned in any one of the interviews (all-or-none contingency). If no delusional statements were made in a day, he not only could stay up late and have his elaborate snack, but he also was given a drink of Scotch whiskey, a favorite of his. Finally, the contingencies on each category were faded over a period of nine days so that the *early bedtime contingency* was no longer in effect during the final seven days prior

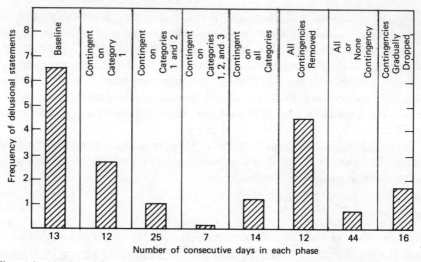

Figure 6. Number of first references in four delusional categories tallied during four daily observational periods.

to discharge. The fading of the contingencies was done without instructing the patient.

2. Office space was provided for tools needed by J. E. for his gardening activity to prevent loss by theft. J. E. was not allowed to store his briefcase for safekeeping in the nurses' station, which had been the pattern for several months.

3. (a) An industrial therapy job in the Camarillo State Hospital TV Studio was provided in an attempt to restore his interest in an old hobby, motion picture photography. Tokens were provided, contingent on task completion. J. E. was paid tokens to restore and edit his collection of self-made 16-millimeter travel films.

(b) The General Relationship Improvement Program (Human Development Institute, Inc., 1967) was scheduled. It is a 10-lesson, programmed learning course in the establishment of direct and expressive interpersonal conversation. A male therapist was the partner in this program.

(c) Gardening, a long favorite pastime for J. E., was continued in the CRU's courtyard, and token payment was provided.

Results

1. Figure 6 shows that the frequency of delusional talk (first references to each category in four daily observations with a possible total of 16) was reduced by more than half when bedtime contingencies were applied to only the first category. Further reduction to one statement per day resulted from adding the

second category. Delusional talk nearly disappeared when the third category was added, but it returned to an average of approximately one delusional statement per day when all four categories were included.

When all contingencies were removed, an average frequency of 4.5 delusional references per day resulted. This was approximately two-thirds of the baseline rate. The "all-or-none" baseline contingency brought the average frequency of delusional references to below one per day. When contingencies were then faded, a slight increase to 1.75 delusional references per day was noted.

2. There was a decrease in the frequency of J. E.'s carrying his briefcase. Briefcase carrying was directly proportional to delusional speech. As delusions decreased in frequency, the "compulsion to carry" decreased to the point where he was even willing to allow his briefcase to sit unguarded for long periods of time.

3. (a) J. E. began to spend two to four hours daily in viewing and repairing his films.

(b) The 10-lesson conversation program was completed, but no test of generalization to others in the environment was performed.

(c) The quality of his gardening work was manifest in the beautification of the CRU courtyard, which deteriorated rapidly after his discharge.

Generalization. The removal of contingencies on a gradual basis was designed as a generalization program. He demonstrated generalization of nondelusional speech to various noncontingent environments. At a "graduation party" at the first author's home, no contingencies were applied and opportunity for delusional verbalization abounded, since many of those attending had never met J. E. before. Many sensitive topics, which in the past had frequently evoked delusions from J. E., were discussed. However, he remained rational and socially appropriate throughout the afternoon.

Placement in a board-and-care home was preceded by instructions to the operators to ignore completely any delusional talk. Provisions were also made for continuation of J. E.'s gardening and photography hobbies.

Follow-up 17 months after discharge indicates an "acceptably low rate" of delusional talk, defined as such since it has not caused concern in the neighborhood or the house. He has pursued gardening with a flourish and has maintained his interest in photography, which is a source of reinforcement for him and provides opportunities to entertain and engage in social interaction with others.

CASE REPORT 2

Patient. J. V., a 45-year-old, black, divorced female, had a 13-year history of multiple hospital admissions. A penal code patient, she was charged with disturbing the peace because of daily episodes of screaming and cursing at the

Welfare Department office where she regularly demanded additional aid. Her psychiatric diagnosis was schizophrenia, paranoid type.

Problem Behaviors

1. High frequency of delusional speech.
2. Verbal abusiveness.
3. Bizarre dressing and grooming.

Procedures

1. (a) Interviews and observations, each 5 minutes in length, were alternated at half-hour intervals. After 14 days of baseline, she was removed from the attention of others (time-out) for 5 minutes whenever she voiced a delusion during an interview. The time-out was continued and medication (chlorpromazine) was reduced from the previous constant rate of 600 to 200 milligrams per day. After 20 days, she was removed from all medication with the time-out contingency still in effect.

(b) An incentive program to gain a staffing and discharge from the hospital, was the final procedure. Again, no medication was given during this procedure.

2. J. V. was removed from the attention of others (time-out) for 5 minutes contingent upon abusive verbalizations.

3. Bizarre clothing and accessories were confiscated (sloppy hair, mascara on lips, rags tied to legs). Alternative, incompatible behavior, such as appropriate dress and grooming, was praised and rewarded with tokens.

Results

1. (a) The average of two delusional responses in interviews and three delusional responses during observations in baseline measurements decreased markedly to 0.2 delusional interviews and observations per day. Removal of contingencies resulted in an increase to an average of 1.2 and 0.7 per day for interviews and observations, respectively. Reduction of medication and the re-establishment of contingencies had little immediate effect bur reduced the delusional interviews and observations to fewer than 1 per day. Removal of all medication did not interfere with the continued decline in delusional expressions. The averages for the final phase were 0.45 delusional interviews and 0.04 delusional observations. Figure 7 presents the data graphically.

(b) The prospect of discharge proved to be highly motivating as J. V. rapidly earned the staffing for return to court. Despite the absence of medication, nine consecutive days passed with no delusional expressions heard.

2. Abusive speech, which was highly correlated with delusional speech, responded readily to time-out. Though abusive speech was not eliminated, J. V. learned to curse under her breath.

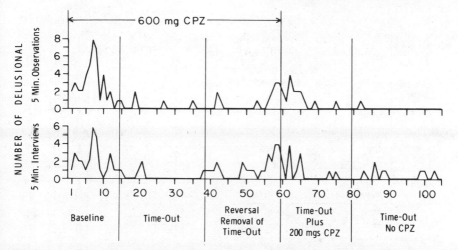

Figure 7. Daily frequency of interviews and observations in which delusional talk occurred. (From R. L. Patterson and J. R. Teigen. Conditioning and posthospital generalization of nondelusional responses in a chronic psychotic patient. *Journal of Applied Behavior Analysis*, **6**:65-70, 1973. Copyright (1973) by the Society for the Experimental Analysis of Behavior, Inc. Reproduced by permission.)

3. Bizarre dress and grooming was eliminated by the procedure outlined above.

Generalization. The fact that contingencies were not applied to observations and yet delusional verbalizations during observations were even lower than during interviews indicates that stimulus generalization occurred.

CASE REPORT 3

Patient. M. N., a 63-year-old, single, white female, had been continuously hospitalized for 26 years. No relatives were located and her life prior to hospitalization was not chronicled so that little was known of her social history. She was not receiving medication.

Problem Behaviors. Delusional speech primarily centered around her personal identity—name, age, place of birth, and family background.

Procedures

1. A psychodrama was planned with the aid of an eminent psychodramatist and entitled "This is your life, M. N." The goal was to gradually change or remove her grandiose delusions within the psychodrama and to measure for generalization outside the sessions.

2. M. N.'s token economy was yoked to her providing two factual state-

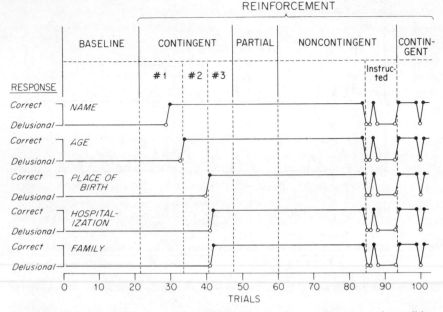

Figure 8. Frequency of delusional and correct responses to five questions across six conditions. (Modified from R. P. Liberman, J. Davis, W. Moon, and J. Moore. Research design for analyzing drug-environment behavior interactions. *Journal of Nervous and Mental Disease*, **156:**432-439, 1973. Copyright (1973) by the Williams & Wilkens Co. Reproduced by permission.)

ments about her personal identity. In a multiple-baseline design, her entire daily needs for tokens were made contingent upon her correctly answering questions regarding her name, age, place and date of birth, place and date of hospitalization, and name of her family. A reversal to a noncontingent condition was carried out after the patient was giving correct answers for weeks, and this was followed by reinstatement of the contingencies.

Results

1. The psychodrama resulted in no increase in rational speech outside of sessions. Although she accepted a number of changes in her life history within some of the psychodrama sessions, she regressed during the last two sessions, exhibiting a high frequency of loose associations, grandiose and paranoid delusional statements, and inappropriate affect.

2. M. N. responded rationally almost immediately as each of the token reinforcement contingencies were applied to her correctly answering questions about her identity on the sequentially multiple baseline. The data are presented in Figure 8 and are described in detail in another publication (Patterson and Teigen, 1973).

Generalization. Though contingencies were applied sequentially to the provision of additional facts, one at a time, after contingencies were applied to the third question M. N. began to answer all six questions factually.

Contingencies of reinforcement were extended to the board-and-care home to which M. N. was discharged. Her daily ration of cigarettes was provided in return for her correctly answering questions regarding her identity and background.

During the day, the manager of the home was instructed to ignore delusional statements. Twice she was heard to comment about her advanced age (instead of her previous delusional insistance that she was 17 years old), and she introduced herself to a neighborhood storekeeper by her real name. A confederate of the authors, unknown to M. N., visited the home and spoke with the patient 52 days after discharge. M. N. gave the "stranger" ambiguous but socially acceptable information about her background. She continues to live outside the hospital 27 months after discharge.

CASE REPORT 4

Patient. H. D., a 38-year-old, single, male black college graduate and army veteran, had spent all but a few months of the previous 16 years in VA hospitals. He was on a penal code commitment for threatening family members with physical harm. Medication remained constant throughout H. D.'s treatment. His psychiatric diagnosis was schizophrenia, paranoid type.

Problem Behavior. High frequency of delusional speech.

Procedures

1. Charging tokens for delusional speech (response cost).

2. Time-out from reinforcement contingent on delusional speech.

3. Providing a drink of his favorite whiskey in exchange for tokens earned by talking rationally.

4. Involvement in ward activities with status as a job supervisor and therapist aide.

5. A program requiring increasing intervals of delusion-free verbal behavior in order to gain a staffing for return to court. Twelve interviews and observations were scheduled on alternating half-hours throughout the day. When an observation was scheduled, the therapist approached within listening distance without engaging H. D. in conversation. During interviews, the therapist spoke with H. D. in a semistructured format for five minutes. H. D. had to be free of delusions for increasing periods of time, initially one hour and eventually five consecutive days in order to gain the staffing. For example, if a delusional statement was noted during an interview on the third day of the four-day interval, H. D. had to restart the four-day interval. Each day H. D. filled in a chart

which provided feedback as to his progress. The chart was prominently displayed on the nursing office door.

Results

Procedures 1, 2, 3, and 4. The programs briefly described in these procedures resulted in a fairly low ratio of delusional talk to rational talk, but providing opportunities for ward activities with status as supervisor was most effective. Response cost and time-out procedures could not be operationalized because the patient became hostile and physically threatening to staff after several days.

5. Earning a predischarge staffing was a reinforcing event for H. D. During the 12 daily interviews over a period of 38 days, 93.3 percent were rational, and 6.7 percent were delusional. H. D. was staffed, found to be "competent" to face the charges against him, and was returned to court.

Generalization. During the final program, separate data on the observations were taken as a measure of generalization, since no contingencies were placed upon his verbalizations during observations. Rational speech was heard during 72 percent of the observations, delusional speech during 5 percent, and silence during 23 percent.

H. D. returned to court where charges were dropped, and he returned to live with his parents and brother. The mother reported that after six weeks he refused to take medication and began drinking heavily but refrained from delusional talk. The drinking behavior resulted in readmission to a VA hospital from which he was eventually released to a board-and-care home in the Los Angeles area. About six weeks before this writing, he phoned the CRU and reported that he is doing well out of the hospital and attends an outpatient clinic program weekly. At the time of this writing, H. D. called again to report he is doing well, although he can afford only a beer or two at a time, a far cry from his earlier grandiose delusions of wealth. He also inquired about other patients whom he remembered.

Hallucinations

The following cases represent an attempt to reduce the frequency of self-reported hallucinations and associated stereotyped behavior of three schizophrenic patients through massed practice techniques (Patterson, 1972). Massed practice can be viewed from Hullian learning theory as conditioned inhibition, or alternatively, from operant principles as a punishment procedure. A response repeated *ad nauseum* becomes associated with the aversive conditions of boredom, satiation, and fatigue through classical conditioning.

In two cases the massed practice procedure was effective, but further experimental verification is required. It is interesting to note that for both B. G. and

B. R. self-report of hallucinations was not correlated with the postural behaviors that were determined by observation to be associated with hallucinations. For example, self-report of auditory hallucinations was not highly correlated with turning away from the interviewer as if to listen to a voice. Indeed, eliminating overt behaviors associated with hallucinations did *not* reduce self-report of hallucinations. Perhaps it is necessary to treat separately verbal self-report of hallucinations and their temporally associated motor behaviors.

CASE REPORT 1

Patient. B. G. was a 34-year-old, single, Caucasian male who was an admitted homosexual. He had been living with another man, when not hospitalized, for at least six years. His hospitalization record extended over the last 12 years during which he had 13 admissions. His current hospital admission came at his own request, only nine days after his previous discharge. He reported that he was afraid to live outside the hospital because of auditory hallucinations. His psychiatric diagnosis was schizophrenia, paranoid type.

Problem Behaviors

1. Auditory hallucinations consisting of voices talking about movie stars, electroconvulsive shock, and saying that he would be tortured into eternity.

2. Deficits in cleaning his room and changing clothes regularly.

Procedures

1. To modify B. G.'s auditory hallucinations, a negative practice procedure was utilized in which B. G. listened to a 30-minute tape recording of a male voice repeating phrases similar to those of the voices reported by B. G. These listening sessions were held once daily for 22 days, twice daily for 10 days, then three times daily for 14 days. B. G. was interviewed from three to five times daily, 10 minutes per interview. The following specific behaviors presumed to be highly correlated with hallucinations were tallied during these interviews: (a) speaking to someone not present; (b) suddenly looking aside as if someone not present had called; and (c) inappropriate laughter when accompanied by (a) or (b) above.

2. Token economy contingencies were utilized to increase room cleaning and clothes changing.

Results

1. The results are presented in Figure 9. Although there was an initial increase in the percentage of observed hallucinations during the first eight days of treatment, hallucinatory behaviors were reduced during the last five days of treatment to an average of 16.6 percent of the interviews compared to a 30 percent average during the five days of baseline.

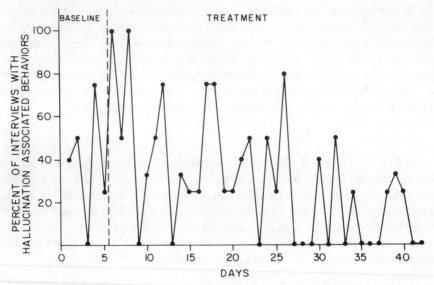

Figure 9.   Percentage of interviews with hallucination-associated behavior.

2. Clothes changing and room cleaning increased to an acceptable level prior to discharge.

Generalization. B. G. was discharged to his own care. Follow-up information obtained from his roommate indicated that the frequency of voices had remained greatly reduced. Four months after discharge B. G. was rehospitalized because of excessive drinking and destruction of property. At the admitting interview B. G. denied having auditory hallucinations. The length of time B. G. remained free of voices is quite long in view of the fact that almost all of his 13 previous admissions had been necessitated by self-reported fear of the voices. It is possible that this aversion-by-repetition procedure may be generally useful in the behavioral treatment of hallucinations, but further experimental verification of its effectiveness is required.

CASE REPORT 2

Patient. B. R. was a 22-year-old black male who had been hospitalized eight times beginning in 1967. His diagnosis was schizophrenia, paranoid type. He had finished high school and had attended a local junior college for one year. He had held only odd jobs and was unmarried. Throughout his stay on the CRU he was kept on a constant dose of phenothiazine (Trifluoperazine, 30 milligrams daily).

Problem Behaviors

1. Auditory hallucinations consisting of both male and female voices alternately praising and damning his sexual prowess.
2. Visual hallucinations of girls.
3. A reaching and grabbing motion made with his hands, which B. R. indicated was to bring the girls that he saw closer to him.

Procedures

1. To modify B. R.'s auditory hallucinations, a negative practice procedure was utilized in which B. R. was instructed to repeat for three daily 30-minute sessions several sentences which closely resembled dominant themes in his auditory hallucinations. Frequency of hallucinations was obtained by having B. R. report during four daily, 10-minute interviews the number and content of his auditory hallucinations.
2. To modify B. R.'s visual hallucinations, a "satiation" procedure was utilized in which B. R. looked at pictures of seminude females that he had selected as being desirable. These viewing sessions were held continuously throughout the day and lasted for 8 hours and 40 minutes per day. The frequency of visual hallucinations was determined by having B. R. report during four daily 10-minute interviews the number of visual hallucinations.
3. To modify the reaching and grabbing motions, a negative practice procedure was utilized in which B. R. was required to repeat constantly the gesture in three daily 30-minute sessions. The number of gestures was recorded during each of the four hallucination report sessions.

Results

1. The report of auditory hallucinations decreased from a nine-day baseline average of 138 reports per day to an average during the last nine days of treatment of 12.8 per day.
2. The report of visual hallucinations increased slightly as a result of treatment from a 10-day baseline average of 2.5 interviews per day with reports of visual hallucinations to a final 10-day treatment average of 3.5 interviews per day with visual hallucinations.
3. The number of hand wavings decreased from an 80-session baseline average of 6.1 per session to an 88-session posttreatment period during which no gestures were observed.

Generalization. B. R. was transferred to a board-and-care home. Unfortunately, it has not been possible to obtain follow-up reports.

Discussion. The negative practice procedure for B. R.'s auditory hallucinations was only partially successful in that they were still being reported by B.

R., although at a lower rate. The visual hallucination program was unsuccessful, and it seemed that looking at pictures acted as a cue for further visual hallucinations. The negative practice procedure for the hand gesture temporarily eliminated this symptom; however, after termination of the sessions of viewing pictures, the hand gestures recurred. The negative practice program was reinstituted and the frequency of the gesture reduced, but not to a zero level as previously.

Confounding the entire procedure is the fact that B. R. was extremely compliant, as is evidenced by his willingness to cooperate with the negative practice regimen, which is extremely tiresome and boring. Such compliance may have led to a high level of report of hallucinations since the demand characteristics of the interviews were biased to the report of hallucinations. Perhaps another measure of the frequency of hallucinations should have been used.

Social Breakdown Syndrome

Within larger neuropsychiatric facilities, there is usually a core of patients who are long-term residents of the institution. These patients have generally learned a variety of maladaptive behaviors that have been shaped and maintained by the custodial environment of the institution. Since all large hospitals are understaffed, with little or no opportunity for interpersonal contact between patients and staff, certain extreme patient behaviors become necessary to elicit staff attention. These behaviors include self-mutilation, obscene speech, standing in the door of the nurses station, and pestiness. If there are limited supplies of items such as coffee and cigarettes, then these items become powerful reinforcers to shape and maintain behaviors such as grabbing them from others.

The next nine case summaries represent the CRU's attempts to modify the inappropriate behaviors of such institutionalized patients. The techniques were quite successful in eight of the nine cases. Three of the patients showed a similar pattern of substantial reduction but not complete elimination in the target behaviors. It is probable that social responses from other patients maintained these behaviors at a low but consistent rate.

CASE REPORT 1

Patient. M. B. was a 36-year-old, divorced female who had been continuously hospitalized for the past 11 years following a postpartum psychosis. She was a high school graduate who had worked as a secretary for several years before the onset of the psychosis. Her diagnosis was schizophrenia, catatonic type (withdrawn).

Problem Behaviors

1. Bizarre posturing and verbalizations frequently described as "praying"

and including (a) standing motionless with eyes rolled back and head slightly elevated, (b) thumb and forefinger held together with arms engaged in a "blessing" motion, and (c) verbally blessing staff members, patients, and inanimate objects such as door knobs and windows.

2. Refusal to comply with requests to perform unit chores.

3. Except for blessing, very low frequency of social interaction with staff members or other patients.

Procedures

1. To modify the complex of behaviors labeled praying, numerous programs were instituted in the following sequence:

(a) Baseline (38 days) frequency of praying was determined by noting any such behaviors during seven daily five-minute observations.

(b) A token economy program in which tokens were used to reward appropriate behaviors, and which could later be exchanged for male companionship, rental of religious items, and staff interaction on topics of a religious nature. Appropriate behaviors were defined as grooming, unit work, and talk about the "real world" (25 days).

(c) A "response-prevention" program in which M. B. spent a fixed amount of time in a restricted area with increasing intervals of time on the unit contingent upon previous periods of prayer-free behavior (56 days).

(d) A program in which M. B. was *rewarded* for each instance of praying. It was hypothesized that praying was being maintained by the staff's assiduous attempts to eliminate the praying. Thus it was made clear to M. B. that the staff wanted her to pray and that praying was part of her therapy program. The program was modified after 13 days with the addition of a "hassler" who followed M. B. around the unit and, once every 10 minutes, prompted her to pray and rewarded her with a special token for praying. The special tokens could be exchanged for time off the unit and for cigarettes (46 days).

(e) Placement in standard unit token economy as M. B. was no longer praying.

(f) After being out on grounds, M. B. returned to the unit and vowed to resume praying (two days after above). *

(g) A program in which M. B. was constantly made to pray in her own special room. M. B. was allowed to escape from the "prayer room" by performing chores, purchasing room time, and praying in church (31 days).

(h) A program similar to (d) above (26 days).

(i) A program in which continued instances of prayer would result in transfer to the less desirable home unit (7 days).

(j) Transfer to home unit.

(k) Throughout all phases, medication (phenothiazines) was kept constant.

Results. M. B.'s praying was only somewhat lower for the 20 days before transfer (2.60 observation with prayer per day) compared to the 38 days of baseline (4.22 per day). M. B.'s appropriate social interactions were considerably more frequent just prior to discharge than during the baseline phase based upon anecdotal reports by CRU ward staff. These were not measured, however.

Generalization. The staff of M. B.'s home unit reported three months later that praying continued unabated. However, they also reported that she continued to interact at a high frequency and was more cooperative in performing requested chores.

Discussion. M. B.'s praying proved refractory to any contingency that could be applied on the CRU except for one brief period as a result of Procedure (d). It is possible that the "reinforcer" for maintaining praying was simply remaining in the hospital. M. B. had mentioned several times that the hospital was her home; and in view of the fact that she had lost contact with her husband, son, and relatives, this was indeed the case. M. B. had seen several other patients leave the CRU for board-and-care homes, and it is possible that she continued to pray in order to stay in the hospital.

CASE REPORT 2

Patient. J. O. was a 39-year-old, Caucasian female who had been continuously hospitalized for the past 18 years. She was divorced, the mother of one child, and had been graduated from a junior college. At the time of admission to the CRU she had no contact with relatives. Her psychiatric diagnosis was schizophrenia, catatonic type (withdrawn).

Problem Behaviors

1. Self-inflicted cigarette burns.
2. Careless smoking behavior resulting in burned clothes.
3. Encouragement of male sexual advances.

Procedures

1 and 2. To modify J. O.'s smoking behavior, a program was initiated which provided scheduled cigarette rewards for not burning herself or her clothing. Each day, J. O. was issued a new set of clothes without burn holes and was then inspected for burns each hour during a short chat with a staff member. If she had remained burn-free since the previous observation, she was given half a cigarette and praised for her exemplary appearance. If she had burned herself, she was not given any cigarettes for the rest of the day. In addition, she was given a bonus of five cigarettes if, by 9 PM, she had not burned herself.

3. To modify J. O.'s sexual permissiveness, appropriate male-female social behaviors were modeled. Cookies, candy, and puffs of a cigarette were given while a male, preferred by J. O., sat and held hands, took walks, spoke, or ate with J. O.

Results

1 and 2. No medication was administered during J. O.'s program. Self-inflicted burns to flesh or clothing decreased from an eight-day baseline average of 1.0 burns per day to 0.24 burns per day for the 46 days of treatment. During the last 14 days on the CRU, J. O. remained burn-free.

3. Sexual acts were reduced from an average of 3.47 observed incidents per day during a seven-day baseline to an average of 0.86 per day the last seven days of treatment.

Generalization. J. O. was discharged to a nursing home, and a one-month follow-up indicated no incidents of self-inflicted burns.

Discussion. The major reason that J. O. had remained hospitalized for 18 years was her self-inflicted cigarette burns. Simply changing the contingencies to provide reinforcement for appropriate smoking behavior reduced her self-inflicted burns and made her suitable for community placement. Indeed, she was a most pleasant patient, cooperative, and very easy to talk to. The nursing home to which J. O. was discharged was willing to continue cigarette rewards for appropriate smoking behavior and to deliver social reinforcement for clean and neat appearance.

CASE REPORT 3

Patient. R. V. was a 52-year-old, divorced male who had been continuously hospitalized for the past 23 years. He had worked as an accountant prior to his initial hospitalization. His diagnosis was schizophrenia, residual type.

Problem Behaviors

1. Touching both patients and staff.
2. Grabbing cigarettes, coffee, soft drinks, and food items from both patients and staff.
3. Poor grooming including hair not combed, face not shaved, clothes disheveled, hands not washed.
4. Refusal to perform requested unit chores.

Procedures

1 and 2. To modify R. V.'s touching and grabbing, a punishment program was initially utilized in which a slap on the hand was delivered whenever R. V. was observed touching or grabbing. Although grabbing was reduced, touching remained at a relatively high level, and a new program was instituted which provided scheduled rewards of special tokens for refraining from touching or grabbing. The initial schedule for reward was one token for each 15 minutes; this was eventually lengthened to two tokens for each 30 minutes. These tokens could be exchanged at any time for coffee or cigarettes at the rate of four tokens

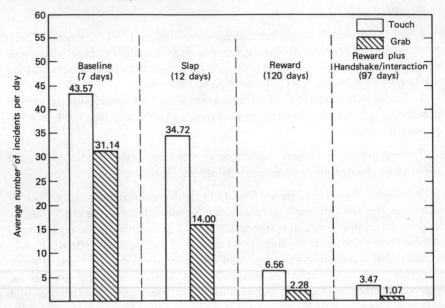

Figure 10.   Average number of observed touches and grabs per day.

per cigarette or cup of coffee. The frequency of touching and grabbing was determined by observing R. V. for one minute every half hour between 9 AM and 9 PM and noting the number of touches or grabs during that observation period. In addition, it was noted that many of R. V.'s touches preceded appropriate social contacts such as a question or a comment. To shape an alternate response to touching, a program of prompted handshaking between R. V. and staff members was initiated in which R. V. received a minimum of five handshakes and/or a 30-second interaction per staff member per day.

3 and 4. To modify R. V.'s poor grooming and refusal to perform unit chores, R. V. was placed in the token economy with tokens delivered contingently upon his maintaining good grooming and complying with task demands. Tokens could later be exchanged for items such as meals, candy, off-unit time, and room time.

Results

1 and 2. Medication was held constant during all phases. The results are presented in Figure 10. Touching decreased by 28 percent during the aversive phase and by 92 percent during the reinforcement plus handshake phase. Grabbing decreased by 55 percent during the aversive phase and by 96 percent during the reinforcement handshake phase.

3 and 4. Based on records of completion of assigned tasks, R. V.'s compliance increased from zero to performance of 70 percent of requested chores.

Generalization. R. V. was transferred to another unit within the hospital. Observations made by the CRU staff one week after discharge indicated that R. V. had generalized the gains made on the CRU. During two continuous 10-minute observation periods, R. V. did not touch or grab even though the opportunity was readily available to grab cigarettes from other patients. The unit staff also reported that R. V. is polite in asking for cigarettes and is cooperative in performing unit chores. He also is an assistant in the occupational therapy shop.

Discussion. Although the frequency of touching and grabbing decreased during the punishment phase, there were undesirable side effects which suggested that a positive approach would be more appropriate. Whenever R. V. was slapped, he would struggle to slap back and would be sullen and uncooperative for a good deal of time thereafter. It is certainly possible that a more intense aversive stimulus was necessary. However, it was decided not to attempt this since even the mildly aversive stimulus of a hand slap would be prohibited in any environment to which R. V. would be transferred.

Interestingly, R. V. seems to be performing even better on his new unit than on the CRU. Considering that patients on R. V.'s new unit are better able to defend themselves than those on the CRU, it is possible that they are providing negative contingencies which are effective in controlling R. V.'s behavior. Also, there is no contingency on his new unit for earning cigarettes through work. All he has to do is ask, thus reinforcing the more appropriate behavior of asking staff rather than grabbing from patients.

CASE REPORT 4

Patient. V. Q. was a 64-year-old, divorced, Caucasian male who had been continuously hospitalized since 1942. He was the father of three children and, by the time of hospitalization on the CRU, had lost contact with any relatives. He had completed only the eighth grade and had held odd jobs as a cook, dishwasher, or general laborer. His psychiatric diagnosis was schizophrenia, chronic undifferentiated type.

Problem Behaviors

1. Loud and obscene speech directed to both patients and staff.
2. An unusual gait frequently described as a "goose-step."
3. Noncompliance with requests to perform unit chores.
4. Poor grooming including not changing clothes, not shaving, and not combing hair.

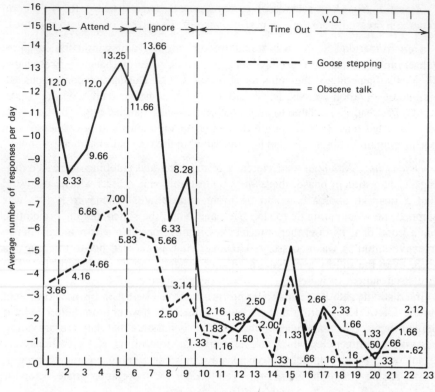

Figure 11. Average frequency per day of observed obscene talk and "goose-stepping," in blocks of seven days.

Procedures

1. Loud and obscene speech was initially attended to for eight days and was then ignored by all staff members. This produced only a small change, and a second program utilizing brief periods (five minutes) of time-out from reinforcement contingent upon loud and obscene speech was utilized. The frequency of loud and obscene talk was determined by observing V. Q. for one minute every half hour between 9 AM and 9 PM and recording whether or not such talk occurred during that time. Medication was held constant.

2. No specific contingencies were used to modify V. Q.'s unusual gait. Instances of "goose-stepping" were tallied at the same time that speech was observed.

3 and 4. To improve both grooming and work behavior, V. Q. was paid tokens for appropriate grooming and performance of assigned chores.

Results

1. The results are presented in Figure 11. Loud and obscene talk was reduced by 30 percent in the ignoral phase and by 84 percent in the time-out phase.

2. Goose-stepping was reduced by 14 percent in the ignoral phase and by 80 percent in the time-out phase.

3 and 4. Based on records of completion of assigned tasks and grooming behaviors, V. Q. was able to earn 30 percent of all possible tokens compared to an initial level of complete noncompliance.

Generalization. V. Q. was discharged to a nursing home with specific verbal instructions detailing the use of contingencies to control his loud and obscene speech. The behavior, however, increased and V. Q. had to be rehospitalized.

Discussion. Although there was a reduction in loud and obscene talk during the extinction phase, a switch to a time-out procedure was made because the behavior increased during the last week of extinction. Also, other patients were still providing attention for V. Q.'s loud and obscene talk.

It is unfortunate that the nursing home environment was not better programmed to deal with V. Q.'s loud and obscene speech, particularly in view of the fact that time-out could have been established easily through the use of outside yards and his own room.

CASE REPORT 5

Patient. J. B. was a 44-year-old, single male who had been hospitalized in various facilities for most of his life. He had not completed the eighth grade, and he had no vocational skills. His psychiatric diagnosis was schizophrenia, simple type.

Problem Behaviors

1. Pesty behavior including standing in the door of the nurses station, asking irrelevant questions, interrupting, and repeating questions.

2. Obscene talk directed to female employees and patients.

Procedures

1. To modify J. B.'s pesty behavior, the CRU staff members were instructed to ignore all examples of pestiness after an eight-day period of continuous attention for such behavior. Each instance of pesty behavior was noted on a data sheet when it occurred.

2. To reduce J. B.'s obscene talk, a program was implemented in which he was interviewed for five minutes, 20 times daily. If obscene talk was emitted

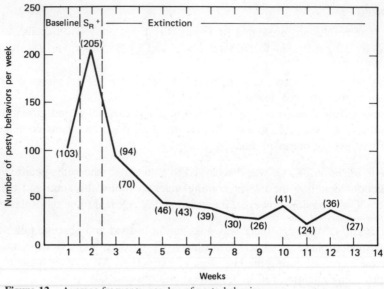

Figure 12. Average frequency per day of pesty behaviors.

during the interview, the interviewer would immediately walk away. If J. B. was able to maintain the five-minute interview without obscene talk, a token was delivered which could later be exchanged for cigarettes, meals, and various food items. Although this program was initially successful, the results were not long-lived. The program was discontinued, and obscene talk was ignored when it occurred. Medication was held constant during all phases.

Results

1. The results are presented in Figure 12 and indicate an approximately 79 percent reduction in the frequency of pesty behaviors.

2. Based on the number of interviews without obscene talk, the extinction plus token reward program was initially successful with 57 percent of the first 70 interviews free of obscene talk compared to only 20 percent for 20 baseline sessions. This declined, however, to only 12.5 percent of sessions without obscene talk for the last 40 interviews.

Generalization. J. B. was transferred back to the unit from which he was originally referred. To aid generalization of behavior change to the home unit, a program was implemented which systematically varied the amount of time J. B. spent on his home unit (from one-half to three hours at a time) and the amount of supervision by the CRU staff (from continuous during stay on the home unit to not at all). Staff members on the home unit were instructed in the contingencies, and extinction for pestiness and obscene talk was modeled. Anecdotal evidence from the home unit three months after discharge indicates continued low frequency of pestiness or obscene talk.

Discussion. Although extinction was difficult to employ considering the content of J. B.'s obscene speech, it nevertheless proved quite effective. In addition, the effort to program J. B.'s home unit was also effective since they had not attempted to use extinction until specifically instructed to do so.

CASE REPORT 6

Patient. B. I. was a 39-year-old, single, Caucasian male who had been continuously hospitalized at Camarillo since 1953. He was profoundly retarded and had undoubtedly been hospitalized most of his life. His diagnosis was psychosis with other cerebral conditions.

Problem Behaviors

1. Inaudible speech.
2. Touching and grabbing both staff and patients.
3. Poor grooming.
4. Noncompliance with requests to perform unit chores.
5. Tearing his shirt.
6. Sexual aggressiveness with females.
7. Smoking in unauthorized locations.
8. Urinating in public.

Procedures

1. To increase voice volume, candy and praise were made contingent upon repeating conversational phrases at an appropriate loudness level. Loudness was monitored in daily sessions with a voice-activated relay. If the relay was triggered during repetition of standard phrases, reinforcement was delivered (Patterson, 1972). Generalization was accomplished by extending these procedures to the general ward environment and maintained by ignoring him unless he spoke loud enough to be easily understood.

2. Incidents of touching and grabbing were punished with a handslap combined with praise—such as a verbal greeting or a handshake—for alternate behavior.

3 and 4. To institute grooming and work behaviors, a shaping paradigm was utilized in which behaviors such as showering were partitioned into small steps that could be performed sequentially. Each step was modeled, prompted, and rewarded with a cigarette or a piece of candy.

5. Shirt-tearing was punished with token fines paired with token rewards for

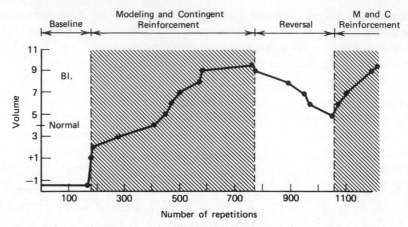

Figure 13. Voice volume level for B. I.

not tearing. This program was terminated after 51 days since B. I. had not torn a shirt in 9 successive days. After 10 months, the behavior recurred and a simplified program was initiated in which he could not enter the dining room with a torn shirt. He had to purchase an untorn shirt for one token but he would miss the meal.

6. During three social interaction sessions per day, B. I. and his female consort were given cigarette and food rewards while they engaged in such behavior as holding hands, taking walks, or eating together. Inappropriate touches were punished with a handslap. Instances of inappropriate sexual behavior were noted when they were observed.

7 and 8. Neither smoking in unauthorized places nor urinating in public reduced when punishment with a variety of aversive stimuli was contingently applied.

9. No medication was administered during any phase of the programs.

Results

1. The results of the voice volume program are graphed in Figure 13 and indicate that volume reached a level louder than normal within 600 repetitions. After a reversal of contingencies with reinforcement for lower volume levels, reacquisition was rapid.

2. Touching reduced by 90 percent from an 11-day baseline of 11.6 touches per day to a treatment average of 1.10 per day.

3 and 4. Based on records of completion of assigned tasks, compliance with requests to perform unit chores increased from near zero to 100 percent by the time of discharge. Grooming behaviors were shaped to the point that B. I.

could shower, shave, and comb his hair, all of which he did not perform when first admitted to the CRU.

5. Shirt-tearing was completely eliminated.

6. The baseline rate of 4.5 inappropriate sexual incidents per day reduced to zero for the last 10 days of the program. The program was then discontinued.

*Generalization.*B. I. was transferred to another unit within the hospital. To aid generalization of behavior change, a program was implemented which varied the amount of "visiting" time B. I. spent on the new unit, the amount of supervision provided by the CRU staff, and the chores to be performed while visiting the new unit. The reward contingencies were modeled for the staff of the transfer unit. Anecdotal reports, one year later, indicate no difficulty with touching, grabbing, shirt-tearing, or inappropriate sexual behaviors. Voice volume has remained at high levels.

Discussion. Although behavior modification techniques frequently have been accused of being too atomistic, the use of several programs to sequentially modify inappropriate behaviors led to the making of a "new man." B. I. was well known among hospital employees for being a difficult and troublesome patient. Indeed, two units refused to have him transferred from the CRU to their units, and it was only with much persuasion that the third unit agreed to take him. However, the behavioral changes have persisted and he is now well regarded by his new unit staff.

CASE REPORT 7

Patient. F. C. was a 61-year-old, single, Caucasian male who had been continuously hospitalized since 1936. He had graduated from high school and been employed as a bookkeeper prior to hospitalization. His psychiatric diagnosis was psychosis with epilepsy.

Problem Behaviors

1. Inaudible speech.
2. Disoriented to day, date, time, and place.
3. Noncompliance with requests to perform unit chores.

Procedures

1. Contingent upon repeating conversational phrases at an appropriate loudness level, edible reinforcers and praise were administered. Loudness level was monitored by the use of a voice-activated relay. If the relay was triggered, candy and praise were delivered.

2. Entrance to the dining room was made contingent upon telling a staff member in an audible voice the answers to a set of nine questions such as the time of the day, the date, the name of the meal, and the day of the week.

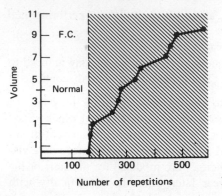

Volume

F.C.

Normal

Number of repetitions

Figure 14. Voice volume level for F. C.

3. Tokens were given contingent upon completion of assigned tasks.

4. Medication throughout all programs consisted only of anticonvulsant drugs.

Results

1. The results are graphed in Figure 14 and indicate an increase in volume level within 425 repetitions to above normal loudness.

2. Compared to a baseline average of five out of nine questions answered correctly, F. C. averaged eight answered correctly for the two weeks prior to discharge.

3. Based on records of completion of assigned tasks F. C. increased his compliance from zero to 70 percent for the two weeks prior to discharge.

Generalization. F. C. was transferred to another unit within the hospital. Follow-up 30 days after transfer indicated some drop in voice volume, although speech was still easily audible. A second follow-up 123 days later indicated that volume had remained at an easily audible level.

Although an attempt was made to program the transfer unit staff to reward F. C.'s task completion, this was not done, and F. C. was not completing any unit chores at the 123-day follow-up.

Discussion. No reversal phase was included in F. C.'s voice volume program because it was felt that reversal would take too long. The same voice volume procedure was utilized with two other patients with whom reversals were carried out. The reversal phase clearly demonstrated reinforcement control of the volume level.

It is interesting to note that these behavioral improvements were made in spite of an organic brain syndrome diagnosis, usually considered to be a poor prognostic sign. It was unfortunate that the transfer unit did not continue to reinforce F. C.'s task completion. Instead, they just let him sit, and they took care of all of his personal needs.

CASE REPORT 8

Patient. E. N., a 41-year-old, single, white male with an eighth-grade education, had been hospitalized all but three of the previous 29 years. He did not receive medication during his stay on the CRU. His psychiatric diagnosis was schizophrenia, residual type.

Problem Behaviors

1. Nonassertiveness; for example, he frequently was exploited by others. Other patients easily persuaded him to give away his money, cigarettes, and clothing. He was unable to disagree with others or to affirm his simple and clearcut rights.
2. Poor grooming; for example, unshaved, clothes dirty and unbuttoned, hair uncombed.
3. Noncompliance with work assignments.

Procedures

1. Appropriately assertive responses to persons in unambiguous situations involving patient rights were prompted and rewarded with praise, a pat on the back, and with natural consequences. Confederates of the staff provided stimuli for self-assertion in four separate situations comprising a multiple-baseline design.

(a) In the hospital canteen E. N. was ignored by a waitress after he placed his order. As the waitress stood idly nearby, E. N. was prompted after a 10-day baseline by a student volunteer to politely repeat his request. The prompt was gradually faded in explicitness and the therapist eventually was also faded from E. N.'s presence in the coffee shop. In order to maintain realism in the setting, E. N. was ignored on less than 25 percent of his requests, on a variable ratio schedule.

(b) In the same setting, E. N. would occasionally be given cold rather than hot coffee. If he did not request hot coffee, he was prompted after a 40-day baseline to do so by the therapist who also praised him for doing so. As above, cold coffee was served less than 25 percent of the time on a variable ratio schedule.

(c) Fellow CRU patients were enlisted to "bum" cigarettes while E. N.'s response was discreetly observed. He was not trained to refuse to give away cigarettes, but data were taken as a generalization measure.

(d) E. N. was cheated at cards by the student volunteer in such a manner that he could readily discriminate the wrongful play. This also was a generalization measure.

2 and 3. Tokens were delivered contingently upon the completion of grooming tasks and assigned unit chores.

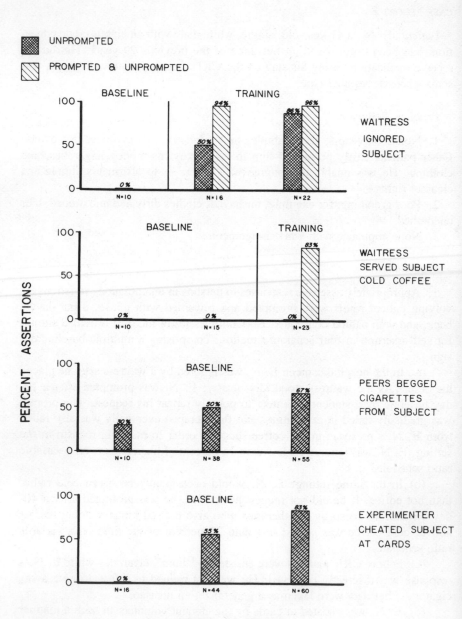

Figure 15. Percentage of assertive responses for all categories with training sequentially applied to the first two.

Results

1. (a) As noted in Figure 15, no assertive responses were emitted during the 10-day trial baseline. Prompting and praise for assertiveness were then initiated and E. N. asserted himself on 38 of the next 40 trials. The 95 percent rate was maintained for an additional 20 trials while prompts and therapist presence were faded.

(b) E. N. did not ask for warm coffee on even one occasion during the 49 baseline trials. Training was given for 23 trials, 19 of which resulted in a request for a cup of hot coffee. However, prompting was necessary throughout. Thus the 83 percent rate reflects only his response to the therapist's prompting, not to the stimulus situation.

(c) and (d) The graph indicates that refusals to give away cigarettes and requests to change the falsified results of the card game increased concurrently with the training given for the other situations. This is more striking when it is noted that no prompting occurred.

2 and 3. Upon admission to the CRU. no grooming behaviors were emitted. With prompting and token rewards, 80 percent of grooming tasks were completed during the last two weeks prior to discharge. No change in room-cleaning tasks resulted from the token program. However, E. N. became a reliable messenger for the CRU.

Generalization. To test generalization of assertive responses, two trials of "poor service" and one of "cold coffee" were arranged in a coffee shop outside the hospital. Although it resembled the hospital coffee shop, the waiter was rather busy and E. N. did not assert himself when ignored. When prompted by a therapist other than the student volunteer, he asked for hot coffee. Later, he asserted himself with still a different therapist when cheated at cards.

To capitalize on these gains, E. N. was discharged to a large, institution-like board-and-care home. "Employment" as a messenger was arranged and constituted a more demanding job due to the size of the new facility. Thus the stimulus conditions were similar to the state hospital and the possibility of generalization increased. At a nine-month follow-up, he was reported to be doing very well with his job, was using public transportation to visit his mother on weekends, and was not being exploited by other residents.

Discussion. The increase in assertiveness in situations similar to those in which training occurred indicates that generalization did occur. Nonassertiveness in patients suffering from a social breakdown syndrome makes them vulnerable to others who would exploit them and thus in need of the protection of the institution. Modeling, prompting, and positive reinforcement for appropriate assertiveness can be provided by nursing staff to enable the patient to solve a wide variety of problems.

CASE REPORT 9

Patient. J. I. is a 30-year-old white male who left high school at the age of 16 to be hospitalized. Fourteen years of institutionalization have caused J. I. to become extremely regressed, although it is noted that J. I. initially held patient jobs as a street curb painter and later as a dishwasher. When J. I. came to the CRU his behavior was extremely bizarre. His diagnosis was chronic, undifferentiated schizophrenia.

Problems

1. Bizarre motor behavior, motor self-stimulation (rubbing body, pulling pants and shirt up and down, flailing arms, and pointing into space).

2. Refusal to talk.

3. Inadequate grooming (failure to wear shoes and socks, button trousers and shirt, and comb hair).

4. Eating too fast (e.g., swallowed a banana, peel and all, without chewing).

5. Scavenging for cigarette butts.

Procedures

1. A study was performed to assess the effects of fluphenazine on J. I.'s (a) percentage of motor self-stimulation and verbal self-stimulation, which were time-sampled 18 times per day, and (b) frequency of eye contact, which was measured six times a day in 10-minute sessions. Eye contact responses were being reinforced and had assumed a stable FR1 rate when the study was begun. An ABA experimental design was used.

2. Since the study produced marked increase in verbal output, a shaping procedure was used to increase rational verbal output and extinguish verbal self-stimulation. Initially, J. I. was prompted to ask for reinforcers. When the prompt was faded, requests remained high due to the reinforcement. Next tokens were substituted for primary reinforcers. He is currently in a phase where responses are being shaped from requests to statements about his environment, which then earn reinforcers.

3. The token economy is being used to modify grooming. Tokens paid for grooming may be exchanged for tangible reinforcers.

4. Eating too fast was handled by making the second portion of his meal contingent on slowly eating the first. Once he was eating slowly, a second phase was added in which J. I. was required to use a certain amount of time to finish eating.

5. No program was developed for scavenging.

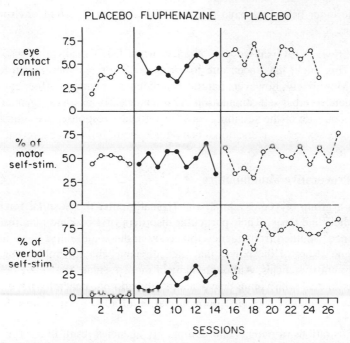

Figure 16. Rate of eye contact and percentage of motor and verbal self-stimulation per session. (From R. P. Liberman, J. Davis, W. Moon, and J. Moore. Research design for analyzing drug-environment behavior interactions. *Journal of Nervous and Mental Disease,* **156:**432-439, 1973. Copyright (1973) by the Williams & Wilkins Co. Reproduced by permission.)

Results

1. The effects of fluphenazine are illustrated in Figure 16. The drug facilitated eye contact, had no effect on motor self-stimulation, and markedly increased the verbal self-stimulation. No reversal was achieved.

2. Rational speech greatly improved due to the shaping program instituted when the study was finished. However, there are only anecdotal data for this.

3. In grooming, J. I. went from a zero baseline of wearing shoes and socks to continual shoe-wearing when paid tokens. Buttoning of trousers and shirt has also improved.

4. Eating has slowed considerably.

5. Scavenging has nearly ceased as a result of earning tokens that may be exchanged for cigarettes.

Generalization. Eye contact is greatly improved outside of the session format. The other behaviors have not been tested under different environmental conditions.

Discussion. A reversal was not obtained when J. I.'s medication was discontinued. This might have been due to traces of the drug remaining in his body tissues. More likely, however, natural contingencies began to affect eye contact and influence verbal self-stimulation. Eye contact, for example, generalized to situations outside of the session. These eye contact responses were usually the initial responses in a conversational behavioral chain, followed by verbal output.

Young Provocative Manipulators

There is a group of young adults who typically enter the hospital for the first time in their late teens. Their particular disorders first become manifest during adolescence. Shuttled from agency to agency in the community, these individuals become aware of the power that their deviant behavior holds over parents and community agencies. Although many of these agencies may have behavioral programs to deal with young provocateurs, they do not generally have the total control of the individual's environment that is afforded by state hospital facilities.

The frustrations of parents and community agencies result in a large number of referrals to the controlled environment of the state hospital. To avoid producing "chronic" patients, many of these young manipulators are referred to the CRU where total environmental structure is arranged to gain control of target behaviors. If this control can be established, the contingencies are rearranged to approximate more closely the natural environmental contingencies. The hospital environment will never match the "outside" environment of the community and, for this reason, generalization of treatment from controlled settings to natural settings represents a major area for research.

CASE REPORT 1

Patient. A. N. was a 20-year-old, white, single male with a high school education and no work history when he came to the CRU. He had been hospitalized at Camarillo State Hospital and at a local community mental health center four times before his admission to the CRU. His current admission was a result of being apprehended for breaking and entering a department store. A. N. was to remain in the hospital until he was "competent" to face court charges. His diagnosis was chronic, undifferentiated schizophrenia.

Problem Behaviors

1. Manipulation of staff, behaviorally manifested in continual pestering, asking questions, demanding privileges, and complaining about programs.

2. Manipulation of other patients, manifested by encouraging them not to comply with staff requests and by providing them with rewards outside of their programs.

Procedures

1. Assertive training. To modify the patient's manipulations of staff, a two-phase program was put into effect. First, A. N. was allowed two 20-minute conversations per day during which he could discuss any subject he wished. For each instance of pestering a staff member, one minute was deducted from the conversation time. Second, A. N. was given individual assertive training sessions utilizing a hierarchy of scenes related to requesting responses from the staff.

2. Contingency contract. Although this program had some effect, the reduction in manipulativeness was short-lived and a difficulty in generalizing appropriate responses from the assertive training sessions to the actual unit situation was noted. Consequently, a modified contingency contract was implemented which offered A. N., in exchange for certain appropriate behaviors, one of three possible recommendations to the court. The possible recommendations varied according to the amount of restraint and control in the posthospital environment, ranging from freedom in the community to referral to a maximum security institution. The final recommendation was contingent on A. N.'s performance on the CRU, including his verbal interaction with staff and patients, helpfulness to staff, argumentativeness, and work. His behavior was rated daily by each shift. If at the end of the specified period of 28 days A. N. had maintained consistently appropriate behavior, he would earn a recommendation for vocational rehabilitation in the community. This required an average daily earning of at least 98 points of a possible 115. A. N. monitored his own performance by daily charting. A. N.'s medication was held constant throughout his stay on the CRU.

Results. A. N. maintained nearly perfect behavior for three weeks while awaiting return to court. Social attention from staff and token earnings for industrious and responsible work behaviors on the unit provided A. N. with a high degree of reinforcement from more natural contingencies operating on a day-to-day basis.

Generalization. A. N. was referred to court with the following recommendations for generalization of improvement:

1. Vocational training, which would have to begin with simple work behaviors and build from there—a work experience focusing on basic, routine tasks. No attention should be paid to his requests for more advanced training until he demonstrates an ability to complete the basics, including being on time, behaving appropriately, and working steadily.

2. Living arrangements should include a curfew, visitation with parents, and maintenance of living quarters. Rules must be clearly and specifically worded. Provision should be made for rewarding appropriate behavior with recognition, attention, or privileges.

Discussion. The staff of the CRU had a powerful lever to use in motivating A. N.'s behavior. The contract had a real threat of punishment (jail) built into it. Other patients like A. N. who are not court referrals are often more difficult to manage because there is not an effective punisher to be coupled with positive reinforcement.

CASE REPORT 2

Patient. W. N. was a 20-year-old, white, single male with a high school education. He had held a variety of odd jobs in the community. His boisterous nature, coupled with physical aggression, resulted in his hospitalization. He had been diagnosed as latent schizophrenic.

Problem Behaviors

1. Verbal aggression (loud yelling, name-calling, arguing).
2. Physical aggression (shoving people).

Procedures

1 and 2. A contingency contract was established to deal with W. N.'s aggressive behavior. W. N. was given certain privileges in return for certain responsibilities. Among his privileges was his right to have therapy sessions, which will be described below. In return, W. N. had to refrain from yelling, name-calling, arguing, pushing, or striking another person. If he failed to comply with the terms of his contract, it would be terminated and he would be immediately discharged to his own care. This was aversive since he had no financial resources or shelter.

Assertive training sessions were conducted with W. N., the staff, and other patients participating. In these sessions incidents of W. N.'s aggressiveness which had recently taken place on the unit were reenacted. Staff participants modeled more appropriate responses and W. N. was prompted to imitate the model. W. N. then practiced the assertive (versus aggressive) response and was given positive verbal feedback. Three *in vivo* practice sessions with young female student volunteers were used both to assess progress and to provide W. N. with opportunities for success in relating to girls.

The General Relationship Improvement Program was administered by nursing personnel. It consists of a 10-lesson, dyadic, programmed learning approach to improvement of an individual's verbal and social skills. Systematic desensitization sessions were carried out with two hierarchies on rejection and criticism.

Five sessions were devoted to relaxation training followed by 10 sessions of desensitization.

Results. Aggressive behavior on the CRU totally disappeared and W. N. negotiated a contract which resulted in his discharge to independent living in the community. The contract provided supportive services of community agencies contingent upon appropriately assertive behavior being maintained by W. N.

Generalization. It was recommended to the aftercare facility that the contingencies of W. N.'s contract should be reviewed regularly and revised to maintain behavioral improvements. Continued direction into realistic vocational and educational endeavors will increase the probability that naturally occurring reinforcers would maintain W. N.'s progress.

Booster sessions of assertive training and systematic desensitization were also recommended. They were built into the contingency contract as rewards for adaptive behavior. These instructions were not systematically carried out, and W. N. was readmitted to Camarillo State Hospital one year later.

Discussion. W. N. spent only 35 days on the CRU and represents a good example of the type of clinical treatment that a controlled unit can provide. W. N. needed an environment in which he could not escape the contingencies of reinforcement. By providing this type of environment a minimal level of appropriate responding could be shaped, thus enabling the patient to reenter the community where more natural reinforcers could be experienced. The importance of programming the aftercare environment to insure generalization is clear in this case. Simply instructing the aftercare staff in the use of contingencies is not sufficient; indeed, intensive training and systematic monitoring of progress appears to be necessary for generalization to occur.

CASE REPORT 3

Patient. J. P. is a 20-year-old, white male who completed high school. J. P. had no work experience prior to his residence on the CRU. J. P. had no previous hospitalization, although he attended a community mental health outpatient facility and a sheltered workshop before coming to the CRU. His diagnosis was schizophrenia, hebephrenic type.

Problem Behaviors

1. Social withdrawal.
2. Bizarre, hypochondriacal, and grandiose speech content with a high rate of talking about being sick and pursuing an acting career.

Procedures

1. Medication (Stelazine). An experimental analysis of drug effects on social

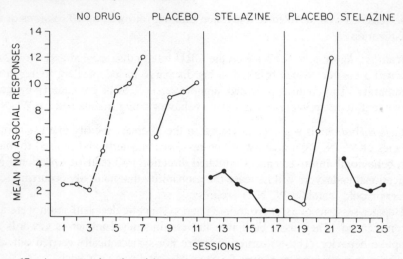

Figure 17. Average number of asocial responses per day. (From R. P. Liberman, J. Davis, and W. Moon. Research design for analyzing drug-environment-behavior interactions. *Journal of Nervous and Mental Disease,* **156:**432-439, 1973. Copyright (1973) by the Williams & Wilkins Co. Reproduced by permission.)

withdrawal and verbal content was undertaken. An AA₁ BA₁B within-subject design was used (A = no drug, A₁ = placebo, B = Stelazine, 60 milligrams daily oral dosage).

Throughout all phases, the daily mean of asocial responses was recorded as a function of drug state. Asocial responses were defined as failure to respond verbally when a staff member initiates a conversation.

2. Bizarre speech was experimentally analyzed in a context that approximates the format of traditional psychotherapy. J. P. has two sessions per day of 15 minutes each. J. P. sits with a nondirective therapist who provides very little verbal feedback to J. P. Feedback is provided by means of two lights operated by the therapist. A red light indicates inappropriate content, a white light indicates acceptable verbal content. The traditional nondirective format is thus simulated by using signals as feedback. A multiple baseline design was used to test the effects of feedback on two bizarre content areas. Bizarre content was time sampled by randomly selecting 25 segments of 15 seconds each from the 15-minute conversation.

Results

1. Stelazine had a marked effect on the frequency of asocial responses as illustrated in Figure 17. It did not, however, affect the content of J. P.'s verbal behavior.

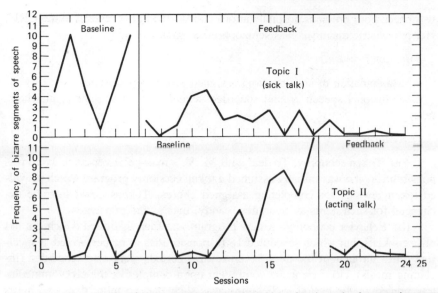

Figure 18. Number of segments with bizarre speech per interview in each of two topic areas, feedback applied sequentially to both topics.

2. Feedback proved to be an effective means of modifying bizarre speech. Feedback reduced both of the bizarre themes to zero. These data are illustrated in Figure 18.

Generalization. Follow-up measurement of asocial responding shows that this behavior is now completely absent. Stelazine has been administered continuously since termination of the experiment.

Negative feedback produced no generalization to situations outside of his 15-minute sessions. From the beginning of the experiment there was no correlation between verbal content in the sessions and verbal content outside of the sessions.

Discussion. It is interesting to note how powerful the medication was in reducing J. P.'s frequency of asocial response, yet weak in its effect on verbal content. Feedback, on the other hand, had a marked effect on specific content areas. The interaction of drug effects with behavioral program effects is an unexplored area which presents itself for further research.

CASE REPORT 4

Patient. M. V. was a 22-year-old, white, single female with a high school education. She had one two-week job experience as a waitress from which she was fired. Four previous hospitalizations culminated in her referral to the CRU. Her psychiatric diagnosis was schizophrenia, paranoid type.

Behavior Problems

1. Manipulation of staff to avoid assigned unit responsibilities.
2. Delusional speech around specified sexual topics (pregnancy, marriage, rape).

Procedures

1. (a) Token economy. To deal with M. V.'s manipulativeness to avoid responsibilities, she was initially assigned a token economy program which provided token rewards for completing assigned chores. Tokens could later be exchanged for such items as cigarettes, candy, meals, and privileges.

(b) Behavior economy. A new program was then instituted which did not utilize tokens, but which scheduled 18 responsibilities to be performed at specified times throughout the day. Seven reward periods were also scheduled (including meals) and were made contingent upon completing the tasks immediately preceding the period. Scheduling was such that no more than two hours elapsed between the end of one reward period and the beginning of another, and no more than four tasks were required to earn a reward. In addition, specified cigarette rewards were given immediately after completing most tasks. Completion or noncompletion of a task was indicated on a 5 × 8 inch "report card" which also summarized her program. Thus, compared to the usual token economy program, the "behavior" economy provided greater specificity, more frequent primary rewards, and simplified, more reliable data-keeping.

2. (a) Time-out for delusional verbalizations. M. V. was interviewed six times a day for five minutes, and the time to onset of the first delusional statement was noted. A "time-out" contingency was to have been utilized. M. V. was withdrawn from the program before the contingency could be applied.

(b) To test the effect of phenothiazines (Stelazine, 60 milligrams daily) she was tested in 54 sessions with medication and 54 sessions without medication. Otherwise, her medication was held constant.

Results

1. (a) Her initial response to the token economy was good, with an average daily token earning of 28 for the period of July 17 to July 28. However, after being AWOL between July 29 and August 3, and after being withdrawn from antipsychotic medication to study its effects on her delusions, M. V.'s token earnings dropped to nine per day between August 4 and August 17.

(b) Utilizing the behavior economy, her work behavior improved to a 71 percent completion rate even though she remained off medication.

2. (a) An instructional phase in the "time-out" contingency was instituted

before M. V. left. Essentially, this was a "threat" period, where she was told of the contingency but was not subject to it. This had no effect on her frequency of delusional reference.

(b) Antipsychotic phenothiazine medication did have an effect on delusions. Time to onset of delusional verbalizations (duration of rational speech) was 32 percent less during sessions when M. V. was not receiving phenothiazines.

Generalization

1. It would seem important that any program with M. V. include the essential elements of the "behavior" economy, a maximum of specificity, structure, and immediacy of rewards. In addition, M. V.'s attempts to manipulate can be greatly reduced by assigning only a limited number of people to have control over her reinforcements.

2. Modification of her delusional speech is also important. Several interventions can be tried: (a) a time-out procedure contingent upon delusional talk has been successful with other patients' (b) a shaping procedure could be utilized in which M. V. would be rewarded socially and with tangible reinforcers for increasingly longer periods of being delusion free; and (c) significant others should ignore her "crazy talk."

It may be necessary to initiate and demonstrate the effectiveness of these interventions in a clinical setting followed by a program to achieve generalization of treatment to a more open setting.

Discussion. M. V. is an interesting case in that she illustrates how a token economy system may not work for certain people. The structure of token systems allows for certain degrees of manipulation. Just as some individuals outside of the hospital find "loopholes" in our legal and tax systems, an intelligent schizophrenic will find "loopholes" in the token economy.

The "behavior economy" was more like a contingency contract because it specified what M. V. had to do to earn certain reinforcers. It was a programmed economy because it was sequential and scheduled according to set times. This system provided fewer "loopholes." Since the system dealt more with unit responsibilities and tasks, it was called a behavior economy instead of a contingency contract.

Destructiveness

Destructiveness, whether to self or to others, is a problem of potentially major proportions because of the harm that can be inflicted by behaviors such as kicking, hitting, biting, scratching, and throwing objects. Following are seven case studies describing the use of several techniques to control assaultiveness directed both toward others (six cases) and toward self (one case).

Four of these cases illustrate the use of a procedure we have labeled "response-prevention." It must be noted that this is not response prevention in the usual sense; that is, it does not prevent an avoidance response from an anxiety-provoking stimulus as in the behavioral treatment of phobias or compulsions.

This response prevention procedure places the patient in a time-out area for a fixed interval of time and allows increasing periods of time on the unit contingent upon previous periods of nonassaultive behavior. For example, a patient may spend one-hour intervals in a time-out area interspersed with periods of on-unit time that each increase by five minutes as long as there has been no assaultive behavior during the preceding on-unit period. Any assaultiveness, including resistance to returning to the time-out area, results in recycling the patient to the minimum amount of on-unit time.

Of the four cases in which the procedure was utilized, two were successful and two were unsuccessful. The successful patients seemed to enjoy interpersonal social contact, whereas the unsuccessful patients rarely interacted with staff or fellow patients. In addition, the unsuccessful patients seemed to have more incidents when they were told to return to the time-out area than they had without the response prevention procedures, and a more traditional approach of time-out for assaultiveness was utilized.

CASE REPORT 1

The self-abusive patient exemplified the occasional conflict between clinical and research demands. Clinically, it was felt essential to protect the patient from the harm that she was inflicting upon herself. Interventions were changed if they did not immediately suppress self-abusive behavior even though they may have proven effective in the long run. Although the series of interventions did result in a cessation of self-abusive behavior, generalization was difficult since no particular intervention could be specified as having been effective and programming of the new environment was thus not possible.

Patient. S. G. was a 16-year-old, Caucasian female who had been hospitalized for most of her life. She was severely retarded with no intelligible speech and unable to care for her own needs. Her diagnosis was schizophrenia, childhood (autistic) type.

Problem Behaviors

1. Self-abusive behaviors including (a) hitting self on body or head, (b) rubbing ears until raw or bleeding, (c) scratching self.
2. Screaming.
3. Incontinence.
4. Lack of expressive speech.

Procedures

1. Painful but harmless electric shock was applied to he arm contingent upon self-abuse. A multiple-baseline design was used in which the shock was administered successively in response to scratching, then scratching and hitting, and finally all self-abuse.

A second procedure was utilized in which staff were instructed to turn their backs and walk away from S. G. when she engaged in self-abuse.

Removal of attention by placing S. G. in an empty, "quiet room" was then made contingent upon self-abuse. In this manner, S. G. could no longer be viewed by staff *or fellow patients*, except through a small one-way viewer in the door for safety purposes. Initially, S. G. was placed in the "quiet room" for two hours after each incident of self-abuse. She then came out on the ward for five minutes. Each successive period out of the "quiet room' was increased by five minutes if she was not self-abusive. Time allowed on the ward recycled to five minutes when an incident of self-abuse occurred. After 11 days, S. G. was allowed to remain on the unit and was placed in the "quiet room" for 15 minutes contingent upon any incident of self-abusive behavior. This was changed after six days to two hours in the "quiet room" for self-abusive behavior.

2. A recording was made of screams which was then played back to S. G. for 30 minutes, three times per day. This was intended to make screaming aversive to her. After six days this was discontinued.

Quinine, an extremely bitter substance, was given orally contingent upon screaming. This phase continued for 20 days.

Screams were subsequently ignored by staff (although recorded on a counter in the nurses station) until her transfer to another unit.

3. Token reinforcement was given when S. G. eliminated in the toilet after being taken to the bathroom and prompted to sit on the toilet. This prompting was reduced from seven times per day to six, she was charged a token for soiling or wetting, and she was required to clean any mess she made.

4. Sign language was taught by a college student who devised hand signs for expressions commonly used in the unit environment such as, "I want to eat," "I want a drink," or "I want to listen to music." The sign was modeled and S. G. was physically prompted to make the sign. Small pieces of food or candy were given for successively better approximations to the sign.

5. No medication was given during any program.

Results

1. Figure 19 shows the number of daily incidents of various forms of self-abuse. Shock did not reduce or eliminate self-abuse, with the possible exception of scratching. The decision to change procedures before reduction of one type

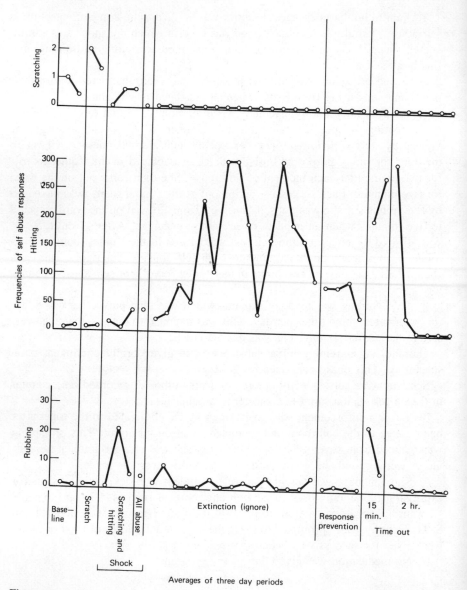

Figure 19. Daily frequency of self-abusive behaviors.

of self-abuse occurred was made clinically rather than experimentally. Hitting and rubbing increased to daily averages of 38.4 hits and 4.3 rubbing incidents when shock was contingent upon all three forms of self-abuse.

When all self-abuse was ignored, self-hitting increased to 154.6 hits per day and ear-rubbing occurred at 1.39 ear-rubs per day.

The response to time-out from reinforcement varied depending upon the ratio of the duration of time in or out of the Quiet Room. During the 11-day phase of two hours in the Quiet Room and five-minute intervals on the unit, hitting averaged 75 per day with one ear-rub during the procedure. When this was changed to 15 minutes in the Quiet Room, hitting increased to an average of 325 per day with 11 ear-rubs per day. When the Quiet Room time was changed to two hours, this initially increased to a 1-day peak of 884 with reduction to zero within 7 days and a continuation of a zero level for 20 days.

2. Listening to a tape of screaming voices and the contingent oral administration of quinine had no demonstrable effects on the frequency of screaming. Ignoring the screaming resulted in extinction of the behavior coincidental with the elimination of self-abuse.

3. Although S. G. had progressively fewer days with soiling or wetting, she did not become completely continent.

4. S. G. learned eight different signs which generalized to staff members other than the student who taught the sign language. She was able to make requests for food and other basic requirements.

Generalization. S. G. was transferred to her original referral unit. An attempt was made to program the use of time-out as possibly the most effective way to continue the improvement made on the CRU. Unfortunately, a one-month follow-up indicated a relapse to pretreatment frequency of self-abuse.

Discussion. The data do not clearly indicate the reason(s) for improvement, which could be attributed to any one of several factors: (a) time-out from reinforcements; (b) social reinforcement for adaptive behavior incompatible with self-destructiveness in a one-to-one relationship with her student therapist; (c) clear and consistent contingencies placed upon behavior by *all* staff; or (d) cyclical decrease of self-destructive behavior may have run its course 90 days after admission with a cyclical peak 75 to 80 days after admission.

It is interesting to note the ineffectiveness of contingent shock. Administration of the shock was quite difficult, requiring that S. G. be chased and held down and the shock be administered. This may have inadvertently reinforced the self-abuse. The time interval between self-abuse and shock was also variable, depending on the amount of chasing necessary to administer the shock. Finally, shock had been administered numerous times in the past and adaptation may have taken place.

CASE REPORT 2

Patient. R. N. was a 20-year-old, single, Caucasian female who had been hospitalized for the past 15 years. She was severely retarded with a diagnosis of schizophrenia, childhood (autistic) type.

Problem Behaviors

1. Assaultive behavior such as pulling hair, biting, and kicking.
2. Yelling, banging doors, and gagging after medication.
3. Lack of self-care and grooming skills.

Procedures

1. Each instance of assaultive behavior was punished by application to the forearm of painful but harmless electric shock.
2. Each instance of yelling, banging doors, or gagging resulted in placement in a time-out area for a minimum of 15 minutes and until all tantrum behavior (banging door, yelling) ceased for one minute. Each instance of behaviors 1 and 2 was noted when it occurred.
3. Grooming and self-care were contingently rewarded with tokens within the framework of the CRU's token economy.
4. The only medication administered during treatment was a minimal dose of anticonvulsant medication.

Results

1. Assaultive behavior decreased from an average of 0.9 incidents per day for a 10-day baseline to 2 incidents in the 30 days prior to discharge.
2. Gagging, yelling, and banging doors decreased from 1.5 incidents per day during the 10-day baseline to no incidents during the 30 days prior to discharge.
3. Based on records of completion of grooming and self-help tasks, these behaviors did not increase.

Generalization. R. N. was transferred to her original referral unit with the following recommendations for generalization of treatment: (a) isolate her in a nonreinforcing area for aggressive acts; (b) ignore loudness, banging, and gagging; (c) reinforce greetings, congeniality, and other appropriate behaviors with attention, food, or brief chats and stroking. R. N.'s improvement did generalize to her home unit where appropriate behavior was reinforced. When transferred to yet another unit, however, her behavior deteriorated to its previous level. The CRU has readmitted R. N. for retraining.

Discussion. It is unfortunate that the behavior change did not persist when R. N. was transferred to the new unit from the referral unit. No contact was initiated between the new unit and the CRU until the new unit could not control her increase in assaultiveness. The "tone" of the contact indicated that the new unit wanted nothing to do with R. N. because she was well known throughout the entire hospital for her assaultive behavior. Unfortunately, much as a self-fulfilling prophecy, her assaultiveness was expected, appropriate behavior was not reinforced, and assaultiveness occurred.

CASE REPORT 3

Patient. K. B. was a 19-year-old, Caucasian male who had been hospitalized for the last six years. He had lived with his elderly grandfather until his hospitalization. His grandfather did not discipline K. B., and K. B. became a management problem in the schools and in the neighborhood. His psychiatric diagnosis was schizophrenia, catatonic (excited) type.

Problem Behaviors

1. Attempting to leave the hospital without permission (AWOL). These attempts included kicking down doors, rushing past staff members out-of-doors, breaking windows, and pacing the halls awaiting an opportunity to leave.

2. Verbal threats of physical harm directed to both staff and patients.

3. Poor grooming including hair not combed, teeth not brushed, clothes disheveled, shoes not worn.

4. Delusional speech.

Procedures

1. and 2. To reduce both K. B.'s AWOL attempts and verbal threats, K. B. was placed on the response-prevention program. This was not successful, and a completely different program (ignore) was then initiated. It was reasoned that K. B.'s AWOL's were maintained by the attention he received when he was caught and returned to the hospital; by the primary reinforcers (food and cigarettes) he received from the relatives he visited; and from the community agencies who caught him. Hence, after contacting various community agencies and instructing them not to respond to K. B., K. B. was given ground privileges and, in effect, allowed to go AWOL as often as he wanted.

3 and 4. No programs were initiated to modify K. B.'s poor grooming and delusional speech.

Results. Medication was kept as constant as possible during K. B.'s stay on the unit. In view of his AWOL's, this was unfortunately rather variable.

Based on the number of assaultive, threatening, or AWOL incidents per day, K. B. was unable to remain free of such incidents for more than two days under the response-prevention program. Under the extinction program K. B. stayed on the hospital grounds for three days before he finally went AWOL. Three AWOL's later the courts, police and jail could no longer tolerate K. B.'s presence in the community. A transfer to an institution with greater security was then arranged by his guardian.

Generalization. No data regarding K. B.'s behavior in the maximum security institution are available.

Discussion. Although an attempt was made to program the community's response to K. B.'s AWOL's, it was not entirely successful. The police repeatedly apprehended him and gave him shelter, a meal, and cigarettes. Hence it was not possible to effectively test an extinction program.

CASE REPORT 4

Patient. S. K. was a 32-year-old, divorced Caucasian female whose first hospitalization had occurred 18 months before her admission to the CRU. She had graduated from a local junior college and had worked as an X-ray technician prior to her hospitalization. Her psychiatric diagnosis was schizophrenia, schizoaffective type.

Problem Behaviors

1. Running through the unit.
2. Throwing water and objects; flooding rooms.
3. Disrobing in public.
4. Screaming and yelling.
5. Banging on windows and doors.

Procedures. A number of programs were instituted which varied the amount and schedule of reinforcement for appropriate behaviors, the amount of ataraxic medication, and punishment for problem behaviors as follows:

Step 1. S. K. was brought to the CRU during the daytime hours and returned to her home unit at night. A DRO program was used with one token given on an FI 15-minute schedule. This was coupled with time-out from reinforcement (one hour) for emission of problem behaviors.

Step 2. The patient was admitted to the CRU and placed routinely on the token economy. The DRO program was changed to a schedule of FI 30 minutes for two tokens, coupled with time-out for 30 minutes upon emission of problem behaviors.

Step 3. S. K.'s antipsychotic medication was discontinued and the DRO schedule was changed to FI 30 minutes for one token. Time-out for problem behaviors was continued.

Step 4. DRO changed to FI 60 minutes for two tokens.

Step 5. The patient's tokens were now given noncontingently at the beginning of the day.

Results

Step 1. The patient made a sharp discrimination between environments. She was well controlled on the CRU yet continued to be disruptive on her home unit.

Step 2. This program reduced the problem behavior to less than one per day.

Step 3. The frequency of occurrence of the problem behaviors initially rose to an average of nine per day upon discontinuance of medication but fell to an average of less than one per day.

Steps 4 and 5. The problem behaviors were not occurring at this point. The total time for all programs was eight weeks.

Generalization. S. K. was released to her own care. A three-month follow-up indicated no recurrence of the problem behaviors.

Discussion. Although it is difficult to determine whether drugs or contingencies were effective since the reversal of both did not affect the rates of emission of the problem behavior, it can be assumed that all aspects of treatment added to the clinical success achieved.

A multiple-baseline design could have rooted out the cogent factors, yet the urgency of the case prompted the staff toward proven methods of behavior modification. When a reversal was attempted, the patient's behavior did not show a decrement. Perhaps by that time her prosocial behaviors had come under the control of natural consequences.

CASE REPORT 5

Patient. T. H. was a 20-year-old, single, Caucasian male who had been hospitalized for the past two years. He was a loner and, during his hospitalization, he had been involved in a number of assaultive incidents. His psychiatric diagnosis was schizophrenia, chronic undifferentiated type.

Problem Behaviors

1. Physical assaultiveness (hitting) directed primarily to female staff members and both male and female patients.

2. Threats of physical assault including gestures and verbal comments.

3. Refusal to perform chores when requested to do so.

4. Delusional speech.

Procedures

1 and 2. To reduce the instances of both threats and actual assaultiveness and to provide immediate protection for patients and personnel, T. H. was placed on the response-prevention program. No effect on T. H.'s assaultiveness was noted.

A new program was then initiated which combined positive reward for appropriate behavior and time-out for assaultiveness. Cigarettes were given contingent on T. H.'s maintaining assaultive-free behavior for specified time periods, while assaultiveness resulted in removal from social stimuli for 15 minutes. The specified time periods for reward, initially fixed at 15 minutes, were systematically changed so that reinforcement was eventually delivered on a variable interval 50-minute schedule.

3. To increase performance of requested unit chores, T. H. was offered half a cigarette in exchange for such tasks as sweeping, mopping, dusting, and cleaning tables.

4. No program was instituted to modify T. H.'s delusional speech.

Results

1 and 2. Instances of both threats and actual assaultiveness were reduced by 90 percent from an average of three incidents per day to an average of one incident every 3 days for the 12 days prior to discharge. Medication was kept constant throughout all phases.

3. T. H.'s compliance with work requests increased from complete refusal initially to 95 percent acceptance.

Generalization. T. H. was transferred back to the unit from which he was originally referred. To aid generalization of behavior change to the home unit, a program was implemented which systematically varied the amount of time T. H. spent on his home unit (from one-half to three hours at a time), the amount of supervision by the CRU staff (from continuous during stay on home unit to not at all), and the chores to be performed on the home unit. The reward contingencies were the same as those on the CRU and no assaultive incidents were noted on the home unit and all chores were successfully completed.

In addition, an attempt was made to utilize only those rewards that could be successfully implemented on his home unit. Thus T. H. was not made part of the token economy system since his home unit did not utilize such a system, and he was not discharged until the reinforcement schedule was shaped to a VI schedule with a rather lengthy average interval.

Anecdotal evidence from the home unit indicates that assaultiveness has returned to a level equal to his pretreatment level.

Discussion. In spite of an attempt to aid generalization of behavior change from the CRU to the home unit, T. H.'s behavior change was relatively short-lived. Unfortunately, it was not possible to program the responses of other patients to T. H.'s threats. Observations by home unit staff indicated that T. H. is easily able to "buffalo" other patients into giving him cigarettes, and the home unit has no consistent procedure to give T. H. cigarettes for appropriate behavior such as unit chores.

CASE REPORT 6

Patient. V. X. was a 28-year-old, single, Caucasian female who had been intermittently hospitalized for the past seven years. She had worked as a secretary prior to her first hospitalization at age 21, and she had graduated from high school and completed several college courses. Her psychiatric diagnosis was schizophrenia, schizoaffective type.

Problem Behaviors

1. Negative self-references including statements such as "I'm dead," "There is no hope," "I'm no good."
2. Assaultive behavior (hitting, kicking, hair-pulling) directed to both staff and patients.

Procedures

1. To modify negative self-references, a massed practice procedure was utilized in which V. X. was interviewed for five minutes, 13 times per day. During each interview, V. X. was told a negative statement about herself. If she responded with her own negative self-reference, she was asked to repeat the reference as many times as she was willing. If she did not respond with a negative self-reference within 15 seconds, another negative statement was presented until the end of the five-minute interview.
2. To modify assaultiveness, a program of time-out for such behavior was at first instituted. This proved ineffective and the response-prevention program was then utilized.

Results

1. Based on the daily percentage of conversation time before V. X. made a negative self-reference, the average percentage was 42.27 for 18 days of baseline. Treatment was initiated for 10 days with a reduction in conversation time before a negative self-reference to 28.30 percent. The procedure was discontinued, and for 33 days there was an increase to 86.12 percent with no negative self-references during the last 9 days before transfer.
2. Figure 20 graphically depicts the results of the response prevention procedure. Points *A, B,* and *C* indicate changes in the amount of on-unit time per interval. Assaultiveness gradually increased before the response-prevention procedure to an average of four incidents per day for the 5 days immediately preceding the program. This was reduced to only six incidents during the 12 days of the program, and to no incidents during the last 5 days preceding transfer to her home unit.

Generalization. After five nonassaultive days in the response-prevention procedure, V. X. was transferred to her home unit. She was discharged shortly

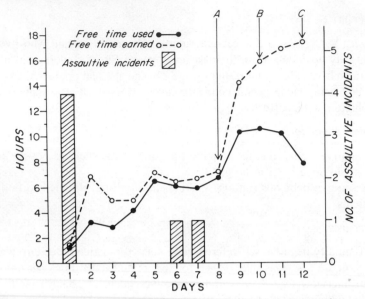

Figure 20. On unit time earned and used by V. X. during the response prevention procedures.

thereafter, and eventually attended college and secured employment as a part-time secretary. However, she decompensated and was rehospitalized nine months thereafter.

Discussion. The use of the response-prevention procedure was markedly effective and was particularly useful in view of the severe damage she could inflict (one female staff member was off for two weeks as a result of a concussion suffered when V. X. threw her to the floor and dragged her across a room).

The results of the negative practice sessions are equivocal, and the improvement during the second baseline cannot be attributed to any easily discernible cause. However, V. X.'s adjustment in the community was the most constructive behavior she had emitted in the past seven years.

CASE REPORT 7

Patient. M. L. was a 20-year-old, single, black male who had been hospitalized numerous times in the past and who had spent many years in various board-and-care homes. His only job had been in a sheltered workshop, and he had not completed his education beyond the fourth grade. His psychiatric diagnosis was schizophrenia, simple type.

Problem Behaviors

1. Temper tantrums including running up and down the halls, screaming, leaping through the air, and breaking windows.

2. No verbal expression of anger or frustration.

3. Failure to complete assigned tasks.

4. Poor grooming including shoes not on, infrequent showers, disheveled clothes.

Procedures

1. To modify the tantrum behaviors, M. L. was placed on a response-prevention program which specified that he spend a fixed amount of time in a restricted area with increasing intervals of time on the unit contingent upon previous periods of appropriate behavior. A daily record was kept of each tantrum.

This was partially effective, but it was noted that tantrums frequently seemed to result from being returned to the restricted area. Hence a new procedure was instituted which provided not only two hours of time-out for a tantrum but also provided time-out for exhibiting any pretantrum behaviors. These behaviors were reliably discriminated by staff members and included rapid pacing, speaking in a tearful voice, and clenching fists with nails dug into his forearm. M. L. was allowed to come out of time-out when he signaled that he felt better and was not going to have a tantrum. If he was still exhibiting pretantrum behavior, time-out was continued. No medication was administered during any phase of the program.

2. To increase M. L.'s verbal expressions of anger, an escape procedure was utilized in which M. L. did not have to go to the time-out area for exhibiting pretantrum behavior if he could express what was bothering him.

3 and 4. Tokens were given contingent upon proper grooming (shoes on, taking a shower) and completion of assigned tasks.

Results

1 and 2. Tantrums were reduced by approximately 75 percent in the response prevention phase from a 7-day baseline average of 2.00 incidents per day to a 44-day average of 0.50 per day with a further reduction to 0.10 incidents per day during the 51-day time-out for pretantrum and verbal expressiveness phase.

3 and 4. Based on records of completion of assigned tasks and grooming behavior, M. L. increased his completion of chores to 100 percent and earned all grooming tokens during the week before discharge.

Generalization. M. L. was transferred to the unit from which he was originally referred. To aid generalization of behavior change, a CRU nursing staff member devised and implemented a program which gradually increased the amount of time M. L. spent on his home unit, the chores he was assigned there, and gradually faded the amount of supervision by the CRU staff. The appropriate manner of eliciting verbal expressions of anger and frustration were also modeled by CRU therapists for all members on the home unit. Follow-up nine months later with the home unit staff indicated that M. L.'s tantrums had not returned and that he was functioning well enough to accept jobs that required responsibility such as running errands.

Discussion. The use of the escape contingency to increase verbal expressions of anger and frustration seemed most important as the home unit reported that M. L. continues to do this. Expressing anger is also helpful for resolving the difficulties that are the cues for anger and frustration.

Dependency, Apathy, and Noncompliance

A large group of patients in state hospitals fall into the category of dependent, apathetic, or noncompliant.

The dependent, apathetic, and noncompliant patient experiences a lack of the environmental contingencies necessary to maintain self-assertive, active accomplishments. This group is generally well groomed, not bizarre in motor and verbal behavior, not dangerous to themselves or others. They are often caught in "the revolving door syndrome" because they lack social and work skills. These patients express the desire to leave the hospital; but when released they return in weeks or months, having thoroughly frustrated the attempts of community agencies to plan for their living and work arrangements. Even welfare support is not sufficient to keep many of these people out of the hospital since they do not adjust to even a minimal demand milieu such as a board-and-care home.

Once out of the hospital, plans for employment seldom materialize, managers of residential care homes lose patience with their apathy, and frequently several "placements" are attempted in search of an environment in which the former patient can "function." The last resort is rehospitalization, but each readmission further diminishes the likelihood for community adjustment.

Some individuals in this category may be making active avoidance responses to escape the aversive or meager positive contingencies applied in the community, such as law enforcement, the rigors of independent functioning and self-support, and the demands of competitive employment. Admission to the protective environment of the institution thus reinforces escape from the demands of societal contingencies.

Whatever the motivation, once in the hospital, the topography of responses looks the same for these individuals. One identifying mark is their constricted consumption of tangible reinforcers and involvement in reinforcing activities.

This presents a problem to reinforcement therapy. Sometimes the individual's desire to get out of the hospital can be used as an incentive and tokens or points may be used to reinforce behaviors. If any reinforcers are present they are generally weak, a situation which presents a challenge to a "shaper" who must program extremely small steps in approximating a terminal response. Reinforcer sampling (or forced practice) has in a few cases resulted in an increase in valence for sampled reinforcers. One fact remains clear for this type of patient: there are fewer treatment approaches available than with other types of patient. For this reason, building reinforcers for the person who is refractory to conventional rewards and activities represents a challenging area for further research.

CASE REPORT 1

Patient. G. X., a 31-year-old, white, single male with a tenth-grade education, had a history of approximately 15 hospital admissions over a span of 12 years. His only employment consisted of door-to-door selling of photo-contracts for a period of two years. His psychiatric diagnosis was schizophrenia, chronic undifferentiated type.

Problem Behaviors. Refusal to do unit chores (apathy) and sloppy grooming.

Procedures. A contingency contract was negotiated and signed by G. X. and CRU staff. The contract required increasing completion of unit work and personal grooming assignments from G. X., in return for discharge from the CRU with help from the social worker to locate aftercare. The token economy provided the vehicle for determining the ratio of completed-to-assigned tasks. Discharge could be earned in as little as three weeks following implementation of the contract if he sustained a 100 percent completion rate.

Results. The data in Figure 21 indicate that the 100 percent rate (30 tokens earned) was reached within four weeks and was maintained for three additional weeks until discharge.

Generalization. Several alternative means of discharge were presented to G. X., with a wide range of support from the environment. Various plans included referral for board-and-care placement, Aid to the Disabled, and assistance with obtaining employment. G. X. chose a plan which included immediate discharge with the address of a potential employer and $25 in cash. Recommendations were made to the community agencies responsible for aftercare services that G. X. be involved in sheltered employment or training. G. X. did not seek employment in the community but immediately obtained Aid to the Disabled and rented a room. After six months he was readmitted to Camarillo State Hospital voluntarily with the complaint that he was "a little bit mixed up and depressed."

Discussion. Discharge was a highly reinforcing event in that it resulted in escape from an environment where basic commodities such as meals and a bed as well as luxuries such as cigarettes, colas, and off-unit time had to be earned. The patient could obtain these items without even minimal task completion in

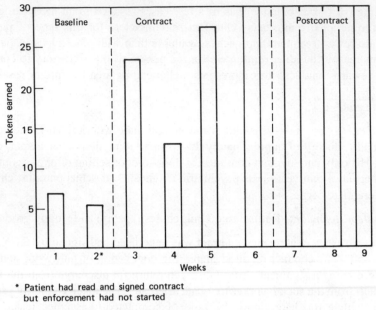

* Patient had read and signed contract
but enforcement had not started

Figure 21. Weekly token earnings.

the community, having a long history of living in residential care settings while receiving Aid to the Disabled. These necessities and luxuries are also available noncontingently in regular hospital units, resulting in increased apathy and dependency.

CASE REPORT 2

Patient. J. D. is a 21-year-old, white male who completed high school with the help of a private tutor. He had no previous job experience. J. D. had no hospitalizations prior to his residence on the CRU. His psychiatric diagnosis was schizophrenia, chronic undifferentiated type.

Problem Behaviors

1. Environmental destruction—ripping clothes and curtains, turning over chairs and objects, and destroying furniture and decorative items.
2. Self-destruction—biting hand.
3. Lack of socialization—little verbal behavior.
4. Nearly mute—very low voice volume.

Procedures

1. Time-out (brief isolation) for environmental destruction.

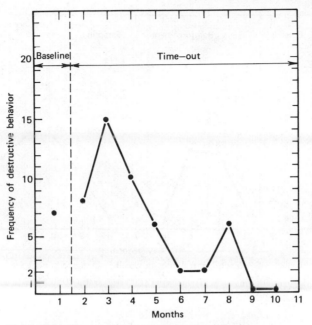

Figure 22. Monthly frequency of assaultive behavior.

2. Inattention by staff for self-destruction (hand-biting).

3. Reinforcer sampling for lack of social interaction: 12 times a day during baseline, a therapist would ask J. D. if he would like to engage in one of three types of social interaction (play catch, talk, or play tic-tac-toe). During the next phase, compliance with one-half of the invitations was made mandatory. Throughout the program, the compliance rate in choice situations was monitored.

4. Shaping of voice volume with the use of instructions and a noise-activated relay was used. J. D. was asked to repeat each of four sentences five times. A multiple-baseline design was used. J. D.'s level of medication was held constant during his stay on the CRU.

Results

1. Time-out had a marked effect on destructive behavior, reducing the frequency to zero for the last two months of residence on the CRU, as may be seen in Figure 22.

2. Staff inattention did not result in a decline in hand-biting behavior. The hand-biting did not appear to be maintained by social consequences.

3. Forced practice resulted in more frequent social participation when given a choice. The results are illustrated in Figure 23.

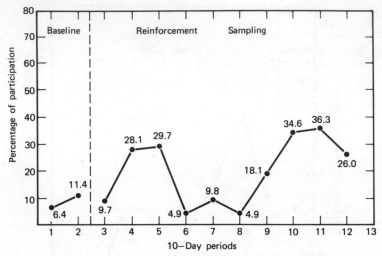

Figure 23.   Percentage of "choice" interactions in which J. D. agreed to engage.

4. A program to test the effectiveness of instructions was implemented. Instructions had no effect over baseline measures. J. D.'s voice volume during these sessions was barely adequate. Because J. D. is still a patient on the CRU, these sessions will be continued and greater demands will be put on his voice volume.

Generalization. When J. D. is discharged, specific instructions will be given to those who control his new environment. These will include instructions that J. D. should not be allowed to escape demands with destructive behavior, biting self, or withdrawing from the environment.

Discussion. J. D. represents a very difficult patient to work with because there is little (other than being alone) that is reinforcing for him. For example, when meals were made contingent on the payment of two tokens per meal (a very small payment), J. D. stopped eating rather than interact to earn tokens. A major area for behavioral study should be patients with constricted repertoires of behavior and reinforcers.

CASE REPORT 3

Patient. S. T., a 29-year-old female, had six previous admissions, three within six months of transfer to CRU. Readmissions resulted when bizarre behavior in public places came to the attention of police. Her psychiatric diagnosis was schizophrenia, paranoid type.

Problem Behaviors

1. Verbal abusiveness and occasional assaultiveness.
2. Noncompliance with assigned tasks.
3. Inappropriate (bizarre) speech, such as "I am married to Elvis Presley," or "You're going to give me shock treatment."

Procedures

1 and 3. Five-minute conversations were scheduled each hour, 17 hours per day. The conversation was to be terminated at the onset of "inappropriate" or abusive speech. Specific examples were provided for guidelines to staff. A late evening chat with snacks with a therapist was made contingent on the cumulative amount of time until the onset of abusive or inappropriate speech.

No response was made to abusive or inappropriate speech outside the hourly interviews. Staff were instructed to ignore such expressions. Physical aggressiveness or assaultiveness resulted in immediate time-out removal to an empty, drab, "quiet room" for 15 minutes.

2. Tasks such as housecleaning duties and folding linen were arranged in such a way that successful completion of the first task for five of six days resulted in advancement to the second step. The second step included two separate tasks. Completion of four successive tasks over a period of one week would result in an off-unit work (Industrial Therapy) assignment. Tokens were provided as an immediate consequence for task completion. Tokens were also provided for promptness, appropriate dress at work, and task completion, and were to be deducted for inappropriate behavior when S. T. was on the off-unit IT assignment. A report card was completed daily by the supervisor who was instructed in the standards expected for the various ratings.

Results

1 and 3. Figure 24 indicates a rapid increase in time earned toward the evening chat. Verbal abusiveness was eliminated almost immediately and inappropriate speech was eliminated in approximately four weeks. When medication was reduced during a three-week period, a brief deterioration resulted. S. T. stabilized when medication was restored to the maintenance dosage. S. T. was totally free of inappropriate speech within the sessions and, more important, outside the session both on the CRU and the off-unit IT assignment for three weeks prior to discharge.

2. The off-unit IT assignment was earned within six weeks. At that time S. T. was completing all four assigned tasks in the proper order. Report cards from the IT supervisor were "perfect" every day after the first day.

Generalization. S. T. was placed in a family care home and employed in a sheltered workshop as an assembly line worker. The family care operator and

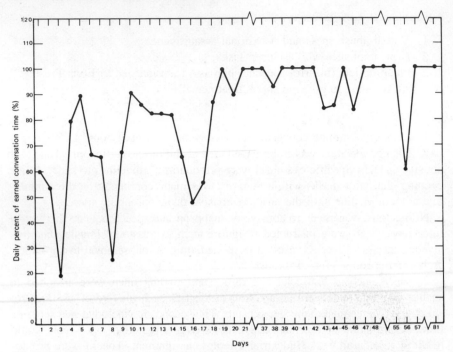

Figure 24.   Daily percentage of evening chat time earned by S. T.

job supervisors were taught to ignore inappropriate behavior and to reward appropriate behavior with praise and attention. S. T. was rehospitalized at Camarillo State Hospital (but not the CRU) briefly several months after discharge but maintained the job in the sheltered workshop (located near the hospital) and continues there at this writing, 13 months after discharge from the CRU.

CASE REPORT 4

Patient. R. T. was a 21-year-old, white male with a high school education. He had no job experience prior to admission to the CRU. R. T. had one previous hospitalization. His psychiatric diagnosis was simple schizophrenia.

Problem Behaviors

1. Poor grooming (refusal to take showers, brush teeth, comb hair, and wear clean clothes).
2. Failure to return on time from walks, outings, and visits.
3. Noncompliance with requests to do elementary tasks (making bed, picking up clothes, refusing to undress before going to bed).
4. Lack of interaction with patients or staff.

Procedures

1. Grooming behaviors were taught by reinforcing successive approximations to adequate standards with verbal praise and tokens which were exchangeable for meals, cigarettes, candy, and other privileges.

2. To learn to return from walks at predesignated times, the patient made a deposit of tokens before leaving for walks; upon return he was refunded a prorated number of tokens based on his promptness.

3. Undressing before going to bed was programmed by allowing the patient to go to bed only if his street clothing was removed.

Tokens were earned by completing housekeeping tasks. During a home visit with his parents, he was given cigarettes, meals, use of record player, and soft drinks contingent upon completing household tasks.

4. An attempt was made to increase social interaction by paying the patient two tokens for each five minutes of "good talk" during interviews. "Good talk" was identified in two daily interviews by means of a rating scale measuring conversational frequency, content, intonation, spontaneity, and emotional mood. To expand environmental contacts, the patient was paid tokens for taking half-hour walks on the hospital grounds and was paid tokens for taking half-hour walks with his family. He also attended an outpatient clinic and participated in their daily activities and coupon incentive program.

R. T. participated in the General Relationship Improvement Program which is designed to (a) increase one's awareness of others and self (b) increase flexibility in self-expression and self-assertion, (c) increase self-respect and self-esteem, and (d) aid in the generalization of socially adaptive behaviors to new situations. To evaluate overall level of functioning R. T. was rated on six separate occasions with three different rating scales: Nurses Observation Scale for Inpatient Evaluation (NOSIE); Psychotic Reaction Profile (PRP); and Elgin Behavior Rating Scale (ELGIN).

Results

1, 2, and 3. Grooming, punctuality, and work behaviors improved from zero compliance to 60 percent compliance.

4. Much more refractory was his lack of social responsiveness, which failed to improve as a result of using the GRIP and paying tokens for social conversation.

The rating scales gave information regarding R. T.'s improvements. The first and last scores can be seen in Table 4.

Generalization. R. T. was participating in a community mental health Day Treatment Program while living on the CRU. Upon discharge from the CRU, R. T. remained as a day care patient in the community mental health center

Table 4. Change of Behavior on Rating Scales

Nurses Observation Scale for Inpatient Evaluation (NOSIE)					
Positive Factors	First	Last	Negative Factors	First	Last
Social competence	14	34	Irritability	12	4
Social interest	8	16	Manifest psychosis	12	0
Personal neatness	8	20	Retardation	14	4
Total positive	30	70	Total negative	38	8
Psychotic Reaction Profile (PRP)					
Factor				First	Last
Withdrawal				32	17
Thinking disorder				8	0
Paranoid belligerence				2	0
Agitated depression				4	1
Elgin Behavior Rating Scale (ELGIN)					
Factor				First	Last
Somatic				2.14	3.43
Social				2.67	3.35
Mental				2.00	2.25
Psychotic				1.33	3.33
Neurotic				2.00	2.00
Antisocial				2.00	2.00
Total				12.14	16.34

where a reinforcement system was used to maintain improvement on the target behaviors.

Discussion. In R. T.'s case, the state hospital, the community mental health center, and his parents all cooperated to structure R. T.'s environment, thereby promoting generalization. R. T. represents one of the most difficult types of patient to treat. He has few reinforcers available, which makes it difficult to structure an incentive program. When presented with a situation in which R. T. may approach another person to ask for something he wants, he preferred to do without, even when the social response was graduated in extremely small increments.

The rating scales all indicated the same trend. R. T. made gradual improvement throughout the rating period, with slightly more accelerated improvement in the earlier ratings.

CASE REPORT 5

Patient. M. M., a divorced, white female in her mid-thirties, had a high school education and had been successfully employed as a clerk-typist for more than five years for a government agency. She had a history of multiple admissions to community mental health inpatient and outpatient facilities in addition to the state hospital. Her constant whining and demands for attention were becoming intolerable to her mother, with whom she lived, and to staff in the various treatment settings. Her diagnosis was chronic, undifferentiated schizophrenia.

Problem Behaviors

1. Repetitive, persistent complaining to staff about medication, rules and regulations, her health, and privileges.
2. Negativism in socialization with her mother.
3. Noncompliance with requests to perform simple tasks.

Procedures

1. (a) The staff was instructed to ignore unreasonable or repetitive requests. Benedryl, a mild sedative to aid sleeping, was available if she was willing to "pay" one token for it. Copies of her individual token economy program were given her and her day was tightly structured with the aid of a written schedule. Negotiations for change in program were possible only with one staff member, her primary therapist.

(b) Three 15-minute conversation periods were scheduled. The conversation was terminated at the onset of a complaint or a demand. The amount of time she conversed in the three sessions without becoming negative or demanding was credited toward an evening "free chat." During this time (free chat) she could talk about anything she wished with no penalty.

2. M. M. lived with her mother when not hospitalized. The mother visited her at the hospital and was prompted by a therapist, through a small earphone receiver, to totally ignore negativism of any sort. She would do this by turning away from and not replying to any negative statement made by her daughter. At the same time, she was taught to respond to appropriate behavior with attention, showing interest and concern. She was instructed to respond to M. M. in a like manner when she was home for a weekend visit.

3. As in 1 above, the token economy provided a medium of exchange. Privileges such as off-unit time, cigarettes, coffee, and home visits were "purchased" with tokens. Tokens were earned by getting up on time, grooming, room-cleaning, and other unit housekeeping chores, as well as secretarial work. All jobs were explicitly defined and daily report cards were filled in by M. M.'s primary therapist to determine the quantity and quality of completion of assigned tasks. Tokens were also earned for completion of tasks at home on weekends. In addition, her mother charged tokens for certain privileges such as staying in bed late and eating out instead of cooking.

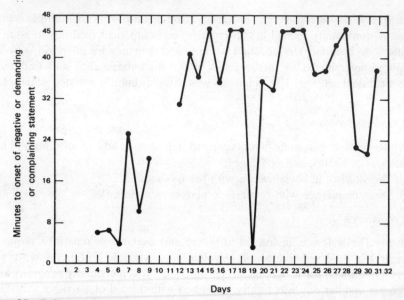

Figure 25. Daily total time to onset of negative or complaining or demanding statements summed over three 15-minute conversations.

Results

1. (a) Anecdotal reports from nursing staff suggested that the several programs reduced the manipulativeness. Perhaps most effective were the specification in writing of her program and the assignment of one therapist through whom all changes had to be channeled.

(b) Although no baseline measures were taken, Figure 25 shows an increase in time to onset of complaints or demands in the three daily conversations. The "free chat" time thus earned appeared to be reinforcing.

2. The mother reported a significant reduction in apathy and noncompliance at home. Joint mother-daughter social events became enjoyable again, although she recognized the need to maintain the program perhaps indefinitely.

3. M. M. responded well to the token economy. Her secretarial skills improved under a schedule of reinforcement wherein she was initially paid after completion of each task, then at the end of the day, and finally only three times per week.

Generalization. M. M. was transferred to her home unit with a simplified, token economy plan that could be supervised by the home unit staff. This was effective for only a short time. Soon M. M. was successful in getting all the coffee, cigarettes, and off-unit time she desired by complaining, arguing, and persistently badgering the nursing staff. Attempts to teach extinction procedures to her home unit staff met with failure.

Placement in a family care home with five other former patients was then arranged by the CRU through a community social service agency. Employment in a sheltered workshop was also arranged, and the mother agreed that she would not let M. M. return home except for brief visits. A series of attempts by M. M. to be rehospitalized in the home unit (where all the necessities and many of the luxuries of life were available noncontingently) followed. Through cooperative planning, the Camarillo State Hospital admissions department, the sheltered workshop, the family care home operator, the community social service supervising the placement, and the mother all agreed with the CRU social worker to resist any attempt on the part of M. M. to change this arrangement. For several weeks M. M. cried, pleaded, and at one time even walked to the hospital from the sheltered workshop demanding admission. M. M. was eventually dismissed from the workshop after three months although an 18-month follow-up indicated she remained in the family care home and she has not been rehospitalized.

Discussion. M. M.'s dependency was effectively reduced by the rigid structuring of her environment to provide rewards only for adaptive (independent) behavior. The most difficult task was to modify the collective responses of a wide range of significant others to her persistent demands. The results provide a source of reinforcement for the CRU's efforts to focus on this most often ignored problem of generalization.

CONCLUSIONS

Applied behavior research and clinical treatment can be an unhappily married "couple" with potential problems that can result from the divergencies in their goals and in the means to achieve their goals. The British behavior therapist Victor Meyer (1972) once told his audience at a conference on behavior modification, "If you take responsibility for treatment, you can't do research." He went on to state that the clinician must use any technique that might bring the desired results and could not worry about controls, generalization, reliability, or matched subjects. Reinforcers for the researcher are demonstrations of experimental control over behavior, publications, and grants. The clinician's reinforcers are different—rapid relief of symptoms and restoration of function; satisfaction of the patient, his relatives, and the nursing staff; and payment of a fee.

We often came to grips with this research-clinical dilemma in the treatment of the patients summarized in the section on Specific Behavioral Interventions with Psychotic Individuals in this chapter. Thus most of the interventions described above are AB designs, untested by control procedures and used in combination in a "shotgun" effort to bring about rapid improvements in behavior. Sufficient improvement in extremely deviant and refractory behaviors reinforced these clinical efforts. However, we were able to obtain some "hard data" utilizing experimental designs and reliability criteria on the modification of such thorny clinical problems as delusional speech, hallucinations, inaudible speech, assaultiveness, social withdrawal, and apathy. Although our clinical-research marriage is not idyllic, we are living with its problems and working toward a more complete consummation.

Treatment failures tend to be more visible and painful when they fall in the *clinical* area, since inadequately controlled or inconclusive *research* tends to be quietly and mercifully "buried" without even an epitaph from a professional journal. However, patients who do not improve, who regress after discharge, or who remain socially undesirable and unwanted despite behavioral improvement tend to serve as constant reminders that we have more questions than we have answers. The young science of behavior will mature and grow strong only to the extent that questions continue to be generated. We feel it is important to terminate the exhortatory and testimonial stage of behavior modification and to begin reporting our failures as well as our accomplishments. This can be done if the effects of behavioral intervention on *consecutive* cases are described and published.

Generalization of behavior across setting and time is currently being developed by the Camarillo-Neuropsychiatric Institute Research Program. The Clinical Research Unit at Camarillo State Hospital, other hospital units, and the Ventura County Community Mental Health Department are being bridged by a behavior modification approach. From the start of the referral process, the CRU staff works closely with the staff of the patient's "home unit" at the state hospital or with relatives and mental health workers in the community. A detailed behavioral assessment is made, including a baseline recording of the target problems. As the treatment program is formulated, the CRU involves the referring therapists in the plan to insure generalization of improvement to the aftercare site. Continuity of care comes about when all responsible therapeutic agents share the same definition of the problem, goals, and method of evaluating or monitoring progress. Specification, observation, and measurement of behavior form the strand that ties together the CRU and its referral network.

Vested interests, ignorance, philosophical and ideological differences, bureaucratic red tape, and woefully inadequate community resources are some of the major barriers to generalization. The consistent employment of contingencies of reinforcement, which is hard won and difficult to maintain in the controlled setting of the CRU, is almost totally lacking elsewhere. Of considerable significance, therefore, is the NIMH supported applied research project to adapt behavior modification to the problems and setting of a typical, comprehensive community mental health center in Ventura County. Methods of behavioral assessment and therapy are being introduced into all facets of the center's program—partial hospitalizations, emergency services, outpatient clinic, inpatient care, and community consultation. The broad, general goals of community mental health are being given substance by the specifics of behavioral engineering. Behavioral techniques generated at the CRU and other research settings are being tested for their effectiveness in the wide variety of problems faced by a community-based program.

We can blame the long-term, clinical failures of some of our former patients on aftercare environments that prompt and reinforce maladaptive behavior, or on our insufficient and poorly planned efforts to anticipate and program for generalization. Thus a challenge to behavior modifiers will be to harness the variety of contingencies from different directions which concurrently have an impact on the patient's behaviors. Of necessity, this systems approach requires more skills of us than straightforward application of behavior therapy. We must become sophisticated in community organization and in the development of mechanisms for interagency communication and planning. It should also be clear to behavior modifiers, whether they be psychologists, psychiatrists, social workers, or paraprofessionals, that the learning model is not the only relevant theory in helping us to understand and treat behavioral disorders. Familiarity with the biological-genetic model and its offspring of psychopharmacology and family planning should be an intrinsic part of the training and practice of mental health workers.

As long as there are individuals with major behavioral deficits and excesses, whether in large state mental hospitals or in small community boarding homes, we must devote our energies and creativity to developing therapeutic interventions that will assist these individuals to learn functional and happier roles in society.

ACKNOWLEDGMENTS

The authors wish to pay tribute to the work of the nurses and technicians who staff the Clinical Research Unit. Their tireless efforts and resiliency in systematically applying behavioral principles and human warmth and respect are ultimately responsible for the success of the treatment programs described in this chapter and for the progress of the field of behavior modification. Special credit is extended to Val Baker, CRU Head Nurse, and Camarillo State Hospital Medical Directors, Drs. Vernon Bugh, Charles Allen and Harry Jones; Hospital Administrator, John Darmer; Chief of Research, Robert Coombs, Ph.D., and Neuropsychiatric Institute Director, Louis Jolyon West, M.D., whose support and encouragement have made our work possible. Credit also goes to Roger Patterson, Ph.D. and F. J. Nicassio, Research Assistant, whose work is reflected in the case summaries. Portions of this chapter have previously appeared in Liberman, R. P., Behavioral modification of schizophrenia: a review. *Schizophrenia Bulletin*, NIMH, 1972, **6**, 37–48.

REFERENCES

Atthowe, J. M., and Krasner, L. A preliminary report on the application of contingent reinforcement procedures (token economy) on a "chronic" psychiatric ward. *Journal of Abnormal Psychology*, 1968, **73**, 53–61.

Ayllon, T., and Azrin, N. *The Token Economy*. New York: Appleton-Century-Crofts, 1968.

Ayllon, T., and Haughton, E. Modification of symptomatic verbal behavior of mental patients. *Behaviour Research and Therapy*, 1964, **2**, 87–97.

Bandura, A. *Principles of Behavior Modification*. New York: Holt, Rinehart and Winston, 1969.

Bootzin, R. R. Magnitude and duration of expectancy effects in behavior modification. Paper read to the 1971 Convention of the American Psychological Association.

Cochran, B. Conference report: Behavior Modification Institute: May 12–14, 1969, Tuscaloosa, Alabama. *Hospital and Community Psychiatry*, 1969, **20**, 16–18.

Davison, G. C. Appraisal of behavior modification techniques with adults in institutional settings. In C. Franks (Ed.), *Behavior Therapy: Appraisal and Status*. New York: McGraw-Hill, 1969.

Ellsworth, J. R. Reinforcement therapy with chronic patients. *Hospital and Community Psychiatry*, 1969, **20**, 238–240.

Fairweather, G. W., Sanders, D. H., Cressler, D. L., and Maynard, H. *Community Life for the Mentally Ill: An Alternative to Institutional Care*. Chicago: Aldine, 1969.

Foster, J. The economics of behavior modification programs. Paper presented at the Annual Convention of the American Psychological Association, Washington, D. C., 1969.

Franks, C. M. (Ed.) *Behavior Therapy: Appraisal and Status*. New York: McGraw-Hill, 1969.

Gericke, O. L. Practical use of operant conditioning procedures in a mental hospital. *Psychiatric Studies and Projects*. American Psychiatric Association, 1965, **3**, 1–10.

Grinspoon, L., Ewalt, J. R., and Shader, R. Long-term treatment of chronic schizophrenia. *International Journal of Psychiatry*, 1967, **4**, 116–128.

Johnson, S., and Martin, S. Developing self-evaluation as a conditioned reinforcer. In B. A. Ashem and E. G. Poser (Eds.), *Behavior Modification with Children*. New York: Pergamon, 1973.

Kale, R. J., Kaye, J. H., Wheland, P. S., and Hopkins, B. L. The effects of reinforcement on the modification, maintenance and generalization of social responses of mental patients. *Journal of Applied Behavior Analysis*, 1968, **1**, 307–314.

Kanfer, F. H. Self-monitoring: Methodological limitations and clinical applications. *Journal of Consulting and Clinical Psychology*, 1970, **35**, 148–152.

Kazdin, A. E., and Bootzin, R. R. The token economy: An evaluative review. *Journal of Applied Behavior Analysis*, 1972, **5**, 343–372.

Kety, S. S. Toward hypotheses for a biochemical component to the vulnerability to schizophrenia. *Seminars in Psychiatry*, 1972, **4**, 233–238.

Liberman, R. A view of behavior modification projects in California. *Behaviour Research and Therapy*, 1968, **6**, 331–341.

Liberman, R. P. Behavior modification with chronic mental patients. *Journal of Chronic Diseases*, 1971, **23**, 803–812. (a)

Liberman, R. P. Behavior modification and community mental health. *California Research Digest*, 1971, **9**, 88–90. (b)

Liberman, R. P. Reinforcement of cohesiveness in group therapy: Behavioral and personality changes. *Archives of General Psychiatry*, 1971, **25**, 128–177. (c)

Liberman, R. P. Reinforcement of social interaction in a group of chronic mental patients. In R. Rubin, H. Fensterheim, J. Henderson, and M. Kushner (Eds.), *Advances in Behavior Therapy*. New York: Academic Press, 1972, pp. 151–159. (a)

Liberman, R. P. *A Guide to Behavioral Analysis & Therapy*. New York: Pergamon, 1972. (b)

Liberman, R. P. Behavior modification of schizophrenia: A review. *NIMH Schizophrenia Bulletin*, 1972, **6**, 37–48.

Liberman, R. P., DeRisi, W. J., King, L. W., Eckman, T., and Wood, D. Behavioral measurement in a community mental health center. In P. Davidson (Ed.), *Program Evaluation, Proceedings of the Fifth Banff Conference on Behavior Modification*, Champaign, Ill.: Research Press, 1974.

Liberman, R. P., King, L. W., and DeRisi, W. J. Building a behavioral bridge to span continuity of care. *exChange*, 1972, **1**, 22–27.

Liberman, R. P., Teigen, J., Patterson, R., and Baker, V. Reducing delusional speech in chronic paranoid schizophrenics. *Journal of Applied Behavior Analysis*, 1973, **6**, 57–64.

McFall, R. M., and Lillesand, D. B. Behavior rehearsal with modeling and coaching in assertion training. *Journal of Abnormal Psychology*, 1971, **77**, 313–323.

May, P. R. A. *The Treatment of Schizophrenia: A Comparative Study of Five Treatment Methods*. New York: Science House, 1968.

Meyer, V. The current status of behavior therapy with emphasis on clinical application. Paper presented to the Fourth Annual Southern California Conference on Behavior Modification, 1972, Los Angeles, Calif.

Padula, H., Glasscote, R., and Cumming, E. *Approaches to the Care of Long-Term Mental Patients*. Washington, D. C.: Joint Information Service of the American Psychiatric Association and the N.I.M.H., 1968.

Patterson, G. R. *Families*. Champaign, Ill.: Research Press, 1971.

Patterson, R. L. A novel treatment for hallucinations. Aversion acquired through repetition. Unpublished manuscript, 1972.

Patterson, R. L., Cooke, C., and Liberman, R. P. Reinforcing the reinforcers: A method of supplying feedback to nursing personnel. *Behavior Therapy*, 1972, **3**, 441–444.

Patterson, R. L., and Teigen, J. R. Conditioning and post-hospital generalization of nondelusional responses in a chronic psychotic patient. *Journal of Applied Behavior Analysis*, 1973, **6**, 65–70.

Paul, G. L. Chronically institutionalized mental patients: Research and treatment. Paper presented to the Third Annual Southern California Conference on Behavior Modification, 1971, Los Angeles, Calif.

Paul, G. L. Chronic mental patient: Current status, future directions. *Psychological Bulletin*, 1969, **71**, 81–94.

Paul, G. L., and Shannon, D. T. Treatment of anxiety through systematic desensitization in therapy groups. *Journal of Abnormal Psychology*, 1966, **71**, 124–135.

Paul, G. L., Tobias, L. L., and Holly, B. L. Maintenance psychotropic drugs in the presence of active treatment programs: A "triple-blind" withdrawal study with long-term mental patients. *Archives of General Psychiatry*, 1972, **27**, 106–115.

Richardson, R. A., Karkalas, Y., and Lal, N. Operant conditioning procedures in the treatment of hallucinations. In R. D. Rubin, H. Fensterheim, J. Henderson, and L. P. Ullmann (Eds.), *Advances in Behavior Therapy, Vol. 4*. New York: Academic Press, 1973.

Rosenthal, D., Wender, P. H., Kety, S. S., Schulsinger, F., Welner, J., and Ostergaard, L. Schizophrenics' offspring reared in adoptive homes. In D. Rosenthal, and S. S. Kety (Eds.), *The Transmission of Schizophrenia*. New York: Pergamon, 1968.

Schaefer, H. H., and Martin, P. *Behavioral Therapy*. New York: McGraw-Hill, 1969.

Schaefer, H. H., and Martin, P. L. Behavior therapy for "apathy" of hospitalized schizophrenics. *Psychological Reports*, 1966, **19**, 1147–1158.

Skinner, B. F. *The Behavior of Organisms*. New York: Appleton-Century, 1938.

Skinner, B. F. *Science and Human Behavior*. New York: Macmillan, 1953.

Ullmann, L., and Krasner, L. (Eds.) *Case Studies in Behavior Modification*. New York: Holt, Rinehart and Winston, 1965.

Wender, P. H. The role of genetics in the etiology of the schizophrenias. *American Journal of Orthopsychiatry*, 1969, **39**, 447–458.

Wing, J. K., Monck, E., Brown, G. W., and Carstairs, G. M. Morbidity in the community of schizophrenic patients discharged from London mental hospitals in 1959. *British Journal of Psychiatry*, 1964, **110**, 10–21.

Yates, A. *Behavior Therapy*. New York: Wiley, 1969.

Zusman, J. Some explanations of the changing appearance of psychotic patients: Antecedents of the Social Breakdown Syndrome Concept. *International Journal of Psychiatry*, 1967, **3**, 216–237.

Author Index

Subject Index